PITCHFORK
POPULISM

TEN POLITICAL FORCES
THAT SHAPED AN ELECTION
AND CONTINUE TO
CHANGE AMERICA

BRADFORD R. KANE

PB Prometheus Books

Guilford, Connecticut

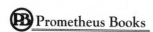 Prometheus Books

An imprint of The Rowman & Littlefield Publishing Group, Inc.
4501 Forbes Blvd., Ste. 200
Lanham, MD 20706
www.rowman.com

Distributed by NATIONAL BOOK NETWORK

Cover design by Liz Mills
Cover image © Garagestock/Shutterstock
Cover design © Prometheus Books

British Library Cataloguing in Publication Information available

Library of Congress Cataloging-in-Publication Data available

ISBN 978-1-63388-582-0 (cloth)
ISBN 978-1-63388-583-7 (e-book)

∞™ The paper used in this publication meets the minimum requirements of American National Standard for Information Sciences—Permanence of Paper for Printed Library Materials, ANSI/NISO Z39.48-1992

To Daniel and Kristyn, Valerie and Dan, Brennan and Ronni, Niko, Antonio, Max, Lisa, Taylor, Hannah, Hillary, Jake, Jeffrey, Sydney, Annabel, Hudson, Eva, Brittany, Brandon, Caiden, Claire, Erika, Chance, Michelle, Brian, and all the other young Americans in their thirties, twenties, and teens who are (or will soon be) beginning to step into leadership roles to guide our country into its next chapter. Regardless of the conditions that you inherit, all of you have the ability, tools, resources, and responsibility to steer the country toward the fulfillment of its highest aspirations and most ideal purpose.

CONTENTS

THE 2016 WAKE-UP CALL

I admit it. I'm guilty. Just like millions of other Americans, I didn't believe that the 2016 campaign could become so macabre. I didn't believe that the Republican Party would allow Donald Trump to be its nominee. And I certainly didn't believe that he would carry the day on November 8, 2016 . . . but then, even Trump and his staff reportedly didn't think that he would actually win.[1]

Like so many of us who care deeply about our politics and our government, I watched every debate, including those among the candidates for the Republican and Democratic nominations and the general election debates. The debates during the primaries were intensely informative, not so much about the issues but, rather, about the political dynamics that motivated various segments of the electorate, and the efforts by the candidates to appeal to those constituencies. Even as the debates provided "car crash" moments—which were amazing, appalling, or shocking, that compelled attention and left viewers aghast—they illuminated the electorate's temperament and appetite.

The debates showcased some issues and tensions that have been with us ever since our country's nascent years. They surfaced with modern adaptations to those historical themes, in the context of contemporary challenges and dilemmas. These included the debates over trade, immigration, taxation, civil liberties, and social-safety-net issues. For example, during the GOP debates on the nexus between national security, civil liberties, and privacy, I heard echoes of Benjamin Franklin stating, "Those who would give up essential Liberty, to purchase a little temporary Safety, deserve neither Liberty nor Safety."[2] I wondered what Mr. Franklin would think if he were watching from on high.

The debates also featured issues and controversies that are products of recent decades, without the long tail of history. These included healthcare reform, climate change and other environmental protections, and, of course, email practices. These issues, too, revealed much about the concerns, predispositions, and ideologies of Americans, as reflected in the way that the candidates positioned themselves.

Providing the subtext to the substance, the stylistic characteristics and demeanor of the candidates were especially arresting. While some candidates adopted a traditional or nuanced approach, others used the debates to bellow bombastic, vituperative, inflammatory rhetoric, in a tone that matched the words. With Donald Trump in the lead in the latter category, it seemed that his approach would ultimately alienate constituencies and disintegrate his candidacy. While I recognized that he was trying to appeal to his base, I thought that the hurdles that he was self-imposing would demolish his electability. The eventual outcome seemed implausible.

The response to Trump's *Access Hollywood* audio was particularly counterintuitive. Virtually everyone agreed that it was offensive and that it confirmed the narrative about him. However, the narrative that it confirmed was interpreted differently by different constituencies. While his opponents found it appalling, disgusting, and disqualifying, his supporters seemed to accept that it was just Donald being Donald, just an entertainer playing to his audience, or just a guy who wasn't worried about being "politically correct." To some voters, it meant that he was unfit for public office, while, to others, it meant that he would say and do things in his own way.

Interpretations may have been similarly divided in response to his other salvos, including his criticism of the "Gold Star" Khan family during the Democratic National Convention, his mockery of a reporter with a disability, his stated willingness to use nuclear weapons, his desire to punish women who have an abortion, his vilification of Judge Gonzalo Curiel's ethnicity, his "lock her up" chant aimed at Democratic nominee Hillary Clinton, his laudatory comments about Vladimir Putin, his refusal to release his tax returns, his "who's gonna pay for the wall?" rally cry that prompts his audience to bellow "Mexico!" his demonization of the media, and his acrimony against anyone who protested at his rallies. Many observers considered these to be "hall of shame" moments, while others would take umbrage at that, suggesting that they were just campaign tactics or rhetorical flourishes that were calculated to appeal to certain constituencies.

The fact that millions of Americans accepted and even embraced Trump despite his injudicious assertions and inflammatory rhetoric is evidence of the electorate's diversity and idiosyncrasies. It signifies a change in what some segments of the electorate wants, hears, sees, accepts, tolerates, relates to, aspires toward, believes, and/or applauds. Some might argue that Trump changed the electorate. More likely, Trump tapped certain previously dormant segments of the electorate that became activated and energized. Trump recognized them, perhaps aided by his familiarity with that cultural cohort through his "reality TV" connection to them. Although Trump didn't create that cohort, he certainly was the beneficiary of its impulses.

My miscalculation about Trump's electoral prospects was in part because I discounted the resonance of historical tensions that remain embedded in today's America, and partly because I didn't recognize that, for millions of voters, Donald Trump's rhetoric and demeanor were assets, not liabilities. Once I realized that the tone and tenor of American politics had shifted since the time when I worked as a counsel in Congress, I began noticing correlations with historical events and trends, as well as the lineage extending from political dynamics that fomented earlier in our nation's history.

The ten American political dynamics that are the subject of this book reflect that linkage between our history, our current challenges, and our future political landscape. They illuminate how we reached this point and where we might be heading from here. That said, the analyses of the ten dynamics cannot please all readers. Thus, a disclaimer is warranted. As with any material that has a political nature, true objectivity is elusive. I believe that the opinions of any one individual are inherently subjective, and mine are no exception. Each of us is limited by our lifelong accumulated experiences, perceptions, and interactions that mold our opinions. In fact, people who purport to be objective and unbiased are either deluding themselves, disingenuous, or illusionists, like the old frontier's vendors of elixirs and potions.

So, for the sake of full disclosure, the following are central tenets of my belief system that guides my perceptions and opinions, and drives my analyses of Trump, his conduct and statements, the Trump administration's actions, and their implications for the post-Trump era:

- the Constitution, Bill of Rights, subsequent seventeen constitutional amendments, and Declaration of Independence are sacrosanct, and adherence to both their language and their spirit must prevail;

- our system of governance, balance of powers, institutions, and rule of law (as outlined by these documents) must not be circumvented, manipulated, ignored, derogated from, nor contravened;
- civility and respectfulness should be accorded to all people in the United States—citizens, residents, and visitors alike—and no one deserves to be vilified (except for convicted criminals, to the extent that judicial process deems that appropriate), nor demeaned by our country's chief executive;
- freedom of the press requires that the media, its practitioners, and their work be treated respectfully, without demonization, denunciation, disparagement, divisive intent, or questioning their patriotism;
- the international order—structures, laws, alliances, organizations, and diplomatic norms—that were principally and thoughtfully established by the United States to provide global stability, protect human rights, preserve environmental sustainability, and discourage warfare must be maintained and reinforced, not diminished or dismantled; and
- deliberate egregious deceptions, falsehoods, and repudiation of facts by the president and people speaking on his behalf are reprehensible, unacceptable, and debilitating to his fitness to govern.

These tenets do not advance a partisan position. They do not seek to gain a political advantage. They are fundamental principles that guide my perceptions and analyses regardless of who occupies the White House, whether that person is a Democrat or a Republican. The lens through which I view the president and his administration is one that seeks stability, reasoned judgment, fairness, civility, upholding the rule of law, and continuity with regard to matters of national security and public safety. In fact, in the past, I have gone to great lengths to limit my partisan activities to the few months prior to an election (to which I believe political partisanship should be confined). In my governmental roles, I often developed and advanced legislation that was calibrated for bipartisan support. After I left government service, I went further, creating the Bipartisan Bridge website to advance bipartisanship and postpartisanship in American government.

But the current landscape is different. The recent usurpation of our Constitution (e.g., the Emoluments Clause), rule of law, institutions of democracy, and norms of civility, respect, decency, and truth compel illumination, transparency, and frankness. Every American has a stake in adherence to our country's time-tested, hard-won, well-developed standards of governance, as well as the thoughtful and visionary domestic and geopolitical policy and strategy that has benefited the United States so demonstrably. We must not readily, willingly, or even reluctantly sacrifice our country's moral leadership or our preeminence in the global community that American leadership has made possible.

For each reader of the ten dynamics in this book, I have a request. Try to imagine and superimpose what Jefferson, Madison, Washington, and Hamilton would think about recent developments if they were around today, and the concerns that they might have.

THE POLITIQUAKE THAT IS RESHAPING AMERICAN POLITICS

T he political earthquake of 2016 resulted from a convergence of political forces and trends that evolved over many years. They were based in demographics, propelled by previously dormant or disengaged constituencies, and aroused by archaic clarion calls that had been relegated to our country's antiquated political past. The combined effect was a campaign that reawakened social, cultural, economic, and legal divisions that inflamed passions on both sides, and will continue to reverberate during Trump's tenure and into the post-Trump era.

The evolution of the ten trends and dynamics that will be discussed created the political environment on which Donald Trump capitalized. They are as deep-seated as our national identity, and as contemporary as our rapidly transforming media channels and challenges. They stem from the diverse racial and ethnic composition of the American people, and lead to increased engagement across the spectrum of constituencies in the political process. They reflect the workings of government and political campaigns, from the role of policy and principles, to the prospects for bipartisanship, and the impact of transparency and accountability. They include major shifts in public opinion on trade and globalization, and the roles of state and federal government. And they culminated in the voter predilections that led to Trump's 2016 victory, which appear to have been incrementally eroding since then, except among his devoted base.

Some of these political dynamics may have been overlooked or minimized in the past, which is at least one of the reasons why conventional wisdom did not envision a Trump victory. But their impact on the election's outcome mandates that they can no longer be dismissed, negated, neglected, or ignored either during an election or in governing. They are now vividly on display, as prominent indicators of the flow of American public life. They have combined to unleash Pitchfork Populism, a movement of disenchanted people who are motivated by fear, resentment, and animosity to resist change and repudiate recent social evolution, while vilifying those who they consider to be "others."

These dynamics are evident in voting behavior. People who voted for Trump did so for many reasons, such as their interest in the issues that Trump raised, the passions that he stoked, their genuine affection toward Trump, their genuine disaffection for Hillary Clinton, and their disenchantment with both political parties, and other reasons. These are legitimate explanations of voter behavior, and all Americans would benefit by understanding them. At the same time, the forces that culminated in Trump's victory do not amount to a permanent transformation of the electorate. As evidenced by the multiplicity of explanations for the outcome, the 2016 election was more of a "perfect storm" in which an assortment of key variables converged at a unique moment. The many contributing factors and emotions indicate that the outcome was propelled by political activation of previously dormant constituencies who lashed out with pent-up force, rather than the result of a long-term structural realignment of the electorate.

The same dynamics that enabled Trump to win, and that drive his tone of governance, can also be harnessed to achieve different outcomes in the future, as long as they are consciously recognized and strategically managed. The pendulum of American politics has a history of swinging in one direction, being halted by the gravity of consequences and new political forces, and then swinging back along a different, sometimes unpredictable, course.

It has become a national pastime to try to understand the 2016 election, the forces propelling the Trump administration, and their implications for policy and governance in the years ahead. The lessons learned from the election are useful in recognizing the dynamics that evolved in recent years and contributed to the outcome, as well as new forces that have emerged and will influence American life for the foreseeable future. They provide frameworks with which to interpret and critique Trump's and his administration's conduct and decision-making. They will also be useful as we evolve past the Trump presidency.

Each of the dynamics that played out during the 2016 election, and that are now in full force, had been gradually building for years. Some of them have deep roots and are the latest incarnation of debates and cultural challenges that date back to the 1700s and our country's origins (e.g., regarding our national identity, racial and ethnic tensions, bipartisanship, and federalism). Others emanate from more recent national conditions, political campaigns, global circumstances, sociocultural divisions, and technological innovations (e.g., democratization of the political process, new media issues, accountability mechanisms, and the globalization of trade).

As these dynamics appeared and gained traction in recent years, some lawmakers may have wistfully and wishfully minimized their importance, attributing them to passing fads and transient waves of popularity. Other decision-makers may have chosen conscious, even calloused, disregard for the popular will. Sometimes, legislative bandages and stopgap half measures were applied to temporarily forestall prominent issues, and mute demands from vocal constituencies. More sustainable or comprehensive solutions to popular calls for action were sometimes intentionally deferred, either by optimism (believing that half measures would be sufficient and that the problems would just go away), or by neglect (believing that the social, cultural, or electoral forces that were asking for attention could be disregarded without ramifications).

Regardless of their origins, each of the currently dominant forces and trends has profound implications and will have an ongoing impact, to one degree or another, on the country's sociocultural and sociopolitical landscapes for many years. The ten dynamics are useful in interpreting Trump's comments about the violence in Charlottesville, Virginia, and his antagonism toward NFL and NBA athletes; his consistent and repetitious statement of falsehoods and his demonization of the media; his transactional approach to decision-making and the regressive policies at his EPA, Justice Department, and other agencies; his tariff battle and his Muslim-focused travel ban; his actions against immigrants and his separation of migrant children from their parents; his destabilization of alliances and his deference to Vladimir Putin; and many other actions and comments by Trump and his administration that raise concerns.

Obviously, these emergent factors will be most prevalent in the executive branch, to the extent that Trump and his aides are able to manage political capital and strategies to exert their will. However, their impact on the executive branch might be short-lived, since the 2020 election could result in a 180-degree change of direction, depending on the outcome. If Trump continues on his path of irascibly offending, irritating, and alienating broad swaths of the electorate, then the likelihood of a 2020 shift to a successor who would reverse course will increase commensurately.

The legislative branch is likely to be subject to the new forces and trends for longer. This is because the sociocultural inclinations that fuel them play out differently in various localities across the country, some of which might adhere to Trumpian positions for a long time. Considering that legislators sometimes secure very long tenures through many reelections, these forces may become intractable in some districts, and continue to be voiced for many years to come, even if the number of adherents diminishes.

The judicial branch might be impacted the longest, since US Supreme Court justices and federal judges receive lifetime appointments. Naturally, this will depend upon the number of Supreme Court justices that Trump is able to appoint. The Trump administration has already appointed an extraordinary number of judges to federal district courts, courts of appeal, and other specialized courts.

Any attempt to contemplate the long-term implications of Trump's presidency requires a healthy dose of speculation, since Trumpism has placed our country in uncharted waters, with a presidency for which there is no precedent. Similarly, new countertrends and forces might emerge that cannot be forecasted, since there is no template for the circumstances that are now exerting their influence on American society and government, which might precipitate new countertrends. Reactions and responses to Trumpism might be equally unforeseeable and *sui generis*, never before having been necessary or envisioned.

Yet, some things are certain. The emergent trends, the broader forces underlying them, and the new political landscape that they launched are very real, and they will have a sweeping impact. They will affect everything, including our national identity, our laws, our economy, and the overall stability of our society. They will continue to guide debates over virtually all areas of domestic policy, from civil liberties and environmental protection, to workforce preparation and economic growth; and from sociocultural norms and the sustainability of our social-safety-net programs, to religion in the public domain and the role of ethics in government. Their imprint will be seen on our foreign policy, from the USA's global geopolitical and economic leadership to preoccupation with our own national security; and from the USA's role in maintaining regional stability and peace in conflict zones to our funding levels for military and diplomatic operations.

Some of the ten dynamics and trends have already materialized with tempestuous force, weighing heavily into the outcome of the 2016 election and steering the Trump administration's actions. Others are still coalescing, and will increasingly affect national policy, politics, laws, and society during Trump's presidency. Just as the roots of each of them preceded the rise of Trump, each dynamic is sure to play a role—to varying degrees—in American life beyond the Trump era.

These ten American political forces provide roadmaps that will benefit the constituencies who can best harness them to fulfill their objectives. Americans of all ideologies would be well served to understand these and other dynamics and trends that are evolving in our country and swaying our shared future. One can envision that, by illuminating these forces and becoming more aware of their impact, we can find ways to improve our country, respect each other, accommodate each other's needs, and help each other succeed in achieving our own versions of the American Dream.

CHAPTER 1

NATIONAL IDENTITY

THE EXPANDING DIVIDE IN OUR NATION'S SPLIT PERSONALITY

S ocial scientists and political philosophers have theorized about what constitutes a "nation."[1] Classical factors that are typically cited include a shared language, religion, history, culture, heritage, and ethnic or racial origins.[2] However, traditional components of nationhood simply do not apply to the United States due to the diverse origins of our population (consisting of Native Americans plus immigrants from around the world).

Yet, there are contemporary factors that bind us as a nation, inspire a sense of shared destiny, and motivate actions for our concerted success and prosperity. We all cheer the American flag and take pride in what it represents. We all readily join in singing the national anthem at many events. But those are just patriotic symbols. We unify quite well, for example, in times of tragedy (e.g., natural disasters and mass shootings) and celebration (e.g., solar eclipses and Fourth of July fireworks). We join forces to fervently chant "U-S-A" when we are in direct competition with other countries, like at the Olympics. But, absent a specific reason to consolidate, we seem inclined to coexist in separate camps, as if aligning with different sports teams.

Americans are an amalgamation of the world's peoples—both indigenous to North America and from every corner of the globe—with diverse stakeholders and no single heritage, religion, race, ethnicity, language, history, or culture shared by everyone. Because of that, the main factors that identify us as a nation, and generate our social cohesion, lie elsewhere. What makes us a nation is more complex than determining who is, or can become, an American. Our laws governing natural-born citizenship are only part of the picture.[3] As a nation whose population is predominantly comprised of immigrants and their descendants, we are an inclusive society in which immigrants adopt, and contribute to, our societal fabric. The diversity of natural-born US citizens is our bedrock. And yet, recognition of the vital historical role of immigrants still leaves room for debate about the conditions under which people from elsewhere can immigrate to the United States today.

Since the American populace is a pluralistic tapestry of diverse threads, the more relevant question is: what comprises "national identity"? St. Augustine offered a classic explanation that can be paraphrased as "a people (or nation) is an assembled multitude of rational beings united by a common agreement on the objects of their love." Modern definitions[4] recognize the more amorphous, abstract, and philosophical determinants of nationhood.[5] As French political theorist Ernest Renan stated it in 1882, "A nation is a soul, a spiritual principle. Two things, which in truth are but one, constitute this soul or spiritual principle. One lies in the past, one in the present. One is the possession in common of a rich legacy of memories; the other is present-day consent, the desire to live together, the will to perpetuate the value of the heritage that one has received in an undivided form."[6]

In the case of the United States, the fundamental essence of our national identity is grounded in our values and governing principles, as enunciated by our founding documents that established rights irrespective of traditional criteria (albeit with glaring exceptions), as well as our choice and consent to be governed by them. None of the classic criteria of nationhood compare, since variances, additions, exceptions, and evolutions neutralize the significance of religion, race, ethnicity, language, or culture.

What unites us most of all are our Constitution, the Bill of Rights, the subsequent constitutional amendments, and the Declaration of Independence (some would include President Lincoln's Second Inaugural Address, Emancipation Proclamation, and Gettysburg Address in the pantheon of principles). These documents, collectively, delineate our values, our system of governance, the powers and limitations of government, our individual and civil rights, and the rule of law that applies to us all. These documents are, however, subject to interpretation, according to the lens (i.e., belief system) through which we view them. This is especially the case when we apply them to emergent issues and new laws.

These documents and their principles are the foundation of our national identity, and the political process is the means by which they are applied (subject to review by the judicial branch). Consequently, political dynamics take center stage in the evolution of our national identity. The better we understand the motivations and worldviews that drive behavior in the political arena, the better we can craft constructive, sustainable paths forward.

Today, our politics and culture are highly polarized. We place an inordinate amount of attention on what divides us, and often take for granted what unites us as a nation. Regrettably, there are valid reasons for that. Many (if not most) Americans lament the intensification of political partisanship between Democrats and Republicans, believing that it has reached an unprecedented and toxic level. Widening gulfs are also evident between rural and urban communities, red and blue states, environmental and fossil-fuel mindsets, and agrarian, industrial, and information-based local economies. These divisions are commonly misunderstood to be symptoms of a recent devolution, attributed to the sociological divide between conservatives and liberals/progressives that has expanded since the 1960s.

Our political, social, and cultural divisions certainly are real, and widening. Although they are legitimately a cause for angst or grief, their linkage to our national heritage also merits recognition. Rather than being a relatively new phenomenon, they are deeply rooted in our nation's origins. Despite the troubling—and sometimes dystopian—consequences of polarization, divisions reflect our country's philosophical diversity and are an extension of motivations along two parallel tracks, each of which contribute significantly to our national identity. Donald Trump is clearly aligned with one side of this chasm and is manifesting it to an unprecedented level.

RUGGED INDIVIDUALISM VERSUS COMMUNITY COLLECTIVISM

Among the many philosophical cornerstones (Renan's "spiritual principles") that have been central to our country's heritage since colonial days are two key creeds that are on opposite ends of the same axis. Each is a lens through which many Americans view our founding principles and documents, as well as current politics and governmental actions. Each has an equal claim to being truly American, and each has had a vital role in driving our progress. As such, they are parallel and equally important elements of our country's split personality and our national identity. They are by no means the only fulcrum on which we balance the diverse elements of our national identity.

But they are a very significant axis around which our society revolves, and each one has a strong influence on our national behavior.

On one side is the ethic of "individualism"[7] or "rugged individualism."[8] It centers on the primacy of individuals—rather than society or the government—and the belief that progress stems from personal inspiration, self-reliance, and assertive action by individuals who diverge from, and transcend, social norms. Adherents to this approach believe in the value of individual pursuits, the self-made person who thrives with an "every man for himself" ethos, libertarian rights that must be insulated from government influence, and personal responsibility that does not look to the government or broader community for support, assistance, or advancement. It is philosophically aligned with capitalism and Social Darwinism, both of which regard individual action as the primary determinant of success and incentivize individual wealth accretion.[9] President Herbert Hoover (1929–1933) popularized the term, for example, in discussing the post-World War I era: "We were challenged with the choice of the American system of 'rugged individualism' or the choice of a European system of diametrically opposed doctrines—doctrines of paternalism and state socialism."[10] He later wrote, "While I can make no claim for having introduced the term 'rugged individualism,' I should be proud to have invented it. It has been used by American leaders for over a half-century in eulogy of those God-fearing men and women of honesty whose stamina and character and fearless assertion of rights led them to make their own way in life."[11]

On the other side is the ethic of "collectivism"[12] or "community collectivism."[13] It centers on the primacy of society—with personal interests being sublimated to benefit the common good—and the belief that progress is achieved through common cause, interdependence, and collective action. Adherents to this approach believe in the importance of social cohesion, basic values shared by all, equal opportunity and justice, reciprocity, protections, norms of public conduct, and collaboration to reinforce those standards and solve shared problems for communal benefit. It is philosophically aligned with a communitarian ethos that recognizes that we're all in this together. This approach was recently characterized by George Lakoff and Glenn Smith, who wrote: "We Americans care about our fellow citizens, we act on that care and build trust, and we do our best not just for ourselves, our families, and our friends and neighbors, but for our country, for each other, for people we have never seen and never will see. American democracy has, over our history, called upon citizens to share an equal responsibility to work together to secure a safe and prosperous future for their families and nation. . . . The American Dream is built upon mutual care and trust."[14] It was also succinctly and comically expressed by Ralph Waldo Emerson who famously quipped, "No member of a crew is praised for the rugged individuality of his rowing."[15]

The two ethics date back to colonial times, and even played a role in the creation of the United States of America. The spirit of community collectivism inspired colonists to join together, and the colonies to coalesce, in opposition to their distant rulers. This was embodied in Benjamin Franklin's famed warning when signing the Declaration of Independence, "We must all hang together, or most assuredly we shall all hang separately." The spirit of rugged individualism inspired many colonists to chart their own course in the new world and take umbrage at restrictions and requirements that were imposed on them by the British king. Their individualism was inherently inconsistent with subjugation by a remote authority, contributing to the sentiment for rebellion. This was embodied in Patrick Henry's vow: "I know not what course others may take, but as for me, give me liberty or give me death."[16]

During the Revolutionary War, there were concerns that individualism led to self-interests that sometimes evolved into rampant personal profiteering. Those who were oriented toward the collective cause were troubled that some people's motivation for victory seemed to be the prospect of personal rank and wealth. General George Washington lamented in 1780, "If I were called upon to draw a picture of the times and of men, I should say that idleness, dissipation, and extravagance seems to have laid hold of most of them. An insatiable thirst for riches seems to have got the better of every order of men."[17]

Examples—past and present—of the rugged individualist ethic (characterized by the belief that the government that governs best is the one that governs least) include: Daniel Shays's Rebellion in Massachusetts in the 1780s against state policies that were thought to cause poverty and property foreclosures; frontiersmen such as Daniel Boone, Davy Crockett, and Kit Carson in the 1700s and 1800s; Lewis and Clark's expedition in the early 1800s; the "nullification" movement in the 1830s by individual states against rule by the federal government; the "captains of industry" or "robber barons" during "the Gilded Age" of the Industrial Revolution in the late 1800s and early 1900s; anything that President Calvin Coolidge (1923–1929) ever thought or did; opposition to the laws advocated by the collectivists; and, most recently, the Tea Party and its progeny the Congressional Freedom Caucus. In policy debates, individualists often champion the interests of privileged individuals who seek insulation from what they regard as government intrusion (leading them to advocate for lower taxes and less regulation), as well as others who see government as an interference in the private lives of its citizens. They oppose national policies that benefit "the Other" and the broader common good (e.g., expansion of government assistance programs), often by taking shelter under the Tenth Amendment's protection of states' rights, which is useful in making an argument for individual liberties.

Examples—past and present—of the collectivist ethic (characterized by the belief that government has an obligation to improve the lives of its citizens) include: the 1700s' independence movement; the political battles over the National Bank during President Andrew Jackson's presidency (1829–1837); the Populism movement of the late 1800s (e.g., Henry George's writings, the Peoples' Party led by Mary Elizabeth Lease in Kansas and others elsewhere, and Coxey's Army's march of unemployed men from Ohio to the capital); President Theodore (Teddy) Roosevelt's (1901–1909) creation of national parks and reforms such as food inspection and antitrust laws; the income tax that originated in the 1890s and culminated during President William H. Taft's tenure (1909–1913); the Progressive Party led by Teddy Roosevelt in 1912; and the environmental movement that insists on responsible stewardship of our natural resources and climate. In policy debates, collectivists often champion the "social safety net" that was propelled by President Franklin Delano Roosevelt (1933–1945) and expanded by some of his successors. Their leadership converted this concept into a primary and intractable part of our political and legal framework, through programs such as Social Security, Medicare, Medicaid, food stamps, crop subsidies, and virtually every initiative and law that was designed to protect civil rights and human rights over the past eighty years.

The two ethics are inextricably intertwined. For example, our economic system is based on the freedom to engage in commerce, choose a job or career, own a business, and accumulate wealth. At the same time, it provides compensation for those who suffer workplace injuries (i.e., workers compensation), pension income for senior citizens who retire after working for many years (i.e., Social Security), healthcare for retired persons and people who cannot otherwise afford it (i.e., Medicare, Medicaid, and other programs), and other hallmarks of financial security and fairness. Our economy combines principles of capitalism and socialism in a way that encourages individual choice and success alongside a collective responsibility for a social safety net that fills economic gaps. The integration of the two approaches contributes to our national identity, prosperity, and sustainability. It is analogous to the wording of our Pledge of Allegiance: "with liberty and justice for all." While all Americans support both aims, "liberty" is especially treasured by the individualists, while "justice" is especially treasured by the collectivists. And yet, they are inseparably combined into one mission statement that we all embrace.

The two historical creeds repeatedly exert their influence in our institutions, economy, and social fabric.[18] Many prominent Americans have been driven by one or the other of them, and in some cases, by both. The dialectic has surfaced in many contexts, including tensions between business and labor, isolationists and interventionists, environmentalists and industrialists, libertarians and egalitarians. Today, rugged individualism is embodied in the entrepreneurial spirit and innovations of our technology, biomedical, entertainment, and other transformational industries, and the people who lead them. Community collectivism is embodied in the partnership and purpose of our world-leading philanthropic, education, nonprofit, and public service sectors, and the people who lead them. A distinction between the two creeds might be that individualism produces transformational leaps forward, while collectivism unifies and strengthens our society for long-term prosperity and success. Obviously, both are indispensable, and both enable us to thrive.

But the two creeds run headlong into each other in our politics, creating a tension that remains prominent in contemporary America. As Paul Ryan, former Speaker of the House of Representatives, declared in 2005, "The fight we are in here, make no mistake about it, is a fight of individualism versus collectivism."[19]

The ideological and political conflict between adherents of the two perspectives has many implications.[20] The contrast between the two includes the scope of people about whom each group is concerned, and their resulting inclinations toward isolationism or interconnectedness. Individualists tend to circumscribe their range of concern more narrowly, focusing on people with whom they identify, such as their family, people who share their ethnicity or religious affiliation, civic groups of interest to them, their town, and their city.[21] Collectivists tend to extend their range of concern more broadly than the scope of the individualists to include people who are not like them, such as their state, the country, Americans facing hardships or disadvantages, refugees, people in other countries who are marginalized or suffering, and the entire world.[22] (Some may extend it to the universe, but that is for astrophysicists to ponder.)

Individualists tend to focus on issues affecting their financial and personal pursuits, security, comfort, and the belief that the government should not interfere with their efforts to achieve them. They are typically driven by competition and the quest for victory. They are generally more short-term focused, since they are motivated by self-interests of individuals, which are physiologically time limited. Because their scope of concern is comparatively narrow, centering on people with whom they identify, individualists have an inherent distrust of "the Other," whom they consider to be unlike them. This manifests in xenophobia and, sometimes, racism. It translates into chants of "build the wall" and policy positions that are rigidly against immigration, trade, and foreign assistance, which are natural targets to blame as scapegoats for perceived social and economic ills. Politically, fear is the message that ignites them, since it aligns with their belief system and their concern about protection of their interests.

Collectivists tend to focus on issues affecting quality of life and are typically willing to sacrifice some enhancement to theirs in order to assist others whose quality of life is impaired. They are typically driven by empathy/ compassion and equality. They are generally more long-term focused, since they are motivated by the community's well-being and sustainability, which continues indefinitely, even after any one person has gone. Because the scope of their concern is comparatively broader, inclusive of people with disparate origins, collectivists celebrate diversity and American multiculturalism. Their views translate into policy positions that are usually supportive of immigrants, asylum seekers, globalism, equal opportunity, and aid to those in need, both domestically and internationally. Politically, hope is the message that ignites them, since it aligns with their belief system and their concern for others' lot in life.

These psychographic and emotional characteristics that distinguish the two groups have been analyzed along with other factors that indicate peoples' adherence to political ideologies. In *Prius or Pickup?: How the Answers to Four Simple Questions Explain America's Great Divide*,[23] two political science professors assess personality preferences and cultural choices that shape our inclinations toward liberal and conservative philosophies (being "fluid" or "fixed"), as well as the resulting worldviews and belief systems. Their four questions and broader analyses of psychological and emotional impulses explain some of the underlying reasons why we adhere to either an individualist or collectivist orientation, and the partisan political messages that resonate with each group.

In foreign policy, the dichotomy is prevalent in the recurring debate on the United States' role in world affairs. The collectivists are oriented toward extending our country's global leadership and interconnected engagement for stability of the rules-based international order through alliances, multilateral agreements, international organizations, and foreign aid funding. Since the end of World War II, and prior to 2017, presidents from both political parties have been consistent in increasing our interaction with foreign partners, recognizing that long-term global stability and prosperity bolsters ours as well. But, at times, our involvement and resources have been hyperextended. The individualists are oriented toward narrowing our scope of interactions through isolationism, protectionism, and xenophobia that reduce our foreign entanglements, or just save money, or both. It had been many decades since this approach prevailed, but Trump has been actively reinstituting it, apparently believing that prosperity and stability among countries is a short-term zero-sum game. However, as our country's level of engagement and international collaboration recedes, so, too, does our level of global leadership.

The divergence between individualists (espousing isolationism) and collectivists (espousing interventionism) has been a recurring theme of our foreign policy. This debate dominated national attention during World War I. Interestingly, President Woodrow Wilson (1913–1921) shifted between both sides of the divide, as his stance on the war underwent a very public transition. He accommodated popular sentiment for isolationism during the early years of the European war and during the 1916 election. But after provocations and incidents that drew the United States into the conflict, he embraced global leadership via his "Fourteen Points for Peace" speech, Treaty of Versailles leadership, and League of Nations efforts, in addition to his creation of federal offices and agencies that enhanced our global role. The debate again took center stage during the 1940 election, when the isolationist and anti-Semitic America First Committee tried to galvanize opposition to entering World War II.[24] Of course, their archaic "America First" slogan was excavated and redeployed into contemporary parlance by Donald Trump during the 2016 election in his effort to vilify globalization.

In domestic policy issues, the dichotomy between individualism and collectivism frames the ongoing debate on the size and role of government. Individualists typically push for a smaller, limited federal government, believing that government should recede in order to reduce taxes (people should pay less of their income for societal objectives), and that personal freedom and liberty should prevail over government rules and regulations that restrain choice. The individualists strive for lower taxes, and with that, lower federal revenues that would diminish the "social safety net." Collectivists strive for a larger, broader federal government, believing that government should improve quality of life, enhance equality and social justice, provide opportunity, and protect the citizenry through regulations and rules on business conduct. The collectivists accept that the services and structures that maintain higher standards are justifiable uses of tax revenues, with proportionately more taxes coming from people with higher incomes.

Debates over the role of government often invoke two value systems: one based on economics, and one based on rights. Among individualists, capitalism is the salient value because it aligns with their belief that each individual is entitled to determine their own course, create their own success, and reap the rewards from their efforts. Individualists view capitalism as an economic form of Social Darwinism, in which people compete to maximize their personal profits and advance their other interests. Among collectivists, democracy is the salient value because it aligns with their belief that each person has an equal right to participate in society, influence their community, and help others succeed for the common good. Collectivists view democracy as the structure that enables everyone to be a stakeholder in building cohesive communities in which everyone can thrive. In the PBS film *The Gilded Age*[25], historian H. W. Brands differentiated the two systems: "The essence of democracy is equality: everybody gets one vote. The essence of capitalism is inequality: rich people are much more powerful than poor people." Historian Nell Irvin Painter followed Brands's contrast by tying it to the role of contemporary government, observing, "The question of wealth versus people ballooned in the Gilded Age. Do our governments represent wealth or do they represent people? That is a fundamental issue which is with us today."

These distinctions are evident in debates over environmental policy and regulation. The collectivist ethic spawned the environmental movement with the call to "save the planet" and laws to protect our air, water, and lands. The movement evolved to focus on climate change, shifting from fossil fuels to renewable energy, and myriad other environmental protections. These efforts reflect collectivists' long-term orientation as stewards with responsibility to bequeath a sustainable environment to future generations, preserving quality-of-life standards for their benefit. The individualist ethic challenges the fundamental philosophy of environmentalism, believing that most laws and regulations for environmental protection fail to consider costs while abridging the liberties of individuals to do what they choose. They often seek to reduce the financial impact of mandates and elevate consumer choice. These efforts reflect individualists' short-term orientation, exemplified by favoring fossil-fuel use and profiteering, prioritizing jobs and costs over clean air and water, and discounting long-term human health consequences.

The convictions held by individualists and collectivists were on display in the late 1990s in reaction to Hillary Clinton's *It Takes a Village*[26], a book that emphasized the importance of societal and communal factors in ensuring the well-being of children. While collectivists celebrated the book, individualists met it with antipathy. Weighing in on that debate at the 1996 Republican National Convention, GOP nominee Senator Robert Dole countered Hillary's philosophy by declaring, "We are told that it takes a village, that is, a collective, and thus the state, to raise a child. . . . I am here to tell you it does not take a village to raise a child. It takes a family to raise a child."[27] Dole rejected the notion of a broader interdependent social network. This debate seemed to have been foreshadowed in 1987 by then-senator Joseph Biden who, when launching his first campaign for president, stated, "For too long in this society, we have celebrated unrestrained individualism over common community."[28]

The dichotomy between the individualists and collectivists is especially prominent in debates relating to the Second Amendment. Issues that impact guns and other firearms evoke intense passion from both sides. The debate does not correlate to a simple division between liberals and conservatives, since many liberals own guns and many conservatives do not. No bright line distinction is fully accurate, since people may have firearms for many reasons, regardless of ideology or culture (e.g., a rifle for hunting, a handgun for protection after being victimized by a crime, a shotgun to protect a rural home to which police cannot quickly respond, etc.). Understanding both sides of the gun debate in terms of the divide in our national identity is useful in recognizing the needs of both cultures, and, hopefully, identifying common ground for reasonable rules that will minimize gun deaths (especially mass killings) while preserving the Second Amendment's "right of the people to keep and bear Arms."

Adherents of "the gun culture" typically object to government intrusion into their lives, have a fundamental bias against regulation, and seek to be self-sufficient as rugged individualists. They are susceptible to the NRA's alarmist arguments against "the camel's nose under the tent," that is, that any law or regulation—no matter how reasonable—could lead to other, more restrictive regulations and laws, which ultimately could culminate in confiscation of firearms. In contrast, most proponents of gun control have no objection to people keeping a firearm at home for protection or sport, but seek measures that prevent abuse and ensure public safety, for the sake of community security. Most gun control advocates support the Second Amendment, since it is, and will remain, part of our Constitution. But they do want firearms to be limited to the Second Amendment's primary modern purposes (protection and hunting), since its original purpose is outdated ("a well-regulated Militia"). They favor laws that promote public safety while preserving gun rights by: conducting background checks (to prevent sales to criminals, people on the "no fly" terror watch list, and high-risk people who are deemed dangerous to themselves or others), preventing mass killings (via semi-automatic rifles, high-capacity magazines, bump stocks), and eliminating loopholes (such as sales at gun shows and over the internet).

If the collectivists commit to protecting Second Amendment rights to allay fears of the "camel's nose," and if the individualists honestly acknowledge that they share an interest in public safety, then the two sides should be able to find common ground and reach consensus on reasonable measures that reassure adherents of both viewpoints.

The distinction between the views of the individualists and collectivists is often blurred. For example, during the effort to pass the Patient Protection and Affordable Care Act (the ACA or Obamacare), many people at presidential and congressional town hall forums adamantly insisted that the government should not touch their healthcare. These vocal opponents tended to be individualists who were skeptical of government intrusion into their lives, believing that they fared better in an unregulated marketplace (perhaps not recognizing their vulnerability to the unrestrained edicts of their health plan, insurer, or HMO). Yet, many of the law's most vocal critics were senior citizens who received healthcare through Medicare, which benefits from the

ACA; when more people have health insurance, cost-shifting to Medicare is reduced. Medicare is the ultimate government-based program and is based on a collectivist ethic. In essence, the senior citizen opponents of Obamacare were arguing for both the individualist and collectivist approaches at the same time, which could be viewed as both ironic and illogical.

A similar incongruity is often seen among advocates for lower taxes and reducing the scope of the federal government, both of which are hallmarks of the individualistic approach. They seek to minimize the amount of income that they contribute to the government, based on the belief that the government spends too much of their tax dollars on inappropriate activities and wasteful programs. Yet, many of the people who most ardently argue for these reductions are beneficiaries of farm assistance, Rural Electric Co-op services, unemployment insurance, children's health programs, food stamps, the Senior Community Service Employment Program, and other federal programs that are made possible by the policies that they advocate against. Here, too, they are on both sides of the dichotomy at the same time.

It is even more complicated when members of a group assert individual rights that are actually based on communal interests or beliefs. For example, some religious or faith-based organizations have asserted that they should be exempt from healthcare essential benefits rules that require them to provide women with contraception coverage (which predates the Affordable Care Act and was reinforced by it). These groups are, in effect, seeking individualistic insulation from the societal collective . . . by being treated as their own community collective!

Both legally and logically, their argument is flawed. In terms of practical effects, it poses an even worse conundrum. It is especially tortuous because it opens the door for any interest group that is organized as a collective around a theme or set of beliefs to assert their own individualistic rights. By seeking *ad hoc* insulation from societal/governmental rules, any group would be able to assert what amounts to a private right of nullification (like South Carolina's nullification effort in the 1830s). Groups could pick and choose the federal laws to which they want to adhere, which would create a patchwork quilt of enclaves around the country with their own rules.

This problem would be exacerbated if corporations were allowed to exert their will in accordance with Mitt Romney's 2011 retort that "corporations are people, my friend"[29] (corporations have the legal status of a "person" for some purposes, but not for all purposes). If these assertions were allowed to flourish, then our laws would be applied differently to each corporate collective.[30] Proliferation of these corporate enclaves would damage national unity by dissembling our national legal structure through fluctuating application of our laws.

PAST PRESIDENTS' INCLINATIONS TOWARD INDIVIDUALISM AND COLLECTIVISM

Strong pendulum-swings between individualistic and collectivistic creeds punctuate American political history. Among our presidents since 1900, the Republicans tended to be rugged individualists, and the Democrats tended to be community collectivists, but not always, and sometimes a president blended the two approaches in his own distinctive way. For example, a president's personality or philosophy might place him in one of the two camps, while pragmatic realities surrounding his presidency placed him in the other.

Use of executive orders (a presidential directive, having the force of law, issued to manage the enforcement of an existing law) can sometimes indicate where a president stands on this duality. A president's frequent use of orders to establish policy might indicate a personality that is more aligned with individualism, since executive orders involve unilateral action rather than collaboration with Congress. However, that is not necessarily the case. Some presidents have used executive orders out of choice and natural inclination. Others have used them out of necessity or opportunism, for example, when their political party is not in control of Congress, and their legislative efforts were being stymied.

During the late 1800s, presidents from both parties were so individualist oriented that major industrialists, entrepreneurs, robber barons, and an overall *laissez faire* attitude predominated. In 1893, during his second Inaugural Address, President Grover Cleveland (1885–1889 and 1893–1897) said, "The lessons of paternalism ought to be unlearned, and the better lesson taught that, while the people should patriotically and cheerfully support their Government, its functions do not include the support of the people."[31] His successor, President William McKinley (1897–1901), championed policies that were hallmarks of the individualist creed, including protectionism, tariffs, trickle-down economics, and the gold standard, which preserved the advantages of the wealthiest Americans. He earlier affirmed his values by declaring, "We cannot gamble with anything so sacred as money,"[32] and "I am a tariff man, standing on a tariff platform."[33] A McKinley campaign poster asserted "protection vs. free trade" and continued with "in the sunshine of protection" vs. "under the cloud of free trade."[34] Another of his posters foreshadowed the parlance of a future president by stating, "My friends, you shall have prosperity with full protection. Believe me."[35]

Teddy Roosevelt (TR), who became president when McKinley was assassinated, was an anomaly, in both style and substance, as the quintessential embodiment of both creeds. By his disposition, he was the ultimate personification of the rugged individual. From his adventurous days as a frontier cowboy and his zealous leadership of the Rough Riders during the Spanish American War, to the outspoken, iconoclastic, trailblazing style that characterized his presidency, TR epitomized the characteristics of individualism. His larger-than-life personality also played a significant role in revitalizing the executive branch after the post-Lincoln succession of predominantly less consequential, weaker presidents (weaker relative to the legislative branch and in comparison with the modern presidency).

At the same time, TR institutionalized tenets of community collectivism within governmental policy and American culture. His reforms have been central to our concept of appropriate government ever since. Under TR's leadership, new laws and enforcement actions created national parks and protected other federal lands, ensured food safety and meat inspection, dismantled monopolies and trusts, conserved natural resources, and regulated businesses. His policies benefited the common good by preserving the environment, outlawing predatory business conduct, and raising quality-of-life standards. His record on race relations was mixed, highlighted by his laudable White House dinner with Booker T. Washington (which was condemned by Southerners), and in contrast with that, his response to the Brownsville Affair, in which TR dishonorably discharged all 167 African American soldiers of the 25th Infantry Regiment who were framed for a murder of a white Brownsville resident.[36]

The Progressive Party agenda on which TR campaigned in 1912 (when seeking to regain the presidency after relinquishing the office) reads like a blueprint for action that was taken by later presidents. He called for women's right to vote, protection of natural resources, labor's right to organize, standards for a "living wage," prohibition of child labor, limiting the workday to eight hours, limiting the workweek to six days, campaign spending limits, registration of lobbyists, and providing federal insurance to the elderly, sick, and jobless.[37] His progressive agenda envisioned an expanded role of government and a contemporary, broader interpretation of the Constitution, to accommodate changes to the status quo. His policies placed him at the vanguard of the collectivists as much as his personality placed him at the helm of the individualists. Although he was a Republican, he served in a period of party realignment and had a major influence on that shift. It could be said that his policies and actions qualify him as the first modern activist Democrat, despite his party affiliation that was defined prior to realignment.

President Wilson (1913–1921) exhibited characteristics of both collectivism and individualism, perhaps hewing more toward the collectivist ethic, as reflected by his laws that lowered tariffs, created the Federal Reserve banking system, and established the Federal Trade Commission to enforce antitrust laws and other regulations. His status as a collectivist was marred by his anti-egalitarianism, in particular his discriminatory racial views and policies against African Americans and Japanese Americans, as well as his Espionage and Sedition Acts. During his final two years, his attorney general, A. Mitchell Palmer, was best known for creating the General Intelligence Unit (which became the FBI), appointing J. Edgar Hoover to run it, and directing him to lead the Palmer Raids, which rounded up socialists and communists, whom he considered to be a threat to principles held by most of the country, including individualists. In foreign affairs, Wilson navigated competing forces propelled by national sentiments about our participation in the European war, and our role in the subsequent world order.

Following Wilson, presidents Warren Harding (1921–1923), Coolidge, and Hoover—as well as President Taft before Wilson—were squarely on the individualists' side of the ledger, doing little to constrain people and companies from acting in their own self-interests, even when that impaired the greater good. Their approach was epitomized by Coolidge's famous quote, "The business of America is business" (or, "The chief business of the American people is business"),[38] and his self-assessment, "Perhaps one of the most important accomplishments of my administration has been minding my own business."[39] The astute observation that "when a great many people are unable to find work, unemployment results," is also attributed to Coolidge.

Franklin D. Roosevelt (FDR) and later Lyndon B. Johnson (1963–1969) were the presidents whose actions most decisively advanced the collectivist approach. FDR created the framework for what we still view as the social safety net, initially with many programs designed during his first hundred days to stabilize the economy and jumpstart job creation during the Great Depression. The crowning achievement of his economic agenda was the establishment of Social Security, to ensure that older Americans would be protected from poverty and its many indignities during their later years when they could no longer be gainfully employed. The Social Security Act also created the Aid to Families with Dependent Children program (Welfare program), which grew in importance over the years. The school lunch program was conceived and developed during FDR's tenure and formally established by the National School Lunch Act that President Harry Truman (1945–1953) signed into law. The Supreme Court's rejection of some of FDR's social welfare programs led him to float the idea of packing the Court with six more justices. While that idea was highly criticized and went nowhere, it did send a message. The Court's originalist, strict interpretation of the Constitution soon evolved toward a more contemporary, contextual interpretation ("the living Constitution").

President Johnson (LBJ) expanded the social safety net and built upon FDR's quality-of-life legacy, most notably with the Medicare and Medicaid programs. He also created the Head Start program and revitalized an expanded Food Stamp program (the first iteration of which was instituted under FDR). LBJ led the establishment of legal protections that remain as vital cornerstones of American social justice, namely, the Civil Rights Act of 1964, the Voting Rights Act of 1965, and the Fair Housing Act (within the Civil Rights Act of 1968). These laws were firmly rooted in the collectivist creed.

Some of the legislation that came to fruition under LBJ had actually been initiated by President John F. Kennedy (1961–1963), most notably the Civil Rights Act of 1964. In addition to his legislative initiatives, President Kennedy (JFK) provided a quintessential enunciation of the community collectivist ethic when, in his Inaugural Address, he gave us the immortal advice, "Ask not what your country can do for you; ask what you can do for your country."[40] That line served as a guidepost for at least a generation or two of Americans.

Of the presidents who served after FDR and before the 2016 election, President Ronald Reagan (1981–1989) was undoubtedly the most avid proponent of the individualist ethic. Reagan explicitly articulated this ideology during a discussion forum titled, "Town Meeting of the World," when Governor Reagan (of California) stated, "I believe the highest aspiration of man should be individual freedom and the development of the individual; that there's a sacredness to individual rights."[41] During his presidency, he continually took actions that adhered to this credo. He did so very prominently in advancing "trickle-down economics," also known as "supply-side economics" and "Reaganomics," and reducing taxes, which, in turn, was his justification for slashing spending on social-safety-net programs. Some of the programs for which he decreased or eliminated funding were Legal Aid Services, Medicaid, food stamps, public housing, Community Development Block Grants, federal education programs, and the Environmental Protection Agency. He also notably opposed raising the minimum wage above $3.50 per hour.

President George Herbert Walker Bush (1989–1993) was usually on the side of the individualists. He often spoke the mantra of personal responsibility, which was intended to decrease the government's role in certain social issues. President Bush coined the phrase "a thousand points of light"[42] as a means to encourage nonprofits and individuals to help people in need through charitable acts, as a substitute for the government providing those services. Bush's "no new taxes" pledge[43] was, at least in part, designed to reduce the federal government's capability to afford a broad safety net of services, and provide the fiscal justification for their curtailment. His goal was to diminish the size, scope, and role of government—both financially and programmatically—while encouraging others to fill the gap of community needs that such a retreat would create.

There were, however, a few major exceptions in which Bush exhibited more of a collectivist approach. The Americans with Disabilities Act of 1990 and the Clean Air Act amendments of 1991 would never have become law without his strong support for the legislation. His budget compromise, in which his base of supporters felt that he violated his "no new taxes" pledge, was another example, and it levied a steep political cost on him. In 1992, he attended the United Nations Conference on Environment and Development (the Rio de Janeiro Earth Summit), although his opposition to some of its work product was notorious.

President William (Bill) Clinton (1993–2001) also tried to achieve a balance between the two creeds. As a leader of the Democratic Leadership Council, which sought to moderate between liberal and conservative ideologies by crafting a centrist "Third Way," he sought compromise and accommodation of divergent interests through mutually palatable solutions.[44] The most prominent example of Clinton's leadership on the collectivist side was his effort to reform the nation's healthcare system, which he undertook during his first two years. During that time, his agenda also included rights for "gays in the military," enforcement of civil rights, a progrowth budget, environmental protections, and other progressive reforms.

Following the reaction to those initiatives and the resounding defeat of Democrats during the 1994 midterm elections, Clinton shifted toward the individualist ethic, embracing "triangulation" between ideologies. In his 1996 State of the Union Address, Clinton declared that "the era of big government is over"[45] to demonstrate his commitment to fiscal responsibility as he headed toward his 1996 reelection campaign. In conformance with that declaration, during the summer of 1996, Clinton signed welfare reform into law (Temporary Assistance to Needy Families [TANF] and its welfare-to-work requirements that replaced Aid to Families with Dependent Children [AFDC][46]), which pleased moderates and conservatives while upsetting progressives. He also signed major legislation that imposed harsher criminal justice sentencing standards, deregulated the telecommunications industry, and deregulated the financial industry (eliminating the 1930s' Glass-Steagall law that imposed firewalls between commercial and investment banks, and between depository institutions and securities firms[47]).

Under Clinton's successor, President George W. Bush (2001–2009), the son of former President George H. W. Bush, the pendulum swung solidly in the individualist direction. Among many examples were his massive tax cuts that disproportionately benefited wealthier Americans, his attempt to privatize Social Security, and his loosening of environmental regulations and enforcement, especially with regard to laws and regulations that favored fossil-fuel industries. And yet, he still recognized the value of the other perspectives when circumstances demanded it. For example, *Washington Post* columnist Dana Milbank recounted Bush's better-late-than-never shift in response to the autumn 2008 financial crisis: "As Bush describes it, he had just been told by Treasury Secretary Hank Paulson that they should spend hundreds of billions of taxpayer dollars to buy up mortgage assets, and he approved the plan in full. 'If we're really looking at another Great Depression,' he recalls saying, 'you can be damn sure I'm going to be Roosevelt, not Hoover.'"[48]

President Barack Obama (2009–2017) redirected the government back toward policies that consistently prioritized community collective benefit. Although he aimed for legislative solutions, when Republicans in Congress thwarted his legislative agenda, Obama resorted to enacting policy through executive orders and administrative actions. In contrast with other presidents whose use of executive orders was an extension of their governing temperament and rugged individualism, Obama was not oriented that way. He mainly used those tools out of pragmatic necessity, as a last resort when facing intransigence from the Tea Party/Freedom Caucus members in the Republican-controlled Congress. As journalist Ron Fournier put it, "At his best, Obama promised to work with Republicans to reduce the deficit in a way that honors both individualism and community."[49]

In addition to the Patient Protection and Affordable Care Act (ACA), Obama led many other collectivist-oriented efforts that sought to improve quality of life for all Americans, including:

- the economic stimulus package (the American Recovery and Reinvestment Act [ARRA] of 2009);
- the financial industry reform law (the Dodd-Frank Wall Street Reform and Consumer Protection Act);
- enhanced enforcement of civil rights (consent decrees by the Department of Justice to monitor police conduct and protect civil rights in Ferguson, Baltimore, Cleveland, Chicago, and other cities);
- stringent enforcement of voting rights (through US Supreme Court cases to uphold the Voting Rights Act of 1965, especially the act's section 5 [preclearance requirements], section 4b [coverage formulas], and section 2 [prohibiting racial gerrymandering]);
- strengthening of women's rights and pay equity (the Lilly Ledbetter Fair Pay Act of 2009);
- assurance of LGBTQ rights (the Don't Ask Don't Tell Repeal Act, the Matthew Shepard and James Byrd Jr. Hate Crimes Prevention Act, and support of same-sex marriage through amicus briefs filed for cases heard by the US Supreme Court);
- expanded environmental protection (COP21 Paris Agreement, and EPA regulations limiting toxic air emissions at power plants and factories, increasing vehicle fuel efficiency, reducing vehicle emissions, increasing energy efficiency in appliances, restricting mountaintop strip mining);
- initiatives to stimulate clean-tech and renewable energy (grants and loans through the ARRA); and

- initiatives to provide all Americans with broadband and wireless access to the internet (Broadband Technology Opportunities Program, BroadbandUSA, and USDA Rural Utilities Programs).

In many of his speeches, President Obama eloquently articulated the necessity and importance of our federal government purposefully acting to benefit the common good for, and elevate the quality of life of, all Americans. However, a comment that he made while campaigning in 2012 stirred controversy. When making a point about government investments in infrastructure and supportive policies like tax breaks and enterprise zones that facilitate the creation of private enterprise, he said, "If you've got a business—you didn't build that."[50] He was making a quintessential point about collectivism, and the ecosystem that it provides so that entrepreneurs can flourish. In fact, Obama led up to that comment with statements such as "if you've been successful, you didn't get there on your own." A broader excerpt surrounding the controversial comment puts it in its proper context: "If you were successful, somebody along the line gave you some help. There was a great teacher somewhere in your life. Somebody helped to create this unbelievable American system that we have that allowed you to thrive. Somebody invested in roads and bridges. If you've got a business—you didn't build that. Somebody else made that happen. The internet didn't get invented on its own. Government research created the internet so that all the companies could make money off the internet."[51] Yet, opponents lambasted him because he took a shortcut in making his point about collective action, which made it easy to take his words out of context.

TRUMP'S EXTREME INDIVIDUALISM DICTATES POLICY

On the spectrum of these two creeds of our national identity, Donald Trump's presidency is unique. He gives the individualism versus collectivism dialectic an unprecedented level of importance by his words and actions. Previous presidents who embraced the individualist creed typically did so due to their philosophies and principles, enabling them to implement policies that reflected their beliefs. Trump is different, which is partly due to his disinterest in learning about historical precedents,[52] and partly due to his personality. Not only does he cling tightly to the individualist ethic in policy matters more than any previous president, he also extends it further. His individualistic personal interests dictate his decision-making *modus operandi* and motivate his conduct and statements. His individualistic persona elevates his "cult of personality" celebrity status and self-glorification to a type of currency, which he leverages when appealing to his supporters for their approval. Their validation of that approach encourages him to fuse his persona and self-interests with policy.

To the extent that policy drives some of Trump's actions, most of his administration's policy initiatives reflect Trump's devotion to the individualist side of the debate that seeks less government involvement or intrusion in commerce, finance, and social justice. Examples include the efforts to:

- overhaul the tax code with lower tax rates for businesses and wealthy Americans, to dramatically decrease their overall tax liability (with only minor tax relief to lower-income Americans), to the detriment of the programs serving the common good that will suffer without sufficient tax revenues;
- repeal and replace Obamacare with a bare bones system that shifts the burden for healthcare costs and coverage away from the government (including Medicaid) and toward personal responsibility;
- deconstruct environmental regulations in order to allow unfettered mining, drilling, fracking, and other extraction of coal, oil, gas, and other fossil fuels to allow individuals' profiteering without regard for the long-term impacts that such activities have on human health and environmental sustainability;
- extract the USA from international agreements that were designed to solve problems through global collective action, for example, the COP21 Paris Agreement, NAFTA, the Trans-Pacific Partnership, and the Iran Nuclear Deal;
- deregulate banks and financial industries to enable greater accumulation of assets by wealthy elites, which will exacerbate the gaps between rich and poor, the privileged class and mainstream society, leaving most Americans vulnerable to corporate practices and predatory excesses; and
- diminish programs and regulatory structures at the Departments of Justice, Labor, Education, Energy, State, Health and Human Services, Housing and Urban Development, the Environmental Protec-

tion Agency, and elsewhere that had been designed to protect rights, provide equal opportunity, stimulate growth, preserve our environment and resources, and protect human health for all Americans.

Many of Trump's supporters celebrate his positions because these policies serve the interests of individuals who benefited from institutionalized advantages prior to Obama's presidency. Many individuals and industries that profited under previous presidencies and regulatory regimes objected to Obama administration actions that diminished their established advantages. As usual, change was disruptive. Obama's focus on equal protection, equal opportunity, quality-of-life improvements for all, environmental protection, lowering our carbon footprint, consumer protections, and strengthening our global alliances were geared toward collective benefit and long-term sustainability. Trump's policies reverse Obama's progressive policies that adapted to contemporary realities and necessities for equality and the common good. The Trump administration aims to reinstate the prior advantages to the detriment of egalitarianism and the long-term prosperity of the broad-based American collective.

Many other Trump supporters celebrate his style of decision-making, which is driven by his individualist impulses. For Trump, individualism revolves around the individual in charge, as was the case with his private business. Trump's tactics, which seem erratic and volatile to some, are seen as crafty and shrewd by his fans who think he is shaking up the process and keeping others off-balance to maximize his leverage. His words and actions convey that he views the government as an extension of himself, as if it belongs to him alone and he can dictate its actions according to his whims. For example, Trump has fabricated spurious allegations without any evidence, in one instance calling for an investigation into the Department of Justice[53] (alleging that his campaign office had been wiretapped), and in another, calling for a new Special Counsel[54] (alleging that an FBI agent had been embedded in his campaign). In both situations, Trump pressured Attorney General Jeff Sessions to diverge from DoJ standards, and excoriated Sessions for not doing what he wanted.

With regard to policy, Trump consistently advances his individual interests. It is not a coincidence that his top priorities were health reform (which would have lowered taxes) and tax reform legislation that includes major tax breaks for wealthy individuals. Tax reductions in the 2017 tax law benefited

Trump and his family dramatically,[55] and the repeal of Obamacare would have also substantially reduced Trump's taxes.[56] Trump's decisions on taxes benefit the broad collective community only incidentally, to the extent that is necessary to make those new laws politically marketable. The common thread apparent from his decisions on taxes is that they are developed with a constituency-of-one in mind: Donald Trump.

On healthcare, it was evident that Trump just wanted a deal, regardless of what it looked like. By repeatedly contradicting himself on health policy, and even criticizing the bill (which he later called "mean") that passed the House with his full support, it was clear that he didn't understand or really even care about the specifics of healthcare legislation. His aims aligned with his individual interests and his lack of concern for collective impact. Trump's primary concerns were that the bill must include tax breaks and that there must be final passage of something, anything, so that he could call it a "win." He was totally indifferent about the vital details that determine the effectiveness of a healthcare system, including issues impacting covered benefits, delivery of services, and payment. Aside from getting a massive tax break, he seemed to believe that healthcare reform doesn't affect him or people like him.

But that is just plain wrong, and it reflects his lack of understanding about healthcare. The repeal of the ACA would jeopardize all Americans, not just those covered by Obamacare. Smart healthcare policy is vital to the collective community, beyond individuals. If millions lose their coverage, then when they need healthcare, they would have to go to emergency rooms, which would increase uncompensated care. Those costs would be shifted to people who do have health coverage, causing everyone's costs to soar. As fewer people have access to preventive care, untreated communicable diseases would rise. Public health contagion would increase, infecting people regardless of coverage. Anyone, including Trump, who encounters other people at work, at a campaign rally, at school, in the supermarket, in the theatre, or at the gym would be at risk. What starts as an erroneously perceived individual risk quickly grows into a major community risk.

Tax breaks that disproportionately benefit the wealthiest Americans—by sharply reducing the corporate tax rate, sheltering millions of dollars from the estate tax, and giving the overwhelming share of personal tax cuts to the wealthy—are a quintessential example of favoring individualism to the detriment of collectivism. These tax cuts, which were in his 2017 tax law, had been atop Trump's presidential wish list, after years of doing all he could to lower or eliminate his own taxes, which he acknowledged publicly and proudly. In interviews during the campaign, he openly spoke about how much he hates paying taxes and does everything he possibly can to lower or completely eliminate his federal tax liability. During his September 26, 2016 debate against Hillary Clinton, Trump even bragged about not paying any federal tax, saying "that makes me smart." The 2017 tax cuts benefit him personally and dramatically—lowering his own taxes by changing the laws that affect him— while exacerbating inequality. Trump's tax cut law will eventually engender resentment among lower-income Americans who only got minor tax cuts that will expire after only a handful of years. They were included so that the administration could claim that the bill helps most Americans, even though those meager measures only amount to a few crumbs from the table of the millionaires and billionaires, who will reap the major benefits. But the impact will not be confined there, and will likely trigger social distortions, disillusionment, and disintegration.

Societal animosity about inequality festers when the accumulation of wealth by individuals is prioritized over the prosperity of the broader community. A 2017 study by fourteen universities on wealth disparities found that the level of inequality in the United States is "probably the highest wealth inequality for any developed country right now," according to the study's lead author, Tim Kohler.[57] "Inequality has a lot of subtle and potentially pernicious effects on societies," Kohler said in a statement.[58] "We could be concerned in the United States, that if [inequality levels] get too high, we could be inviting revolution, or we could be inviting state collapse." The tax cuts and other laws that increase inequality will have long-term negative impact. People with less financial means will increasingly feel dislocated from society, as if the deck were stacked against them. There will likely be economic stagnation among those who seek upward mobility but can't catch a break to get ahead. There may be a rise in economic crimes, and possibly in violent or physical crimes that result from personal hardship and feelings of futility. There will likely be even more political discord, partisanship, and voter rebellion, possibly to the point of class warfare. These risks will jeopardize the well-being of the entire American community, including the rich.

The repeal of financial industry regulations, corporate accountability measures, and consumer protections (which prevent the type of banking and lending practices that led to the 2008 economic collapse) could put the country at risk of another fiscal crisis. Although some well-tailored revisions to the Dodd-Frank law were appropriate and enacted in 2018 (along with others that were overly permissive), wholesale repeal of the law, or dismantling the Consumer Financial Protection Bureau, would enable rampant profiteering at the expense of the collective. Removing communally minded safeguards allows self-interested banks and individualistic bankers to instill predatory lending practices. Irresponsible corporate practices, obstacles to economic opportunity and social mobility, and reductions in consumers' financial bargaining power may flourish. If consumers lack access to capital and face dire consequences from banks' unreasonable and unregulated rules, there could be a new wave of economic victims burdened with financial hardships. The federal government might again be called in to provide a safety net or bailout to financial institutions at great cost, both financially and politically.

On trade, Trump apparently has individual interests, although we don't know what they are since he never released his tax records. But it appears that he and/or his businesses faced disadvantages due to some trade rules, which fueled his animosity. He is now trying to settle that score by renegotiating or canceling a number of major trade pacts, and by imposing tariffs, regardless of the consequences to the collective society. (Note: trade is discussed further in chapter 7.)

On immigration, Trump's travel ban vilifying Muslims also stems from his individualistic stance and idiosyncrasies. He has absolutely no affinity for the people against whom the travel ban discriminated, making it easy for him to reject their needs and ambitions. He regards his own ambitions and background as the benchmark for which individualistic pursuits are meritorious, making it easy for him to impose adverse treatment on people who, from his perspective, are not like him. He considers them unworthy of empathy, accommodation, or compassion. His antipathy is evident in his effort to prevent refugees from coming to our country. A limit is set each year on refugee admissions into the United States, with far less actually admitted. In 2016, the limit was 110,000. In 2017, Trump lowered the cap to 45,000; and in 2018, he lowered it again to 30,000.[59]

Trump's pernicious attitude led to his decision to penalize asylum seekers and unauthorized immigrants by separating children from their parents.[60] Although Attorney General Sessions announced the policy, it stemmed from Trump's White House.[61] Trump's support of that inhumane policy was reinforced in July 2018 when, deflecting a question about the government's violation of the court-mandated deadline to reunite families, he declared, "I have a solution. Tell people not to come to our country illegally. That's the solution. Don't come to our country illegally. Come like other people do. Come legally."[62] When Trump was then asked if "you're punishing the children because their parents are coming?" he did not refute the punitive intent, responding, "We have laws. We have borders. Don't come to our country illegally."[63] It takes a dose of rugged individualism to migrate to another country, but apparently, Trump only likes his version of what an individualist is.

As an ardent individualist, when Trump has a policy inclination, it usually aims to reduce the government's role and spending (except for defense and his pet projects, such as building a wall along the border with Mexico), and hence, reduce his taxes. His agenda generates strident opposition from advocates, activists, interest groups, elected officials, and communities that are adversely impacted by the funding and regulatory cutbacks. Opponents recognize the harm to society that his policies inflict on services, issues, and programs. They fiercely resist policies that undermine the fabric of society that our collective community gained through decades of dedication and hard-fought battles. And when we do not hear much from Trump about a particular policy, it appears that he doesn't have a personal or political stake in the matter, either for or against a particular outcome.

Trump's policies, which ignore the collectivist rationale of existing laws, propel negative repercussions. Beneficiaries of government protections are at risk, as his administration threatens policies and programs that safeguard civil rights, voting rights, clean air, clean water, fair labor standards, worker safety, and educational and economic equal opportunity. Decimation of these rights and laws will tear social cohesion, exacerbate wealth gaps, and build animosity between communities. Individualist policies that encourage an "every person for himself/herself" attitude will impose severe consequences. Increases in poverty, homelessness, crime, drug addiction, and decreased economic productivity are predictable long-term results from such a climate. Counter-reactions to Trump's policies might also include actions that disregard social norms by bending rules and breaking laws to secure self-interests. These occurrences will definitely impact Trump's friends and supporters, along with all other Americans.

Perhaps even more troubling, cabinet officers typically follow the president's lead by aligning their policy decisions with his policies. In the case of Trump's cabinet officials, that translates to decisions that prioritize the largess of wealthy individualists at the expense of the needs of the broader collective community, whose needs should be at the forefront of any cabinet member's thoughts.

TRUMP'S EXTREME INDIVIDUALISM
MAKES GOVERNMENT PERSONAL

Trump's affinity for individualism far transcends traditional boundaries. His devotion to individualism is literal. He applies it not just as a matter of policy and ideology, but also as a personal tool, in a way that we've never before seen in a US president. Both his words and his actions reveal that Trump expects his appointees and staff to accord priority above all else to his reputational, pecuniary, and electoral interests. Many incidents—such as those in which he required appointees to be loyal to him personally—demonstrate that his primary motivation is to preserve, protect, promote, and defend *his own* interests.

He sometimes widens the scope of his concern beyond his and his children's interests, but even then, it is problematic. For example, when gender is a factor, he extends the scope of his concern to men under scrutiny. When his staffer, Rob Porter, was accused of domestic abuse by his former wife and denied a security clearance by the FBI, Trump came to his aid and continued to support him even after Porter was forced out of his job.[64] When Fox News executive, Bill Shine, was unemployed due to his role in covering up sexual abuse by Roger Ailes and Bill O'Reilly, Trump hired him as a deputy chief of staff.[65] Most profoundly, when Brett Kavanaugh was accused of sexual misconduct, Trump doubled down in support of him,[66] vocally lamented that men are vulnerable to having their careers ruined by women's allegations, and even ridiculed the accuser at a political event.[67] It is no mere coincidence that, the following month, Secretary DeVos released new rules about sexual assault and harassment at colleges that tilt enforcement procedures in favor of the accused (usually men).[68]

It seems that there are two reasons for Trump's concern for men who are accused of improprieties. First, his defense of them aims to reinforce his defense of himself. Trump has been accused of sexual misconduct by nineteen women, all of whose allegations he claimed were fake news, going as far as to call them liars.[69] Second, and just as important, as an ardent individualist, Trump seems to believe that he is licensed to serve his individual interests, without restraint, modulation, or consequence. He seems to resent anyone who calls for empathy or compassion to be injected into the calculation. Trump apparently identified with Kavanaugh being an aggressive defender of his own individual behavior, regardless of the veracity of his defense, particularly since Kavanaugh was being confronted by activists in the #MeToo movement.

On matters of national policy (e.g., tax breaks, bank regulation, healthcare, trade, tariffs, fossil-fuel profiteering), Trump does not seek to benefit the common good or the broad-based American collective. Instead, when he broadens his range of concerns, he most often goes to bat for people like him and people whom he aspires to be like: the wealthy, privileged class, such as members of his country clubs, and celebrities. Supporting their interests is akin to supporting his own. Additionally, because Trump quests for approval and values people who pay homage to him, he rewards those who profess their loyalty or devotion to him. To secure and reward the support of his base, he is willing to take policy positions that cater to their beliefs and excite them, as long as their interests do not conflict with his own. Although Trump's rural and middle America base is not like him, they share his anger and resentment toward the establishment, celebrate his deviance from traditional norms, and validate his belief that he is the individual who matters, even when his policies are disadvantageous to them. The symbiotic relationship between Trump and his base plays out on many policy fronts.

Trump manufactured a public image of himself as a strong-willed, self-made, rugged individualist, and his base seems to have embraced that image, irrespective of facts to the contrary. They may be unaware of all of Trump's legacy advantages from his father, finances, and schools—and his questionable business practices—that put him on a glide path toward wealth. His base may be so enamored with his celebrity, brash demeanor, and authoritarian bombast that they willfully dismiss facts about his true nature. They may simply envy his inherited wealth and disregard for norms. In turn, their adoration inspires Trump to amplify his branded persona. Their adulation reinforces Trump's belief in his own image and encourages him to take it to an extreme, resulting in a hyperbolic caricature of a superior rugged individualist.

Trump's conduct and policies can be explained more by personality and psychology than by public policy or political philosophy. The Goldwater rule,[70] named for 1964 GOP presidential nominee Senator Barry Goldwater, restrained comments about a public official's psychological fitness without a professional face-to-face evaluation. But many believe that it does not apply to Trump.[71] Despite protestations from his acolytes, Trump's psychological and mental status is a public matter, not the exclusive domain of psychiatrists who evaluate him as a patient. In contrast with his predecessors, whose decisions were based on their perception of national interests, Trump acts on his personal interests. Trump insists that he *is* the policy, and the policy is what he wants. Therefore, the only way to understand his policy is to understand his psychological composition and needs that drive his decisions. His daily ubiquity and the transparency of his tweets and comments—far beyond that of past presidents—inundates every American with insight into his character, motivations, objectives, needs, and temperament.[72] He chose to rip away the veneer and expose his impulses. Rather than hide his psychological fabric, he has placed it in the public record. Informed by the deluge of his daily behaviors, each of us can evaluate him and interpret his conduct in the context of every other human interaction that we've ever had. It would be irresponsible of the public not to do so, since he has transformed his personality and psychology into governmental and national behavior, therefore inviting our scrutiny.

While fusing his persona and policy, Trump glorifies himself as the archetype of individualism. The lofty status that he accords himself was reflected in his declaration that "I alone can fix it," when accepting the Republican nomination.[73] His self-devotion was even more explicit in a 2017 interview during which he proclaimed, "The one that matters is me. I'm the only one that matters."[74] He went further during a 2018 interview with Fox News in which he fabricated a disaster scenario to claim his indispensability, asserting, "If I ever got impeached, I think the market would crash. I think everybody would be very poor."[75]

Yet, unlike authentic rugged individualists, he is plagued by dependency on others. He quenches his thirst for validation by soliciting tributes and praise (from Russia's President Putin, Israel's Prime Minister Netanyahu, the Philippines' President Duterte, Saudi Arabia's Crown Prince Salman, etc.), which seem to be as vital to him as air and water are to most people. He bullies others in an attempt to build up his stature (referring to politicians and pundits by derogatory nicknames like "Little Marco" Rubio [US Senator from Florida], "Low Energy Jeb" Bush [former Florida governor and rival for the 2016 GOP presidential nomination], "Liddle' Adam Schiff" [Democratic Congressman from California], and "Sleepy eyes Chuck Todd" [NBC political director and host of *Meet the Press*]). He boasts his preeminence even when he is an amateur ("I know more about ISIS than the generals do").[76] He proclaims his superiority even when such claim is baseless ("Nobody loves the Bible more than I do"[77]) or antithetical to his conduct ("No one has more respect for women than me"[78]). He shifts the blame for his failures onto others ("Can you believe that Mitch McConnell, who has screamed Repeal & Replace for 7 years, couldn't get it done").[79] He is obsessed with winning, as if wins will establish his worth ("My whole life is about winning. I always win. . . . My whole life is about winning. I don't lose often. I almost never lose").[80]

Common sense and basic life experience teaches us that anyone who consistently utters such epithets and basks in self-aggrandizement has an obvious need to inflate their image to overcompensate for low self-esteem. He often injects claims of intellectual prowess inappropriately, as when he complimented himself as a "very stable genius" during the 2018 NATO meeting.[81] He repeatedly cites his Electoral College victory, even when entirely out of context, as if to assert his worthiness, as in his press conference with Putin in Helsinki.[82] The intended audience for these comments may actually be himself, as it seems that he says them to justify being president, and reassure himself that he belongs. Our parents taught us that these behaviors indicate an emotionally destitute, weak person, and we don't need a psychiatrist's evaluation to confirm that. Even so, many psychologists and psychiatrists have publicized their professional opinions[83] about Trump's mental and emotional status, with similar findings.[84]

A strikingly fatuous display of Trump's dependence on approbation and affirmation occurred in June 2017, at his first cabinet meeting, that opened with the most sycophantic cacophony of humiliating brown-nosing that has probably ever been imposed upon senior officials in our government's history.[85] Trump's cabinet members took turns showering him with compliments and praise saying that they were "deeply honored," "thrilled," and "privileged" for the "great honor to work with you," and that "it was a great honor traveling with you . . . and an even greater honor to be here serving in your cabinet." Short-tenured chief of staff Reince Priebus climbed to the top of the dunghill by declaring, "On behalf of the entire senior staff around you, Mr. President, we thank you for the opportunity and the blessing that you've given us to serve your agenda."[86] The genuflection stopped just short of referring to him as their wonderful dear leader. One could only imagine how quickly

Truman or Eisenhower would have cut off such talk and directed everyone to get back to business. Although that display was the apex of absurdity, similar obsequiousness is commonly uttered from the press secretary's podium, any lectern from which Trump is being introduced with him standing nearby, and anywhere else where Trump could be watching, which includes televised interviews and congressional hearings.

Trump conveys the impression that he harbors a narcissistic delusion of being the ultimate individualist, supreme in all endeavors. His ignominious August 15, 2017 press conference at Trump Tower about the Charlottesville violence was a typical example. Trump's comments were filled with so many newsworthy calamities ("You also had some very fine people on both sides") that the media did not have the bandwidth to cover them all. In one over-looked claim about the video of the violence, Trump declared, "I watched those very closely, much more closely than you people watched it."[87] This claim is nonsensical on many levels. First, he had no way of knowing how closely anyone else watched the video, or how a whole roomful of reporters watched it. Second, he assumed that other people did not watch it well or cor-rectly, which he had no basis to assert. Third, he conveyed his belief that he is better at watching things than anyone else, and that all others must defer to his superior watching powers.

That comment fits within a lineage of Trump's statements of individ-ual superiority, including, "Nobody has more respect for women than I do"; "Nobody's better to people with disabilities than me"; "There's nobody that's done so much for equality as I have"; "Nobody knows the system better than me"; "Nobody's more conservative than me"; and "I will be the greatest jobs president that God ever created."[88] Trump's statements bring to mind his doctor's declaration during the campaign, which suffered from similar flaws: "If elected, Mr. Trump, I can state unequivocally, will be the healthiest individual ever elected to the presidency." We later learned that Trump did, indeed, dictate that language to the doctor for use in the letter, as many had suspected.[89] As 2018 came to a close, Trump unleashed one of his most ironic and outlandish boasts, claiming that "nobody knows more about technology than me."[90] Vint Cerf and Tim Berners-Lee (who are among the creators of the internet), Bill Gates and Steve Wozniak (who are among the creators of personal computing), and tens of millions of tech professionals worldwide are evidence to the contrary. Even high school students pose a stark contrast to

Trump who (aside from his use of Twitter) is devoid of basic computer skills and well-known as a technological Luddite.[91]

Taken together, these boasts convey that Trump either believes that he is a historically supreme being—superior to all others in all ways—or is overcompensating mightily for his limitations and closely guarded feelings of inadequacy. Alternatively, he may be hypersensitive about being exposed as a fraud: as a businessman who went bankrupt multiple times, as a TV personality based on a false image, and as a candidate who allegedly needed illegal help from Russians to win. His hyperbolic statements of false superiority may be designed to prevent exposure of his faults, failings, and fallacies.

Trump is so eager to project himself as a powerful, dominant, rugged, individualistic leader that he acts in ways that damage his own best interests. For example, after he fired FBI director James Comey, White House staff issued an official rationale for the firing, claiming that it was because of reasons laid out in a recommendation by the Justice Department. But Trump, wanting to show that he is in control, and the dominant force in the government, contradicted the official explanation. In a televised interview, NBC's Lester Holt asked him whether he fired Comey because of the Justice Department's recommendation. Trump responded, "I was going to fire Comey. My decision." In response to Holt's follow-up question, Trump said, "I was going to fire regardless of recommendation," and reiterated, "But regardless of recommendation, I was going to fire Comey."[92] It almost seemed like a Jack Nicholson and Tom Cruise scene from the film *A Few Good Men*, with Lester Holt demanding of Trump, "Colonel Trump, did you order the Code Red," and Trump responding, "You're goddamn right I did!"

Trump reprised that role in December 2018 when he met with then-House Minority Leader Nancy Pelosi and Senate Minority Leader Chuck Schumer about funding the government. He again sought to proclaim his individual dominance by insisting on funds for a border wall while negotiating over keeping government open through a Continuing Resolution. As Trump escalated the tension during a photo op for the media, he blurted out, "I am proud to shut down the government . . . I will take the mantle. I will be the one to shut it down. I'm not going to blame you for it . . . I will take the mantle of shutting it down."[93]

The stock market is another tool that Trump uses to show that he is a powerful individual. When market indices rose dramatically during his first year in office, Trump touted their success, attributing the gains to his presence and policies. Analysts thought that Trump's motive was for stocks to rise and speculated about whether he would disavow responsibility for market declines. Although Trump took credit for the rise, financial growth is only one of his goals. He also uses the markets to proclaim his control. In early 2018, Trump announced his plan to impose tariffs on steel and aluminum, despite warnings against starting a trade war that would lower stock prices. When countries reciprocated, Trump doubled-down, imposing more tariffs on more goods, which continued the decline of stock prices. Then, he unleashed a series of tweets and comments demonizing Amazon, ostensibly to drive down the price of its stock (likely due to his animus toward Amazon's CEO Jeff Bezos, who also owns the *Washington Post*). Lawmakers from both parties asked him to stop attacking Amazon, but instead of complying, he again doubled-down with more aggressive statements, further toying with the stock's price. By targeting the stock market as a whole, or specific companies, Trump apparently relishes the ability to make stock prices rise and fall according to his caprice, to reward or penalize companies and their leaders.

Another case of Trump's self-indulgent need to showcase his unique power was his pardon of Arizona's controversial Sheriff Joe Arpaio, who was convicted of contempt of court for failing to comply with a court order. Trump did not consult with the Department of Justice, Arpaio had not yet been sentenced, and Arpaio had not even submitted a request for a pardon. Trump issued the pardon as an individual favor, to demonstrate to his base how powerful he is. He probably also used the pardon as a means to send a message to anyone who is under Special Counsel Robert Mueller's scrutiny in the Russia probe, letting them know that a pardon might await them, too, if they are convicted after refusing to divulge Trump's secrets. Trump was flexing his muscles, as the individual who can make the government do what he wants it to do.

But in so doing, Trump damaged national interests by pardoning a government official who refused to follow court orders. By issuing the pardon, Trump elevated his individualist interests above the collective national interest. That began a series of pardons—presumably replicating the feeling of powerfulness—that he granted without the customary scrutiny by the Justice Department. With each pardon, in effect, he proclaimed that making Trump happy is more important than the rule of law. Yet, this country is based on the rule of law, and Trump has set himself up to eventually be reminded of that in an unpleasant and consequential way by Congress, the courts, and the facts that Special Counsel Mueller details in his full report. He is trying to usurp governmental authority so that it serves his will, as if our federal government were an extension of himself, existing just to execute his dictates. Our democracy does not allow that.

In the summer of 2018, Trump found another tool that he could use to capriciously impose his will with virtually no restraint. After former CIA director John Brennan criticized Trump for his embarrassing and unpatriotic comments at the Helsinki Summit with Vladimir Putin, and the damage that Trump's conduct did to US interests, Trump revoked Brennan's security clearance, and threatened to revoke clearances from other critics. While the executive branch has the right to revoke such clearances, doing so to punish someone for expressing their opinion is an affront to the First Amendment's right of free speech. Trump either did not understand that or simply did not care, being much more dedicated to his own image and feelings than to the Constitution and national security. Trump's authority over security clearances enabled him to serve his individual interests, both by hitting back at a critic and by shifting national attention away from the top news story at the time that was disadvantageous to him, namely, Omarosa Manigault Newman's highly condemnatory book, *Unhinged*.[94]

In September 2018, Trump attempted to unilaterally advance his individual interests through yet another mechanism with no constraints. He ordered certain documents that he believed were favorable to his legal defense against Special Counsel Mueller's investigation to be declassified and publicly released.[95] While a president has the legal authority to declassify documents, Trump's motive was highly suspect. Declassification can compromise national security, jeopardizing the intelligence community's sources and methods, which can have protracted negative effects. Trump's planned release of those particular pages and passages sought to impair Mueller's investigation, support his own interests without regard for other consequences, and bias public opinion about the Trump family's involvement with Russians. It appeared that obstruction of justice was Trump's goal. Although Trump bowed to pressure from the intelligence community and retracted his order to declassify the documents, the message underlying the order was clear. The timing was also relevant, as it may have been an effort to distract media attention away from the major news of the day that was disadvantageous to Trump, like former campaign chairman Paul Manafort's agreement to cooperate with Mueller.

In February 2019, Trump resorted to an extreme tool of individual authority in his obsessive effort to build a border wall. He unilaterally usurped government power by declaring a national emergency where none existed. By fabricating and falsifying an emergency, he sought to redirect funds that Congress explicitly refused to allocate, which circumvented Congress's power under Article One of the Constitution to decide how federal funds are to be spent.[96] Lawsuits were quickly initiated to prevent this violation, and his declaration is unlikely to withstand legal scrutiny because: (a) although circumstances at the border did not change significantly during his first two years, he had not previously considered the situation to be an emergency; (b) when he declared an emergency, he said that he didn't need to do it, and was doing it just to speed up the process; and (c) the actual, factual border conditions did not pose a national security threat nor otherwise constitute a national emergency.[97] The only threats at the border were personal to Trump. Contrary to his promises to his base, he had not built the wall, and Mexico did not agree to pay for it. Trump's self-interests were at risk, and he acted on those to the detriment of national interests. He disregarded our Constitution, the future impact on our government, our democratic processes, and the effect on Republicans who were forced to choose between supporting him or the rule of law.

Trump's self-centered individualism takes many forms, including unabashed and unabated narcissism. In one glaring example, when eleven Jews were murdered in a Pittsburgh synagogue, instead of canceling a rally on the same day out of respect and mourning for the victims, he held the rally and jovially lamented, "I said, 'Maybe I should cancel this arrangement because I have a bad hair day.'"[98] The juxtaposition of his complaint about the rain's effect on his hair while the nation mourned a mass-killing hate crime was appalling, illuminating his incapacity for empathy, his narcissistic priorities, and his total self-absorption. An especially bizarre display of these characteristics occurred when Trump met with hurricane survivors in Puerto Rico in 2017. Amid a throng of people who had lost their homes, their belongings, and possibly some loved ones, Trump deemed it appropriate to toss rolls of paper towels into the crowd, like basketballs.[99] He later said, "I was having fun," maybe believing that the paper towels had cleaned up their lives, soaked up the rains, and solved their misery in the process.[100] Trump's conduct and comments repeatedly demonstrate that his individualistic narcissism leaves no room for communal empathy, even for people whose lives were devastated.[101]

Empathy for people in need is a personality trait that is more prevalent among community collectivists than rugged individualists, based on the relative scope and breadth of their concern for others. Empathy can even be viewed as a motive for paying taxes, since tax revenues help the broader collective. In that context, the paper towel incident speaks volumes: Trump's inability to muster empathy for suffering victims created a void that he instead filled with his self-enamored conduct. As the boss sets standards for the staff, Trump's lack of empathy was epitomized in another incident by his aide, Kelly Riddell Sadler, who dismissed then terminally ill Senator John McCain's opposition to a Trump nominee by saying, "It doesn't matter, he's dying anyway."[102] Trump's aversion to empathy, and the tone he sets for his administration, might explain why he is unwaveringly cemented as an individualist, even though most individualists are not bereft of empathetic capacity.

The dual creeds of our national identity also come into play in Trump's reaction to criticism. He doesn't understand when Americans care more about the collective well-being of the American people than about the individual who resides in the White House. Because Trump runs the government as an extension of himself, orchestrated around his own best interests, he mistakes criticism of him to be criticism of the country. As a result, he continually demonizes the media (which he also does to urge distrust of the media so that his base will not accept news reports about Special Counsel Mueller's findings). He often asserts that the media is "the enemy of the people."[103] At a rally in Arizona in August 2017, he questioned the patriotism of the media, telling the crowd, "I really think they don't like our country."[104] It is as if his need for ego reinforcement is sustained by superimposing his individual interests on the entire country.

It is not surprising that Trump disdains the many marches and demonstrations in which Americans voice their opposition to both his policies and him personally, as they are a very visual form of criticism. It is quite possible that he views the marchers from the lens of a Hoover-esque individualist who scornfully dismisses the collectivists as dependent laggards who can't fend for themselves, and instead whine and plead to the government to give them things or protect them. It is likely that he considers the marchers as products of a failed philosophy or "loser" mentality. Since Trump, like other individualists, strives to be less interconnected with the country and the world than the collectivists are, he is antagonistic toward those who extend relationships with, and reliance on, a broader network of stakeholders. In lashing out against his critics within and outside of government, Trump fails to recognize the sanctity of the right to criticize the president. Our Congress, our courts, and, indeed, our Constitution were constructed to support and defend the rights, protections, and shared values that are embodied in those marchers.

Trump's self-centered version of individualism emboldens him to act as though the law does not apply to him. That contradicts our national values and compels scrutiny from Congress as it did from Special Counsel Mueller. In addition to Trump's concern about the investigation into matters involving Russians, his indifference to constraints on his own pursuits emboldens him to profiteer from his hotels, especially the one in Washington, DC, where foreign officials purposefully stay when in DC to meet with him or his staff. Trump behaves as if he is above the law, in direct violation of the Constitution's Emoluments Clause.[105] Although Trump's profiteering has not been the focal point of the initial hearings by congressional investigators, that may change, and these issues are primed for scrutiny by the courts, especially since his offenses against the Emoluments Clause are ongoing.[106]

Since Trump's self-interested pursuits are on a collision course with the rule of law, he has unleashed an incessant flow of fallacies in an effort to exonerate himself, including his repetitious "no collusion" mantra. Trump and his acolytes have tried many strategies to attack Mueller's, his staff's, and the FBI's credibility through deceptions, distortions, and false theories (e.g., fabricated conflicts of interest that Trump alleged when he tried to fire Mueller in 2017,[107] the firing of Deputy Director Andrew McCabe,[108] hysteria over text messages from an investigator whom Mueller removed from the case when he learned about the messages,[109] and the concocted illusion of an FBI "secret society" undermining Trump that conspiracy theorists claimed was revealed by those text messages[110]). Yet, Trump's actions are not surprising. As journalist Howard Fineman said in January 2018, "In a game of brute survival, the durability of institutions doesn't matter to the people in the ballgame, and that's where we're at."[111]

Trump's narcissistic individualism is also expensive. His use of federal resources to indulge his desire to spend weekends at his hotels are costly in terms of Air Force One, the Secret Service detail, staffing, lodging for Secret Service and White House staff, and myriad other logistics. Many taxpayers are offended by this extravagant and elitist use of taxpayer dollars, particularly while Trump's administration pushes policies that would disadvantage working-class Americans. Trump is indifferent about requiring middle- and lower-income Americans to pay for his self-gratifying luxuries and doesn't seem to care about the appearance of abuse that it generates.

Trump's individual excesses have also set a tone of fiscal indifference that his cabinet members seem to feel liberated to follow.[112] Many cabinet members are multimillionaires or even billionaires who may feel that they have license to squander federal resources as capriciously as the boss does. Such was the case when Secretary Steven Mnuchin's wife enjoyed a vacation by joining her husband on a trip, with transportation provided by a White House jet. After her offensive tweets about her ride and her designer clothes went viral, Mnuchin reimbursed the government for her airfare. But what if she hadn't tweeted? There is no reason to believe that they would have reimbursed the government if they hadn't been exposed. Former veterans' affairs secretary David Shulkin and his wife cavorted on a similar vacation at government expense, which they reimbursed only after it was publicly exposed. Health and human services secretary Tom Price was forced to resign after disclosure of his profligate use of private jets. Former interior secretary Ryan Zinke and former EPA administrator Scott Pruitt (both of whom were later forced to resign for multiple offenses) were castigated for their unnecessary flights and first-class travel, resulting in promises to travel in coach class henceforth. These incidents raise concern about other lavish expenses incurred by Trump administration officials and paid by US taxpayers that have not yet come to light.

If the problem were limited to Trump's individualistic policies, that would be enough to galvanize opponents. But Trump's subjugation of national interests to his own personal, individual interests escalates resentment and resistance. His self-promotional style, self-adulatory statements, and self-aggrandizing ethical abuses have intensified opposition to policy and practices that are borne from his narcissism and deep-seated antipathy toward the peoples' collective needs.

IMPORTANCE DURING TRUMP'S TENURE AND THE POST-TRUMP ERA

Trump has capitalized on the trend toward small government individualism and has taken it so far that it has the potential to fragment—if not undermine—our social cohesion. In light of what he has shown so far, it is necessary to consider how to avoid the worst outcomes. Can his individual-centric efforts be contained? Can the degenerative impacts of Trump's personalization of government be mitigated? Can the two competing creeds be reconciled in a constructive way that builds a shared national identity? How can Americans redirect the current pattern? What possible solutions are available and practical?

Although Trump is immune to moral suasion and reminders about our laws, his unbridled, unrepentant, self-centric individualism can be kept in check by the investigations that are being conducted by many congressional committees, aided by insights garnered from Special Counsel Mueller's evidentiary findings in his full report. The guilty verdicts against Paul Manafort and the guilty pleas by Trump's former attorney, Michael Cohen,[113] already altered Trump's approach, and the eventual results of the many ongoing investigations may be so consequential that they could dramatically shift the political landscape. With the Democrats in control of the House of Representatives in the 116th Congress as a result of the 2018 midterm election, they have begun to impose "checks and balances" accountability and expose Trump's practices. The scope of actions that the House is willing to take to expand its investigations and act on Robert Mueller's findings is much broader than it would have been if the GOP had retained control of the House.

Trump's capricious and imperious uses of his powers to grant pardons, revoke security clearances, declassify documents, and declare emergencies expose the need for reform. His abuse of these powers compels establishment of legally enforceable standards.

Congress should craft criteria and procedures that must be followed with regard to granting pardons, revoking clearances, and declassifying documents. Once the legislation is enacted into law, the Department of Justice should develop regulations that specify operational details. At a minimum, legislation should: (a) direct the Department of Justice to evaluate the merits of any proposed pardon, revocation, or declassification; (b) require public disclosure of the evaluation, with a reasonable public comment period, prior to any final action; and (c) invalidate an action that fails to conform to the criteria and procedures.

Congress should amend the National Emergencies Act to clarify that the president's authority to declare an emergency can only be invoked in response to a bona fide national emergency. Legislation should establish criteria for appropriate uses of that authority, for example: (a) there must be a threat to public safety or national security as certified by the CIA, FBI, Department of Defense, the Federal Emergency Management Agency (FEMA), or other federal agency with the capacity to make a factual (nonpolitical) determination of this type; (b) the threat must either be imminent or so consequential that remedial action must be initiated immediately; and (c) the impetus for the declaration must either emanate from new circumstances (not a stable, endemic situation) or a substantial, verifiable, recent intensification of exigent conditions that compel the designation of an emergency.

Trump's use of his powers is emblematic of his mindset. Although both rugged individualism and community collectivism have been ascendant during the past century, with Trump at the helm, individualism is now dominant. America is most unified and functions at its best when parity balances the two ideologies, minimizing polarization. In recent decades, when one side of our cultural heritage is incentivized and intensified while the other is obstructed and marginalized, animosity grows among those who feel excluded. Eventually the pendulum swings back the other way, the roles are reversed, and the animosities amplify with each cycle. The net result is an increasingly fractious society, and that does not portend well for future swings of the pendulum. The two creeds are not mutually exclusive, and both deserve respect, like when Senator Cory Booker dignified both while expressing his preference, saying, "I respect and value the ideals of rugged individualism and self-reliance. But rugged individualism didn't defeat the British; it didn't get us to the moon, build our nation's highways, or map the human genome. We did that together. This is the high call of patriotism."[114]

The solution may lie in a hybrid between the two creeds. A coequal coexistence is possible between the rights of individuals and the needs of the broad national community through a framework that responds to both. The voting patterns of the 2018 midterm election highlighted the cultural divide between rural America (in which individualism prevails) and urban/suburban America (in which collectivism prevails), as well as the need to accommodate both. Long-term cultural, social, economic, and political sustainability (rather than harmony, which is a much less realistic goal than sustainability) could be advanced through a type of cultural coalescence between the two legitimate, engrained mindsets. It would incorporate the essential qualities of both creeds, validate both belief systems, and serve as a foundation upon which policies are crafted to satisfy the most indispensable elements of each in ways that can be supported by Republicans and Democrats in Congress.

Although a detailed evaluation of the interplay between the two creeds on every important issue would be unwieldy, an example of the give-and-take between the two approaches offers a path forward.

Equality is one of the most fundamental concepts in our legal and cultural frameworks, if not the single most important. It is a cornerstone of our country's founding document, stated in our Declaration of Independence: "all *people* are created equal" (with an adjustment that Mr. Jefferson would welcome today if he had a do-over). It is a central theme in our constitutional amendments, myriad laws, social norms, and daily life operations throughout America. As such, it is one of the indispensable principles that should be advanced at every opportunity. Any law, regulation, or other government action that derogates from this principle is automatically suspect. The conscientious administration and promotion of equality in all governmental programs and services, protection of rights, and provision of opportunities is vital to the best interests of all Americans: rich and poor, advantaged and disadvantaged, across all demographic classifications. These concepts are rooted in collectivist notions of government serving the greater good, for all communities. A purely individualist approach would fall short of this mark, as it would have an exclusionary and elitist effect, with disparate benefits and privileges.

At the same time, equal opportunity does not translate to equal outcomes for every person. This is where the precept of rugged individualism takes hold. Since some people are more ambitious and persevering than others, governmental policy may incentivize individual distinction and success. Regulatory environments and policy frameworks should make it easy for every person to access all the necessary tools—education, business skills, capital, business resources, a decent standard of living, etc.—for any individual to pursue the livelihood of their choosing, so that they can succeed. These rights and opportunities should inure to all individuals in America. By being equally accessible to every American—providing opportunity to each person and the rewards of success to those who work to attain them—the individualistic and collectivistic principles converge.

Yet, the liberty to pursue opportunities should not be unrestrained. It should not enable industry leaders and major companies to unfairly leverage their market advantages, for example, by preventing new entrants into the marketplace. Policies should benefit entrepreneurs, small businesses, people from traditionally marginalized communities, and other individuals whose main asset is their vision or aspirations. Policies should not be co-opted to benefit those who already have major assets, influence, market dominance, bargaining power, or other structural advantages. The policies that support rugged individualism should be tailored to promote educational and economic advancement, social mobility, and attainment of basic quality-of-life standards, as opposed to amplifying the success of established enterprises, accentuating market dominance, or allowing unbridled profiteering.

Corporate policies and behavior have a vital role in achieving this balance. Corporate social responsibility (CSR) and corporate citizenship programs have been established in recent years at countless major companies and have become recognized as intrinsic to business sustainability.[115] CSR has been elevated to board agendas, senior officers are tasked with CSR program development and implementation, and CSR programs are highlighted in annual reports. While corporate growth and success is essentially rooted in individualism, CSR programs are rooted in collectivism, because it is good business for a company to demonstrate that it supports its community and is a good citizen within it. CSR programs can and do meaningfully enhance equality, opportunity, and other goals. In the years ahead, annually updated CSR Scorecards would be useful in tracking corporations' achievements on these and other environmental, social, and economic metrics. High performance on CSR Scorecards could be incentivized by providing the company with some type of Seal of Approval from a governmental or nongovernmental body, while consumers would be encouraged to patronize companies with such a seal.

The fusion of the two creeds should be appealing to even the most ardent Trump supporters. They, too, want success for themselves, their families, and members of their communities, through access to education, jobs, entrepreneurial tools, and small business resources. More often than not, Trump's supporters share the characteristics of individualists. They seek their own prosperity, not that of Fortune 500 corporations that have profiteered at their expense. During the 2008–2009 recession and subsequent recovery, many Trump supporters were exploited and victimized by big banks and major corporations through predatory practices, lending abuses, and unequal bargaining power. They realize that the success of Fortune 500 companies does not return substantial benefit to them.

It is very likely that the disillusionment and discontent that Trump supporters voiced during 2016 was partly the result of feeling ignored, neglected, and abandoned by corporate America, and being excluded from the economic rebound that others experienced after the recession. Despite their own rugged individualism, Trump voters, in effect, wanted to share in the success of the community collective.

In crafting hybrids among the two ethics, the president has a unique responsibility. The President of the United States, no matter who serves in that role, is the *de facto* CEO of the nation's community collective. Many other influencers and actors advance the interests of individuals and rugged individualists, for example, through client relationships or marketing to select groups. In contrast, the president is uniquely situated to advance the interests of our entire society. That is implicit within the job description, akin to a fiduciary duty to promote the sustenance, prosperity, and welfare of the American community. That duty certainly has been interpreted differently by each president. But those presidents whose interpretation prioritized the interests of a narrow cohort over the broader community collective, or who unfairly tilted the playing field in favor of a demographic or economic group to the disadvantage of others, are widely viewed as some of our worst presidents.

Donald Trump epitomizes the use of the presidency for the advantage of a narrow subset of Americans. He prioritizes and bolsters the interests of the select few, namely, himself, his family, the wealthiest among us, and others whom he likes or deems worthy of his support. A typical example is his tax law that funneled the overwhelming majority of personal tax breaks to the wealthy. He also acts with disdain toward people with whom he does not identify. Obvious examples include his travel bans, actions against DACA "Dreamers," disparagement of immigrants from Haiti and African countries, and countless comments, tweets, and Justice Department actions that vilify minorities.

Americans should take action to ensure that there will be no future president who is inclined to operate in dereliction of his or her duty to the entire society of American people. Ideally, the president is a unifier. At a minimum, the president is the president for all Americans. Anyone can serve individuals; but the president is supposed to—and is required to—serve the entire American community collective. Prior to casting their votes, the electorate is entitled to know how each person who aspires to the office will interpret that responsibility.

While there are limits to what can be done, at the very least, these issues should become a standard element of each presidential campaign. They need to be raised during the primary process, while voters are choosing among multiple candidates with whom they might be pleased. Waiting until the general election would be too late, since, at that point, voters face a dialectic between ideologies, and these issues could be considered incidental compared to litmus-test-level matters. Thus, each party's debates during the primary elections should include questions to each of the candidates such as:

- Our nation has a long heritage of promoting both rugged individualists and community collectivists. What role do these two legacies play in your thinking about the role of government?
- Which of these two traditions would you prioritize over the other, and why?
- As president, you would be the chief executive officer who serves the interests of the entire community collective, promoting the public interest. What does that mean to you, and what steps would you take to ensure that broad-based public interest is central to your decision-making?

These questions would not provide airtight assurances that a candidate would, as president, act in the best interests of the public, or achieve an appropriate balance between the two tracks of our nation's split personality. However, these questions, or others that raise the same issues, would illuminate each candidate's thinking on the matter, illustrate the degree of their understanding about these competing forces, and foreshadow some of the factors that would be central to the candidate's governance. There is every reason to incorporate these issues into the election of the person who will be the steward of these responsibilities. They are a small step toward ensuring that each future president will be mindful of his or her duty to serve our entire society. Given what has happened when these questions were not raised, they certainly are worth asking.

CHAPTER 2

DEMOGRAPHICS

THE CURRENT AND EMERGING STATUS
OF RACIAL AND ETHNIC TENSIONS

The racial and ethnic composition of our country is continually evolving toward numerical parity between whites and communities of color. The implications of this gradual trend are profound and will impact many arenas, from politics and economics, to civic planning and culture, including even the use of the term "minority."

For some, the statistical parity between white and nonwhite populations will generate optimism and encouragement, since parity is likely to boost opportunity and equality. For others, particularly those who feel that parity puts them at a disadvantage, it will generate anxiety and animosity that necessitate structural reassurances of fairness. And for many more, parity will generate a shrug of the shoulders, on the notion that it doesn't even matter since we are all Americans, regardless of which box we check, and how many Census form self-identification boxes there are from which to choose.

In the meantime, as we head toward numerical parity and after we reach that point, we must continue to inculcate a culture of equity and fairness for all Americans. While working toward that future, Americans must resist efforts to the contrary, such as those that were initiated by former Attorney General Jeff Sessions during Trump's first two years. Progress will be incremental, and there are sure to be setbacks along the way. Yet, by consistently advancing fairness, opportunity, and equality across the board for nonwhites and whites alike, resentment and fear will dissipate over time as interactions and familiarity increase, laying the groundwork for constructive coexistence, even if harmony is too great a goal.

DEMOGRAPHIC TRANSITION AND ITS EFFECT
ON RECENT AMERICAN POLITICS

Since World War II, the percentage of the total US population that is white has been gradually declining, while most other demographic groups have been incrementally increasing their share of the population. According to the United States Census Bureau, in 1950, 89.5 percent of the population was white, 10 percent of the population was black, and Native American and Asian/Pacific Islanders each accounted for 0.2 percent of the population (Latino/Hispanic heritage was not recorded until 1970).[1] In 1970, Census Bureau figures showed that whites accounted for 87.5 percent, blacks were 11.1 percent, Native Americans were 0.4 percent, Asian/Pacific Islanders were 0.8 percent, and Latino/Hispanic Americans (of any race) accounted for 4.4 or 4.5 percent of the population (apparently with some double-counting between race and ethnicity).[2]

In each decennial Census since then, the white population's percentage of the total population declined incrementally and slightly. In 2010, the most recent Census found that whites accounted for 72.4 percent of the total population.[3] From 1970 through 2010, the black and Native American populations increased incrementally and slightly in each Census, with blacks accounting for 12.6 percent and Native Americans reaching 0.9 percent of the total population in 2010.[4] The Asian/Pacific Islander and Latino/Hispanic populations rose at a higher rate over that period, with Asian/Pacific Islanders reaching 5 percent and Latinos/Hispanics (of any race) reaching 16.3 percent of the total population in 2010.[5]

The Census Bureau has developed projections for the share of the population that will be comprised of minorities in the next few decades and states that "'minority' refers to people who reported their ethnicity and race as something other than non-Hispanic White alone in the decennial census."[6] According to the bureau, minority groups combined to account for 36.3 percent of the population in 2010, and the bureau estimates that the percentage of minorities will increase to 39.9 percent in 2020, 44.5 percent in 2030, 49.2 percent in 2040, and 50.1 percent in 2042.[7] Obviously, a key aspect of these estimates is that, by 2042, the combined share of minority groups will make minorities the new majority.

Our communities of color have faced structural inequities since the inception of the United States, and severe inequities persist today. Although progress has been made on many fronts, inequality remains insidious and pervasive. For example, in 2015, the median income for white households was $62,950, yet only $36,898 for black households.[8] In 2010, the median income of black men was just 68 percent of their white counterparts.[9] In the latter months of 2017, the unemployment rate among blacks was 7 percent but 3.4 percent among whites, reflecting a longtime trend of black unemployment being twice that of white unemployment.[10] Among job applicants, researchers found that a black applicant without any criminal record is less likely to receive a callback or a job offer than a white applicant who does have a criminal record.[11]

These and other statistics demonstrate the lack of parity that exists in many aspects of American life that limit the upward economic, political, and social mobility of minorities. As demographics evolve toward numerical parity between minorities and whites, the urgency of solutions to resolve inequities will increase. Since policies and programs take time to produce their intended results, both governmental and nongovernmental initiatives need to be established as soon as possible to increase the pace toward a level playing field. This is necessary both for the sake of inclusive fairness, and for the sake of averting protracted injustices that would exacerbate social friction and its many harsh consequences.

Demographics and politics have been inextricably intertwined throughout American history, playing an important role in many contexts, including presidential elections and in policy decision-making following elections. The demographic shifts and democratization of the political process that have occurred since World War II have amplified the role of racial and ethnic factors in campaigns, governance, and policy. Since the 1960s, the language, strategy, policies, and appointment power of presidents have energized stakeholders on different sides of racial and ethnic issues. Some prominent examples include:

- Lyndon Johnson's "Great Society" initiative aimed to eliminate poverty and racial justice throughout the country. Yet, when he signed the Civil Rights Act of 1964 into law, the president reportedly said to his staff, "We have lost the South for a generation," signaling the law's anticipated backlash among Southern whites.
- Richard Nixon's "Southern Strategy" aimed to capitalize on white Southerners' resistance to change and their antipathy for the new laws

that were enacted under LBJ's leadership. Nixon spoke of "states' rights" and "law and order" as placeholders for overt racial references, while third-party candidate Alabama governor George Wallace used explicitly racist language that harkened back to South Carolina senator Strom Thurmond's Dixiecrats. Both Nixon's and Wallace's approaches exacerbated racial tensions.

- Jimmy Carter's term (1977–1981) was a time of transition on issues of race and ethnicity that included implementation of reforms rooted in the 1960s and early 1970s, as well as reactions and resistance to some of them (e.g., school busing of public school students, and the Bakke court case in which the US Supreme Court dealt a blow to Affirmative Action and quotas[12]).

- Ronald Reagan continued to leverage the concerns of white voters during his campaign and his presidency by using racially coded language in asserting his policies on "forced busing," the "welfare state," "states' rights," the "war on drugs," and his opposition to Affirmative Action.

- George H. W. Bush stoked racial divisions during his campaign with his ad about Willie Horton (an African American who committed a heinous crime while on a weekend furlough from his life sentence for murder), and during his presidency by inaction after the Rodney King police brutality case, which led to the 1992 Los Angeles city riots after the police officers responsible were acquitted. Bush also nominated conservative Clarence Thomas to the US Supreme Court after the death of civil rights champion Justice Thurgood Marshall.

- Bill Clinton was the first president to make inclusion and empowerment of minorities and women a priority in his presidential appointments and in many of his policies, which sought to rectify racial disparities (but not all, which led to criticism for parts of his criminal justice and welfare reform laws that were seen as having a discriminatory effect).

- George W. Bush appointed numerous minorities to prominent cabinet and senior staff positions, although his and their policy views and initiatives were not advantageous to communities of color, taking particularly regressive actions on Affirmative Action and voting rights issues.

- Barack Obama appointed many minorities and women at all levels, advancing policies aiding opportunity and quality of life for all Americans, while still being criticized by some communities of color for not going far enough to replace racial disparities with a level playing field.

This was due to his desire to not be seen as favoring the needs of African Americans over those of other Americans.

TRUMP'S BASE AND HOW TRUMP ENDEARS HIMSELF TO THEM

The demographic transformation of the US electorate is likely to have an increasingly consequential impact on American politics and government as our population evolves toward statistical parity between whites and non-whites. The emotions accompanying this change have been steadily amplifying in recent years and were especially evident among Trump's base of voters during the 2016 campaign.

Trump's most strident support is commonly among people who are white, male, older, working class, in lower income brackets, and without a college education.[13] It is neither incidental nor accidental that there was a strong correlation between support for Trump and lower education levels, which even Trump acknowledged when he crudely proclaimed, "I love the poorly educated."[14] White evangelicals were also among his most loyal supporters, and their overwhelming support for him continues despite his words and actions that violate their stated principles.[15] Although some of his voters were in other social strata, with college degrees and higher income levels, they were not the archetype of Trump's 2016 base voters.[16] It is highly likely that most would self-identify as individualists rather than collectivists, in some cases due to their affinity for economic or personal liberty, and in other cases due to their anti-immigrant and antitrade views.

Many of the white, working-class voters in Trump's base expressed feelings of powerlessness in recent years, as though they were bypassed by the nation's overall prosperity.[17] They were resentful toward those who gained ground while they perceived themselves losing ground, including those who benefited from Affirmative Action. Rightly or wrongly, many of them felt as though they had been bludgeoned by the 2008–2009 economic crisis, excluded from recovery efforts, ignored by the Obama administration, and forced to fend for themselves without any assistance from the federal government. Trump spoke directly to them during his Inaugural Address, saying, "The establishment protected itself but not the citizens of our country. Their victories have not been your victories. Their triumphs have not been your triumphs. And while they celebrated in our nation's capital, there was little to celebrate for struggling families all across our land. That all changes starting right here and right now. . . . The forgotten men and women of our country will be forgotten no longer."[18]

New York Times columnist David Brooks suggests that the predicament facing these Americans is emblematic of a deep cultural divide that has been long in the making. Writing about "the less-educated masses," Brooks explains, "Their pain is indivisible: economic stress, community breakdown, ethnic bigotry, and a loss of social status and self-worth. When people feel their world is vanishing, they are easy prey for fact-free magical thinking and demagogues who blame immigrants. We need a better form of nationalism, a vision of patriotism that gives dignity to those who have been disrespected, emphasizes that we are one nation, and is confident and open to the world."[19] By Brooks's description, the Americans who confront these challenges were primed for someone like Donald Trump to come along and offer his message. They may have even been hoping beyond hope for a candidate like him to recognize them, and when he did, they eagerly reciprocated by pledging their allegiance to him.

When they voted in previous elections, Trump's base voted for Republicans more often than not, since they typically identified with conservative and/or libertarian policies. Still, some had voted for Democrats, possibly on the basis of labor, wage, and other economic issues that would have motivated union members and other working-class voters. A sizeable percentage of Trump's base voters had not been regular voters, presumably because they felt marginalized by both political parties. They registered their anger with their 2016 votes for Trump, supporting the candidate who had given voice to their fears, enmity, and resentment.

Some people who voted for Trump in 2016 adulated him and were among his base voters, while others voted for him for other reasons and are not among his devoted base.[20] Trump's base voters were so committed to him that they would have supported him no matter what policies and polemics he conjured up. These are the intensely loyal followers whom he referenced when he said, "I could stand in the middle of Fifth Avenue and shoot somebody and I wouldn't lose any voters."[21] Whether or not they agree with everything he says, they express a tribal devotion to him. Since they identify with him, they feel that an affront to him is an affront to them. When Trump characterizes himself as a victim (of the media, the political establishment, or whomever, from one day to the next), the base joins him in feeling victimized. Since Trump is the personification of their cause, disrespect aimed at Trump is interpreted by his followers as disrespect aimed at them. When he hits back, they feel like they threw the punch. Because he validates them, they feel empowered. Since Trump lashes out against the establishment of both parties, his base voters are emboldened to reject people in both parties who rejected and disrespected them over the years. Their tribe is partly pro-Trump and partly just against anyone who is anti-Trump. They are on Team Trump and he is their champion.[22]

Larry Sabato, a professor of politics and the director of the University of Virginia's Center for Politics and a renowned guru of electoral politics, takes it a step further. Sabato described Trump's hardcore supporters by explaining, "I would say the most distinctive thing about him other than his obnoxiousness is that his followers aren't a base. They're a cult. This is a cult. They've ceded their independent thinking to this man. This is the most intense cult that I can remember in American politics."[23]

Trump ran a very white-centric campaign, often disparaging and insulting blacks, Latinos/Hispanics, immigrants, Muslims, and people of non-European origin, among others. Even when he launched his campaign, he made a point of insulting Mexicans. Later, when Trump asserted that Judge Curiel couldn't fairly preside over a case involving Trump because Curiel is Mexican (which isn't even true, since Judge Curiel was born in Indiana), even Republican leaders agreed that Trump's comment was racist.[24] Trump's sweeping and disparaging generalizations about African American society were offensive each time that he broached the topic, like when he imparted his "what have you got to lose" gambit.[25] He vilified the Islamic faith; soon after becoming president, he issued a travel ban that aimed to prevent people from countries with overwhelmingly Muslim populations from coming to America. Trump spoke the language of white grievance, anti-immigrant xenophobia, cultural myopia, and ethnocentric disparagement. It is as if Trump, who grew up in Queens, emulated a certain fictional Queens resident from a 1970s television sitcom in which the character's bigotry was a tool for contrast and condemnation. For Trump, Archie Bunker from *All in the Family* appears to have been a role model.

Trump's support among white Americans grew as he elevated their status in the social hierarchy through white "identity politics."[26] He did this by giving voice to white grievance, resentment of Affirmative Action, and those who advocate for white privilege.[27] In doing so, Trump solidified his support among the small subset of people who openly harbor or espouse white supremacist and neo-Nazi beliefs.[28] To be clear, by no means are all or most members of Trump's base white supremacists and/or neo-Nazis. For that matter, it is offensive, insulting, and just plain wrong to attribute those hate-filled ideologies to Trump's entire base. However, it is even more insulting, offensive, and wrong to suggest that white supremacists and neo-Nazis are not among Trump's base. They most certainly are.[29] As Melissa Ryan, author of the *Ctrl Alt-Right Delete* newsletter, wrote, "Whether you call them neo-Nazis, the alt-right, or white nationalists, Trump—an overt racist who refers to black-majority nations as 'shithole countries'—simply knows them as a key constituency and a significant portion of his political base."[30] It is a good bet that anyone who is patently racist or supports white supremacist ideology is a solid Trump supporter (even though not all Trump supporters are white supremacists). In Trump, they found their champion. Trump's white-priority campaign gave license to white supremacists and neo-Nazis to come out of the shadows and pursue their objectives.

Although overt racism is the most contemptible, latent racial bias and white privilege are also pernicious. They are the vile progeny of our nation's racist origins that W. E. B. Du Bois connected to contemporary problems: "The white group of laborers, while they received a low wage, were compensated in part by a sort of public and psychological wage. They were given public deference and titles of courtesy because they were white. They were admitted freely with all classes of white people to public functions, public parks, and the best schools. The police were drawn from their ranks, and the courts, dependent on their votes, treated them with such leniency as to encourage lawlessness."[31] While writing about conditions in 1860–1880, Du Bois framed the modern awareness of white privilege and the mindset of white superiority.

As was obvious at Trump's rallies and in publicized interviews with his supporters, many people in Trump's base propagate implicit bias, benign neglect, and subtle white supremacy that surfaces in different aspects of mainstream society, including government programs and policies. Whether conscious or unconscious, these views are corrosive. They breed social disunity, cultural apprehension, xenophobia, and voluntary segregation that encourage racial and ethnic groups to grow apart. Unlike openly racist whites, who are comparatively few in number, there are many latently biased whites in America, and their attitudes found refuge in Trump's words and actions. Professor Eddie Glaude Jr. connected the economic and racial motivations of Trump voters, explaining that they were fueled by "economic anxiety joined with the idea that government is taking things from hardworking people and giving them to undeserving black and brown people, people who don't attend my church."[32]

By making common cause with white Americans who harbor latent racially biased views, and questioning the legitimacy of minorities' interests, Trump reinvigorated and pseudo-validated the anachronistic beliefs that Du Bois decried. Trump says that he is not racist or xenophobic, maybe because he thinks he is just being himself, and he has so internalized racism and bigotry that he doesn't recognize it. But that is the nature of unconscious bias and latent racism. His words and actions speak volumes. Trump repeatedly attacks the esteemed Congresswoman Maxine Waters as having a "low IQ,"[33] despite her extraordinary intellect and legendary career.[34] In August 2018, Trump insulted the intelligence of two formidable African Americans in the same tweet, writing, "Lebron James was just interviewed by the dumbest man on television, Don Lemon. He made Lebron look smart, which isn't easy to do."[35] Deliberately and unjustifiably assaulting anyone's intelligence is offensive. But when that attack is applied repeatedly to African Americans, and is the main invective hurled at African Americans, it is plain old racism.[36] And the perpetrator is racist.

Compounding matters, Trump's January 2018 reference to African countries and Haiti as "shithole countries" during a meeting about immigration moved Trump's sentiments from latent racism to patent racism.[37] Any contention to the contrary was neutered by his follow-up comment, expressing his desire for more immigrants from Norway, a country whose population is overwhelmingly white.[38] In response to a February 2018 public opinion poll that asked 1,337 adults, "Do you think Donald Trump is a racist or is not a racist?," 57 percent of all respondents said that they believe Trump to be a racist, with 47 percent of whites and 84 percent of African Americans saying that they believe he is a racist.[39] Concern about what Trump's conduct reveals was succinctly stated in an editorial from the *Arizona Republic*, after the pardon of former Arizona sheriff Joe Arpaio: "By pardoning Arpaio, Trump made it clear that institutional racism is not just OK with him. It is a goal."[40]

It is admirable when Americans become engaged in the political process, exercise their rights, and speak up for their beliefs and their interests.

Unfortunately, many within Trump's base do so with antagonism, antipathy, bigotry, and even aggression toward others who express other values or do not look like them. It is problematic when anyone pollutes the political arena with venom and hostile behavior, and Trump rallies during his campaign were visibly and vocally filled with both. The rallies often had a feeling akin to the Old West, or the scene in *Frankenstein* when the town folk marched down the street with pitchforks and torches, ready to unleash their fears and anger at the source of their discontent. The friction may have historical precedent, with anachronistic echoes of frontiersmen in President Andrew Jackson's era, the anti-immigrant backlash to the two world wars, white supremacist rallies in the 1920s that recurred through the civil rights era, and other episodes of incivility, xenophobia, and hatred. But our nation has evolved and there is no place for bigotry and racial/ethnic antipathy amid the sensibilities and laws of modern America. Pitchfork Populism is not acceptable in a civilized nation that is based on the rule of law, rights, equality, justice, and mutual respect.

During the campaign, Trump engaged in racial and ethnic disparagement to build and galvanize his base among people who share his white-centric views, and he continues to do the same as president.[41] As acclaimed journalist and author Ta-Nehisi Coates wrote, "It is often said that Trump has no real ideology, which is not true—his ideology is white supremacy, in all its truculent and sanctimonious power."[42] Trump stoked discord at his campaign rallies, which normalized the animus and encouraged uncivil actions spawned by those emotions.[43] Trump sometimes even went so far as to encourage violence. For example, worried that there might be a protester with a tomato at a 2016 rally, he implored his adoring throng to "knock the crap out of them, would you? Seriously. Okay? Just knock the hell—I promise you, I will pay for the legal fees. I promise, I promise."[44] In turn, his base unleashed racially and ethnically motivated aggression, as "Trump's campaign rallies were associated with a rise in violence when they came to town."[45] After Trump's victory, there was a surge in racially motivated violence and other acts of hatred, as if Trump's views granted his supporters license to commit those acts.[46]

As president, Trump's racial aggression has escalated with conduct ranging from subtle (dog-whistle antagonism against NFL players protesting racism and NBA players refusing to visit the White House[47]), to structural (policies, issues, and entitlement programs[48]), and overt (sympathizing with the Charlottesville terrorists by saying that there were "some very fine people on both sides," insults about Rep. Waters and basketball star LeBron James, and his "shithole countries" remark[49]). Renowned historian John Meacham poignantly alluded to this pattern when he observed that "Trump is an extreme manifestation of forces that had been subterranean, but real, for a long time."[50] At his September 2018 press conference in New York, Trump falsely claimed that he won the women's vote in 2016, getting 52 percent of women's votes, when in reality he got 52 percent of *white* women's votes. His claim marginalized nonwhite women, as if black, Latina, and all other non-white women don't matter or don't exist.

The mobilization of Trump's white-centric base has been attributed to their fear of losing their status and statistical dominance, fear of nonwhite Americans gaining influence, fear of white privilege and political power dissipating, and fear of change.[51] They resent the loss of white Americans' control of the national discourse and priority in our national identity, as if it were a zero-sum game.[52] They resent the need to accommodate the legislative, policy, and funding needs of minority stakeholders. They resent the effect that it will have on their dominance of government, politics, and the drawing of congressional and other political districts. They resent the possibility that others who do not look like them might achieve the American Dream ahead of them.[53] The web of fear and resentment in which they are entangled is of their own making, driven by self-interested, impractical, antiquated attitudes that are reinforced, consciously and unconsciously, through explicit actions and implicit bias.

Fear and resentment beget destructive consequences. They lead to distrust of our institutions, including government, the media, financial centers, and any other institutions that can be interpreted as sources of power that restrain the aggrieved from attaining their rightful lot in life. Whether or not justifiable, that distrust can further metastasize into a broader fear that institutions are collaborating in collective action, which spawns conspiracy theories. Such was the case in 2018 when "Q-Anon" became a popular, albeit unknown, figure who gave voice to such fears by making outlandish and baseless claims that a broad-based conspiracy was afoot involving Barack Obama and Hillary Clinton, with subsequent extensions of the absurdities including Robert Mueller and Kim Jong-un. The "Q-Anon" conspiracy was used as an alarmist tool to urge support for Donald Trump as the savior against the forces of evil.[54] The ideology of conspiracy, such as what Q-Anon espouses, invites obedience to an authoritarian, believing that such a champion is necessary to crack the conspiratorial establishment's stranglehold on society.

Fear and resentment also lead to distrust of dissimilar people (the "Other"). That distrust spawns racism, xenophobia, demonization, and intolerance, all of which are contemporary forms of scapegoating. These mindsets were central to Trump's thirty-five-day shutdown of the government (from December 22, 2018 to January 25, 2019). The shutdown resulted from Trump's insistence on getting funds for a southern border wall to fulfill his campaign promise to his base. Despite the absence of a factual basis to justify the wall's necessity or efficacy, he knew that people with racist and xenophobic views would applaud him for his stance, since his "build the wall" promise was based on fear and intolerance. Trump was so convinced that demonizing "others" who migrate from south of the border would endear him to his base that he assured Speaker Nancy Pelosi and Senate Minority Leader Chuck Schumer that he would take the full blame for it.

It is worth reflecting on FDR's admonition that "the only thing we have to fear is fear itself." Just as that was sound advice about fear, it is also appropriate to declare that the only thing we have to hate is hatred, and the only thing toward which we should be intolerant is intolerance. These warnings against hatred and intolerance should apply to people at political rallies just as they apply anywhere else in America, whether they are driven by white-centric emotions or anything else. Hatred and intolerance are contemptible no matter what group of Americans are the recipients, and that includes both Trump's opponents and his supporters.

THE FALLACIES OF "MAKE AMERICA GREAT AGAIN"

Trump's base clings to the wistful mirage of 1950s America,[55] when white individuals who went to work and paid their bills were rewarded with social, cultural, political, and economic advantages, without fearing, resenting, or even having to think about nonwhite Americans who were being denied those same rewards and benefits. Today, working-class, non-college-educated whites among Trump's base feel aggrieved by that which helps nonwhites, and—to add insult to injury, in their view—by having to even compete with them for jobs. To those in Trump's base, the "Make America Great Again" slogan equates to "Give me the same unfair advantages that my grandparents had, before they had to share them in a more equitable society." But there's only so much space on a bumper sticker.

The Trumpian 1950s mindset is fallacious on many levels. It reveals a presumption of inherent entitlement, insisting on continued access to advantages, and the unlevel playing field that allotted those advantages to previous generations. Proponents of that mindset are diffident or even oblivious to the denial of similar advantages to previous generations of nonwhite Americans. They seek to maintain their own status without regard to whether all Americans should be given the same opportunities and advantages. It is a symptom of an "I've got mine" attitude that does not extend concern to the success of other groups or to society as a whole.

In sociologist Michael Eric Dyson's 2017 book, *Tears We Cannot Stop: A Sermon to White America*, in which he shares his perspectives on race as an appeal to white Americans, he writes, "Race has no meaning outside of the cultures we live in and the worlds we fashion out of its force and energy. Whiteness is an advantage and privilege because you have made it so, not because the universe demands it."[56] He explains that "whiteness has privilege and power connected to it, no matter how poor you are," and that "whiteness is a privilege, a declared, willful innocence."[57] Among Dyson's especially poignant observations is that "One of the greatest privileges of whiteness is not to see color, not to see race, and not to pay a price for ignoring it."[58]

Although some white Americans recognize these dynamics, others do not. The fact that many whites refute these concepts, either out of willful ignorance or a belief that doing so would be detrimental to their interests, is confirmation of Dyson's point. His observations are reflected in studies on "implicit bias" and "unconscious cultural associations," which have gained traction in sociological thought, and spawned training tools such as the Implicit Association Test by Harvard's Project Implicit.[59] Although implicit bias can take many forms, two broad categories are apparent: (a) institutional implicit bias, which is evident when institutions have inculcated a bias, such as our criminal justice system arresting, convicting, and incarcerating more nonwhites than whites, and employee hiring processes that, in effect, prefer white applicants over nonwhite applicants even when both are qualified; and (b) individual implicit bias, which is evident in individuals' systematic (conscious or unconscious) inclinations and presumptions, as with adverse stereotypes about nonwhites and favorable assumptions about whites. The latter is the type that Trump exploits and evokes with his divisive rhetoric, and which is very visible among the crowds at his rallies. Trump's white, older, working-class, non-college-educated, and evangelical supporters are either unaware of the bias that is being disseminated to them or are complicit by embracing it. Either way, they show no desire to challenge those biases or level the playing field. They appear to be more concerned that their long-held economic and societal advantages are eroding.

In his latest book, *How Fascism Works*, Yale professor Jason Stanley offers his insight into the mindset of those who seek revitalization of a bygone era, writing, "Fascist politics invokes a pure mythic past tragically destroyed. . . . In the rhetoric of extreme nationalists, such a glorious past has been lost by the humiliation brought on by globalism, liberal cosmopolitanism, and respect for 'universal values' such as equality. These values are supposed to have made the nation weak in the face of real and threatening challenges to the nation's existence. These myths are generally based on fantasies of a nonexistent past uniformity, which survives in the small towns and countryside that remain relatively unpolluted by the liberal decadence of the cities."[60] Noting their attachment to the past, he explains, "Corruption, to the fascist politician, is really about the corruption of purity rather than of law. Officially, the fascist politician's denunciations of corruption sound like a denunciation of political corruption. But such talk is intended to evoke corruption in the sense of the usurpation of traditional order."[61] Stanley cites President Obama, women, Muslims, Jews, African Americans, LGBTQ Americans, and "cosmopolitans" as examples of those who disrupt the traditional order from the point of view of those who aim to preserve it. The underlying objective—whether conscious or subconscious—of many in Trump's base is a return to the 1950s traditional order.

Many white Americans seem to think of race in a way that can be analogized by art. One artist, a painter, starts with a white canvas. The painter adds a few dots of color in some places, and maybe even shades an area or two. But it's still essentially a white canvas. From this perspective, whiteness is the default position, and anything that adds color infringes upon the whiteness. In contrast, another artist constructs a mosaic from small tiles. There are tiles of many colors, many are white, many have distinctive colors, and some have their own unique blends of colors. There is no single-color starting point, no default position, and no assumption that one particular color should be prevalent. The tiles fit together to form the outline of our country, with a resplendent design and swirling patterns from one end to the other. The tiles complement each other, and, once they are shaped together, they take on a unified purpose as a beautiful work of art depicting the nation.

In addition to its deformed attitudes toward nonwhite Americans, the Trumpian mindset's wistful longing for a return to previous eras imagines that our country's white population had been homogeneous and harmonious in those times, as if it were "great" for all white people. This ignores historical truths. As far back as our colonial days, there have been tensions within the white population composed of immigrants and their descendants from countries with different sensibilities, cultural habits, career inclinations, and urban versus rural living areas, which led to different quality-of-life standards and levels of success.

When America first became a nation, there was a prevalence of white Americans with British, French, or Dutch origins. In the first half of the 1800s, major waves of white immigrants came from Ireland, Germany, and Scandinavia, and in the latter decades of the century, especially large waves of whites came to America from Italy, Russia, Poland, and other eastern, southern, and northern European countries, while immigration from some regions was discouraged or outright prohibited, as by the Chinese Exclusion Act of 1882. During the early 1900s, Europeans immigrated to America to the extent possible under our increasingly restrictive immigrant quota laws, such as the Emergency Quota Act of 1921 and the Immigration Act of 1924, which set annual limits on the number of immigrants who would be admitted from each country, and intentionally welcomed more from western and northern Europe than from elsewhere.

These groups of new Americans, many of them white, were subjected to discrimination, menial labor in hazardous workplaces with unconscionably long workdays, dilapidated and dangerous housing with overcrowded living space, and violence without police protection, all of which combined to perpetuate endemic and inescapable poverty. They did not achieve social mobility or attain the American Dream at the same pace, in the same manner, or to the same degree. Ours was a very fragmented society in which white people with particular ethnic or national origins tended to live in depressed regions, cities, and neighborhoods—slums and ghettos—where there was a concentration of people with similar origins and very little chance of escape through education or economic success. For most of them, there was no "great" in "Make America Great Again." That slogan is pure historical revisionism, and factually inaccurate.

Between the end of World War II and the onset of democratization and activism that began in the 1960s, the United States was in a unique phase.

While other countries were rebuilding from massive destruction to homes, factories, and infrastructure, America did not face similar obstacles, enabling it to become the world's only economic powerhouse. For many, it was an era of extraordinary opportunity, prosperity, and placidity, typified by President Dwight Eisenhower's leadership style, and television shows that were popular in the 1950s and early 1960s such as *Ozzie and Harriet, Father Knows Best,* and *Leave It to Beaver.* Discrimination against groups of white Americans by other white Americans dissipated as a strong economy and public works initiatives provided broad-based education and employment opportunities that enabled marginalized communities to transcend structural social, ethnic, and linguistic barriers. In addition, the GI Bill enabled many World War II veterans to get a college education and buy a home.

The GI Bill assisted whites more than nonwhites, due to the disproportionately white composition of our military forces. Moreover, African Americans were treated with a greater degree of equality by European allies and civilians, and returned home with a sense of achievement and inclusion from their war service. However, they found that social standards and recognition of rights in the United States had not evolved commensurately.[62] Minorities continued to face persistent inequality, discrimination, and segregation even while the rising tide of economic prosperity lifted whites. The paradox was exemplified in 1948, when President Harry S. Truman desegregated the military, and South Carolina senator Strom Thurmond ran for the presidency as the candidate of the segregationist and racist States' Rights Democratic Party (the Dixiecrats).

In the postwar period, American society was acclimating to a newfound global dominance, while only beginning to confront racism and unresolved inequities. There was some incipient progress in the 1950s, such as the US Supreme Court's *Brown v. Board of Education* decision in 1954, Rosa Parks's defiance and the Montgomery Bus Boycott in 1955 and 1956, and the desegregation of Little Rock Central High School in 1957. But those steps mainly elevated the debate on civil rights and equality to prominence on the national scene. Major substantive changes to our legal and institutional structures did not occur until the mid-1960s. Once they did, those advances only initiated a process of social and cultural transformation that would take decades to begin shifting attitudes. Despite successes, that process is still ongoing, with much remaining to be achieved for a full transformation to complete equality in all facets of American life.

Apparently, people who wear "Make America Great Again" hats are either attached to a wistful notion that never even happened (such as imaginary harmony and prosperity for all whites during America's first century and a half[63]) or are reflecting on a brief aberrational period of white prosperity that resulted from tragic war consequences (1950s America[64]). Either way, in asserting their desire to "take our country back," Trumpians seem to believe that the country can and should resurrect an inequitable society in which white working-class advantages are institutionalized to the detriment of all other Americans. Their belief is illusory, self-interested, pernicious, inequitable, impractical, and uninformed.

RISING INFLUENCE OF MINORITIES IN AMERICA

The Oxford English Dictionary defines "minority" as "the smaller number or part, especially a number or part representing less than half of the whole." In the context of demographics, renowned sociologist Louis Wirth defined a "minority group" as: "a group of people who, because of their physical or cultural characteristics, are singled out from the others in the society in which they live for differential and unequal treatment, and who therefore regard themselves as objects of collective discrimination."[65]

Historically, each of our country's minority racial and ethnic groups fit the dictionary definition as they are numerically less than half of the whole population. Each group also fits Louis Wirth's multi-part description of what constitutes a minority group. Today, many of Wirth's elements still apply to African Americans, Latinos/Hispanics, Asian/Pacific Island Americans, and Native Americans.

As America evolves, how will we characterize a "minority group" that might be singled out for targeted marketing or statistical purposes, but that is no longer singled out for "differential and unequal treatment," due to progress on civil rights and other laws that prohibit discrimination? What if the members of the group no longer "regard themselves as objects of collective discrimination"? In that case, if there's a difference of opinion among members of the group, are some members part of a "minority group" while others are not? These questions may begin to affect American society when attitudes evolve to match the law.

A practical question that will soon be very relevant is: what happens to the characterization of minority groups when the aggregate population of all minority groups is more than half of the total population? According to the US Census Bureau's projections, that will occur in 2042, when non-white Americans (who self-identify as something other than "non-Latino/Hispanic white") are expected to account for 50.1 percent of the total national population. At that point, with a majority-minority population, will white Americans be regarded as a minority, even though they will still comprise a plurality of the population? Will white Americans be considered to be a single group despite the strong identification of many whites with their national origin subgroup? Will some people oppose the aggregation of minority groups into a collective majority? Will these critics be called out for adherence to a hypocritical double-standard, since white subgroups with different national origins and ancestries are routinely aggregated into a singular category of white Americans?

These are not merely academic questions. They will have actual ramifications that impact political influence, policy outcomes, legal rights, emotional responses, and attitudinal perceptions.

By accounting for the predominant share of the electorate, nonwhite constituencies will probably have enhanced electoral influence, and nonwhite candidates may become competitive in more districts. The potential to determine electoral outcomes will still be subject to the drawing of districts, and the Voting Rights Act might even (ironically) protect the rights of white voters from having their electoral influence diluted through overly aggressive gerrymandering, while still continuing to protect communities of color.

When communities of color comprise the larger share of the overall electorate, with a corresponding potential to impact elections, they will have more capacity to influence governmental agendas and policy decisions. As the nonwhite share of the population increases, communities of color will garner increased funding for governmental programs that are allocated on a population basis (e.g., healthcare, food assistance, infrastructure development, housing, education, etc.[66]). Just like today, the influence of communities of color and their elected representatives will still depend upon their ability to leverage their numerical strength, provide funding for candidates, navigate myriad political forces, and orchestrate desired outcomes. Numbers alone will not determine outcomes.

The reactions of white Americans to this demographic transition will be very important. Even when whites become less than 50 percent of the population, they will still be the single largest racial group, constituting a plurality of the population, though not a majority. As the single largest group, whites might not experience a tangible depletion of their political influence. For many whites, the shift from majority to plurality status might evoke a collective "whatever," because their lives will not be appreciably altered. Since the overwhelming majority of the white population is not obsessed with delusional notions of reversing history to return to the 1950s, most whites will accept the world in which they are acculturated. The transition to whites being a plurality will be gradual, and most will adjust to the notion that "we're all minorities; we're all Americans."

However, there are sure to be some whites who do not greet the change with such sagacious equanimity. As we have seen from many among Trump's base, some whites resist change, reject egalitarian objectives, and rebel against diminution of advantages to which they believe they are entitled. These white Americans are beholden to the fears and resentments discussed earlier. As we have seen throughout history, fears and resentments are best overcome by familiarity and engagement. As the nonwhite population increases, there will probably be an incremental rise in interactions between whites and nonwhites, as a natural consequence of the numerical parity and societal integration that it brings. Because familiarity and engagement breed collegial relationships and friendships, this concern will largely dissipate, at least for most of the population.

Still, as we approach the 2042 shift in demographics, the anxieties of some whites will probably intensify despite increased engagement and familiarity. The concerns of these whites may be rooted in history, or even in their own conscience. Since they may be aware that white people mistreated and oppressed communities of color during the era of institutionalized white dominance (especially the 1950s and earlier), they may fear that they will be similarly mistreated and disadvantaged in an era when minorities, aggregated together, are the majority. For whites who have anxieties about demographics, it may be a product of conscious recognition of past injustices or subliminal feelings of guilt that breed paranoia, as if the shoe being on the other foot would spawn retribution.

However, this emotional concern is absurd. First, whites will still be the largest single component of the population, and thus will not be marginalized politically, economically, or culturally. Second, communities of color advocate for new frameworks that establish a level playing field and an egalitarian society to uplift all through pragmatic, forward-looking solutions, not anything that penalizes or withholds opportunity from others. Third, all of the laws that protect civil rights and provide equal opportunity will continue to do so, protecting and providing for the interests of white Americans just as they do for nonwhites. Fourth, there is just no factual basis for this emotional reaction.

As we approach 2042, it is possible that our society will evolve to the point that there will be less resistance from today's Trumpians.

- First, the swift and unexpected rise of Trump gave voice to latent concerns that, having been aired, may gradually recede, as often occurs following an emotional release.
- Second, although some people feel emboldened to engage in bigotry, such as that which occurred in Charlottesville, acts like that offend mainstream society and possibly many in Trump's base, leading many to confine their irascibility to select outlets like Trump rallies.
- Third, bigotry that turns to violence goes too far for many of those in Trump's base, since no one wants to be associated with crazy people, like the Florida man who sent bombs to Democratic politicians or the Pennsylvania mass murderer who killed worshippers in a synagogue. This may spur the base to recoil, repudiate violence, and tamp down its hostility.
- Fourth, if Trump's presidency impairs his base's finances with tariffs on farm products or tax breaks that mainly benefited the wealthy, not them, the base may become disillusioned, retract their support, and disengage, satisfied with having scored a major victory against the political establishment by electing Trump, which also dissipated their anger at politicians.
- Fifth, since the demographic shift from a white majority to a plurality will occur incrementally, the whites who are currently concerned may acclimate incrementally.
- Sixth, those who resist demographic change will eventually realize its inevitability, the futility of pushing back, and its economic benefits, like more customers, sales, and a larger workforce from which to hire.
- Seventh, older Americans, who are a major cohort of Trump's base and who express concerns about dilution of the assistance programs

on which they depend, will gradually be replaced in the electorate by younger Americans whose sensibilities are influenced by contemporary demographics and attitudes.

Trump's base and other white Americans may either resist or welcome the demographic changes that lie ahead. Despite the many factors that could impact the trajectory, there is reason to believe that there will be incremental adaptation to circumstances. As we head toward 2042, if leaders in the post-Trump era emphasize civility, coalescence, and the need to address the challenges of Trumpians alongside those of other Americans, then the likelihood of a long-term trend toward acceptance of the new, diverse realities will increase, even though there are likely to be growing pains along the way.

DEMOGRAPHIC SHIFTS MAY PRODUCE POLITICAL, SOCIAL, AND CONCEPTUAL CHANGES

As demographics evolve, the language with which we address these issues and groups also needs to evolve. Our current use of the terms "minorities" and "minority groups," while statistically accurate, are infused with a derogatory and sometimes repressive association. When applied to human beings, those terms not only describe numerical values, but also connote a structural dearth of power and influence that is proportionately inferior to those with larger numerical values, that is, the majority. Minority and majority designations are appropriately used to describe collective, relative political power in a legislature. However, the term "minorities," when applied to racial/ethnic groups, serves as a consistent and deprecating reminder that people in these groups historically had less influence or importance. The stratification of minority groups—rather than their consolidated treatment as the majority of the population—diminishes the power of each component group, and restrains the influence of each.

When nonwhite minority groups, aggregated together, become the majority of the population in 2042 or near then, it will be erroneous to refer to nonwhite Americans as minorities. The term will become an anachronism, with primarily historical significance. Our lexicon will need to expand and evolve to acknowledge the shift in demographic statistics and the societal influence that accompanies it. The new reality should be expressed in new terminology that conveys nonwhites' consolidated power when it is advantageous to do so while continuing to recognize each constituent group in ways that maintain their unique identities without being subsumed into the aggregation.

A more accurate—albeit cumbersome—moniker might be "New Majority Americans," "the Modern Majority," or "Historically Categorized Americans" (which borrows from the nomenclature of "Historically Black Colleges and Universities"). These phrases invoke the emergence of the new realities or the historical categorization of minorities, respectively, moving beyond previous characterizations, and placing emphasis on being American rather than being a member of a minority group. Rather than perpetuating the verbiage that marginalized each group of minorities from wielding its full strength, these phrases consolidate communities of color into an influential collective that has forward-looking, empowering significance. While the phrases might be too much of a mouthful to be embraced for common parlance, there might be some other name that achieves the same objective while doing so more artfully.

The consolidation of political influence by "the Modern Majority" (or another moniker for the future nonwhite majority) would be particularly consequential in advancing key emerging issues that are becoming prominent in the American policy landscape. For example, consolidation of a coalition in support of "Black Lives Matter" could advance the movement. "Black Lives Matter" became the slogan that succinctly articulated the demand for African Americans to receive equal justice under the law at parity with that ensured to white Americans. The demand extends to all aspects of due process and criminal justice, including fair and equal standards by police when assessing who warrants their suspicion, verbal interaction by police, physical engagement by police, fair conduct during an arrest, arrest rates, equal protection of African American communities, equal treatment by the judicial system in affording due process, fair trials, fair sentencing, equal treatment during incarceration, etc. Even more broadly, the BLM community gives voice to the injustice of systematically devaluing Americans based on racial characteristics, whether by overt racism or unconscious bias.

The BLM community justifiably bristled at politicians who responded by saying that "All Lives Matter." The discontent was because not all lives were being mistreated and marginalized; not all lives were being treated as if they didn't matter. Black lives were being treated adversely, not white lives. It is implicitly understood and agreed that all lives matter, and the

BLM community's leaders would probably acknowledge that. However, when one group is being singled out for substandard treatment—inferior to the treatment provided to the overall population—then the rallying cry for reform must fit the problem. When some Americans are being denied the dignity, respect, and justice that should be accorded to all Americans, then remedies must be crafted to help them and solve that specific problem.[67] Hence, "Black Lives Matter" captures the issue correctly. The replacement of "Black" with "All" misstates the problem, falsely asserts color-blindness, deflects the appropriate focus, and dilutes the necessary objective.[68]

Recognition and acceptance that "we're all minorities, we're all Americans" is an aspirational vision for white and nonwhite Americans alike. It does not eliminate the need for activism when problems surface. The BLM community has a vital societal role in advancing the Fourteenth Amendment's "equal protection of the laws," and it will remain highly relevant while disparities in representation and treatment persist. When true equal protection is eventually achieved, then the "Black Lives Matter" slogan will be a moot issue, because all lives will indeed matter and be treated equally. Until then, unfortunately, the BLM movement does matter.

A moniker like "the Modern Majority" can be helpful in achieving BLM's goals by consolidating the influence of traditional minority groups into a unified powerful bloc. As appalling as it is for African Americans to suffer from substandard treatment, it is just as unacceptable for Latinos/Hispanics, Native Americans, and Asian/Pacific Islander Americans to be subjected to adverse treatment. BLM opponents would prefer a "divide and conquer" approach whereby African Americans are isolated and stand alone (along with some compatriots who support the cause) rather than face a unified, powerful coalition. As a matter of sheer political power, the unified voice of 51 percent of Americans—through its voting power, campaign contributions, congressional representation, etc.—can compel reform more effectively than what roughly a third of that number could accomplish.

A unified "Modern Majority" can be a powerful force on vital issues such as equity where disparities and structural inequality are endemic. This includes environmental equity in response to the Flint, Michigan, water quality tragedy and toxic air emissions from industrial facilities and coal-fired power plants. The coalition could galvanize support for economic equity initiatives, such as addressing the wealth gap, hiring practices, loan qualifications, and income disparities. A unified voice can improve justice equity relating to law enforcement practices, arrests, prosecutions, convictions, and sentencing. The community could enhance educational equity through reforms that rectify disparate funding among public schools and limited access to high-performing schools. It could extend to health equity by providing access to affordable quality care, enabling access to fresh nutritious food, and resolving disparate health outcomes.

The collection of data about key equity metrics is a meaningful starting point. Patterns of inequity can be revealed by correlating the data with the location of the activity being tracked (per nine-digit zip code area or Census block). Data could expose inequities in service reliability, such as the number of electric and water service outages in each area and their duration, and the frequency of road maintenance. Data collection could identify disparate levels of K-12 education spending and funding for social services in each area. Data metrics can illuminate inequitable recruitment and hiring at various job classification levels, track the availability of financing in each area to prevent gaps, and spot inequitable allocations of economic development investment. Data collection and mapping can enhance quality of life by identifying inequities in access to recreational facilities, public transportation, and fresh produce vendors.[69] The equity metrics that are selected would enable government agencies, nonprofit service organizations, corporations, and individuals to monitor conditions, revise programs, improve service delivery, and facilitate planning.[70] An equity metrics system would enhance transparency and responsiveness and, as data collection becomes robust, would be a useful decision-making tool.

In all campaigns for equity, the unified voice of 51 percent of Americans can compel reform more effectively than if the effort were consigned to just a subdivision of this majority. Institutionalizing a culture of equity within all government agencies, embedding it in all government services, and applying it throughout all areas of public policy is a major effort that should not be relegated to the statistically smaller demographic groups who are most jeopardized by inequity.

In select instances, "the Modern Majority" could be interpreted even more expansively for additional policy impacts. Taken together with Louis Wirth's definition of minority groups, the term could encompass many more Americans, creating an even larger coalition for specific issues where it would aid the policy goal. In accordance with Wirth's criteria, women in America were historically a "group of people who, because of their physical or cultural characteristics, (were) singled out from the others in the society in which they live for differential and unequal treatment, and who therefore regard themselves as objects of collective discrimination."[71]

Even though women are roughly half of the population and half of the electorate, their voting patterns and policy preferences do not mirror those of men within their racial and ethnic groups. Compared to men in each racial or ethnic group, women's voting habits tend to track the voting preferences of nonwhite communities, with the degree of the variance differing among racial and ethnic groups (including among white voters).[72]

It would be advantageous to include women in "the Modern Majority" rubric when building a coalition for action on policy or legislative issues that would expand equity or opportunities for those who had traditionally been disadvantaged. For example, it might be especially appropriate regarding issues of wage and income inequality, and healthcare cost and access disparities, all of which afflict both women and communities of color. It would also be useful in policy analyses that forecast impacts of legislation.

However, the inclusion of women in a broader interpretation of "the Modern Majority" should only be applied selectively so that, for example, funding for programs that are designed for communities of color are not diverted to support affluent white women (e.g., government contracting set-aside programs, in which a percentage of procurement dollars are designated for contracts with companies owned by minorities). It should be applied as more of a strategic partnership between women and the coalition of communities of color.

IMPORTANCE DURING TRUMP'S TENURE AND THE POST-TRUMP ERA

Although the vast majority of Americans, led by those in younger age groups, increasingly embrace equal opportunity, diversity, and a multicultural society,[73] the Trump administration is battling this humanistic impulse. That position stems directly from Donald Trump himself, as is clear from his explicit comments as candidate and president, his exploitation of white "identity politics," and his choices of when to act and when not to act on racial and ethnic issues that arise. The political reward that Trump reaps from his racial positions and comments is epitomized by the devotion that he engenders among white evangelicals, who comprise about 35 percent of the Republican coalition.[74] Michael Eric Dyson characterizes Trump's orientation on issues involving race by asserting that "Donald Trump is the epitome, not only of white innocence and white privilege, but also of white power, white rage, and, yes, even of white supremacy."[75]

In the first two years of Trump's presidency, many actions were taken that adversely impacted nonwhites. The Department of Homeland Security (DHS) defunded organizations that receive support through its Countering Violent Extremism Task Force, which opposes white supremacists and neo-Nazis, even though there has been a dramatic rise in domestic terrorism perpetrated by these groups. This action sent an implicit message that the Trump administration was either not concerned about or not offended by the racially and ethnically motivated hate crimes that domestic terrorists commit. At the same time, DHS enhanced its efforts against terrorist acts by those connected with, or inspired by, Al-Qaeda, ISIS, and other radical Islamist extremists, even though they are not as prevalent within the United States as domestic terrorists. DHS also escalated its anti-immigrant efforts through the anti-Muslim travel ban, raids by Immigration and Customs Enforcement (ICE) officers to detain working-class immigrants who have not committed any crimes that could be found in a penal code, and ICE's separation of migrant children from their parents. The administration's apparent aims are to instill fear throughout the immigrant population and to encourage immigrants to voluntarily leave the country, while turning a blind eye toward hate crimes perpetrated by domestic terrorists.

The Department of Justice also aggressively instituted policies that benefit whites to the detriment of communities of color. These policies were directed by former Attorney General Sessions, who has a long history of trying to turn the clock back to the days of white dominance and inherent white advantage, dating back to his time as a US attorney in Alabama and throughout his tenure in the Senate.[76] His record shows that he is a longtime opponent of Affirmative Action and non-European immigration, although he might accept nonwhites entering universities and jobs as long as there are no whites who want those slots.[77] The idea of a level playing field on which nonwhites compete with whites for employment and educational opportunities seems to be offensive to him.

In 2017, Sessions redirected use of civil rights law to help whites, alleging discrimination against them, and to scale back Affirmative Action.[78] A

memo by Sessions initiated a program using "investigations and possible litigation related to intentional race-based discrimination in college and university admissions."[79] His plan was opposed by civil service attorneys in the
department's Civil Rights Division's Educational Opportunities Section,
causing Sessions to utilize attorneys who were Trump's political appointees.
His use of civil rights law—which was designed to protect minorities—to
assist whites is, at best, paradoxical, and is more aptly cynical, malevolent,
and dystopian. But to Jeff Sessions it is good policy. And to Trump it is great
politics, since it is another way to cater to the grievance mentality of his
base, which resents civil rights laws interfering with their feelings of entitlement. Trump benefits since the message reaches his base that action is being
taken to aid their interests. In July 2018, Sessions went further by rescind-
ing Obama-era "guidance memos" that allowed colleges and universities to
consider applicants' race as one among many factors.[80] Although this action
was ostensibly taken to energize Trump's base, Sessions cited a lawsuit initiated by Asian Americans challenging Harvard's admission practices,[81] even
though his comment was merely a facade for a broad policy that exceeded
the scope of the Harvard situation.

When it comes to law enforcement and police conduct, Sessions's record
demonstrates that he does not treat all races equally. He initiated a Department of Justice policy that is intended to increase enforcement of, and seek
maximum criminal sentences for, low-level, nonviolent crimes, like drug possession, that are presumed to disproportionately impact communities of
color.[82] The department abandoned Obama-era consent decrees that were
imposed on local police departments to prevent racist enforcement practices and police brutality.[83] Sessions also threatened to withhold federal funds
from Sanctuary Cities that refuse to direct their local police departments to
become the enforcers of federal immigration laws.[84]

The administration's other efforts that targeted diversity and inclusion
include: the Election Integrity Commission, which was expected to be used
to purge nonwhites from voter rolls before it was terminated due to broad
bipartisan condemnation;[85] Secretary Betsy DeVos's orders to scale back
investigations into civil rights violations at public schools and universities, halt
prioritized action on sexual assault reports, stop reviews of disciplinary actions
that disproportionately target minority students, and sharply reduce the budget and personnel of the department's Office of Civil Rights;[86] DeVos's claim
that schools can report undocumented students to immigration officials, even

though the US Supreme Court has ruled otherwise;[87] and the administration's plan to resurrect the War on Drugs, expected to target nonwhite populations.[88] When DeVos mischaracterized Historically Black Colleges and Universities (HBCU) as "real pioneers when it comes to school choice," her ignorance of the historical discrimination that necessitated HBCUs offended many, as did the administration's indifference to the issue.[89]

On June 16, 2017, the US Commission on Civil Rights tied all of these regressions together when it expressed its concerns about the Trump administration's budget cuts for civil rights enforcement and the resulting impairment of civil rights. The commission criticized the administration's pattern of civil rights deconstruction and initiated an investigation into federal enforcement.[90] The commission cited concerns about policies and/or budget cuts at seven federal departments and agencies: the departments of Justice, Education, Labor, Housing and Urban Development, and Health and Human Services, as well as the Environmental Protection Agency, and the Legal Services Corporation.

Although demographic trends are heading toward statistical parity where "we're all minorities, we're all Americans," Trump has said and done many things that reveal a desire to reverse trends and take us back to the 1950s. He can't. Rather than resist demographics, he would better serve the country, including his base, by doing what he can to make that transition harmonious. But don't count on it. For political expediency, Trump is much more likely to be divisive, as he was with his comments about NFL/NBA players and the Charlottesville violence. He will most surely continue to inflame discord, give voice to his base's grievance mentality, and guide his administration toward more policies that cynically promote white preference while unnecessarily intensifying racial, ethnic, and cultural divisions. He will do this to solidify his base, partly for electoral purposes and, more importantly, to frighten congressional Republicans into believing that they will lose his base's support and their own elections if they stand up against him. This is most important to Trump as a way to mute consequences from Special Counsel Mueller's and Congress's investigations. Trump has shown himself willing to use race-based issues to do that.

The Trump administration might be able to notch some policy wins while it has the chance to do so. However, especially on issues involving racial and ethnic equal opportunity, any victories that they garner will surely be fleeting, lasting only until the next president has the chance to reinstitute policies that reflect American values. Younger Americans and future generations who are acculturated in an environment of racial/ethnic statistical parity are the destiny that Dr. Martin Luther King Jr. envisioned when he famously said, "The arc of the moral universe is long, but it bends toward justice."[91]

To facilitate a transition to an era of tolerance, acceptance, and equity, more can be done to inculcate these values and perspectives within younger (and future) Americans who will set the tone in years to come. Rather than trying to convert older Americans (whose age will matriculate them out of the electorate by natural means over time) and Trump's base (whose share of the population will also diminish over time, as discussed in chapter 10), it is more important to ensure that the voters and leaders in 2042 and beyond will embrace America's emerging tapestry.

As we prepare our youth to be tomorrow's voters and leaders, it is unquestioned that American history is, and should continue to be, a required course in high school. However, that course is basically a civics lesson about current events from previous years, decades, and centuries. Due to the relative power of constituencies in our country's initial centuries, the teaching of US history is skewed toward the actions and roles of white men.

As vital as history is, a civics course about contemporary current events is equally important and should be taught on equal footing. There is an opportunity to instill modern sensibilities through contemporary perspectives, featuring contemporary leaders. High school curricula should be augmented with a required course on Diversity in Contemporary America, focusing on wide-ranging constituencies and demographic groups, and the men and women whose contributions benefit all Americans.

The course would highlight cultures and leaders from many racial and ethnic backgrounds, and their impact on many aspects of American society, such as health and medicine, law and government, business and social entrepreneurship, science and technology, arts and education, and environmental protection and innovation. It would showcase cultural traditions and characteristics that are integrated into mainstream American life, as well as people who have had a prominent role in recent achievements. Because of its focus on contemporary leaders and their contributions, students will likely be inspired by some of them as role models, and guest lecturers would be available.

The course could further broaden its reach with the use of contemporary technology. Classes in different parts of the country could have exchanges, or joint lectures, by use of video Skype (or other live, real-time interfaces), and share the findings of their research, studies, and teachings. Since the focus of the course is diversity in contemporary America, exchanges would ideally pair classes that have significantly different racial or ethnic compositions and that are located in different social settings (i.e., urban, suburban, and rural), in order to maximize the breadth of perspectives. In light of the cultural divide between rural and urban communities that was evident in 2016 and 2018 voting behavior, it would be especially beneficial to pair student groups from these two environments.

Another way to build familiarity and understanding between cultural groups is for communities to form Family Cultural Exchange Clubs (FCECs). Through such a program, families consisting of at least one parent and one child could form neighborhood clubs designed to spend time with families of other ethnic and racial backgrounds. In some neighborhoods, the clubs themselves would be a showcase of diversity. In these cases, at club meetings, families could be randomly paired with other families, initially for joint outings and eventually for dinner parties at each other's homes. Other clubs may be homogeneous, or, within a diversified club—there may simply not be enough families of various backgrounds to enable one-to-one pairings of all the families. In both of these situations, a club could pair itself with a club from another part of town that has an imbalance of families from a different racial or ethnic group. An informal network of clubs could facilitate the pairings.

Local governments would be the key to making this happen. By sponsoring the system, they would show their support, give reassurance to those who might have reservations, encourage the growth of FCECs throughout the area rather than in just an isolated instance, and coordinate the collaboration between clubs in disparate parts of their city or county. State involvement could further encourage this approach, and be a resource for various local governments who seek to interact with FCECs in neighboring parts of the state.

Whatever logistics are chosen, multiple-family outings would enable parents and children to share in the experience of getting to know a family of a different background. If it is true that a lack of understanding breeds fear of the unknown that, in turn, breeds racism and prejudice, then FCECs would provide an opportunity to build familiarity, commonality, and an understanding of different perspectives and concerns. By spending time together on outings and in each other's homes, it is likely that participating families will develop a comfort level and even a friendship, chipping away at America's most pervasive societal shortcoming, one family at a time.

Education and familiarity are fundamental to the normalization and acceptance of diversity. Conversely, ignorance and separation lead to apprehension, suspicion, unconscious bias, distrust, "Other-ness," exclusion, and acrimony. As we gravitate toward statistical parity in America, proactive engagement is essential to build confidence, collaboration, and conscious egalitarianism. While FCECs and a required high school course are not panaceas, they are worthwhile steps in the march toward a more inclusive and intentionally intertwined society.

CHAPTER 3

ISSUES

THE IMPORTANCE OF POLICY AND PRINCIPLES

T he phrase "content is king" was popularized in the 1990s by Viacom's Sumner Redstone, about entertainment, and Microsoft's Bill Gates, about websites. Regardless of who said it first, it has been an accepted maxim ever since. It makes the point that consumers' decisions are principally driven by the substantive material that they want or need. Content prevails over form; substance prevails over process. Considerations such as convenience, delivery mechanisms, hardware tools, warranties, and other bells and whistles are merely value-adds that might be nice, but are not the main reason that drives a buyer to make a purchase.

In politics, too, content is king: policies, principles, and positions on issues are the essence of campaigns and governing. Voters are influenced by a candidate's personality and character, but they still want to know what a candidate would do in office. Of course, that works both ways: candidates who have comprehensively articulated their positions on a vast array of issues probably will not succeed on that alone if the voters perceive them as unlikeable, unrelatable, or inauthentic. Although shortcomings in either personality or policy can be perilous, it is very rare for candidates to win an election after a campaign in which they offer only slogans in place of specifics.

To be successful, politicians typically need to convince voters that they would be responsible stewards. A key to that is the disclosure of details concerning the policies that they would enact if allowed to hold the reins of government. Candidates usually reveal to voters the issues of concern to them, the specifics of the policies that they would pursue, and the principles or philosophies that motivate the solutions that they espouse. For example, it usually does not suffice for candidates to claim that they would enact great tax reform without explaining what that means: how they would adjust corporate and personal income taxes, what tax rates they would propose, how it would affect taxpayers at all income and asset levels, how it would affect tax deductions, the net gain or loss in federal revenues, what new taxes would need to be imposed to make up the difference, etc. Platitudes like "I'll get the economy going" and "everyone's going to have great healthcare" are neither policies nor principles but just puerile palaver. Although most voters probably don't delve into details on every issue, they do want details on the issues of greatest importance to them. Their decisions are driven in large part by the specific content or substance that is presented by candidates.

During the campaign, Donald Trump did not provide specifics about the issues that he claimed he would act upon. He offered slogans and aspirations on many issues, but did not include details describing what he would do about them. Continuing that pattern as president, Trump has suffered from the hazards of policy that is not based on fundamental principles, consultation with experts, and well-reasoned policy processes. In contrast with policy norms, most of Trump's decisions are driven by his temperament, emotions, biases, and self-interests, as well as his beliefs about what would please his base of supporters. These idiosyncrasies are no substitute for a sound policy methodology. When public policy is bereft of philosophical underpinnings, it is merely the whim of the person who offers it, and it is tied only to that person's caprice. That is the manner of an autocrat, not an American president.

THE IMPORTANCE OF POLICY AND PRINCIPLES

Policy is the cornerstone of government and the core of both legislative branch mandates and executive branch initiatives. Policy drives the structuring of budgets, the allocation of human and fiscal resources, the regulation of industries, the administration of justice, the rules by which government operates, the requisition and provision of goods and services, and virtually all other governmental activities and interactions with the citizenry.

For candidates, policy is also one of the cornerstones of political campaigns. It is one of the principal means by which candidates can demonstrate their understanding of, and concern for, the needs and life conditions of the electorate. Ideally, policy should be tailored to the challenges that voters face, and connect with voters on a human, personal level. A candidate's policies should resonate with voters' life experiences, and not merely pass muster as focus-group-tested good political sense. Voters typically expect and demand a cogent policy foundation that conveys candidates' purposes for seeking office. Without it, candidates appear to be vapid, devoid of a rationale for their candidacy, even if they have personal appeal. The absence of a solid policy framework signifies that candidates are running for office more for personal achievement than for public service that makes a meaningful impact on society. There are exceptions, but not often.

For elected officials, the policy framework reflects their *raison d'être*, and can serve as a means to benchmark their performance in office. Their policies and positions can be useful in assessing whether they delivered on their campaign promises, how they addressed key issues that arose during their tenure, their level of engagement and leadership on issues of importance to their constituents, and/or whether they took on additional policy challenges. Aided by today's panoply of media outlets and information resources, constituents can monitor this progress. The degree to which officials collaborate with their colleagues to achieve policy objectives is another vital element of their performance, although that is more difficult to assess from a distance.

Elected officials' principles, and their adherence to them, provide an important lens through which to view their policies and performance.

- For some officials, principles are immutable, at the core of every decision, and there is no room for divergence from them. That can be a double-sided coin, earning legislators plaudits for being unwaveringly dedicated to their principles, while also generating criticism for being too dogmatically opposed to compromise (e.g., the late senator John McCain of Arizona on torture,[1] and senators Ron Wyden of Oregon and Rand Paul of Kentucky on privacy issues and limiting government acquisition of personal data[2]).
- For other officials, principles are circumstantial, and relatively adaptable in the pursuit of successful policy. Here, too, it is a double-sided coin, earning legislators plaudits for being flexible in order to achieve pragmatic results, while also generating criticism for being opportunistic and not taking a firm stand on policy options (e.g., former senator Bob Corker of Tennessee on tax cuts, which he first opposed on the grounds of the fiscal impact, and then supported even though his concern had not been addressed[3]).
- In the middle ground are pragmatic public officials who have solid principles and go to great lengths to adhere to them, while also being mindful

of the need to legislate successfully. These legislators earn plaudits for knowing when a good bargain that offers meaningful gains is attainable and justifies some flexibility, while generating criticism from purists for prioritizing progress over principles (e.g., senators Joe Manchin of West Virginia and Pat Toomey of Pennsylvania on background checks for gun purchases, despite their history of supporting NRA positions[4]).

Overlaying each of these styles is the maxim "where you sit is where you stand." In essence, where one stands on an issue is influenced by how that issue personally affects the person. This is not just endemic among legislators and judges but also virtually everyone, to one degree or another. Many people operate solely by "where they sit," whereas others reach far beyond themselves, their own interests, and their own realm of familiarity to support worthy causes and people in need. Ohio senator Rob Portman's stance on gay marriage was a case of this maxim in action.[5] For years, he vehemently opposed gay rights. In 2011, his son came out as gay, and in 2013, Portman switched to favor gay marriage. Although Portman's new position was laudable, and reflected a broader shift in popular opinion, it was clearly influenced by "where he sat" on the issue, once he realized that it personally affected his son. It raises the question whether he would switch to a pro-choice stance (he has a 100 percent rating from the National Right to Life Committee) if a family member had an abortion; whether he would support reasonable gun control (he has an A rating from the NRA) if a family member were a victim of a shooting; whether he would support raising the national minimum wage (he has voted against raising it) if it were needed by a family member; and whether he would support Obamacare (he has voted to repeal it) if a family member needed the coverage.

Policy and principles can chart a course for stability and sustainability. They define the mission, vision, purpose, and objectives of an administration, enabling it to advance in its chosen direction, act efficiently, and incorporate others into its decision-making. By continually engaging in strategic planning and scenario planning, a government can maintain the viability, reliability, and consistency of its actions. A policy framework, along with the principles embedded within it, are essential inputs into those planning processes. There will always be some *ad hoc* decision-making, particularly in response to unforeseeable situations and outlier events. But policy development that can be anticipated and planned should be managed proactively with fidelity to an administration's core principles, values, and objectives.

This is important not just for a government to function effectively, but also for the governed to plan accordingly. Predictability is important for all those who are affected by governmental actions. Just as financial markets loathe uncertainty because it inhibits planning and hinders business decisions, governmental conduct that is erratic, incongruous, and mercurial presents uncertainty that inhibits business and personal planning, and hinders life decisions.

Without a coherent policy framework that is based on cogent principles, a government is aimless, treating decisions and situations as *sui generis* events that are devoid of any connective tissue between them. In such a climate, government decisions and actions are prone to being inconsistent, and are likely to be viewed as arbitrary and capricious. If the executive branch is constantly in flux, frequently shifting directions without a discernible pattern to its behavior, then the legislative branch has no guidance on how to calibrate its agenda and actions, and constituents are immobilized, awaiting clarity.

An administration that eschews policy and principles might do so for a number of reasons. For example, it might not recognize their importance; it might opt for flexibility in times of national crisis; it might not have the talent and skills to develop principles and policy; or it might not have the vision to want to do so. But one other situation is especially relevant to the Trump administration.

TRUMP'S RELATIONSHIP TO POLICY AND PRINCIPLES

Donald Trump is not ideological—he used to advocate for policies that were crafted by liberal Democrats—and only rarely cares about policy details. Both of these characteristics are showcased by his frequent reversals of his views from one meeting to the next and contradictions of his own positions. He typically speaks in platitudes, avoids details, and has a toolkit of diversionary tactics that he uses in place of substance, especially when he wants to divert the attention of the media or his constituents. Sometimes his avoidance of details is due to his lack of policy knowledge and his lack of curiosity to learn specifics, such as when, during a primary debate, he apparently did not know what the term "nuclear triad"[6] meant (he was so evasive that Florida senator Marco Rubio graciously answered the question for him, doing so in a manner that also educated Trump on the issue).[7] Trump's lack of policy depth was on display in 2017 when his provocative comments toward North Korea threatened action that would violate US policy and the Law of Armed Conflict's four basic principles: military necessity, distinction (between combatants and civilians), proportionality, and limitation (avoidance of unnecessary suffering).[8] Particularly on matters of national security, policy details are not academic exercises; they can be the difference between peace and war, stability and massive carnage.

Trump substituted slogans for substance. He provided no evidence that he knew policy details (other than, to some extent, on trade and tax issues). This was clear by how frequently he changed positions on many issues during the campaign (e.g., abortion, nuclear war, climate change, the "Dreamers"), which he continued to do as president. In lieu of consistent, informed policy, Trump relies on his judgment, which he asserts is superior to that of virtually all others.[9] But that is a boast that validates the opposite conclusion, regardless of who says it.

Instead of basing his policies and opinions on detailed understanding and knowledge, Trump typically regards each decision as an isolated transaction that is independent from consistent policy. His decisions and actions are driven by his interests, instincts, and emotions to fit his momentary needs and whims. During his campaign, Trump said that he would govern on an *ad hoc* basis, applying his negotiation and decision-making skills to issues as they arise, which foreshadowed his transaction-based approach.

As president, despite his boastful claims of being a supreme negotiator and dealmaker, his track record proves otherwise, as has been the case in negotiations around DACA, gun control, border wall funding, and government shutdowns. When negotiating trade and other international deals, he settles for minor concessions and declares them to be great victories (as he did following his first meeting with North Korea's Kim Jong-un, despite receiving nothing that substantially and verifiably reduces the nuclear threat posed by North Korea), and relinquishes his bargaining leverage without receiving anything in return (as he did when he moved the US embassy in Israel to Jerusalem). In other instances, Trump remains intransigent, achieves nothing, and blames others, as he did at meetings of the G7 and G20 where he refused to join the other countries in unified policies and joint communiqués about issues. Oddly, the instances in which he achieves a deal are when he negotiates against himself or against his own political party to give him political cover, as he did to get Obamacare reform passed by the House (even though that tactic still failed to get the "repeal and replace" legislation through the Senate). During the 2019 government shutdown, he also negotiated against Senate Majority Leader McConnell, who wanted Trump to accept the bipartisan negotiated deal that Trump was disparaging. Trump finally agreed to support it in exchange for McConnell supporting Trump's declaration of a national emergency, which McConnell considered repugnant. By negotiating against his own party, the shutdown ended.

Throughout his life, Trump has treated most of his business and personal activities like a series of transactions that he can reject when he no longer considers them beneficial.[10] He aims to control everything in his midst to promote his self-interests and self-enrichment, requiring others to comply with his control. His well-documented business practice was to enter into a transaction with a contractor, receive the benefit of the transaction, renege on the contract,[11] contrive a reason for doing so,[12] pay pennies on the dollar instead of full payment,[13] threaten a lawsuit,[14] and please himself that the only thing he lost was the chance to transact with that contractor again.[15] Trump's myopic focus on his self-enrichment also led him, as an adult, to collude with his father in shielding millions of dollars from tax liability by transferring his father's assets to him and his siblings.[16]

New York Times columnist David Brooks observed the transactional nature of Trump's relationships and linked it to Trump's past and present, stating, "Through his business life, he's not had a series of relationships based on friendship, trust, and reciprocity, and affection. He's had relationships based strictly on self-interest and the urge to dominate. And he just feels comfortable in one kind of relationship. And, frankly, that's even true within his White House. He has relationships based on who's useful to who, not 'we are a band of brothers in this together.'"[17]

As president, Trump is replicating his lifelong transactional *modus operandi*, getting the value that he wants from each person and each issue, and then treating them as if they are fungible and dispensable. These practices may explain Trump's infatuation with authoritarians and autocrats who have no restraints on their conduct, enabling them to do what they please without accountability. But our government does not operate that way.

A transactional approach to governing foregoes principle-based, consistent, coherent policy, and instead revolves around an authoritarian individual—in this case, the president—who is not tethered by policy. It is especially insidious because it ignores the relationship between our three branches of government and hence disregards our Constitution.

- A transactional approach diminishes the relationships—both personal and institutional—between the president and the Congress, and between the president and the courts.
- A transactional approach treats every issue as its own isolated demand, drama, and power struggle, as if nothing before it or after it matters, disregarding both stakeholders and consequences.
- A transactional approach emboldens the president to think that he can unilaterally abrogate alliances, agreements, and strategies that were incrementally cultivated by many preceding presidents.
- A transactional approach negates our collaborative, mutually respectful, and responsive system of accountability with checks and balances by replacing it with an imperious, ego-centric, imprudent system based on command-and-control, personal whim, and the "cult of personality."
- A transactional approach assumes that Congress and the courts are subservient to the president, and that they should abide by his decisions, even when capricious, impulsive, or driven by self-interests.
- A transactional approach reduces issues to mere bargaining chips that can be cynically offered and withheld for the sake of deal-making, regardless of their critical value to constituencies.
- A transactional approach provides neither consistency between policies nor guidance on decision-making processes and determinations on forthcoming issues.
- A transactional approach deludes the president into believing that he can narcissistically undermine, insult, degrade, or threaten anyone and anything to get his way, without consequences for future issues or concern for others on whom he must rely for future results, as if there are no relationships and no carryover from one issue to the next.
- A transactional approach enables the president to serve his own personal interests, domestically and internationally, without concern for restraint from the law or longtime strategic allies.
- A transactional approach by the president emboldens other stakeholders, like domestic legislators or other countries, to apply a transactional approach in response, which can result in their unwillingness to support

the president or the United States when their interests are not thoroughly aligned with his.

A government can withstand occasional transactional determinations, and it can even flounder along with a transactional approach, in lieu of policy, for a little while. But if a transactional approach persists for an extended period, it runs the risk of creating a government that suffers serially from instability, entropy, disintegration, a crisis of confidence, and paralysis. It sows the seeds of dysfunction and can ultimately lead to authoritarianism and a constitutional crisis.

Trump campaigned as a populist who might use some authoritarian means, but what America got is an authoritarian who offers some populist rhetoric.[18] Trump is not really a populist at all, since he does not empower the masses for their own benefit. Instead, he motivates them to empower him, enabling his embrace of authoritarianism and nationalism, which appeals to a narrow slice of the electorate and operates without consistency. By embracing those themes to tap into the fears, resentment, and anger of his base, Trump championed Pitchfork Populism, a sanitized cousin of mob rule. He uses it as a tool of retribution for perceived wrongs. His vitriolic message is contrary to economic populism that is policy based and expands its appeal to a broad cross-section of voters. Authoritarianism, which benefits from a transactional approach to governing, is incompatible with American democracy.[19]

During a 2017 interview, Trump displayed his quest to govern as an autocrat when he responded to a question by declaring, "I have absolute right to do what I want to do with the Justice Department."[20] Trump may think that he does, but many federal laws say otherwise. In June 2018, Trump stated in a tweet that "I have the absolute right to pardon myself," which would make him the judge and jury of his own actions, in effect placing him above the law.[21] Such a pardon would also function as an admission of guilt.[22] His assertions conjure echoes of ex-President Nixon's conversations with interviewer David Frost, when Nixon declared, "Well, when the president does it, that means that it is not illegal."[23] Both men's comments are oblivious to the president's obligation to operate within the boundaries of the law.

A transactional approach that is acceptable for a centrally controlled, family owned, for-profit business without shareholders does not apply to a highly networked system with checks and balances that is based on the rule of law, serving the public interest, and responding to 325 million shareholders.

If Trump hyperextends presidential authority toward the realm of autocracy, most Americans, including senators and representatives, will not passively watch as the Constitution disintegrates. Whether for the sake of upholding constitutional principles or for the sake of their own reelection prospects, legislators will rein in blatant transgressions and reject a legacy of being complicit with them.

To further extend his authority, Trump raises the notion of sovereignty, which he cites to clear a path for doing what he wants without restraint from global stakeholders, critics, agreements, and organizations. Sovereignty was the central theme of his 2018 speech at the UN General Assembly. He said, "We will never surrender America's sovereignty to an unelected, unaccountable, global bureaucracy,"[24] which expanded on his use of the term at the 2017 meeting.[25] It is a corollary to his "America First" mantra, as a justification for his actions, even while he hypocritically imposes on the sovereignty of others.[26] Trump rejects international limits on his decision-making, and even seeks to marginalize domestic influences that limit his transactional whims on the global stage.[27] In the past, sovereignty was cited at the UN mainly by autocrats and authoritarians who used it to deflect global scrutiny of their practices. By invoking the shield of sovereignty, Trump embraced the autocrats' message in order to take action that offends the world order, evades reproach for doing so, and seeks the same deference from his domestic audience. Even more troubling, an American president extolling sovereignty means that authoritarian leaders in other countries, including the most heinous dictators, can cite his comments as precedent and validation for their unconscionable conduct, such as violations of human rights.[28]

Trump's transactionalism is also evident in his self-glorifying imposition of tariffs. In his September 8, 2018, comments to reporters, he boasted, "There's another $267 billion (in tariffs on Chinese goods) ready to go, on short notice, *if I want*" (emphasis added). Prior to Trump, no president treated tariffs, which have a national economic impact, as a tool of personal pique or power. As stated on the website led by Erick Erickson, a leading conservative: "What Trump really cares about is Making America Great Again through great, compelling television in which one Donald J. Trump is the star, the hero, and the mythical demigod who overcomes impossible odds to achieve glorious victory."[29]

Trump goes so far as to superimpose his interests on the entire country. He regularly assaults the media, even vilifying them as "the enemy of the people" for not supporting him, as if it were their job to do so. After the FBI's lawful court-approved raid on the office of his attorney, Michael Cohen, Trump lambasted the FBI, asserting that it was "an attack on our country in a true sense. It's an attack on what we all stand for."[30] Trump attacked Special Counsel Mueller's investigation, falsely claiming that it is a "Fake and Corrupt Russia investigation, headed up by the all Democrat loyalists," and falsely alleging that "Mueller is most conflicted of all."[31] Trump wanted to use the Justice Department as his personal private investigators to expose White House staff who leaked information to the media in 2017,[32] and the senior official who wrote an anonymous op-ed in 2018.[33] Conversely, he condemned the department in 2018 for taking action against two of his allies in Congress who engaged in blatantly unlawful conduct.[34]

Trump's transactional conduct indicates that he believes that the country is an extension of himself, or, as King Louis XIV of France famously said, "*L'état, c'est moi*,"[35] which translates to "the State, it is I," or "I am the State."[36] In many ways, on many issues, and especially with regard to investigations, Trump acts as if he disdains our constitutional system of checks and balances.[37]

TRUMP'S AUTHORITARIAN TRANSACTIONAL CONDUCT

Trump's transactional approach was center stage during the 2016 campaign, and remained his core operating mode during his first two years in office. As candidate and president, he presents a deluge of platitudes but a dearth of specifics. His general statements on a wide range of issues only hint at policy, often as a "word salad" of disconnected keywords, without clarifying his positions or committing to solutions. His pronouncements typically lack details and concrete principles to guide them. His treatment of issues has been cursory, mentioning a topic, as if "checking the box" for that issue, asserting that he'd make it great, and then continuing along a stream of consciousness to the next issue. As a candidate, he sent the signal that, given the chance, his decisions would be driven by his whims and he would govern as an authoritarian: not by facts and policy but by personal fiat. As president, that has become a salient characteristic of his actions.

On healthcare, Trump lambasted Obamacare during his campaign and after, and promised to give America great healthcare without giving any policy specifics about what he would do to make it great. When pressed for details, he didn't provide clarity, instead offering more aspirational objectives for his healthcare plan. A few days before his inauguration, he promised "insurance for everybody"[38] (akin to universal coverage), before retreating soon afterward to universal access (i.e., you can have it if you can afford it, which leaves millions uncovered). When Trump was asked about healthcare legislation being considered in Congress and his fallacious statements about what it would achieve,[39] he was unable to coherently explain or logically justify his positions. This showed that he had no real understanding about healthcare policy. His shifting and contradictory views revealed that he had no principles or ideological attachment to the issue, and that he was, essentially, a policy agnostic. He went so far as to criticize the bill passed by the House, calling it "mean," even though it was amended in the way that he specified.[40] The failure of the health reform effort was partly due to Trump's lack of health policy knowledge and principles, and partly due to the irreconcilable competing ideologies of Republicans, which could have been resolved if there had been presidential leadership and advocacy for one approach or another. It was evident that Trump just wanted to pass anything on healthcare, to claim it as a personal win.

On trade and other international agreements, Trump offered plenty of slogans but no policy solutions during his campaign. He lambasted NAFTA, the Trans-Pacific Partnership (TPP), the Paris Agreement (COP21), the Iran Nuclear Deal, and other existing and proposed agreements. He routinely asserted that America made bad and even "stupid" agreements, especially those on trade, due to the inability of US negotiators to craft good deals. Beyond these general criticisms, his ire extended to particular industries, like steel, along with an unsupported boast that he could get a better deal for US steel. But he wouldn't (or couldn't) discuss policy details like World Trade Organization rules, particular provisions of trade agreements that were injurious to the United States, countervailing duties, or how to impose tariffs without starting a trade war. He never proposed any specific changes, and his "America First" chant was so amorphous that it wasn't a principle that could be crafted into action. Trump's approach was much more of a marketing or branding pitch (his expertise) than a policy.

Shortly after he took office, Trump unilaterally extracted the United States from the TPP and COP21 (which he could not do as easily with NAFTA and the Iran Nuclear Deal). In May 2018, he withdrew America from the Iran Deal, even though doing so was entirely counterproductive, since Iran had already received the main benefit of the agreement (unfreezing economic relations and billions of dollars). On trade, Trump has done little to improve agreements or initiate new ones. His rebranding of NAFTA in late 2018 was largely cosmetic, changing the name so that he could claim it as a win, and most of the changes that he made mirrored changes that had been included in Obama's TPP. Trump's ill-conceived tariffs on steel and aluminum that he imposed in March 2018 lacked economic prudence, as they were antithetical to economic growth and seemed to be politically motivated (to appease his base and distract from other issues). The tariffs triggered countermeasures from other countries, which exposed many other US industries, as well as consumers, to higher costs.[41] As with other issues, Trump's deficit of cogent principles and policy understanding produced detrimental outcomes.

On immigration issues, Trump does have a guiding principle—regrettably a nefarious one—and his policy is tainted by it. Just like his policy to separate migrant families who he considers to be ethnically undesirable, Trump's initial travel ban applied to countries with predominantly Muslim populations: Somalia, Sudan, Iraq, Iran, Syria, Yemen, and Libya.[42] The second version of the ban did not include Iraq, and the third version omitted Sudan, while adding North Korea and certain Venezuelan officials to deflect criticism that the ban only targeted Muslims.[43] His acolytes argued that the ban was not anti-Muslim because not every Muslim-majority country was included. But the anti-Muslim bias was clear because the ban only excluded a country with a large Muslim population if it did not have some special reason to be in Trump's good graces. The ban was directed at Muslim countries that do not have either:

- an existing or proposed Trump hotel or other Trump property (owned or licensed);[44]
- an important military relationship with the United States;
- an important oil or other economic relationship with the United States; or
- a close strategic or economic relationship with one or more European Union countries.

In Trump's eyes, these extenuating factors were redeeming qualities that warranted exemption from the travel ban. Even though there was a principle underlying the travel ban, it was malevolent. The ban is an ill-conceived policy that embodies Trump's anti-Muslim rhetoric, and offends American values about religious tests. Although Trump's staff reworked the travel ban, trying to mask its original intent by adding two non-Muslim countries, that deception was undermined by his January 2018 comment about "shithole countries" during a meeting with senators about immigration. Trump followed that comment by voicing his desire for more Norwegian immigrants, exposing his racial criteria for immigration. After many courts found that the travel bans violated the Constitution, the US Supreme Court upheld the third version (by a 5-to-4 vote) in a troubling decision that naively elevated the importance of Venezuela's and North Korea's inclusion, feigned ignorance of Trump's expressly anti-Muslim intent, and accepted the fallacy that the travel ban didn't target a religious group.

Tax issues are another major exception to the rule of Trump's indifference to policy and are among the few issues with which he has experience. He also probably cares more about them than any other, for personal reasons. He has railed against the tax code for many years; tax reform was one of his two highest policy priorities, and his desire to ease his own tax burden may have been one of his primary motivations to run for president. He has said that he does his best to use the tax code to avoid paying taxes, or at least pay as little as possible ("that makes me smart"[45]), and his ambition for tax reform was surely guided by that principle. He has also spoken about tax issues much more coherently than he was able to discuss healthcare or immigration.

Trump will benefit greatly from the 2018 tax law's "pass through"[46] and "carried interest"[47] provisions. He also wanted the new tax law to fully eliminate the estate tax, for his children's benefit; although he didn't get that, he succeeded in getting a dramatic rise in the exemption from that tax. These provisions mainly benefit millionaires and billionaires like him. As for tax cuts for his base voters, he abandoned his campaign promises, giving them mere tokens. Working-class taxpayers will receive tax relief that may amount to a few hundred dollars, which will expire after only a handful of years. It seems that this inequity is becoming apparent to many of his white, working-class, non-college-educated voters due to, in some cases, their shrinking tax refunds and, in other cases, their higher than expected tax bills. Their sense of injustice is likely to increase in parallel with their tax burden as more of the tax law's provisions take root. The disparity of being cynically given only a few scraps from Trump's banquet table will likely offend many of his base voters and could cause many of them to become disenchanted with him.

On foreign policy and global affairs, Trump is all over the map. This is due to his transactional approach to foreign policy that revolves around his personal whims, reversing course according to his caprice, temperament, and interests, while hoping that adversaries bend to his will without fighting back. Trump admitted this about his foreign policy when, in response to an interviewer's question about the effect on policy of understaffing at the State Department, he declared, "The one that matters is me. I'm the only one that matters because when it comes to it, that's what the policy is going to be."[48]

Trump's affinity for authoritarians and autocrats compounds the problem of foreign policy, as it compromises American values and global moral leadership. His relationship with Saudi Arabia showcases the pitfalls of his self-centered approach. Drips of information about Trump's ties to the Saudi royal family became waves after the murder of journalist Jamal Khashoggi by Saudi agents. Khashoggi disappeared[49] on October 2, 2018, after entering the Saudi's consulate in Istanbul, Turkey, and the intelligence community probably informed Trump about this. At a rally on October 3, Trump said, "We protect Saudi Arabia. . . . And I love the king, King Salman. But I said, 'King, we're protecting you; you might not be there for two weeks without us.'" On October 5, Saudi Crown Prince Mohammed bin Salman told an interviewer, "I love working with him (Trump)."[50] The Crown Prince probably said that to solidify Trump's support, knowing what was about to come to light. On October 6, the press reported Khashoggi's disappearance and apparent murder inside the Saudi consulate in Istanbul.[51] Shortly thereafter, US intelligence officials who heard the audio recording of what transpired confirmed that Khashoggi was murdered and asserted that it occurred at the direction of the Crown Prince.[52] This sequence of events shows that Trump's personal interests and support of Saudi Arabia's authoritarian regime empowered them to violate human rights and press freedoms, and do what they did to Khashoggi. The mutual love between the leaders made the Saudis feel that they had license to deal with Khashoggi as heinously as they wished. And it sent a similar message to other autocrats.

Trump's mercurial transactional approach is typified by his interaction with China. While campaigning, he antagonized China by calling it a currency manipulator, accusing it of trade improprieties, and using his promise to be tough on China as a rally applause line. When he met China's leader, he reversed course, sounding as if President Xi Jinping was his best buddy and China was his favorite partner. Next, he deliberately irked China with regard to their militarized islands in the South Asia Sea, the perpetual issue of Taiwan, and China's association with North Korea. After China objected, Trump backed off and switched to a conciliatory tone, especially once he discovered how much he needed China's help with North Korea. In early 2018, he alternately applauded China (when Xi Jinping became president for life) and vilified China (for the US trade deficit with them), making China a primary target of many new tariffs. In May 2018, he obsequiously took orders from Xi (promising to help ZTE, a Chinese telecom company) and irascibly criticized China for its trade practices at the same time, jeopardizing the trade talks that were progressing at that time. In September 2018, when asked about Xi being his friend, Trump told the worldwide audience, "Maybe he's not anymore," which was tantamount to diplomatic malpractice, and defied any notion of friendship. Trump's approach toward China is both transactional and emotion-driven, creating a policy that is as stable as a balloon in a hurricane.

Trump has been just as inconsistent in dealing with many other countries. During his first two years in office, he:

- accepted a budding "bromance" with President Macron, yet completely reversed his attitude toward France in favor of an adversarial stance over tariffs and his rejection of international agreements;[53]
- lambasted Mexico and Mexicans when imposing tariffs and excoriating immigrants yet tamped down his vitriol when negotiating revisions to the trade agreement,[54] and then ratcheting it up again at his rallies and during his fight with Congress over funding to "build the wall";
- stated his plan to end the US military role in Syria yet bombed Syrian targets twice and approved a prolonged US presence;[55] then, after a phone call with Turkish president Erdogan,[56] Trump shifted by declaring the defeat of ISIS and the end of the US military role in Syria (despite objections from his staff, the military, and the intelligence community); then he reversed course again by directing hundreds of military personnel to remain in Syria indefinitely;[57]
- intensified his antagonism toward Germany during the June 2018 meeting of the G7 countries yet claims to have a great relationship with Chancellor Angela Merkel;[58]
- withheld support for NATO's Article 5 (that an attack on one NATO member is an attack against all NATO members) yet eventually confirmed, albeit reluctantly, that the US would abide by it;[59]

- claimed that he would broker a peace deal between the Israelis and Palestinians yet crippled the effort by moving the US embassy to Jerusalem without concessions to the Palestinians, closing the office of the Palestinian Mission in the United States, and revoking visas from their diplomats;[60]
- planned a February 2018 state visit to the UK yet canceled his trip on the pretense of not liking the new US embassy in London, despite common knowledge that he actually canceled because of the likelihood of massive protests awaiting him[61] (which did materialize during his hastily organized visit in July 2018, causing him to avoid London, the site of the biggest protests); and
- vilified North Korea and Kim Jong-un with provocative epithets and threats of war yet abruptly reversed course by praising the oppressive dictator as "honorable,"[62] which defied any standard of reasoned judgment, diplomacy, or prudence, after which he progressively ramped up his accolades to the point that he absurdly declared, "We fell in love."[63]

Before Trump reversed his approach toward North Korea, his conduct was unconscionably dangerous, escalating the risk of an apocalypse. Placing millions of people in jeopardy of nuclear annihilation is not an acceptable tactic of negotiation. Outreach initiated by South Korea led to a high-stakes meeting of Trump and Kim Jong-un, and Trump's approach to the meeting was very revealing. Rather than having his staff develop detailed, meaningful policies in advance—that would produce tangible, verifiable steps for future actions—Trump mostly improvised, yielding only a skeletal, ill-defined, amorphous statement of four goals. Rather than crafting an enduring interaction that would benefit from support of our allies, Trump went it alone, treating it as a brief transaction, hours after offending our closest allies at the G7 meeting. Rather than calibrating the process and policy for its impact on other adversaries, Trump saw it as a two-party transaction without broader implications, even though the world watched to inform their strategies. Accentuating his errors, Trump continually praised Kim, saluted his general, and gave an unjustifiably rosy assessment of the outcome, which strengthened Kim's position. Assessing the meeting, David Brooks said, "He did a good thing in the worst possible way."[64]

His transactional approach to such a consequential shift in policy emphasizes two key recurring trends. First, Trump likes dealing one-on-one instead of meeting in a group where he is just one of many. Maybe this is because it makes him feel important, it makes the policy talk more comprehensible, it enables him to take all the credit, or for another reason. Second, Trump likes dealing with authoritarian autocrats who have little or no constraints on their process and policy making, and who can freewheel according to their whim, without accountability. Maybe this is because he is unable to be well prepared on policy, he feels uneasy when his opponent is well prepared with structured goals, or he envies their unmitigated authority, due to his individualistic nature. Whatever the reason, it is appalling that a US president has such an affinity for authoritarian autocrats.

In contrast with his mercurial shifts, Trump's policy, positions, principles, and relations have been ironclad in the case of Russia. Trump is unfailingly deferential, amiable, obsequious, accommodative, and sycophantic toward Vladimir Putin: a recipe for failure in transactional relations. The reason for his obeisance might become known when the entirety of Special Counsel Mueller's report is released. It might be that Trump embraces Putin because Putin has financial and/or personal "kompromat" (compromising material or information) on him,[65] or because Trump admires authoritarians. Regardless, it is obvious and troubling that Trump bestows his most cooperative working relationship, consistent support, and transactional deference upon our principal geopolitical rival and global adversary. Although Trump allows the intelligence community to convey a different message and policy, he consistently aligns his own opinions with Putin's, from his unwillingness to criticize Putin to his insistence that "others" may also have interfered with the 2016 election (which conflicts with the intelligence community's evidence).[66]

Trump's subservience toward Putin was vividly on display at their summit in Helsinki, Finland, in July 2018.[67] Why Trump said that he needed hours to assess Putin's intentions (despite having previously met with Putin for hours) after needing only the first minute to assess Kim Jong-un's intentions remains an incongruous mystery. It may have been just an excuse to have a secretive meeting with Putin. Before that meeting, at their "press availability," Trump's demeanor spoke volumes. Unlike his usual style at such events, his body language and facial expressions were subdued, he spoke only briefly, didn't take reporters' questions, and, very uncharacteristically, he deferred to Putin to speak first.

Later that day, their press conference was an epic fiasco. Trump looked and acted scared. His remarks raised major concerns about his allegiance, competence, coherence, and even his patriotism, resulting in bipartisan rebukes.[68] In response to a question about Russia's cyber-attack on the 2016 election, Trump even refused to support the conclusion of his own intelligence community that Russia was the culprit, giving equal weight to Putin's denial.[69] There was broad consensus that Trump damaged US global leadership and credibility.[70] In appearance, Trump was rigid and downcast, while Putin was smiling and strutting.[71] Trump's voice was submissive and restrained, without its usual tone and flourishes. In terms of his transactional approach, Trump was bankrupt, diminishing our country's stature. Trump's weakness reinforced concerns that Putin has kompromat on him, which Putin wields to give himself superior bargaining power.[72] In the transactional world in which Trump resides, kompromat may have dictated the outcome.[73]

Trump's obsequiousness toward Putin has serious policy ramifications. Jeremy Bash, who formerly served as chief of staff at the CIA and the Department of Defense, summarized the widely held concerns, saying, "The president has been unwilling to listen to the Intelligence Assessments about Russia. He basically said to his briefers, 'I got this. There's nothing you need to tell me about Russia. I know everything.' So, if you have not just an 'America First' policy toward Russia, but a 'Me First' policy, where the president knows everything, can handle everything by himself, then there's not much role for intelligence, there's not going to be much role for facts, and we're not going to get the policy right."[74] Although Bash was speaking about Trump's conduct toward Russia, the dynamics that he illuminated apply broadly to Trump's policy decision-making process.

On many issues, both domestic and foreign, Trump vacillates and contradicts himself. His tendency to do this reflects a lack of core principles and policy insights, and explains why his opinions gravitate toward the last person who speaks to him. Using a transactional approach that revolves around his personal interests, he speaks publicly (to convey a false image of strength) on matters that should be managed privately, causing him to publicly reverse his position later (conveying his weakness). Examples include:

- On women's reproductive rights: He was pro-choice before switching to pro-life, and he told MSNBC's Chris Matthews in a televised interview that he would criminalize abortion before being universally criticized by stakeholders across the ideological spectrum and retracting that extreme stance.

- On the Foreign Intelligence Surveillance Act: He tweeted his opposition to Section 702 before his intelligence chiefs rushed to the White House to explain to him that he is actually in favor of 702, after which he sent out a tweet that contradicted the earlier version and expressed his strong support.
- On the government shutdown in early 2018: He said he supported a "clean DACA" bill before being told what it meant, and switching to demand border security funding in exchange for DACA. He then reiterated that he supports a "clean DACA" bill, which reemphasized the internal inconsistency of his comments.[75]
- On the government shutdown in December 2018: He assured Senate Republicans that he would sign the bill to keep the government open through February 8. Before the Senate passed the continuing resolution to fund eight agencies, talk show hosts and the House Freedom Caucus criticized Trump, and he reversed course, refusing to sign the legislation and causing much of the government to shut down.[76]
- On avoiding a government shutdown later in 2018: He indicated to Senate Majority Leader Mitch McConnell and House Speaker Paul Ryan that he was receptive to their plan to avoid a government shutdown prior to the midterm election[77] before he called for a September shutdown of the government over immigration issues in a tweet just four days later.[78]
- On climate change: He told Pope Francis, Al Gore, various European heads of state, and other stakeholders that he would seriously consider upholding America's commitment to the COP21 Paris Agreement before he decided to cancel our participation in the agreement.
- On manufacturing: He professed to support a "Buy America" approach before it was exposed that Trump ties, steel for his buildings, and other products, including his daughter's brands, were made overseas in less developed countries, after which he has largely ignored the issue.
- On guns: At a meeting with legislators on February 28, 2018, he declared his solid support for broad gun control and safety measures[79] before meeting with the NRA, after which he reversed course on some reforms (banning assault rifles, expanding background checks, and raising the age requirement for purchase of a firearm to twenty-one), added NRA policies to the agenda (encouraging guns in schools and firearm training for teachers), reduced support for background checks

to the "Fix NICS" bill (that merely implements current law), deferred reforms by calling for a study by a commission (led by Secretary Betsy DeVos, who supports arming teachers), and deferred to states for action on other reforms (e.g., allowing risk protection orders, and raising the age of purchase).[80]

- On immigration: On June 15, 2018, Trump expressed his opposition to the immigration reform bill that had been developed by the House Republican leadership before his spokesperson reversed his position later that day, stating Trump's support for that package and adding that Trump opposed the "discharge petition" that would have advanced a different immigration bill.[81] After Trump reiterated his support when speaking to the House GOP Caucus, he reversed again on June 22, opposing it in a tweet, saying, "Republicans should stop wasting their time on immigration."[82] Then, on June 27, Trump reversed yet again, issuing a tweet that urged Republicans to pass the bill.[83] In another turnabout after the bill failed, on June 30, Trump claimed that he had never supported it, even though his earlier tweet proved that claim to be false.[84]

- On Russia: There are numerous reversals and contradictions. Some were by Trump, while others came from his staff. They began before he was inaugurated and have never stopped. They increased in number and magnitude since his Helsinki summit with Putin, which probably has a lot to do with their two hour private meeting without staff. The contradictions and reversals include whether Trump believes Putin directed Russia's attack on the 2016 election, Trump's claim that Putin did not want Trump to win the election even though Putin said he did, and Trump's support for Putin's self-serving suggestion to allow Russian investigators to question US citizens in exchange for US investigators questioning Russians suspected of interfering with the election.

Trump's reversals and contradictions occur because, on most issues, he is motivated by neither principles nor policy. Instead, he uses his transactional approach to get "wins" that promote his brand, satisfy his ego, and serve his base whose support he needs politically and as a psychological buffer from Mueller's and Congress's investigations. When his or his base's wishes or beliefs coincide with those of conservative Republicans, then Trump is willing to speak the conservatives' language to maximize their support. But their ideology is not what drives his decision-making. They are merely an expedient ally when his self-interests or his base's views coincide with theirs.

For example, Trump has become the darling of the American Legislative Exchange Council (ALEC), which advocates for states to enact conservative business and economic policies. ALEC's embrace of Trump, and vice versa, was an opportunistic marriage of convenience, despite ALEC's initial opposition to his protectionist assault on trade.[85]

Similarly, Trump solidified his support among white evangelicals by taking steps that fit their ideology but that he likely took for the sake of his political interests. Examples include: moving the US embassy in Israel to Jerusalem, appointing conservative judges and agency heads, inhibiting equality for transgendered Americans, seeking reductions of women's reproductive rights, and supporting church participation in politics (i.e., halting the restriction that was imposed by the Johnson Amendment, named for Senator Lyndon B. Johnson, who authored the 1954 amendment to the tax code prohibiting political activity by nonprofits).[86] Even Trump's appointment of conservative justices to the Supreme Court was transactional rather than ideological. Although evangelicals were passionate about justices being selected from the list prepared by the Federalist Society and the Heritage Foundation, Trump's main motivation was political, to solidify his support among evangelicals, and hence, Republicans.[87]

It is likely that Republican legislators, conservatives, and many evangelicals will increasingly apply a transactional approach in response to his.[88] They are likely to remain his allies only when doing so is convenient or expedient to advance their interests, without loyalty to Trump. This will not bode well for Trump if Mueller's findings are adverse to his political status. If that happens, they might eagerly shift their allegiance to Vice President Pence, whose passion for their ideology is well-established.

Trump has introduced so many oddities, incongruities, and inanities to US domestic and foreign policy that it might be tempting to shrug in futility and declare it all inexplicable. For example, it seems implausible to reconcile his variegated actions and postures regarding Russia, Ukraine, China, North Korea, the Philippines, Turkey, Syria, Israel, Palestine, Saudi Arabia, Iran, Haiti, Cuba, Mexico, Canada, Poland, Germany, France, the United Kingdom, and many other countries. Compounding the challenge of making sense of his divergent predispositions toward them, he has alienated many of our closest allies, while embracing and even coddling some of our longtime adversaries, including those with an authoritarian leader.

Yet, there are actually a number of elements that are consistently evident in Trump's thinking and policy actions on both domestic and foreign issues. The tapestry of Trump's decision-making can be distilled into the following five components, each one of which leads to the next:

1) Narcissism: Trump is driven by his own psychological needs and personal interests (detailed in chapter 1), not US national interests. To satisfy his quest for attention and approval, he asserts that he is the smartest, most capable, most supreme person, and seeks affirmation of that from others. He acts as if he is the ultimate arbiter of what is best, and even of what is truth.[89] Even though he exhibits weakness and low self-esteem, and overcompensates for them, he either doesn't realize that, or is not willing to let that deter him from pursuing his own interests. He acts on his own whims and caprice, instead of knowledge, facts, science, and expert advice. Foreign leaders recognize Trump's narcissism, and some satisfy his need for praise by flattering him in order to manipulate US policy, as in the Saudis' celebration of him, complimentary letters from North Korea's Kim Jong-un, and Japan's Prime Minister Abe nominating Trump for a Nobel Prize apparently at Trump's request.[90]

2) Anger: Trump harbors animosity against anyone who inflicted a slight against him, real or perceived. He is angry at much of the world, including people, organizations, and systems that rejected him, criticized him, impeded him from doing what he wanted, or withheld the affirmation and approval that he seeks. The targets of his ire include the NFL (for not allowing him to own a franchise),[91] business leaders (for abandoning his business councils, and a history of not accepting him),[92] US tax law (for its impact on his finances, which he tries to avoid),[93] the intelligence community (for the Steele dossier, their objections to his disrespect of the CIA and FBI, and criticizing him for not accepting their findings about Russia's interference in the 2016 election),[94] the amorphous "establishment" (for its skepticism and disapproval of him, and protecting US institutions from his actions),[95] and perhaps most of all, President Obama (as discussed in chapter 10).[96]

3) Deconstruction: Trump seeks retribution against his adversaries, to settle the score and establish his supremacy. The first part of this process is to deconstruct, destabilize, and dismantle much of what preceded his presidency, which he views as the establishment that slighted him. He tears down US principles, including civil rights, environmental protection, presidential accountability, DACA, family unity among migrants and refugees, and Obamacare. He destabilizes international structures and relationships, as with the Iran Nuclear Deal, the Paris Agreement, TPP, NAFTA, NATO, G7, and "3M": Merkel, Macron, and May. He typically acts without first learning and understanding the details, purpose, and history of what he is affecting, or the consequences of his actions.

4) Replacement: In seeking retribution, Trump attempts to reconstruct the country and the world in his image, according to his whim. His transactional approach facilitates that without constraints like norms of governance and constitutional checks and balances. He conducts a series of transactions—domestically and internationally—in his own style, doing things differently for its own sake. As the self-appointed arbiter of what is best, he believes that his view is inherently the smarter and correct approach. Policy is an extension of Trump himself, and he aims to replace policy, laws, and structures as he sees fit. Where he has no strong opinion, his staff and appointees can fill the vacuum, which still gives him credit for reconstructing government.

5) Authoritarianism: Trump emulates autocrats, authoritarians, dictators, and so-called strong men. As the entire world saw in Helsinki, Trump most admires, and is most deferential to, Russia's Vladimir Putin. Trump's admiration—or envy—of these rulers is evident in his congratulations to China's Xi Jinping when he became president for life, and his complimentary and supportive comments toward Turkey's Recep Tayyip Erdogan, Saudi Arabia's Salman bin Abdulaziz Al Saud, Egypt's Abdel Fattah el-Sisi, the Philippines' Rodrigo Duterte, and Poland's Andrzej Duda. Trump seems to regard them as role models due to their expansive powers, scope of control, lack of accountability, and extreme authority to execute and enforce their edicts, all of which he strives to replicate. Their authority is consistent with Trump's desire to reward people who are nice to him, and punish those who are not.

Trump's approach to policy and decision-making is in stark contrast to that of his predecessors. Prior presidents began with principles or ideological beliefs, which they effectuated by developing strategy and then policy. Trump, however, begins with transactions as the objective, to gain "wins." He then reverses the process to identify a policy and an underlying principle. As problematic as this is to people with leadership experience, governmental insight, or decision-making acumen, his approach resonates with his base. Of the five components, above, his base is energized by his "anger," which they share, and his desire to "deconstruct" the status quo, which was a source of their angst. Given their fervent affection for those two elements of his approach, they are willing to embrace his choices for "replacement" of the status quo, accept his "authoritarianism," and simply disregard his "narcissism."

Trump wanted to win the election for the sake of winning, retaliating against Obama and others, and addressing a few issues that impeded him and his businesses. He was not motivated to run for office for the sake of enacting a specific policy vision for the country. With the rare exception of taxes, which impacts him more than anything else in government, he doesn't know much about policy details. With the exceptions of tax reform, immigration, and trade agreements, he doesn't seem to care much about the underlying principles that lead to his policy. It is an offense against democracy to tailor public policy for personal gain or protection. Yet, Trump has demonstrated a pattern of enacting policy as an extension of his own personal best interests.

POLICY DECISIONS IN THE ABSENCE
OF CONSISTENT PRINCIPLES

Trump's ambivalence toward policy specifics and principles raises many questions. In the absence of policy vision or leadership from the president, what happens? What course does the administration take?

Many of Trump's cabinet appointees filled the gap by aggressively asserting their own policy agendas based on traditional conservative ideology that they cultivated before working on behalf of the American people. In some cases, appointees had worked in the private sector and transported their prior industry-cultivated objectives to their new federal positions, as was the case with secretaries of commerce Wilbur Ross, education Betsy DeVos, health and human services Alex Azar, and treasury Steve Mnuchin. Some appointees came from other government roles and brought a variety of agendas and goals with them to their new positions, such as former attorney general Jeff Sessions, former interior secretary Ryan Zinke, and former EPA administrator Scott Pruitt. Often, this produced tragic consequences. For example, Pruitt, who had been the attorney general of Oklahoma and a legislator before that, was known to be closely tied to the state's fossil-fuel industries, from which he received massive campaign contributions, and for which he provided regulatory relief and other favorable outcomes. As EPA administrator, Pruitt implemented the fossil-fuel industry's policy wish lists to an extreme degree, dismantling a plethora of regulations that impacted them.[97]

The policy shifts pouring forth from the Department of Justice are among the most venal. Although these are not industry-driven the way that the EPA's changes are, they are driven by conservative orthodoxy that is not even aligned with Trump's past comments. The department's policies are largely the result of having former attorney general Jeff Sessions at the helm, who brought to the job the same antiquated, divisive, race-baiting, ultraconservative beliefs that he honed as a senator from Alabama.

As attorney general, Sessions had a regressive impact that recalibrated which rights and whose rights the Department of Justice would enforce.[98] Among the actions that Sessions initiated were measures to:

- dismantle Affirmative Action at universities, and shift the focus of civil rights enforcement[99] to alleged discrimination against whites, by joining lawsuits where white students (and, in a case against Harvard, Asian American students) claim to have been denied admission due to such programs;[100]
- delay or revoke Justice Department consent decrees that, in concert with local police departments, established reforms of procedures and protocols to rectify patterns of discriminatory and socially unjust police conduct (e.g., profiling, arrest rates by demographic groups, firearms use, etc.);[101]
- direct prosecutors to "pursue the most serious, readily provable offense," along with maximum-length sentences, even for nonviolent, low-level drug offenses, reversing an Obama-era policy;[102]
- withhold funds from cities and other jurisdictions that self-identify as Sanctuary Cities (cities that prohibit their law enforcement officers from detaining undocumented immigrants who have not committed a

crime and otherwise enforcing federal immigration law while conducting their usual policing responsibilities);[103]
- allow employers to discriminate against LGBTQ employees by the Justice Department filing an amicus brief in favor of the employer in the
Zarda v. Altitude Express case (which was decided in favor of the employee
by a federal court of appeals in New York);[104] and
- allow voters to be purged from the voter registration rolls (process
begins when a voter does not vote in one federal election, and the
voter is purged from the roll if they do not vote in a second federal
election), despite the discriminatory impact on certain demographic
groups (via *Husted v. A. Philip Randolph Institute*, decided by the US
Supreme Court in 2018).[105]

Some of these actions were taken by Sessions and his political unit over
objections from the department's career staff attorneys, particularly the Civil
Rights Division's attorneys, who refused to be complicit.[106] Sessions's most
long-term impact will be felt in the judiciary. By November 2018, Sessions
and the White House had already nominated, and the Republican-majority
US Senate had confirmed, a historically high number of conservative judges,
with lifetime tenures, to federal courts: fifty-three to district courts and twenty-
nine to courts of appeals, in addition to two Supreme Court justices.[107]

Reprehensible policies and decisions might also be ongoing at many
other agencies and departments that have yet to be the subject of public
scrutiny. They may be relatively unnoticed, and below the radar of the
media, because national attention has been riveted on Trump's myriad other
governmental and personal improprieties (e.g., his alleged collusion with
Russians and the resulting investigations, his alleged violation of the Constitution's Emoluments Clause and other ethical transgressions, his North
Korea dramas, his multifarious tariffs, his culture war against the NFL and
the NBA, his sexual affairs and his payments to prevent them from reaching
the public's notice, his daily Twitter rants and distractions, the improprieties of his appointees, etc.). Although the media has appropriately focused
on Trump's Russian issues and other legal problems, as well as many governmental matters that demand scrutiny, those issues divert attention from
actions at federal departments. In many instances, ethical improprieties of
cabinet officials have received appropriate media attention. However, the
focus on individual improprieties might be siphoning media resources away

from policy and other substantive actions at those departments that would normally warrant scrutiny and compel public awareness.

Appointees at sub-cabinet levels (e.g., deputy secretaries, assistant secretaries, deputy assistant secretaries, and the like) also have the ability to redirect policy within their departments and agencies. However, the Trump administration has nominated relatively few people to sub-cabinet posts. Most of these positions remain vacant or filled by Obama holdovers,[108] and Trump's administration has had a very difficult time recruiting people to fill these posts.[109] Rather than voicing concern about this, Trump has portrayed the lack of appointees as intentional, for the sake of saving money (which is largely just a public posture to save face), despite the restraint that it imposes on achieving his own objectives. The result is that policy in departments with few Trump appointees has not changed as much as it might have. At the same time, policy has shifted dramatically in other departments where many traditional conservatives have been appointed, or where its issues have been atop the administration's agenda.

Since relatively few policy experts have been brought in to fill vacancies at many departments, policy shifts have been undertaken selectively, mainly on high-profile issues like Obamacare, immigration, tax cuts, and tariffs. This is creating an interesting phenomenon. The ever-cautious Greek philosopher Aristotle taught us that "nature abhors a vacuum," which is as true in politics as it is in physics. The administration's policy vacuum creates opportunity for other forces and actors to fill the void, at least in the near-term.

One fascinating consequence of this policy and staffing vacuum is that, without new staff in place to redirect policy, career bureaucrats maintain existing policy.[110] This means that, in effect, the Obama administration's policy remains in place in many areas, which continues programs, projects, agencies, and structures on the same paths that were previously established. At a minimum, key methodologies, considerations, factors, and goals are often still in place, continuing to inform the decision-making process at the staff and management levels. Once matters reach the executive level within a department, they are certainly subject to reevaluation and redirection, which may or may not occur. But even then, the executive offices make their assessments within the context of the work product generated at the staff and management levels, which were based on the preexisting policy guidelines.

The policy vacuum also opens the door for senators and representatives to fill the void. Legislators are able to propose policy on issues and programs of special concern to them. They certainly can do so through legislation, and they can also make recommendations to a department by way of a letter or meeting, which would launch a departmental analysis of their proposal. Recommendations of this sort are routinely taken seriously, and in the absence of some other direction from the White House or departmental policy, they might be given more weight and have a greater likelihood of adoption.

Domestic policy issues that are outside of the media spotlight and public controversy are especially ripe for departmental staff and legislators to influence departments' policy and decision-making. By not getting much attention from advocates, activists, or other stakeholders, there might be more flexibility for a department to take action. Thus, internal (staff and management) and external (legislators) players can weigh heavily on domestic issues, through the executive and legislative branches. These influencers can impact a multitude of smaller yet consequential issues within each department, such as the allocation of grants, designation of projects, location-specific federal lands management, and weighing in on federal regulations. This would not apply to high-profile issues such as healthcare, tax reform, gun control, and immigration because the president is vested in these issues, and they are already being shaped by a critical mass of governmental and outside stakeholders. The more visible and contentious the issue, the less room there is for this type of low-key influence.

FOREIGN POLICY DECISIONS IN THE ABSENCE OF CONSISTENT PRINCIPLES AND STRATEGY

Foreign policy is affected differently when there is a vacuum of presidential influence. Officially, Congress has a coequal role in foreign policy. Legislators routinely raise issues, ask questions, make requests, and offer recommendations, and they certainly can propose legislation that would affect foreign affairs. But in all practicality, the executive branch is where the tools to formulate and implement foreign policy are concentrated. Foreign policy decisions typically involve consultations with international stakeholders, including consideration of the interests of competing power centers (i.e., foreign governments). Engagement of this much broader array of actors focuses on interaction and coordination with our network of global partners and allies. That network and other relationships are managed by the State and Defense

Departments on diplomacy and security matters, respectively, representing the United States on the global stage. Legislators do not have parallel staff resources or authority to implement strategies with America's global stake-holders, although their requests for support to conduct international fact-finding and investigative missions certainly are routinely accommodated.

Regarding the formulation and implementation of foreign policy, State Department management and staff have a central role, especially if there is a vacuum of input from above. They continue to do their job, whether that is within the framework of the preceding president's policy or new policy that is established by the current president or departmental secretary. When the Trump administration redirects policy, the management and staff adjust accordingly. Yet, on many global and country-specific issues, neither Trump nor others in his administration have done so. In some instances, Trump's administration has taken no action, while in other cases, staff has made policy statements that have been subsequently contradicted, thus providing no clear guidance on the direction that policy should take. In such cases, the policy that was in place during the Obama administration could continue in effect, churning forward until there is either a directive to develop a new policy or a clearly delineated shift in policy, beyond an applause line at a rally.

The inability to establish and implement a cogent Trump foreign policy is partly due to White House management decisions and institutional barriers that have been imposed upon the Department of State. As Jim Prince, executive director of the Democracy Council (a global policy development think tank), points out, "The across-the-board hiring freeze at the State Department limits transfers, reassignments, and staffing of new offices, even though offsetting cuts would normally have allowed them to occur. Draconian restrictions on career professionals, such as limitations on their participation in inter-agency communications or interaction with Congressional oversight committees, as well as the disempowering of authority for offices below the executive level, also degrade the implementation of our foreign and national security policy, and the actual formulation of policy."[111]

Through the Trump administration's first two years, there has been no Trump Doctrine on foreign policy. One meaningful principle has emerged, however, that could have a role in a broader policy framework at some point. The use of chemical weapons by Bashar al-Assad against his own people in Syria generated worldwide revulsion and condemnation, including from

Trump. He ordered missile attacks twice in response to Assad's depravity, although the limited missile responses had only a minor effect and were as much about Trump flexing his military muscles as it was an effort to curtail Assad's capabilities. While a prohibition against chemical weapons constitutes neither a foreign policy nor a doctrine, it certainly could be part of one. So, although it is only a start, it is at least a meaningful guidepost.

Aside from that, there is no indication of what would comprise a cogent, constructive Trump doctrine or foreign policy. So far, there have been only a few consistent—but very problematic—themes that can be gleaned from Trump's actions:

- transactional personal relations: Trump engages leaders on an *ad hoc* basis via conversations and their personal chemistry—actual, imagined, or utilitarian—which often is unaligned with official US positions (e.g., President Xi of China, President Macron of France, Crown Prince Salman of Saudi Arabia, Prime Minister Netanyahu of Israel, Prime Minister Abe of Japan, President Putin of Russia);
- personal interests over national interests: Trump has been highly deferential to countries in which he has financial or other personal interests (e.g., his apparent indebtedness to Russians and financial relationship with Saudis; Trump-owned or licensed hotels and golf courses in the United Arab Emirates, Turkey, India, the Philippines, Indonesia, Canada, South Korea, Uruguay, Panama, Ireland, and Scotland[112]; Trump's and his daughter's manufacturing interests in Asian countries);
- receding from global leadership: under the guise of "America First," Trump minimized America's role in multilateral international agreements (e.g., the Paris Accord on Climate Change, the Trans-Pacific Partnership, and the Iran Nuclear Deal), favored unilateralism and xenophobia over globalism and collaboration (as in his 2018 speech to the UN General Assembly), and reduced US leadership in many regions (e.g., the US military presence in Syria and Iraq, aid to Pakistan, and Middle East peace negotiations, which he debilitated by prematurely moving the US embassy to Jerusalem); and
- embracing authoritarian or autocratic rulers: Trump expresses his admiration of "strong-man" leaders, like Putin and Duterte, toward whom he has been supportive, perhaps because he emulates them.

These themes do not constitute a foreign policy doctrine. Even if they did, it certainly would not be a doctrine that could be considered responsible, appropriate, sustainable, or aligned with America's long-term national interests. Trump has put forth a few broad foreign policy concepts, like fighting terrorists, putting "America First," and restricting immigration, and some isolated region-specific directives regarding North Korea, chemical weapons in Syria, and Middle East peace before Trump sacrificed our leadership role. But they lack the coherence and consistency to constitute a stable, predictive foreign policy that is sufficient to guide expectations about America's reactions to issues that may arise.

Until there is a new, legitimate, cogent foreign policy doctrine that signals our country's intentions and forecasts our global conduct, Trump's foreign policy is just an amalgamation of *ad hoc* impulses. Until then, the vacuum may be filled with some of the principles that comprised the "Obama Doctrine," which consequently guided State Department actions. Although there was no official or definitive articulation of the Obama Doctrine, it was more than just "apply sound judgment, not rigid dogma" (which is a better way of expressing "don't do stupid stuff" that was attributed to Obama and Secretary Clinton). The Obama Doctrine and Obama's foreign policy were largely based on fundamental principles that reflected long-held American values. As stated by Ben Rhodes, Obama's deputy national security advisor, Obama "was advocating an inclusive global view rooted in common humanity and international order."[113] The Obama administration was unable to effectuate everything that President Obama articulated, in some cases because it inherited some global and regional commitments from which it could not summarily extricate the United States, like the wars in Iraq, Afghanistan, and imprisonments at Guantanamo Bay, and in other cases because Obama expressed geopolitical aspirations that mainly served as a "North Star" overall objective for policy rather than the policy itself.

The Obama Doctrine appeared to center on four categories of principles or metrics that guided US international activity and may continue to do so in the absence of other directives:

- "Our commitment to the universal values that are the source of our strength," as stated by President Obama on April 25, 2016, in Hannover, Germany, principal among which are:

- human rights, including prevention against oppression, injustice, and hunger;
- civil rights, including equality, nondiscrimination, and the worth and dignity of each person;
- rule of law, democracy promotion, and strengthening of democratic institutions;
- opportunity and inclusion in economic, quality of life, and civic affairs;
- peaceful coexistence between and among peoples; and
- labor rights and protections, and consumer protections.

- International cooperation and interdependence among the community of nations with regard to:

  - security, elimination of terrorism, and peaceful resolution of conflicts;
  - economic growth and prosperity, ideally through integrated economies;
  - environmental protection, especially clean air and water, and combating climate change;
  - investment in human capital, infrastructure, and financial structures; and
  - public health improvement, disease reduction, and the prevention of epidemics.

- Self-determination rights for people to choose their national and local governments without intervention from external interests, including:

  - prohibition of territorial aggrandizement by adjacent or other foreign countries;
  - elimination of influence from foreign political, economic, and military interests;
  - assurance of freedom of speech, assembly, and organizing for political purposes; and
  - protection of the rights of minority populations, including rights to engage in civic affairs.

- Elimination of, and safeguarding against, the rise of repressive authoritarian and autocratic rulers within a country's internal political system by protecting:

- ∘ voter enfranchisement for all citizens, equally, without risk of adverse consequences;
- ∘ democratic institutions and nongovernmental organizations (NGOs) that protect civil liberties and civic engagement;
- ∘ rights of minority populations, including rights to engage in civic affairs; and
- ∘ freedom of speech, assembly, and organizing for political purposes.

These Obama principles assert key factors that drive our country's decisions to support or oppose foreign governments, and guide our responses to international occurrences. They reflect American values that are largely shared by countries that are governed by democracies, and were cultivated by decades of American leadership. They are inextricably intertwined within our culture, institutions, and government, with broad consensus among Americans who hold diverse ideologies. As such, there is no values-based rationale for departure from them. These principles are the bedrock upon which our foreign policy can remain consistent, reliable, predictable, and effective, to the extent that career professionals at the State Department and elsewhere in the administration are emboldened to apply them.

Trump's antipathy for anything associated with Obama might cause him to repudiate these principles, even though they express American values and were developed over the past hundred-plus years by presidents of both parties. More likely, a Trump Doctrine would retain those that conform to his views and apply his transactional approach to reprioritize some principles over others. Three of the principles are especially compatible with Trump's interests and seem likely to guide his policy: (a) economic growth and prosperity, which Trump generally supports despite his tariffs and antagonism toward trade deals; (b) the elimination of terrorism (Trump continued Obama's strategies against ISIS and in Afghanistan); and (c) self-determination of national and local governments, which comports with an America First reduced US global presence. The least likely to be applied is the fourth category, as indicated by Trump's supportive conduct toward authoritarian and autocratic leaders. Even if Trump maintains some of these principles, he is likely to apply them with a unilateral, win-lose approach in which he imposes his will (regardless of the interests of other countries), or, if unable to do so, withdraws our participation. He shuns international collaboration, win-win objectives, multilateral cooperation, and interdependence, while extending his self-centered worldview into foreign affairs.

Trump does not grasp the long-term negative consequences of his approach. His actions show that he doesn't understand the importance of America's leadership in global efforts, initiatives, and agreements. If the United States cannot be counted upon to lead on a regular basis—and even worse, if Trump continually offends the world community—then even our longtime partners will not be ready or willing to support our efforts when they are requested to do so. If the United States becomes viewed by the world community as a country that simply throws its weight around, acting like the "ugly American" that is entitled to whatever it wants without concern for global stability, equanimity, or mutual prosperity, then other countries will turn toward China, Russia, and other powers as their principal strategic allies and economic partners. As our engagement declines, our power will certainly diminish.

Ironically, Trump often does what he criticized Obama for doing. Obama opted to "lead from behind" in Libya because our allies were situated in closer proximity and had more exigent interests in the region. They were better positioned to take the lead. We supported them with material and resources, but our allies were the most kinetically engaged. We benefited by having our objectives implemented by others, at less risk to our personnel. Despite chastising Obama for this approach, Trump has replicated it, and even exceeded it. Without a strategy or long-term plan, Trump has retracted our military, diplomatic, cultural, and financial leadership from various conflict zones (e.g., Russia's incursion into Ukraine, Iraq's sectarian violence, Syria's devastating civil war, Pakistan's antiterrorist efforts, and Israeli-Palestinian negotiations that halted when Trump prematurely moved our embassy to Jerusalem without concessions to the Palestinians, sacrificing our "honest broker" role). Trump also carried out Obama's will in Syria by twice ordering missile attacks to counter Assad's use of chemicals against his own people. Despite Trump's effort to extract the United States from Syria, he reasserts the US militarily when he feels that Assad has crossed Obama's "red line" against the use of chemical warfare.

Trump's idea of leadership seems to be limited to doing what we want—more precisely, what he wants—and telling others to fall in line whether they like it or not; in other words, if you're not with us, then you're against us. But

global affairs do not succeed that way. Leadership requires consensus building, consistent engagement, strategic planning, responsive accommodation,
and helping our partners achieve their objectives as well as our own. Trump's
self-interested transactionalism impairs our global stature, marginalizes our
relationships, and obliviates our moral leadership. American leadership is
based on our ideals, values, and principles, as well as our judicious application of them. But Trump acts as though our leadership is based only on our
money and his bellicosity. He uses threats of force and finances, like with-
holding financial aid or imposing or releasing economic sanctions, to compel
action or support. Yet, even if that occasionally compels short-term compliance with a particular demand, it engenders animosity that, over time, breeds
resentment and a search for alternative partners and sources of support.

Interestingly, former ambassador to the United Nations Nikki Haley was
unaligned with Trump's approach. In many instances, she addressed the
UN Security Council with a markedly different tone than that which Trump
employs, most notably by condemning Russia for reprehensible conduct.
Maybe it was because she insisted on imparting a forceful institutional presence that maintains long-held American principles. Maybe Trump intentionally engaged in a good-cop/bad-cop strategy that allowed Haley to enunciate
traditional values in an insular diplomatic forum. Maybe Haley's mission
was to reassure global diplomats of American continuity in order to mitigate
Trump's weakening of important alliances. Maybe Trump just doesn't care
what the United Nations does or what our ambassador does in that forum.
Whatever the reason, it seems that Haley was granted the latitude to engage
the world community with a tenor that our secretaries of state and others
have not been able or allowed to provide.

Aside from Ambassador Haley's niche, if Trump opts to completely
repudiate Obama's principles, it would be contrary to our national heritage,
national identity, national interests, and international leadership. The Obama
Doctrine principles were actually developed over the course of decades, by
many presidents with diverse ideologies, building upon each other. Disavowal
of all of these principles would cause a counterproductive disintegration of
our moral authority, and a recalibration of what America represents. A comprehensive departure would most assuredly be temporary, too, since these
principles are embedded in our culture, supported by a broad consensus with
diverse viewpoints. Republican and Democratic stakeholders would reinstate

these American values at their first opportunity to do so, under the leadership of the next president, regardless of their party affiliation.

In the absence of Trump administration policies and principles that formally and substantively revise the Obama Doctrine, foreign policy decision-making could easily rely on Obama Doctrine principles as our default position in response to international events and developments. It is natural and appropriate that State Department management and staff continue to apply them when evaluating proactive and reactive strategies regarding country-specific, regional, and global circumstances. In effect, Obama's principles could operate as a "when in doubt, go with it" framework to fill any foreign policy vacuum that exists.

IMPORTANCE DURING TRUMP'S TENURE AND THE POST-TRUMP ERA

It is clear that principles-based policy will not be the primary driver of Trump's strategy and decision-making, unlike other presidencies. A major reason for this is Trump's *modus operandi* in which his transactional approach and cult-of-personality style are his defining characteristics. After watershed events, political pundits often speculate that Trump will adapt to changing circumstances and "pivot" in style or substance. Some thought he might pivot to a presidential tone when he hired John Kelly to be his chief of staff,[114] while others thought he might pivot to a pragmatic policy approach when he met with Democratic leaders to discuss the federal debt limit and the Deferred Action for Childhood Arrivals (DACA) legislation.[115] Their analyses assumed he would adopt a standard orientation toward public policy and would respect the factors that usually contribute to decision-making. It is as if these pundits assessed what they would do, rather than what Trump would do.

But Trump doesn't function that way. His lens is his self-interest, and that doesn't allow for a pivot.[116] By operating with a transactional and personality-based approach, he does not account for changing circumstances that would normally dictate the propriety of a pivot. David Frum, who served in President George W. Bush's White House, expressed his concerns about Trump's mechanisms and motivations, saying, "Trumpism is not a set of ideas. It's a system of power. Donald Trump has no policy ideas. He's not even really a populist. . . . What he's deadly serious about, and very effective at, is enriching himself, [and] shutting down the institutions of government that would normally catch him. Right now, the president is receiving streams of undisclosed millions of dollars from business partners in the Philippines, Turkey, the United Arab Emirates, India. No one knows how much he's receiving."[117]

Trump obsequiously caters to the desires of his fawning base, whose support he believes buttresses his claim to the office, as their Pitchfork Populist in Chief. Many of his decisions are guided by what he thinks his base wants or what he promised them during the campaign, even though that is often detrimental to his broader political standing, and worse still for the country overall. Yet, Trump has said that he doesn't need to bow to his base because they are the voters who would support him even if he were to "stand in the middle of Fifth Avenue and shoot somebody." Their support is immutable, regardless of the policy directions he chooses. So, if he doesn't need to worry about them, why does he worry about them? Why does he make politically unwise choices in their name? Does he worry that they would abandon him if he did not oppose gun control reforms, DACA, Muslim and Central American immigration, the Paris Agreement, the Trans-Pacific Partnership, and the Iran Nuclear Agreement? Does he think they would defect if he did not shut the government down in December 2018 over funding for his border wall?

It is possible that Trump believes his base's support is tentative, itself transactional, and always needing reinforcement. It is also possible that Trump invokes his base just to give himself cover, or an excuse to do what he simply wants to do, by fiat. His base may just be a utilitarian guise to exert his transactional, authoritarian impulses (i.e., Frum's "system of power" and the "L'état, c'est moi"[118] concept). Trump is captive to his narcissistic emotional needs and its consequent self-interested imposition of his authority. His transactional conduct reveals his belief that the country and the world should bend to his will, adopt his perceptions, and adhere to his dictates. He does not adjust to the policy landscape because he does not consider that landscape to be as important as his own desires. His words and actions show that, in his view, what is good for him is good for the country, instead of the other way around. His prioritization of self over country led to his patriotism being called into question when he sided with Vladimir Putin against the US intelligence community during their press conference in Helsinki, Finland.[119]

Now that we have seen the dangers of a president whose core policy is his self-interest, and whose self-interest becomes policy, something should be done to protect against a recurrence in a future election. Since the absence of a cogent, rational policy framework is a red flag that warns of a possible lack of qualifications to serve as president, it may be useful for experts to weigh in, during the primary campaign season, on whether candidates are in fact qualified. Although this exceeds the Constitution's criteria for the presidency, making any such approval unenforceable, it could still be useful information to voters.

One solution might be to assemble a bipartisan panel of political "Brahmin," that is, experienced political professionals who have served in previous administrations and are highly respected. They would meet with each of the viable candidates in all competitive political parties, ask them whatever questions they deem appropriate, and determine whether the candidates are credible. The standards for credibility would focus on whether a candidate: (a) understands the role of the presidency and the president's responsibility to the public, (b) applies reasoned judgment, (c) is fit to serve, and (d) is devoid of conflicts of interest and nefarious motives for seeking the presidency. The process would not evaluate candidates' policy positions. It would merely guard against the most obvious pitfalls and self-interests driving a candidacy. While they're at it, the "Brahmin" could pose the questions suggested at the end of chapter 1, to determine whether a candidate has a solid grasp of the responsibilities of the office being sought.

Another reason Trump lacks a coherent, consistent policy strategy is, as previously noted, the White House's inability or unwillingness to recruit experienced professionals to fill the departments' key policy roles. For example, when Trump announced that Rex Tillerson would be replaced as secretary of state (almost fourteen months into Trump's presidency), the department had twenty vacancies among assistant secretary and undersecretary positions for which there were not even any nominees, and forty-two vacant ambassadorial positions without nominees.[120] Prompted by Trump's antipathy toward State Department bureaucrats—who have long been recognized as experienced, dedicated career professionals with subject matter expertise—"Tillerson dismantled large parts of the department: as the White House proposed a 31% budget reduction, the department accepted the lowest number of new Foreign Service officers in years. Sixty percent of the highest-ranked diplomats have departed. . . . In Trump's first nine months, more than 79,000 full-time workers quit or retired—a 42% increase over that [same] period in Obama's Presidency. To Trump and his allies, the departures have been liberating, a purge of obstructionists."[121]

By not having enough of the right people in the right positions, the administration has a sporadic policy orientation that is occasionally focused (e.g., the tax bill), in some cases inconsistent (e.g., immigration and DACA), and at other times absent (e.g., many foreign policy issues). Trump's team swarms some high-profile issues, and ignores others that are not percolating. Due to the multitude of key vacancies, its policy efforts are subject to reliance on alternative sources of input. Even when Trump does appoint someone to a key role, it may create more policy confusion, as was the case with the appointment of National Security Advisor John Bolton, an architect of the Iraq War.[122] Bolton's view favoring global extension of US power by military means sometimes conflicts with his boss's worldview (e.g., Trump's vitriol against the Iraq War and his America First isolationism), and sometimes amplifies it (e.g., their shared antipathy toward Iran and hostility toward North Korea, at least before Kim Jong-un's meager gestures and personal letters inspired Trump's mollified approach and amorous language).[123]

During the campaign, Trump, in effect, ran against both the Democratic candidate and the Republican Party. By doing so, both campaign and candidate alienated many experienced GOP staffers. Trump's personal style and multifarious offenses along the way reinforced their distaste for lending their talents to his success. After Republican Party chair Reince Priebus and others saw Trump's nomination as a *fait accompli* and gave in to the inevitable, some Republican staff tried to warm up to his candidacy. When Priebus was named White House chief of staff, a trickle of experienced staffers did accept positions, perhaps strongly influenced by party loyalty.

From the start of Trump's presidency, his personnel office has been seen having a difficult time recruiting quality staff for sub-cabinet-level appointee positions in various departments.[124] Sometimes, candidates were rejected because they were not sufficiently loyal to Trump.[125] In other cases, qualified, experienced Republicans were unwilling to serve due to Trump's behavior, temperament, or positions, in addition to "incoherent and unclear leadership" at agencies.[126] Many candidates had business backgrounds that required extensive vetting for financial conflicts of interest, which some did not pass.[127] Missteps and signs of dysfunction in the White House were further disincentives, especially Trump's public castigation of his senior staff (e.g., Reince Priebus) and cabinet officials (e.g., Jeff Sessions).[128] The wariness of prospective appointees was further compounded by the congressional investigations into Russian interference and the appointment of the special counsel.[129]

Experienced staff had no desire to take a new job that could put them at risk of being dragged into the investigations, which could burden them with legal bills and even legal jeopardy.[130]

The events of August 2017 further deflated the enthusiasm of prospective appointees. Trump's tweets and statements about North Korea showed, to anyone who wasn't already convinced, that he is terribly ill-equipped for sensitive aspects of the job, exhibits precarious judgment, and seldom abides by the reasoned judgment of experienced staff. Then, Trump's response to the Charlottesville violence and his infamous Trump Tower press conference demonstrated that he is morally bankrupt, as he aligned himself with the most contemptible hate groups in America. Trump's racist statements in January 2018 about Haiti, Africa (as if it were one country), and Norway (in contrast to the other countries) intensified concern about his racist tendencies. Trump's calamitous July 2018 press conference with Putin in Helsinki further damaged his standing and credibility as the guardian of national interests. With GOP elected officials beginning to repudiate him (selectively in public and frequently off-the-record), it is clear that House and Senate Republicans are calculating the cost of fealty and silence. If Trump continues to offend American values and sensibilities, it is likely that more Republicans will voice their discontent, and that could also impact a prospective appointee's decision to serve in the White House or an agency.

These events have a chilling effect on efforts to recruit experienced staff. Potential staff members have little to gain by boarding a ship that is taking on water, and probably contemplate their exit strategy before they even enter. They have lots to lose, including their reputation (having the Trump presidency on a résumé may hurt within GOP networks more than it helps) and their integrity, which experienced staff would not sacrifice blithely. Ruth Marcus, deputy editor of the *Washington Post*, distilled it by observing that "everybody who comes within the orbit (of this president) just ends up being diminished by it."[131]

As a result, it increasingly appears that Trump's talent pool will have to make do with the staff that is already in place, without the addition of many more. When needs arise, Trump often moves people around (e.g., redeploying John Kelly as chief of staff, Kirstjen Nielsen as secretary of homeland security, and Mike Pompeo as secretary of state) rather than finding new talent for senior roles. Understaffing and management-level gaps will likely cause departments to scale down their policy function and shift their focus to operational efficiency and program implementation. Some departments and agencies will increasingly be guided by alternative policy mechanisms, for example, the State Department, which will have to rely on resourceful improvisation without reinforcement while many policy and ambassadorial positions remain vacant. Inexperienced staffers might be promoted into some of those posts, which will create yet another problem if people with scant credentials are placed into pivotal policy positions that have important responsibilities.

The net result of these staffing challenges is that Trump's policy apparatus may be relegated to lumbering forward on parallel tracks. The most prominent track will be the one with Donald Trump at the helm. Major policy issues will continue to emanate from his office or his Twitter account on an *ad hoc*, transactional basis, and change course just as chaotically. These pronouncements will equate less to policy and more to self-absorbed indulgences. This substitute for policy development is destined to engender resentment in Congress, where principles-based policy is the currency of legislators and legislating. Conflicts between Congress and the White House over both the substance and process of policy making are inevitable, especially now that Republicans got the tax relief that was their main objective for Trump's tenure, and the Democrats have taken control in the House of Representatives.

A second track would be the development of new policies by cabinet-level leaders or by career civil servants who step up to the plate to address policy development needs. The latter efforts are those that might be created by management-level staff or that could percolate up from other staff levels. We have begun to see this play out, for example, in low-key trade negotiations with Argentina to allow US pork products into their country,[132] and with Colombia to allow avocados grown there to be sold in the United States.[133] These new initiatives might also be informed by input from legislators, lobbyists, trade associations, economists, and public policy think tanks.

The third track, instead of new policy, would be the continuation of existing departmental policies through bureaucratic continuity. When the White House or a cabinet officer redirects policy, then that prevails. However, at every department, there are myriad policies that fly below the radar, and they, too, have significant impacts on a national scale. As has been observed following each presidential transition, many of these policies continue along the paths that were established under the direction of the preceding administration. Thus, Trump's shortage of sub-cabinet-level appointees, in effect, empowers career civil service bureaucrats or holdover appointees to continue pre-Trump policies. Many low-profile policies may benefit from continuity and be able to survive into the post-Trump era.

In response to Trump, the Democratic Party faces its own policy dilemma. After Trump's election, which also extended the GOP's control of Congress, Democrats embarked on a soul searching journey. The process intensified after the 2018 midterm election, as attention shifted to the 2020 presidential election. Democrats are evaluating the best ways to reach and motivate the most voters with the most compelling messages in order to position their party for success. Whatever direction they choose, policy will be at the heart of their appeal, and many politicos will audition to show that they are the presidential candidate who can best connect the policy to voters' lives. The debate about the messages and messengers that would be ideal generally distinguishes between two main orientations.

To hasten the onset of the post-Trump era, one group of Democrats believes that the message should be tailored to inspire minorities, women, youth, LGBTQ voters, and others who solidly and actively support Democrats. To bolster participation and voter turnout among these constituencies, Democrats have expanded voter registration, enhanced outreach, encouraged new candidates, and elevated progressive policies that appeal to them. To motivate and mobilize their base, this wing of the party believes that its presidential nominee in 2020 should either be a woman, a person of color, or someone with biographical and demographic characteristics that would arouse their most consistent and passionate voters. This is a type of base-oriented strategy, and its proponents see "identity politics" as a solution.

Ironically, "identity politics" is actually more established in the GOP where it is implicitly institutionalized through sensibilities that favor whites, especially white men. Because Democrats broke down the barriers to enfranchisement of all demographics and embraced diversity, "identity politics" became associated with Democratic candidates. Thus, today's "identity politics" is actually a misnomer, as it is primarily a reflection of the wide swath of society and demographics that engages politically and becomes elected as part of the Democratic Party. Yet, "identity politics" continues to be a dominant force on the Republican side of the aisle, with the advantaged identity being whites. That is easily confirmed by a search for nonwhite faces on the Republican side of the aisle during a State of the Union speech.

Some beneficiaries of "identity politics" consider it to be condescending or demeaning. They object to others marginalizing them by giving their physical characteristics—as a woman, minority, person with a disability, etc.—primacy in defining their candidacy, rather than being defined by their campaign's policy goals. They object to being reduced to their demographics, and the assumption that they will mainly champion social justice issues, without honoring their entire message and vision. Those objections are legitimate. Yet, the term "identity politics" could be said to fit candidates who lack a substantial track record or policy fluency across a spectrum of issues, and instead base their candidacy on their biography, demographics, or a single issue. Candidates whose identity (ethnicity, gender, sexual orientation, etc.) is a focus of their candidacy are differentiated from candidates whose policies (experience and expertise on a wide range of issues) are the core of their candidacy while also having politically appealing racial, ethnic, gender, or sexual orientation characteristics. The distinction between the two is nuanced.

Another group of Democrats shuns the notion of "identity politics" in favor of a message based on economic policy and other issues with broad-based appeal. If candidates' demographic and personal characteristics are relegated to the background, then they are not "identity politics" candidates. This wing of the party opts for a broadly inclusive economic message that appeals to the middle class and people striving to rise into the middle class, across all demographic groups, including working-class whites. Their approach is based on the notion that Americans of all descriptions—including independents and Republicans—have suffered economically, and all have an equal stake in elevating prosperity, improving quality of life, and leveling the economic playing field. It centers on economic opportunity and fairness, and it seeks to attract voters beyond the Democrats' traditional core, while risking lower enthusiasm among its base voters. The potential reach of this approach may broader than that of "identity politics." (Further discussion of these strategies and candidates that embody them is in chapter 10.)

Rather than choose between "identity politics" and economic egalitarianism, the Democrats should craft and pursue a fusion of the two. They are not mutually exclusive, and are, in fact, complementary. There are precedents for hybrid solutions that unite the party, dating back to 1896 when William Jennings Bryan called for economic fairness and opportunity for all, to attract support from rural and urban workers alike. A modern hybrid could include policies for equal economic opportunity, job skills training, job growth, wage increases, and economic fairness that would benefit all middle-class and lower-income Americans. It could promise a return to hallowed norms—the rule of law, equality and justice for all, global alliances, and the international order that the US constructed—with a unifying theme such as "this is obvious." This platform could appeal to all demographic groups, including those who are central to the "identity politics" strategy—such as communities of color, women, LGBTQ groups, religious minorities, and youth—as well as working-class and college-educated whites.

As we evolve toward numerical parity between whites and nonwhites in the post-Trump era, it is counterproductive to elevate identity factors above all others. Doing so also ignores the maxim that politics is about addition (attracting), not subtraction (alienating). Focusing on a candidate's demographic characteristics for the sake of capitalizing on "identity politics" could alienate many voters. If the Democrats do that when selecting their presidential candidate for 2020, voters may regard it as a cynical, patronizing, pandering ploy that is more concerned with the messenger than the message, rooted in marketing and branding. It is also unnecessary, since identity characteristics are readily apparent, and the demographic transition toward a nonwhite majority will increasingly empower diverse candidates.

There is a vibrant debate over what factors matter most to voters and motivate their support. Differences between the parties have also been observed, with Democrats typically being drawn to candidates who provide detailed policy solutions, and Republicans usually being drawn to candidates who articulate broad principles.[134] In both cases, both the message and the messenger matter. While an outsized focus on candidates' identity is risky, their racial, ethnic, gender, and sexual orientation attributes are valuable assets alongside their principles, policies, and priorities.

Democrats would be well served to choose a candidate who can articulate policies and represent voters in ways that transcend his or her own genetic identity. "Identity politics" should focus on the politics of voters' identities, not the candidate's. Policy would be the candidate's driving force, while turning "identity politics" upside-down, speaking to others' identities in a selfless and universal manner, rather than celebrating the candidate's own identity association or characteristics. For example, along with a broad-based economic message, a male candidate should have strong credentials on issues of high importance to women; a female candidate should have the same on issues of importance to men; a white candidate should have strong credentials on issues of importance to nonwhites; a nonwhite candidate should have the same toward issues of importance to whites; and so forth. This variation on "identity politics," in which a candidate's strengths reach beyond their own genetic identity, can widely expand the candidate's appeal to more groups of voters.

Especially after enduring a presidency that is run by the politics of personality, voters from all political parties will have a strong appetite for the return of principles and policy to their central role in the political process. In 2020 and thereafter in the post-Trump era, voters will reward candidates who have strong core principles and cogent, forward-looking policies, regardless of what she or he looks like.

CHAPTER 4

EMPOWERMENT

THE DEMOCRATIZATION OF
OUR POLITICAL PROCESS

Throughout most of American political history, the selection of each party's presidential candidates was centrally controlled, orchestrated by party leaders, major funders, and other powerful stakeholders. Insiders made the decisions, classically in smoke-filled rooms, and later through caucuses comprised of invited elites. The rank-and-file were then expected to "fall in line": organizing, campaigning, and voting for the chosen candidate.

That centralized control of the system has been changing in recent decades. The selection of nominees was democratized through the switch to primary elections (in most states), the proliferation of mass media and its transparency, and popular sentiment for inclusion. Despite these changes, the Republican and Democratic parties continue to determine the factors that guide the way they choose their presidential nominees. As their systems evolved in recent decades, adjusting to the rising forces of democratization, the two parties have embraced different approaches in choosing their nominees. In 2016, the usual approaches of both parties came to a crashing halt, and they departed from their typical practices.

In the years ahead, the trend toward democratization of our political processes is likely to accelerate as new voices are enfranchised, enabling an increasingly diverse spectrum of people and opinions to influence our politics and government. More Americans are becoming motivated and encouraged to participate in the political process and become candidates. Rising inclusion is amplifying the impact of virtually all racial, ethnic, age, gender, sexual orientation, and other demographic groups, as well as Americans with diverse ideological preferences. The way that we choose our leaders and voice our opinions will evolve through expanded involvement, activism, and opportunities to run for office.

PRESIDENTIAL NOMINEES 1960 THROUGH 2016

From 1960 through 2012, when there was not a Republican incumbent seeking reelection, the Republican Party nominated the person who was deemed to be "next in line" to lead the party. In each case, the eventual Republican nominee had either: (a) matriculated up from being the current vice president (Nixon in 1960, George H. W. Bush in 1988); (b) placed second in a previous cycle's contested primaries (Reagan in 1980, McCain in 2008, Romney in 2012); (c) had a long career as an elected official, during which they were a leader of the party (Goldwater in 1964, Nixon in 1968, Dole in 1996); or (d) been a governor of a major state, along with the unique advantage of being the namesake son of a previous president (George W. Bush in 2000).

In a stark repudiation of this practice, Donald Trump won his party's nomination despite having none of those characteristics. A number of other candidates had solid claims to being the "next in line" candidate for the nomination. Trump was clearly not the choice of the GOP establishment, and he overcame many obstacles that the establishment erected to prevent him from capturing the Republican nomination. Without reliving the entire primary season, most Americans will remember the many strategies and machinations by candidates, commentators, and party insiders that were designed to favor any candidate other than Trump. It was easy to lose track of how many Republican elected officials and other influential leaders either prognosticated or swore that Donald Trump would never get their party's nomination.

From 1960 through 2012, when there was not a Democratic incumbent seeking reelection, the Democratic Party has not nominated a "next in line" presidential candidate, except for three times when it did so to nominate an incumbent or former vice president (Hubert Humphrey in 1968, Walter Mondale in 1984, and Al Gore in 2000). The eventual Democratic nominees in the 1960, 1972, 1976, 1988, 1992, 2004, and 2008 elections had not been the presumed front-runner throughout the process, had faced strong opposition, and emerged from a pack of contenders. In most of those cases, some other politician had been regarded as the "next in line" candidate early in the process, but either chose not to run or was defeated.

Ironically, by nominating Hillary Clinton in 2016, the Democratic Party departed from its usual practice and embraced the Republican Party's typical approach that favored the "next in line" candidate. Her "next in line" status emanated from the 2008 primary election outcome, augmented by her subsequent dutiful service as secretary of state in the administration of the person who defeated her in 2008. Even before Hillary Clinton formally declared her candidacy, Democratic Party chairperson Debbie Wasserman-Schultz ceded control of vital DNC operations to Hillary Clinton's campaign—including fundraising, communications, and strategy—to stack the deck in her favor.[1] As later became clear, Wasserman-Schultz was not alone, as CNN commentator Donna Brazile shared debate questions with Clinton's campaign prior to a CNN town hall.[2] This became a major irritant that alienated many of Bernie Sanders's supporters (in addition to other tension points, such as policy differences on trade).[3] During the general election campaign, it was difficult for Clinton to attract and mobilize Sanders's supporters and donors, as well as other voters who felt that she had been unduly thrust upon them by the party's early machinations to limit the field of candidates.[4]

Both Trump's grassroots support and Clinton's grassroots challenges illuminate the same phenomenon. In today's America, the voters are no longer eager to be told what to do by party leaders. The base of each party wants to have a say in the selection process. The masses do not want to be force-fed by the party establishment. Millions of Americans are energized to watch debates, organize, volunteer, contribute funds, attend caucuses, and vote. With direct access to so many parts of the process, voters feel empowered to decide who they want to support, and they don't appreciate top-down pressure that directs them toward a candidate who is not their preference.

A similar dynamic can be seen with policy positions and other reasons to support a candidate. Voters want to decide what matters to them and the positions with which they agree, rather than passively accepting information from party leaders. The candidate that best speaks to their concerns, emphasizes their issues, understands their challenges, connects with them on a human level, and proposes solutions to their problems will gain their interest and support. When considering a candidate's positions, voters care whether those policies are rooted in passion and authenticity, or are merely the product of political calculations, focus-group testing, and opportunistic calibration like that found in a party platform.

With the deluge of information (and, in some cases, misinformation) that is available these days via broadcast TV, twenty-four-hour cable TV news, talk radio, newspapers, Google, Facebook, Twitter, email blasts, and internet-everything, voters have the opportunity to be informed (or, at least, feel that they are). This access to information, combined with multiple avenues to participate (via social media as well as rallies and campaigning), enables voters to be engaged and involved in the political process more than ever before. Engagement breeds a feeling of empowerment, which conveys a sense of being a stakeholder in, and possibly even impacting, the process. Wielding this newfound political power, many voters are encouraged to influence the process rather than simply follow the top-down dictates of the party establishment.

The net result is that the political process has been democratized—opened to inclusive participation—to a greater extent than in the past. Virtually any American can now become informed, engaged, empowered, and influential. Along with that comes greater opportunity for activism. People can speak out and impact the electoral flow when they feel that their voice is not otherwise being heard.

EVOLUTION TOWARD INCLUSION

Although the democratization of the electorate tangibly influenced the 2016 campaign and election, it did not happen overnight. It has been an incremental evolution spanning decades. The democratization that benefited prospective candidates, enabling a wider swath of citizens to toss their hat into the ring and run for office, has followed a similar path.

Through most of American history prior to the mid-1960s, only a very elite slice of society had even the hope or possibility of being elected to Congress, governorships, or other higher offices. Officeholders were, by and large, cut from the same privileged cloth. Despite President Lincoln's characterization in his Gettysburg Address, during most of American history, the government was not of, by, and for all the people. As statistics on past members of Congress indicate, government was principally owned and operated by males who were white, who were middle-aged or older, and who had enough money to purchase power and enjoy the luxury of public life.

Following the Civil War and continuing until the 1960s, the spectrum of opinions was generally narrower than it is today, although reasonable minds differed on issues and spawned some legendary legislative battles (including a caning or two). Compromise on legislative matters was usually achievable. After even the harshest fights and filibusters, comity among lawmakers usually prevailed. Destroying each other's character or career was rare, although there were some famously venomous campaign fights, such as those between

John Quincy Adams and Andrew Jackson, and between Grover Cleveland and Benjamin Harrison. But when it came to governing, politicians shutting down the federal government because of a failure to agree on a budget would have been unthinkable. Their pals at the country club wouldn't hear of it. The collaborative nature of politicians stemmed from the commonalities between political opponents, and was evidence of their mutual respect for institutions in which they cohabitated.

With the transformation of our society that began in the 1960s, the opportunity to participate in our government was vastly expanded to millions of Americans who had traditionally been excluded. This change came about due to the combined effect of the Voting Rights Act of 1965, the shifting landscape of demographics, the mobilization of political factions, and the new expectation of inclusion and fairness for all Americans embodied in the Civil Rights Acts of 1964 and 1968. The result was that racial and ethnic minorities, women, and young Americans in their twenties and thirties became politically empowered. They ascended to congressional, mayoral, gubernatorial, and other elected offices in numbers that were previously unimaginable, making government more reflective of the electorate.

Today, government leaders are characterized by lifestyles, historical backgrounds, and heartfelt political philosophies that are as diverse as those of the constituents they represent. Prior to the late 1960s, there had been only a sprinkling of diversity among congressional members. In the 115th Congress (2017–2018), both the House and Senate were beginning to look more like the people of the United States. Even with substantial gains in the 2018 midterm election, Congress still has further to go, especially in the Senate, which is a great distance from even resembling demographic parity, but the gains cannot be overstated.

- In 1971, there were 13 African American members of Congress, and they created the Congressional Black Caucus.[5] In 2017, the CBC had 49 Democratic members (including two senators).[6] Along with 3 Republicans (2 in the House, 1 in the Senate), there was a total of 52 African Americans in Congress,[7] and that number rose to 57 at the onset of the 116th Congress in 2019 (55 members of the CBC plus one Republican African American in each chamber).[8]
- In 1976, 5 Hispanic members of Congress created the Congressional Hispanic Caucus,[9] which, in 2017, had 31 members (including

two senators), all of whom are Democrats.[10] Combined with the 6 Republican members of the Congressional Hispanic Conference,[11] there were 37 Hispanic/Latino members of Congress in 2018, with that combined total rising to 42 in 2019.[12]

- The Congressional Asian Pacific American Caucus (CAPAC) was created in 1994, and in 2017 there were 22 members of the CAPAC leadership and executive board (including 4 senators).[13] The CAPAC increased in 2019 with the addition of 3 newly elected Asian/Pacific Americans.[14]
- The Congressional Caucus for Women's Issues was founded in 1977 (as the Congresswomen's Caucus) with 15 women members of Congress.[15] In 2017, there were 89 women members of the House of Representatives, along with 23 women senators, for a total of 112 Caucus members.[16] At the onset of the 116th Congress in 2019, those numbers rose to 106 in the House (including nonvoting delegates) and 25 in the Senate, for a total of 131 women in Congress.[17] (Imagine how the leaders of the Whig Party in the 1850s would have reacted to that, as well as the idea of rooms being set aside just for congresswomen, right by the House floor!)

Although women and people of color remain far short of electoral representation that equates to their demographic representation, the pace toward parity has increased. Much more progress is needed for diversity in Congress—in terms of racial, ethnic, gender, sexual preference, and other characteristics—to match that of the electorate, along with similar gains in state and local governments. Yet, even though change is happening incrementally, America's political process has begun to embrace the inclusionary standards that it set for itself hundreds of years ago. American democracy is flourishing compared to its status just sixty years ago.

Women in particular have been mobilized in reaction to Trump. He has been a catalyst for women to become activists and candidates due to his extensive record of misogyny and philandering (e.g., the Access Hollywood audio, many allegations of sexual harassment and predatory behavior that surfaced during the 2016 campaign, his marital infidelities with Stormy Daniels and Karen McDougal). With Trump's conduct as the backdrop, the public's revulsion intensified with the revelations of sexual abuse by Harvey Weinstein, Matt Lauer, Louis C.K., and a multitude of other men with economic and/or decision-making power. That spawned the #MeToo and Time's Up movements, which have accelerated the drive toward gender equity in politics and policy. Ironically, Trump and other miscreants unintentionally inspired many women to take action against offensive behavior and seize the mantle of political leadership.

After the 2016 election, organizations that assist female candidates saw unprecedented surges in women seeking office and preparatory skills.[18] In February 2018, EMILY's List projected that 50 women would run for Senate seats and 431 for House seats, and the group reported being contacted by over 30,000 women who considered running for office.[19] The actual numbers even exceeded estimates, with 53 Senate and 476 House candidates. EMERGE, an organization that trains women to become candidates at all levels of government, was inundated with trainees,[20] and many of its alumni won their elections.[21]

A new national attitude welcomes and encourages women to become candidates for public office. Past gains were limited, and even 1992's "year of the woman" surge undervalued women through the implicit message that it was an impermanent feature or event, instead of a new standard. Now, women are recognized as vital stakeholders and essential partners in all aspects of the political process and political leadership. Women in leadership roles have become normalized, and momentum for women to reach parity seems certain to continue. The current trend is sustainable because it is embedded in the public consciousness, and voters no longer accept the notion of women being relegated merely to token roles. The urgency of electoral gender equity is widely recognized, and with it, the political landscape has shifted toward a new chapter of inclusivity.

Public sentiment favoring more women legislators and the perspectives that they bring was amplified by Republicans' mishandling of sexual misconduct allegations against Brett Kavanaugh when the Senate Judiciary Committee considered his nomination to the Supreme Court. The all-male GOP contingent's outrage against injury to Kavanaugh's reputation, which mirrored Trump's outrage, was in stark contrast to their criticism of women's accusations about Kavanaugh, and both were appalling. The Republicans' dread of even being seen speaking to Dr. Christine Blasey Ford (which they delegated to a female prosecutor) revealed their fear of questioning her without displaying misogyny (they cited the optics, but if they spoke to her with respect and empathy, optics would not have been an issue). Chairman Grassley's assessment of the reason why there weren't any female GOP senators on the committee exacerbated the tension. Grassley's assessment that "it's a lot of work; maybe they don't want to do it" revealed an almost Neanderthal bias against women's capabilities.[22]

The need for women's voices was exemplified by the two female "she-roes" who confronted Senator Jeff Flake in an elevator prior to the committee's vote on Kavanaugh. Their passionate influence prompted Flake's call for the FBI to investigate Dr. Ford's allegations of sexual abuse, which might have been consequential if the White House had not imposed unjustifiably strict limits on whom the FBI could interview. The White House prevented the FBI from following up on leads suggested by Dr. Ford, and even predetermined some accusations by other women to not be credible, rather than risk having the FBI investigate them and find otherwise.

Each time Trump was asked about the message the women's allegations against Kavanaugh sent to young men, he lamented that sexual misconduct could ruin a man's career, rather than recognizing the need for respectful behavior, empathy, and adherence to rules of consent. Having been accused of sexual misconduct by many women for many years, Trump projected his own fallacious claim of "false charges" onto other men who are accused of sexual misconduct, as if to bolster his own defense. He basically twisted men into being the victims of women. In so doing, Trump once again most likely inspired more women to become politically active. Trump's and Kavanaugh's conduct, which placed sexual harassment in the national spotlight again, became an impetus for action in Congress. In December 2018, Congress adopted new rules against sexual harassment by legislators, to support claims by victims and shift responsibility to the accused,[23] with Rep. Jackie Speier and some other legislators pushing for even stronger enforcement.[24]

The democratization of the political process that is empowering women will also democratize policy and legislation. The influx of female legislators and executive branch officials also changes the nature of issues, as women object to the designation of some issues as "women's issues" and reject being pigeonholed into that subset of concerns. The notion of "women's issues" is inherently condescending, as women are not a monolith with unitary opinions and circumscribed interests. Women are impacted by, and care about, all issues—national security and foreign affairs, agriculture and commerce, environment and energy, taxation and government oversight—in addition to women's health, reproductive rights, child care, sexual harassment, and gender equity. At the same time, all issues that are important to women are also important to their husbands, fathers, sons, brothers, friends, neighbors, and colleagues. The term "women's issues" has become antiquated as more women become legislators, engage in the entire spectrum of issues, and inspire people to care about the concerns of everyone in the national collective, beyond their own immediate interests.

Women and minorities certainly have achieved progress toward electoral and political inclusion, and more is certainly forthcoming. Still, those advances do not translate to commensurate progress in our streets, neighborhoods, cities, universities, careers, and corporate board rooms. Despite many gains, our broader society remains at an earlier stage of the empowerment process. In some states, legislatures continue to pass laws that maintain the political, electoral, and economic advantages of historically empowered groups: whites, men, and the wealthy. Some laws erect barriers that restrict voting eligibility in targeted situations. They aim to impede certain racial, ethnic, age, and other demographic groups from activating the full power of their inclusion, and they often achieve their desired effect.

Highly visible electoral opportunities for government offices are ripe for gains that will increase diversity and present a more representative democracy. Yet, to some extent, the democratization of Congress and state legislatures paints a patina of progress over societal circumstances in which exclusion too often prevails over inclusion. Victory is not defined by electoral triumph, but rather, by the policy reforms that are enacted thereafter, such as those that advance democracy, equality, participation, and enfranchisement. A broader challenge remains among the less scrutinized and publicly visible jobs, educational pathways, and countless other roles where women, minorities, LGBTQ Americans, people with disabilities, and all others must also be welcomed, leading toward equity and opportunity.

DEMOCRATIZATION SPAWNS DIVERGENT OUTCOMES

The inclusionary drawing of district boundaries (adhering to the Voting Rights Act) has facilitated electoral opportunities for historically marginalized populations. But it has also generated some opposite results. When the drawing of districts consolidates communities of color into a district that enables racial and ethnic minorities to wield political power in those districts (rather than diluting their voting power across multiple districts), other nearby districts are deprived of the ideological balance that communities of color would have infused. Those nearby districts are then dominated by predominantly white populations that, in many states, tend to favor more conservative candidates. By concentrating like-minded constituents into districts that are heavily skewed toward a political party (aka, "cracking and packing"),[25] a larger number of adjacent districts are predisposed to favor candidates with very different mindsets and political philosophies. Sometimes this outcome is intentional, as a means to mute the influence of communities of color in districts other than the one in which they are consolidated.

When like-minded voters are concentrated in separate districts, primary elections become more important, since the party registration of voters in each district tilts heavily in one direction or the other. To win the primary, candidates embrace more extreme positions than they would have if they needed to appeal to voters with a broader range of political preferences, and there is little or no need to adjust their policy positions to win the general election. As a result, many officials now arrive in Congress (and state legislatures) with hard-line inclinations.

In recent years, this has especially been the case with the Tea Party movement. Beginning in 2010, a large and powerful contingent of Tea Party Republicans won congressional races. That group morphed into the Congressional Freedom Caucus, which remains a significant voting bloc in the House. The Tea Party and Freedom Caucus Republicans benefited from redistricting with party-centric concentrations. Similar to what occurred with Democrats, their success is a product of the democratization of the political process and the empowerment of the grassroots voters in their districts. Typically, in the districts where they succeeded, the only contested election is the primary, since Democrats have little or no chance of victory in a general election there. If Republican Party politics in their districts were still centrally controlled by establishment leaders from the business-oriented or country-club wing of the party, then it would have been unlikely for Republicans of this new breed to win the many congressional seats that they gained since 2010.

Some of these legislators built their political careers by opposing particular issues or interests that are well represented by other lawmakers. Some campaigned on promises to reverse precedent and progress, uproot traditional procedures, restrain the federal government, shut down whole federal departments, and refuse to cooperate with opposing forces. Some were elected by promoting distrust, divisiveness, and intransigence. Strident campaigns leave the victor with what they believe is a mandate to carry the election's parsimony with them to their new jobs. In such cases, when officials arrive in office with the stated intention of waging partisan battles, even the prospects of compromise and negotiation are, to them, repugnant. This became a monumental obstacle for former Speakers John Boehner and Paul Ryan, who were often unable to consolidate the regressive Tea Party and Freedom Caucus members with traditional conservatives and members of the Republican Main Street Partnership.

As more districts are heavily weighted toward one party or the other, Congress is becoming an amalgamation of polar opposites. The influx of legislators with extreme views feeds divisiveness and legislative polarization—even paralysis—since, for many, their *raison d'être* is to steadfastly adhere to their hard-line positions. Although there are still many legislators from both parties who work with colleagues on both sides of the aisle, some legislators (especially members of the Freedom Caucus) feel that their mandate from their voters is to refuse to communicate, compromise, or even respectfully engage with members of the other party. The cure to this problem lies in redistricting reform (like in California), which can be structured in many ways and is being explored in some states.

In addition to the decennial redrawing of districts, increased opportunities to participate have made both the Republican and Democratic parties into coalitions of diverse members. However, the type of diversity differs between the two parties. Democrats are much more diverse in terms of the identity—racial, ethnic, LGBTQ, religious, and other demographic characteristics—of their elected and represented members, with active and influential participation from each community. Democrats often seek consensus between their moderate and progressive wings on the basis of key fundamental values and principles that they typically share. In contrast, the GOP's diversity centers on ideological and socioeconomic differences, as they have much more homogeneity in terms of their members' and elected officials' racial, ethnic, and other demographic identities. Adherence to ideology often makes it difficult to reach consensus among wings of the Republican Party.

The impact of this is that Republican identity politics (i.e., white-centric politics) provide Democrats with a natural point of contrast, as they factor diverse identity characteristics into their calculations. In turn, that stimulates the GOP's reaction, pushing back against the Democrats' broad demographic outreach. Increased involvement and participation by the

Democratic Party's constituencies has exacerbated anxieties among other groups. While the Republican Party has its competing factions—and its ideological coalition posed challenges to Speakers Boehner and Ryan—the Democrats' elevation of diverse "identity politics" contributed to Trump's traction with many white voters.

DEMOCRATIZATION, COUNTER-REACTIONS, AND POLICY DEBATES

During the 1960s, America experienced an unprecedented era of activism. The combined forces of the civil rights movement, the Baby Boom generation, student activism, antiwar protests, and environmental awareness generated a groundswell of civic and political engagement. Diversity in the political process surged as these movements inspired many people to engage in grassroots activism and electoral politics, and the Voting Rights Act of 1965 facilitated their enfranchisement. Alongside that progress, rights and equality were solidified by many of the Supreme Court's decisions during the leadership of Chief Justice Earl Warren.

Following urban unrest and riots in many cities during the mid-1960s that illuminated societal divisions, in 1967, President Johnson convened the National Advisory Commission on Civil Disorders or the "Kerner Commission," to study the situation and propose solutions.[26] In 1968, the Kerner Report recommended development of a broad-scale federal initiative with four main proposals that framed subsequent policy initiatives:[27]

- Welfare: establishment of a base level of income support, especially where jobs are not available and where wages are at inadequate levels;
- Housing: development of a National Open Housing Law with six million new middle-income and low-income units, especially in smaller and dispersed buildings, rather than high-rise projects;
- Jobs: creation of two million new jobs in government and the private sector with opportunities for advancement through job training that is subsidized by federal funds or tax credits; and
- Education: allocation of grants to promote integration, and during the transition to integration, provision of special compensatory aid to improve schools in marginalized communities.

The civil rights movement, together with reactions to the Warren Commission (which investigated the assassination of President Kennedy), the Vietnam War, and Watergate, brought an emergent awareness of inequities and discontent, as well as activism to resolve them. Expanded opportunities for candidates from diverse communities enabled a new and broader breed of legislators to be elected to Congress during the 1960s and 1970s. This wave of legislators instituted laws and programs that reflected the agenda of the 1968 Poor People's Campaign[28] and the Kerner Report's proposals. These included strengthening the social safety net and protecting civil rights and individual liberties, as well as establishing environmental protections and improving government accountability.

These developments generated a counterreaction among social conservatives who objected to the Democrats' liberal policies and the Warren Court's decisions. During the 1970s, conservatives developed long-term strategies to regain power in all three branches of government, at both the federal and state levels. Republicans' strategies included the use of language and messaging that would widen the appeal of their policies. They vilified judicial activism to tilt public opinion toward favoring the appointment of conservative judges and justices. Their counteractivism benefited from the democratization of the political process, just as liberal Democrats had previously benefited. This led to the election of President Reagan in 1980, and the election of many conservative Republicans to Congress throughout the decade. Their success also energized the evangelical movement to mobilize into the political force that it has been ever since. In the decades that followed, conservative presidents, legislators, and interest groups have collaborated to appoint conservatives to all levels of the judiciary and deny liberal appointees whenever possible. Their efforts originally intended to rein in judicial activism evolved into an attempt to *facilitate* judicial activism, only with an opposite judicial philosophy. By appointing a cavalcade of conservative crusaders, the GOP has enabled the courts to reverse decades of progress, dating back to the Warren Court and earlier. Their long-term efforts culminated in the 2018 confirmation of Brett Kavanaugh to the Supreme Court, which gave ardent conservatives a solid five-justice voting bloc majority on the Court.

During the late 1980s, constituencies that had been disempowered and neglected by Reagan became reengaged, spurring a new wave of left-leaning activism. In counterreaction to conservatives' policies and Reagan's governance, many liberals were elected to Congress. Following the 1986 midterm election, Democrats controlled both chambers. Although President George H. W. Bush succeeded Reagan, keeping the presidency in Republican hands, his election was widely viewed as a result of Governor Michael Dukakis's ineptitude as a candidate, despite the electorate's discontent with Reagan's policies and the Iran-Contra scandal. Bush's style of governance embraced a more centrist approach, as reflected by his budget compromise, multilateral approach to foreign affairs, and support for both the Americans with Disabilities Act and the Clean Air Act amendments of 1990.

President Clinton embraced both liberal and moderate approaches, seeking to appeal to a broad spectrum of energized forces. Clinton espoused many liberal policies, most prominently the need for universal healthcare coverage. At the same time, he presented himself as a moderate, having led the centrist Democratic Leadership Council, which spawned the "third way" and "triangulation" philosophies of governing, and his pronouncement of the need to reinvent the federal government. Yet, in the 1994 midterm election, largely in reaction to his healthcare legislation and his effort to establish LGBT rights in the military, a number of conservative Republicans were elected, shifting control of the House to Republicans for the first time since the 1950s.

The trend toward democratization has continued during the 2000s, energizing and activating additional constituencies at different times. While political activism and dissent were muted and even discouraged during the aftermath of September 11, enabling the "Patriot Act," the initiation of the Iraq War, the creation of the Department of Homeland Security, and the GOP's congressional gains in the 2002 midterm election, that was only a temporary pause. Since the 1990s and increasingly in the 2000s, the GOP has been transitioning from a party of conservatives, who sought to conserve the status quo, to a party of regressive reformers (some might say reactionary radicals) who seek to reverse progress and reimpose the status quo of a bygone era. The George W. Bush administration's ill-conceived Iraq War, fossil-fuel devotion, climate change denial, LGBTQ vilification, and Hurricane Katrina response were among many debacles that propelled youth engagement and environmental activism during the latter half of Bush's presidency.

A resurgence of liberal activism took hold in the 2006 midterm election, swinging the pendulum of congressional control back to the Democrats. That change in sentiment, along with the economic crisis of 2008 and other significant factors, culminated in the election of President Obama. In turn, the forces of democratization fueled the rise of the Tea Party energized against

Obama and his policies, especially Obamacare. The success of the Tea Party and other Republicans in the 2010 midterm election shifted control of the House back to the GOP, which maintained control until the Democrats' gains in the 2018 midterm election. The GOP's policies and prominence also helped fuel the rise of the short-lived Occupy Movement, which enfranchised people who had not been politically engaged, many of whom later reemerged as Bernie Sanders supporters.

Trump's victory in 2016 was, in large part, a continuation of this pattern, as he energized a sizeable faction of the electorate that had previously been disregarded due to its low participation rate and discontent with both parties. Rather than discount them as being disengaged or dormant, he recognized them, activated them, gave them a shared identity as a group, validated their predicaments, related to their frustration with politics, voiced their concerns, and catalyzed them into a political force. His promise to appoint conservative judges and justices was vital, inspiring conservatives and even evangelicals to support him despite the philandering behavior and apocryphal rhetoric they would normally consider disqualifying. As with other demographic and interest groups that become activated, it is likely that Trump's base will remain engaged and continue to be a force in electoral politics for years to come, especially since his appointment of Neil Gorsuch and Brett Kavanaugh to the Supreme Court fulfilled their top priority. They, too, are part of the American heritage of empowerment and participation.

As president, Trump has inadvertently energized a massive wave of political engagement among those who object to his policies, persona, parlance, presence, and/or performance. The success of the Democrats in the 2018 midterm election, giving them control of the House of Representatives, was largely a counterreaction to Trump. Their gains were propelled by women, minorities, youth, and people with a college-level education. Opinion polls, focus groups, marches, rallies, and social media showed that most people in these groups opposed Trump's and his administration's tone and actions. For example, after the February 2018 mass killing at Marjory Stoneman Douglas High School, the students of Parkland, Florida, led an impressive crusade for gun reform and voter mobilization. They are emblematic of the new wave of youth activists who become politically engaged even before reaching voting age, and are wielding their influence on policy and voting. These newly activated groups, as well as Trump's base, will remain formidable forces as the democratization of the political process continues.

Prior to the 1960s, the range of issues and policy ideas that received governmental attention was relatively narrow, because the officials who were in position to raise them had a relatively narrow range of ideologies, interests, and sensibilities. People whose concerns and causes did not fit that narrow scope had very little prospect of being elected to an office from which they could advance other objectives. The electorate did not have significant influence and were relegated to supporting the policy options force-fed to them. Power was centrally controlled by power brokers and elites who selected candidates and dictated the acceptable range of policy options, without significantly adapting to grassroots input.

Of course, presidents have been the exceptions. When a president had the courage and vision to steer the ship in a new direction, then the rest of the government has often followed suit. That is among the reasons why we honor the presidents who were great leaders. In order for them to make the mark that they did, they had to challenge the orthodoxy, prevail, and guide the country on uncharted waters.

Since the 1960s, each era of liberal or conservative dominance, and each wave of presidential and congressional control, has been fueled by activism on policy issues. Each time that the political climate moved in a new direction, the move was propelled by the empowerment and engagement of additional demographic, socioeconomic, and/or issue-oriented constituencies. Archaic, top-down political control has given way to democratization, enfranchising virtually all sectors of society who are able to exert their power and garner the forces necessary to extol their cause. The ideologies and candidates that stimulate the greatest issue activism can prevail, or at least sway the debate, over time.

A consequence of increased participation is that with each new electoral wave driven by polarized interests, the intensity of the rhetoric escalates, and policy positions become more defined. Both sides of the political divide become increasingly wedded to particular policies and positions, making each side more contentious and intractable.

Even though this escalation brings more fractiousness, discord, and acrimony to Congress, state legislatures, and government overall, there is a silver lining to the disorder. Paradoxically, the turmoil stems from the achievements of democracy and the empowerment of vastly divergent sectors of society that had been precluded from participation through most of our country's history. Rather than being restricted to the sidelines as observers, Americans with diverse backgrounds and views are entering the arena in large-scale numbers. Our country is on an irreversible glide path that is increasing, and even accelerating, toward greater democratization of all sectors of the electorate.

While democratization is an inherently positive development for a democracy, it also poses perils. In particular, constituencies whose dissatisfaction or resentment motivates them to join the electorate are easily manipulated by false promises to level the playing field. Exploitation of their discontent can lead to Pitchfork Populism. These concerns were presciently articulated by H. L. Mencken, who wrote in 1920, "The larger the mob, the harder the test. In small areas, before small electorates, a first-rate man occasionally fights his way through, carrying even the mob with him by the force of his personality. But when the field is nationwide, and the fight must be waged chiefly at second and third hand, and the force of personality cannot so readily make itself felt, then all the odds are on the man who is, intrinsically, the most devious and mediocre—the man who can most adeptly disperse the notion that his mind is a virtual vacuum. The presidency tends, year by year, to go to such men. As democracy is perfected, the office represents, more and more closely, the inner soul of the people. On some great and glorious day, the plain folks of the land will reach their heart's desire at last, and the White House will be adorned by a downright moron."[29] Even if Mencken were engaging in hyperbole, his words were still a very astute *caveat emptor* about the dangers of a faux-populist pretense.

IMPORTANCE DURING TRUMP'S TENURE AND THE POST-TRUMP ERA

Democratization of the political process is all about inclusion and empowerment. In the case of both, the more you have, the more you want. Inclusion begets greater inclusion; empowerment begets more empowerment. Trump's supporters have been, and likely will continue to be, beneficiaries of this trend, extending into the post-Trump era. They have been recognized, their opinions are being studied and understood, they are becoming politically organized, and their beliefs have been validated. As a result, voters in Trump's base are positioned to continue exerting their influence on future elections.

At the same time, inclusion and empowerment of some people makes others realize that they, too, want to jump into the pool, as is their right.

When there is a strong impetus or necessity to join the political process, it expedites the flow toward engagement. With Donald Trump as president, there is no need to look far to find the poster child that inspires millions of Americans toward activism, albeit not in the way that he might have had in mind. One of the unintended consequences of his presidency is that his daily malfeasances and absurdities are producing new cadres of political activists, as exemplified by the Parkland students and the surge of female candidates.

Unfortunately, Trump's misdeeds have included taking direct aim at the tools of our democracy. Some of his and his administration's actions have sought to curtail and even reverse democratic progress, discourage factual public discourse, and manipulate the mechanics of democracy. For example:

- Trump's Advisory Commission on Election Integrity was a thinly veiled attempt to acquire data about voters in every state and was expected to be used to purge voters from the rolls. It was terminated because state officials—Republicans and Democrats—refused to participate.
- Jeff Sessions repudiated well-established standards for enforcement of the Voting Rights Act (e.g., gerrymandered districts) and supported the purging of voter registration rolls in a process that many believe will have a discriminatory impact[30] (Sessions supported the overly aggressive efforts of Ohio's secretary of state to purge voters from the voter registration rolls, which led to a case, *Husted v. A. Philip Randolph Institute*, decided by the US Supreme Court in June 2018).[31]
- Trump's vilification of the media and government officials, and his claims of "fake news," aim to weaken public confidence in news reports and government actions that are disadvantageous to him. He seeks to diminish trust so that people will not know whom to believe, leading to apathy and less political participation by opponents.
- Trump's falsehoods, fabrications, deceptions, and distortions of the truth seek to establish a false narrative for the public to embrace, while muting opposing views. His consistent repetition of falsehoods aims to normalize his false narrative so that it pervades the consciousness of those who are receptive to his influence, in hopes that his words will become accepted as fact. He uses this tactic to bias public debate, insulate himself from justice and the consequences of the truth, and impair the forces of democracy and grassroots activism that challenge him.

- Trump operates as an authoritarian with his capricious and narcissistic transactional approach, policy contradictions, contempt for democratic institutions, and disrespect for law enforcement officials (e.g., Jim Comey, Andrew McCabe, Jeff Sessions, and Robert Mueller). His support of autocrats while musing about replicating China's shift to a president-for-life is a shameless vitiation of democracy. His incipient autocratic tendencies are antithetical to democracy, despite his effort to normalize them.

These actions constitute a blatant attack on, and affront to, principles of enfranchisement and democracy. But Trump can't win. Throughout our history, when a rogue miscreant picks a fight with our resilient democratic institutions, national values, history, sensibilities, and Constitution, the miscreant who seeks to upend the basis of our society eventually loses. The more that Trump does to quash inclusion and empowerment, the more he energizes his opponents and spawns new ones.

Trump's appointees to senior positions also run afoul of inclusion and diversity principles. His initial team fell woefully short of the standards set by recent presidents, and his subsequent appointments exacerbate the problem. First, almost everyone is white. Second, Trump is familiar with them either due to their existing roles in his administration, or their roles on the cable news shows that he watches. It seems that Trump does not even try to recruit beyond his range of vision, nor empower others to do so on his behalf. Third, he is highly influenced by a person's physical appearance, and whether he likes their look for the role, as if the Trump White House is being produced as a television docudrama. Fourth, rather than hiring experts with diverse views who would explore a range of options for each issue that comes before them, Trump increasingly hires people who he believes will agree with him.

This can be seen in a quick overview of Trump's notable appointments and nominees in 2017 and 2018:

- Larry Kudlow, as chair of the National Economic Council, was a longtime commentator on CNBC, and has been a longtime friend of Trump's, with whom he consulted frequently.
- Jerome Powell, as chairman of the Federal Reserve, was attractive to Trump, as explained by Larry Kudlow on CNBC, February 27, 2018,

"The rumor was—I wasn't in the meeting—when Trump interviewed Powell he told associates, 'The guy looks like a Central Banker.'"

- Ronny Jackson, as secretary of veterans' affairs (before withdrawing), was his doctor, spoke with him often, implausibly claimed that Trump weighs 239 pounds, and was assessed by Trump: "He's like central casting. He became like a Hollywood star" (via audio recorded at Mar-a-Lago).
- Mike Pompeo, as secretary of state, with whom Trump became familiar and comfortable due to the daily intelligence briefings that Pompeo personally provided to Trump as CIA director, was a Trump favorite because of the jocular rapport they developed together.
- John Bolton, as national security advisor, was a longtime commentator on Fox News, imparting brash, strident, hawkish views following his controversial service in George W. Bush's administration.
- Mercedes Schlapp, as director of strategic communications, became familiar to Trump because she was a Fox News contributor.
- Heather Nauert, as under secretary of state for public diplomacy and public affairs, and later, as ambassador to the United Nations (before withdrawing), was known to Trump as a Fox News anchor and host following roles at other news outlets, and whose appearance may have appealed to Trump.
- Joe diGenova, a Fox News contributor, and his wife, Victoria Toensing, were said to be joining Trump's (personal) legal team, but were subsequently rejected by Trump, in part because "the president was turned off because they looked disheveled when they came to meet with him," as reported by Darren Samuelsohn of Politico on March 27, 2018.
- Bill Shine, as deputy chief of staff for communications, was the longtime co-president of Fox News and Fox Business channels, which he left in the wake of sexual harassment allegations against Roger Ailes and Bill O'Reilly that tarnished Shine for his failure to take remedial action.

Despite obstacles and challenges, democratization can extend to more phases of the political process, be achieved with new tools and avenues for participation, and can produce an array of benefits and outcomes. Even with all the progress that has been made in recent decades, there's surely more to come, along with the help of the courts when needed. Opportunities for political engagement may reach more voters and communities, be enhanced by new hardware and software technologies, increase interaction between constituents and their legislators in state houses and Congress, and enable more people from diverse backgrounds to run for office. Democratization is sure to accelerate, as it always does, with new ways to become involved and make an impact, as occurred in the 2018 midterms and is likely to occur in the 2020 presidential election. Once people become engaged, they often remain engaged thereafter, which could foretell further inclusion and empowerment in the post-Trump era.

In today's highly charged political atmosphere, the door of opportunity is wide open for people who want to participate, especially for those who seek to become advocates. For example, there are many training and mentorship programs that help people gain advocacy skills and prepare them to be effective. Further access to training would enfranchise even more participants, both as a career and as a complementary skill set that is applied when needed. Since colleges and universities aim to equip young adults to contribute to society, in addition to preparing them for the workforce, they should be willing to offer courses that prepare students to become activists, advocates, and candidates. Many students want to become involved but don't know where or how to begin. Courses that teach skills which are essential to these activities, and illuminate practical ways to apply them, would fulfill an important need for students while helping the institution to achieve its mandate.

Similarly, programs for postdegree continuing education can also play a vital role. They can provide training on advocacy, activism, and candidacy to meet the needs of people who are already in the workforce. Programs could even be offered in the workplace. Such courses would also be in the best interests of the employer, since training in advocacy could also be applied by employees when they are called upon to advocate on their company's behalf, whether in the context of sales, community affairs, or government relations.

Whether one aims to participate as an activist at the grassroots level, an advocate who interfaces with government officials, or a candidate who runs for office, the barriers to entry continually descend. For those who are passionate and energetic, it is also possible to take advantage of the partisan, contentious climate, since stakeholders seek people who can become leaders on key issues. Even though women and people of color have already had significant electoral success in recent decades, the public appetite welcomes even more people from diverse backgrounds to step up to the plate.

Younger Americans deserve special attention in any discussion of democratization of politics, inclusion, and empowerment, since they have the most to gain from opening the process. Naturally, they have the longest future of political engagement, stretching ahead for decades. As long-term stakeholders in our democracy, they are highly motivated to join the process. Since they have the most direct connection to modern America and the most contemporary sensibilities, without being tethered to antiquated behavioral norms, young people tend to find Trump unnerving and offensive.[32] Younger Americans fill the streets during demonstrations and are a solid barometer of what behavior is no longer acceptable. Many have been inspired to take action to counter Trump's conduct, with many more sure to follow. They are the next leaders of a vital part of our heritage, as political activism is one of the most quintessentially American ways to channel energies toward a positive, productive purpose. Trump's presidency will provide them with more opportunities for necessary activism than ever before.

The influx of young Americans into the political process raises issues about the connection between their activism and the trend toward increased use of technology tools in political and issue campaigns. Since younger cohorts are, generally speaking, more sophisticated users of technology tools than Americans in older age brackets, they will benefit the most by the increased reliance on websites, apps, cloud-based data, and mobile computing in all aspects of the political process. The extension of ubiquitous broadband and the advent of 5G mobile networks will enable new tools and capabilities for people to become informed and inform others, facilitating a broader level of political participation.

Ironically, though, use of technology does not necessarily translate to greater inclusion and empowerment. Studies have found that high-frequency users of smartphones and other devices have both positive and negative reactions to their use.[33] Frequent use of social networking can instill opposite feelings of connectedness and isolation, as well as both productivity and futility.[34] Youth are connected, but only to a limited degree, at a depth that does not replicate face-to-face interaction. When politically divisive online discussions escalate to aggressive language and animosity, they engender feelings of revulsion, causing people to recoil from online political interaction. Since users can self-select the stories they want to read and videos they want to see, they often end up in their own self-constructed silos or echo chambers, without benefiting from constructive interaction and enhanced awareness of other perspectives.[35] The lack of a shared experience among people with diverse views compounds feelings of isolation.

Interestingly, reactions differ amidst stable versus turbulent political environments.[36] In normal times amidst prosperity, social stability, and low decibel political noise, people tend to remain in their unfulfilling personalized political silos, insulated from broader debates and interaction.[37] Conversely, when society is in an uproar—following a terrorist attack, police brutality incident, or international crisis—technology users tend to reach beyond their self-manufactured digital bubbles to engage with others, hear from a broader universe of people, and be influenced by new inputs.[38] These interactions have been found to be more gratifying, as they expand the normal boundaries of connectedness, and enable users to feel like they are part of a broader shared experience.

This directly impacts young people's engagement in the political process because, even though smartphones and other devices add convenience, they are no substitute for genuine interpersonal political interaction. It may seem as though convenience promotes inclusion, and that empowerment grows from that. It may seem like young people would be satisfied by attending political events remotely, making GOTV calls from their home, hitting the "Like" button on politicians' pages, and participating in conversations on Reddit, but they aren't as fulfilling as interacting in a group setting. This is both surprising, since young Americans seem to prefer everything via technology, and not surprising at all, since politics is the ultimate people business, "of, by, and for" us all.

Yet, as we approach 2020 and subsequent campaigns, new technologies such as artificial intelligence, augmented/virtual reality, data analytics, and gaming platforms might reinvent ways in which voters, campaigns, political candidates, and others interact. For example, rather than walking a precinct and knocking on doors, the combination of AI, AR/VR, and data analytics might enable volunteers to engage with voters face-to-face, yet remotely, reaching more homes in a shorter period of time. Elected officials might be able to use gaming technology to replicate a workday in the legislature, allowing constituents to experience the work life of a legislator in a fun and engaging manner. It might become commonplace to attend candidate town hall forums remotely through AR/VR, by total technological immersion, where participants can even interact with the candidate.

In light of the separate advantages of digital and in-person engagement in the electoral process, both will probably be part of the secret sauce to greater inclusion and empowerment of young Americans. Most activities would best be engaged in a real world, face-to-face sense. At the same time, there would also be room for online, issue-based community projects.

Participation among ideologically diverse groups should be encouraged, to inspire participants to go beyond their usual comfort zone. Democratization of the process only happens if people want to participate, and they are more likely to want to participate if their encounters are mutually respectful and genuinely informative. By breaking down barriers through gratifying and thoughtful exchanges, users could have an enriching experience that educates, illuminates, stimulates empathy, and inspires young voters to become more involved.

CHAPTER 5

MEDIA

THE BATTLE FOR TRUTH AND FACTS

T he democratization of the political process has occurred in tandem with, and partly because of, the democratization of media, information, and technology. Societal attitudes favoring inclusion and enfranchisement, which awakened in the 1960s and accelerated ever since then, have expanded the national appetite for news and information. Technological innovations since that time have opened the doors for a virtually limitless array of news sources to become viable and find audiences that are eager to receive news from a wide range of perspectives.

However, along with the democratization of news and media have come new battles over truth, accuracy, reliability, and facts. During the 2016 election, Russians used social media platforms to disseminate distortions of truth, mislead those who were vulnerable to their nefarious messaging, intensify partisan passions, and exacerbate social divisions. Donald Trump has intensified those battles, pitting his version of truth and reality against that of responsible media outlets and journalists on a daily basis. Intentional deceptions manipulate public perceptions and sentiments, presenting risks of long-term damage to our media institutions and the public discourse that relies on them. The alternative reality that Trump imparts is calculated to insulate him from justice, vilify government institutions, demonize his opponents, and marginalize minorities, each of which impairs our Constitution, rule of law, and societal norms.

The challenge to truth and facts that Trump and his staff propagate necessitates concerted action and resilience by all principled stakeholders to ensure that verifiable truth, genuine accuracy, actual reliability, and authentic facts prevail. There is an emerging recognition that access to new audiences through new media platforms are accompanied by new responsibilities. Deceptive practices can be countered through reforms, such as policy and operational innovations, and public awareness of both the problems and the solutions.

DEMOCRATIZATION OF THE MEDIA:
THE GOOD, THE BAD, AND THE UGLY

In the 1960s and 1970s, the main sources for news were the major newspapers and print news services, news radio and NPR, and the three major broadcast television channels, as well as PBS, all of which had large, cross-cultural audiences. In the 1980s, technological innovation made it possible to further feed the national hunger for news through cable television channels exclusively dedicated to news coverage.

In the 1990s, the proliferation of the internet changed everything. News reached us faster from websites of major news outlets, and from diverse perspectives, as many new sources reached large audiences through web access. That trend accelerated since the early 2000s through a tsunami of "new media" outlets, social networking sites, and smartphone apps. Websites, online tools, and social networking platforms such as Facebook, Twitter, Google, LinkedIn, Reddit, Instagram, and many others became primary sources for news and information. These and other online tools are the principal conduit not only to news but also to political activism, advocacy, civic engagement, and information about policy issues, especially among younger Americans. Interaction with people in younger age groups—to provide media and information to them, recruit them to volunteer for a campaign, or ask for their vote—necessitates reaching them through their preferred communication channels. That reality increasingly entails use of social media accessed through mobile devices.

The proliferation of devices with which to receive content has made access to media ubiquitous: anything, anywhere, anytime. Now, each consumer of media has virtually unlimited choices, ease of access, and total control to search for articles and videos of interest, from any editorial perspective.

The democratization of media and information is inherently positive, like any enhancement of democracy. Americans hew toward increased choice, affordability, and inclusion, all of which are enabled by the explosive combination of social networking, "new media" websites, apps, and mobile computing. Today's information landscape empowers more people from more diverse backgrounds to contribute to the public discourse, connect with others, amplify their message, and even run for public office. Societal cohesion and community engagement are bolstered by advocacy, collaboration, and collective action for the common good. New technologies also present powerful tools that rugged individualists can apply toward achievement of their ambitions.

However, the positive force of democratization is accompanied by an other-side-of-the-coin, often with negative consequences. The internet itself, which is a hallmark of megademocratization, demonstrates both the best and the worst consequences of ubiquitous access. It enables teenagers in India to study marketable software skills, farmers in Uganda to check on current crop prices, and parents in Nebraska to learn about their child's health condition. At the same time, the internet also enables criminals to engage in identity theft, hackers to spread computer viruses, and terrorist organizations to disseminate their propaganda and recruit people who are vulnerable to their worldview.

One of the negative aspects of the internet is that news sources now race to produce and publish material as quickly as possible, ahead of the competition. To win that race and be noticed, some less reputable outlets are willing to publish material without vetting it appropriately, and sometimes they do so completely irresponsibly and erroneously. The amount of attention that a post receives largely depends on how well it appeals to emotions, how well it is marketed, and the degree to which its language and images are provocative. This "click-bait culture," which is notorious for presenting misleading and manipulative posts, is dominated by amateurs and exploiters who are more interested in driving traffic and "going viral" than providing insight, illumination, and truth. Its purveyors would rather gain followers than respect. They would rather gain clicks than win a Pulitzer.

While social media websites and services are not inherently disreputable, they are vulnerable to misuse by people and institutions with malevolent intentions. These sites claim that they are merely technology platforms, not content publishers or media sources, since the content posted on them is user generated. This stance has been used to justify their reluctance to take responsibility for the content made available on their platforms that, in 2016, enabled Russians and other miscreants to gain access to vast American audiences. Facebook and other social media sites came under scrutiny in 2018, and reforms are beginning to be developed that will place some responsibility on them to establish and enforce safeguards.

Another negative result of media democratization is the fragmentation of the news audience. With so many websites from which to choose, each consumer of news can choose information sources that reflect their viewpoint or political philosophy. Advances in data analytics, machine learning, and artificial intelligence have accentuated the fragmentation. Google, Facebook, and other platforms routinely tailor each person's newsfeed based on what they viewed in the past, their preferences, and how much time they previously spent viewing content. In choosing news websites, consumers can limit themselves to sources with editorial leanings that reflect their own, receive content from a wide array of viewpoints, or even check out what opponents are saying.

Since people can choose from among virtually limitless sources that have specific perspectives, the country no longer has a shared news experience like it did in the days of Walter Cronkite's broadcasts. As a result, there is a narrower scope of commonly accepted facts and truth. Subjective reports can masquerade as objective news. Genuine news can be assaulted as subjective or fake by those who find it undesirable.

Uglier still, today's technologies allow virtually anyone to disseminate half-baked opinions or completely flawed, untrue, or nonsensical stories—disguised as news—to gain an audience. In some cases, their motives are more nefarious than just making money, reaching all the way to deliberate deception and propaganda that poisons the well of popular opinion, as we witnessed during the 2016 campaign. Just as new media adds new ways to communicate, it also creates new opportunities to inject fabrications, falsehoods, and "fake news" into the public discourse, which can misdirect policy debates, inflame emotions, trigger hate speech, and hijack public opinion. Facebook's facilitation of Cambridge Analytica's notorious data mining practices is an egregious example.[1] Crowdsourcing, which generates diverse content from virtually anyone, can also exacerbate the problem of unreliable information, as it might not be responsibly generated or posted.

These are among the ugly, other-side-of-the-coin consequences of media democratization. They come with the territory and will remain part of the media landscape because, with few exceptions, our devotion to the First Amendment restricts action that would aggressively limit who can participate in media generation or what they can write (or post material) about.

STEPS TO REDUCE CYNICISM AND ENHANCE TRUTH

The problems inherent in media democratization can and should be countered with exposure, transparency, and accountability to root out the people and practices that are reckless, dishonest, or devious. Remedies are challenging, in light of First Amendment protections. Yet, some reasonable steps are increasingly necessary, and a couple of approaches might offer a starting point.

First, the "new media" arena lacks a curator. While its openness is an asset, its unchecked "Wild West" demeanor is not. In previous eras, the gatekeeper role resided with the publisher. That was true in the 1800s, when only a handful of wealthy newspaper owners controlled the message. It was also true in the 1900s with the rise of radio and eventually television, both of which were capital-intensive operations that could only be operated by a handful of institutions. They curated news relatively responsibly, for the sake of both journalistic integrity and company profitability, protecting their reputation and their investment.

When news was limited to print, radio, and television, the gatekeeper functioned as a filter, creating a different problem. Audiences were limited to the narrow range of topics and opinions that the curators permitted. That may explain why there was also a proliferation of community newspapers and ethnicity-specific newspapers that widened the scope of thought, even though their distribution levels were diminutive compared to that of the major media players. Although newspapers, radio, and television were centrally and narrowly controlled, their editorial integrity was generally reliable. Most adhered to responsible journalistic procedures and engaged in due diligence.

Today, internet and social media assets do not necessarily abide by journalistic standards. The openness of social media, with its absence of barriers to entry, poses another double-sided coin of consequences. Expanded participation is good. Irresponsible (and especially reckless) behavior is bad.

This raises the question of whether there is a need to devise a solution to promote integrity and honesty while not inhibiting the free flow of thought and information. The objective would be to encourage media outlets, online media, and social networking sites to establish a curator that reviews content to prevent obvious malfeasance and abuse, while not going so far as to become a gatekeeper that restricts freedom of expression and diversity of opinions. There should be a focus on journalistic standards (integrity and truthfulness) rather than journalistic practices (operations and procedures), because adherence to specific journalistic practices is resource-intensive and inherently exclusionary, necessitating funding that is inaccessible to small players. Journalistic standards, on the other hand, are not expensive, as they are based on a commitment to make responsible publication decisions.

A "Good Journalistic Standards Seal of Approval" would be useful and could be managed by a nonprofit, nongovernmental organization. It would be akin to the Green Seal[2] program that began certifying environmentally sound products and practices in the 1990s. It could be led by nonpartisan respected media authorities (e.g., professors, retired journalists, retired judges, nonprofits focused on media accuracy) and maintain a list of online media and other information sources that conform with accepted journalistic standards. It would also maintain another list of sources that are derelict. Major media outlets could be affiliated with the effort, taking the form of an advisory board. The advisory board would provide guidance and its assent to the effort as early adopters of standards while not controlling decision-making. This approach would not address all possible perils, since an individual could still post something fallacious on their own Facebook (or other) page. But at least the most trafficked outlets and other low-hanging fruit would be reviewed.

The more challenging issue intertwined with social media is the naive, gullible, and/or ill-informed precondition that afflicts many consumers of media. In the past, when supermarket tabloids like the *National Enquirer* were the principal domain of nonsensical media, few, if any, people actually believed that "Martians Appear at the Galleria," or that there was any merit in the "New Ice Cream Diet." Even the least sophisticated among us knew that certain things were "fake news."

With today's deluge of media outlets, most news consumers can't keep up with which stories and outlets are safe or responsible, and which are devious. Many social media users seek quick news updates—headlines or short articles of 250–300 words—to give them a general sense of what's happening, rather than delving deeper into detailed, long-form articles. Often, users access social media from their smartphones, which are more convenient for accessing short articles than lengthy ones. Thus, cursory click-bait updates are more appealing to these users than a longer Reuters or *New York Times* article, or a thorough Vox.com or *Atlantic* analysis. Also, users who seek quick-hit updates are probably unlikely to consider the source of a headline or brief article. When accessing news on a smartphone, most users will probably not research it. As a result, people often ingest content without reflecting on its authenticity or accuracy, which incentivizes click-bait manipulative postings.

In addition to relying on a Good Journalistic Standards Seal of Approval, media users should be encouraged to consider the source of content. News sources should place the name of the author and publication above the article's headline, in a font as large as the headline. Efforts should be undertaken to educate the electorate about media content and conduct so as to minimize their naiveté, gullibility, and lack of informed awareness. Ideally, programs would be developed to enable voters to become judicious consumers of news, so that they can distinguish a legitimate story from a hoax. Yet, that is a profound and comprehensive endeavor, since discernment stems from critical reasoning and intellectual rigor, neither of which can be mandated. Long-term solutions probably depend on school districts' educational standards and curricula that educate teens before they become voters. Regrettably, a national initiative of this type is unlikely since it is probably not too high on Secretary Betsy DeVos's agenda.

FRAGMENTATION OF THE MEDIA AND ITS AUDIENCES

The democratization of the media market and the fragmentation of the media audience continually raise questions about the existence of media bias. For many years, newspapers have been accused of having political biases in accordance with the political predispositions of their editors and ownership. Concern about bias was intensified by cable television news practices.[3] As a strategy conceived by Republican operative Roger Ailes, Fox News consciously adopted a business model by which it presented news through the lens of conservative ideology. Some years later, MSNBC decided to be the counterpoint to Fox, offering a left-leaning orientation during the hours when it provided opinion-focused content. The major broadcast television networks, as well as CNN, did not apply an intentional editorial bias like that of Fox and MSNBC, and even went to great lengths to provide diverse viewpoints. Although networks occasionally have a slight tilt in their coverage of some topics (e.g., after a mass killing), that is largely due to the sensibilities of their personnel rather than a corporate business decision.

In recent years, the issue of bias has become even more pronounced due to the proliferation of online news sources, blogs, and websites that repost political content, and social media sites on which political topics are among the most popular user-generated posts. Since these media sources, like other internet-based content, are accessed by users self-selecting the material of interest to them, they have played an especially prominent role in the fragmentation of the media audience. People easily choose which sites to visit, which articles to read, which videos to watch, and which stories to believe.

An email that circulated among conservatives in early 2017, when Trump began intensifying his allegation of "fake news," crystallized the divisiveness of the issue and typified the meme of bias that Trump and his followers were asserting. The email alleged that CNN, MSNBC, and CBS were providing "only politically biased news stories," while Fox was "the only factual and truthful balanced network." It may be convenient to either reject this characterization as a hyperbolic double-standard or accept it as an acknowledgment that some degree of bias exists everywhere. One could also parse the oddity of that three-network grouping. But it may be more useful to note a few observations about the email's allegation.

First, branding plays a role. Fox's longtime tagline declared it "Fair and Balanced." Avid viewers of Fox have been fed that brand message repeatedly. It is well recognized that branding is essentially a form of self-interested marketing. It is often effective, since messages eventually sink in. Repetitive branding can transform a notion, or even a fallacy, into an accepted fact among those who receive it frequently, as seems to be the case with Fox. The same can be said for CNN's use of the slogan "The Most Trusted Name in News." Both slogans are statements of opinion, without empirical evidence to substantiate them. In neither case is the slogan based on an objective industry standard.

Second, and very importantly, the content on each cable news channel is geared toward the predilections of its anticipated audience. The subject matter and editorial tone that are aired on each cable channel are designed to appeal to that channel's targeted viewers, just like the way that the previously mentioned conservative email resonates with its intended recipients. This targeting is no accident; in fact, it is quite calculated. Each network is owned by one of the corporate media conglomerates, each network needs to make money by advertising, and advertisement rates are determined by viewership trends, or Nielsen ratings. Thus, each network aims its programming to appeal to certain targeted segments of the potential viewing audience. All of the networks are very sophisticated in their research and efforts to stratify the population according to numerous key demographics like age, race/ethnicity, income level, education level, and urban/suburban/rural lifestyle.

Third, each network starts with roughly the same news stories. The networks then prioritize, assess, and present those stories in ways that they think will appeal to their targeted audiences and satisfy their audiences' news appetites. That is done by selecting lead stories, the amount of time to allot to each story, the messages to run on the chyron banners at the bottom of the screen, the degree to which interviewers ask challenging questions of some guests more or less than others, and even the theatrics employed in the delivery of stories by anchors and reporters. There are also some time slots on each of the channels that are dedicated to presenting straight news, while other time slots are more focused on editorial or opinion presentations.

By and large, all of the cable news channels navigate the same considerations. They each slant their straight news coverage to one degree or another (some more than others), with major editorial variances during their opinion or commentary hours. As such, it is a fallacy to categorically label specific cable news channels as either "politically biased" or "factual and truthful."

Fourth, the fragmentation that news channels desire to secure a reliable and loyal audience poses challenges when a media outlet conducts public opinion polls. Many media outlets engage in polling to gauge voter sentiment on political candidates, job approval ratings of elected officials, public policy options, and other prominent issues. Since some outlets now have audiences that are concentrated on one side or another of the political spectrum, polling only members of their audience would end with commensurately skewed results. To poll a representative cross-section of the electorate, media outlets partner with other outlets that have different and complementary readers or viewers (e.g., polls conducted jointly by MSNBC and the *Wall Street Journal*). Failure to include media partners that can reach to other sectors of the electorate would produce misleading, misinterpreted, and inaccurate results.

MEDIA BIAS IN THE AGE OF TRUMP

That same 2017 email, so typical of many messaging efforts by Trump supporters, alleged that bias is so extreme that CNN, MSNBC, and CBS are on a "Trump bashing rampage." While this is an emotion-driven, hyperbolic overstatement, it is effective with its audience because it reinforces the meme regularly repeated in conservative media. It is the natural and necessary result of Trump's calculated effort to brand the media as his perpetual opponent. He thrives on that image of the media, which he uses to rally his base. Trump claims that he is being victimized by the media, equates an attack on him with an attack on his supporters, urges his base to share his resentment, alleges that the media is dismissive of his base's interests and concerns, and secures his base's devotion by fighting the establishment that, he alleges, wants to marginalize them.

The assertion of a liberal media bias is a fallacy. It is an intentionally fabricated myth, as evidenced by its perpetrators' cynical disavowal of the actual parity between conservative-leaning and liberal-leaning media outlets and personnel. Even if there had been a bias many years ago, the playing field was leveled in recent decades by Fox, conservative talk radio, and a plethora of politically conservative websites and blogs that have shifted the balance to the right.[4] If there were a liberal bias, then the policies and personalities of both presidents Bush and the Republicans who controlled Congress in recent years would have generated the same level of media scrutiny and consternation that is being applied today toward Trump. But that did not happen. Those other politicians certainly got their share of scrutiny and criticism, as government leaders always do. But it did not reach the intensity that now exists toward Trump. Republican legislators also sometimes criticize Trump, and they would not appreciate their criticism causing them to be characterized as liberals. Conversely, if there were a liberal bias throughout the media, then Obama would have been insulated from criticism. But, in addition to receiving fair criticism for some policies that spawned vibrant debates, Obama was subjected to a cacophony of unjustifiable antipathy and excoriated by many in the media world.

It often seems as though Trump wants to be the recipient of negative bias from the media because he leverages it to burnish his image with his base. He invites negative bias by his disregard for basic standards of public conduct and speech, diminishing the presidency itself. As he curries favor among his base, he offends American values and most of the country, which compels criticism by decent, fair-minded Americans, including the media. The media and the electorate recoil at Trump's incivility and lack of compassion toward people whom he doesn't like. They justifiably renounce his vilification of the media, his incessantly reckless and juvenile use of social media, his arrogant indifference to constitutional norms including the Emoluments Clause and the separation of powers, and his obsequiousness to our main international rival, Russia, while behaving as though he is beholden to its leader.

Trump continues to say and do things that we have never before witnessed by a public official in this country. Some people like it, and some don't. Either way, it is unprecedented. No current or historical American public official has ever said things that so many large constituencies find hurtful, insulting, demeaning, and vindictive. The long view of American political history and acceptable public behavior is the lens through which much of the media sees Trump. Whether one likes or dislikes him, his speech and actions are undeniably in violation of traditional American standards. The media's criticism of Trump is not inspired by a liberal bias, but rather is driven by the media's bias in favor of American values and responsible, rational, respectful conduct.

In response to criticism, Trump himself is overtly critical of the media. He consistently antagonizes them, attacking them as "the enemy of the people," and labeling reputable outlets as "fake news" and "fake media."[5] During the campaign, he was sometimes even aggressive, such as when he called out MSNBC's Katy Tur[6] to subject her to his audience's acrimony, and mocked a reporter with a disability.[7] Although other presidents have disliked their press coverage, Trump is likely the first to publicly insinuate that reporters are unpatriotic, as he did when he told an Arizona rally, "And they're bad people. And I really think they don't like our country."[8]

Trump's aggressive disparagement of the media has generated condemnation across the ideological spectrum. Even some prominent Fox News personalities have been highly critical of his attacks.[9] When the White House suspended the press pass of CNN reporter Jim Acosta, a broad coalition of media across the ideological spectrum supported CNN's lawsuit to restore Acosta's access in recognition that the White House's action was an infringement on press freedom.[10]

The essential role of the press in a vibrant democracy was eloquently and poignantly expressed by Judge Murray Gurfein, who presided over the Pentagon Papers case in 1971. Judge Gurfein wrote in his court opinion, "A cantankerous press, an obstinate press, an ubiquitous press must be suffered by those in authority in order to preserve the even greater values of freedom of expression and the right of the people to know."[11] Recently, Martin Barron, executive editor of the *Washington Post*, applied those principles to the Trump administration. When asked about the ramifications of the president saying that the media is "the enemy of the people," Barron assessed, "There could be long-term consequences that have a corrosive effect on the institution of the media and the press in this country. I'm very concerned about that. Donald Trump initially condemned us, and then tried to delegitimize us, and then even dehumanized us, saying that we were the lowest form of humanity. And then, when that wasn't enough, he said we were the lowest form of life itself. It's very corrosive. The press is a fundamental institution in this country. We're provided for in the First Amendment of the Constitution. There's a reason that the Founders did that. The purpose is to hold government accountable."[12]

Maybe Trump deliberately disparages journalists simply because they don't provide the glowing coverage that he requires to confuse his supporters or curry favor with them. Maybe Trump is trying to position his supporters against the media so that they won't believe any news detrimental to him. Maybe Trump believes everything that he says about the media. Any or all of these three interpretations could explain why he fights back with the tools of his office. It speaks volumes that his administration opposed AT&T's purchase of Time Warner[13] (including CNN, which Trump often vilifies) and has threatened action against the *Washington Post*[14] (which Trump also repudiates), while endorsing the (conservative-oriented) Sinclair Broadcast Group's proposed purchase[15] of Tribune Media's local news stations, even though Sinclair already owns over two hundred local stations.

Trump's main area of expertise also adds to the media's skepticism. Even Trump's opponents recognize that he is outstanding at branding, whether it be for his own brand (MAGA) or that of his opponents ("Little Marco" [Rubio], "Lyin' Ted" [Cruz], "Low Energy Jeb" [Bush], and "Crooked Hillary" [Clinton]). But branding is thin soup. Whether branding a politician or laundry soap, branding is based on platitudes, images, and emotional themes. It is devoid of factual substantiation. Many in the media do not respect Trump's substitution of branding in place of specific policies and principles. Their view of Trump is influenced by his habit of shunning substance in deference to slogans.

The perception of media bias is highly subjective, tied to one's policy preferences. Although a large share of Fox's viewers are offended by Trump's personal conduct and speech, they tend to agree with his policy choices and agenda priorities. As a result, they are willing to suppress their opinions about his persona. To conservatives and Fox viewers, Trump's appointment of Neil Gorsuch and Brett Kavanaugh to the Supreme Court mattered much more than anything else the president says or does. Thus, they are willing to cut Trump a lot of slack and accept his claims of media bias against him, as long as he continues to take public action that comports with their political and policy views.

TRUMP'S BATTLE WITH TRUTH AND FACTS

Deliberately deceptive pronouncements were a troubling aspect of Trump's campaign, and have become even more problematic during his presidency. Communications generated by Trump and his staff routinely depart from traditional White House standards. By the 801st day of his presidency, Trump had already told 9,451 lies and inaccuracies, according to the *Washington Post*'s Fact Checker database.[16] As Dan Balz, the dean of White House reporters, wrote, "Trump's capacity to make things up is one of the defining features of his presidency. His loose adherence to the truth, when it suits his political purposes, seems to know few limits."[17] Trump's incessant distortion of facts, truth, and reality has escalated the need for consumers of media to discern which assertions by Trump, and which news sources reporting about Trump, are fact-based and credible.

George Orwell's prescience is legendary, so perhaps he foresaw the coming of someone like Trump when, in "Politics and the English Language," he wrote, "Political language . . . is designed to make lies sound truthful and murder respectable, and to give an appearance of solidity to pure wind."[18] We can't say he didn't warn us. Maybe Trump's language and tweets are actually a tribute to Orwell's *1984*, in which the political party's slogan was "War is peace. Freedom is slavery. Ignorance is strength."[19] If it turns out that Orwell is Trump's favorite author, and Trump has just been echoing Orwell's warnings about the evils of deception, then we may need to reconsider Trump as a satirist.

Trump incessantly engages in distinctly Orwellian language and behavior. In countless instances during his campaign, Trump simply ignored facts,[20] made up his own, claimed that it was the real truth, assigned interpretations of facts that were the reverse of reality, castigated anyone in disagreement, impugned the character of his critics, refused to address anything adverse to his view, and vilified those who sought his accountability.[21] His principal tactics included projection and preemption. He projected his shortcomings onto others and preempted their valid accusations, in an attempt to inoculate himself by making it seem like they were retaliating with the same points that he alleged. He repeated his distortions of facts as often as possible in an effort to get his audience to assimilate his version into their thoughts, giving it a patina of truth in the minds of the malleable.[22] Media outlets reinforced his messages, albeit inadvertently, by repeating reports about comments or conduct that they found appalling or baffling. As dystopian as Trump's practices were for a candidate, still worse is that he has continued them as president, with projection and preemption among the weapons that he frequently wields against his adversaries.[23]

Trump's deceptions and proliferation of a dystopian reality, designed for public adoption, are not without precedent in American history. Whenever they occurred, they were venal and pernicious, tarnishing our national character with infamy. Falsehoods, popular sentiment, news reporting, passage of laws, and government enforcement allowed slavery of African Americans, displacement and genocide of Native Americans, ethnocentric discrimination against certain immigrants, and disenfranchisement of women. While Trump's complex web of fabrications does not plummet to the depths of the historic tragedies that included mass killings, it still poses a clear and present danger to our democracy and civil liberties.

Since the first days of Trump's administration, Trump and his spokespeople have continually propagated utter fabrications and falsehoods, like the size of the crowd at the inauguration, and Trump's claim that the media started his fight with the intelligence community, even though his tweets and speeches clarify that he initiated it.[24] As Kellyanne Conway unwittingly admitted in early 2017, the Trump administration presents its own "alternative facts."[25] In the administration's first months, the myriad falsehoods and deceptions professed by Trump and his staff already crippled their credibility, perhaps irretrievably.[26] As NBC News anchor Andrea Mitchell observed, just a few months into the Trump administration, "I have never seen anything like this where people just flat-out lie. It's really disconcerting to see the podium in the White House briefing room being used to mislead or misdirect or obfuscate."[27]

Trump acts as though facts, truth, and reality are fungible and negotiable. He sets the country and world on notice that this will be a recurring and constant practice.[28] This is partly because Trump tries to never admit anything, never give in, never show vulnerability, and never acknowledge a mistake. It is as if he were governed by the old maxim "never let them see you sweat," which begets a cycle of falsehoods to cover up the previous ones. With that approach, even failures can be handled with a fallacious "declare victory and go home" whitewash. Trump uses this tactic often, for example, in deliberately mischaracterizing the outcomes of his summits with North Korea's Kim Jong-un and Russia's Vladimir Putin, his meetings with the G7 and our NATO allies, and his tariff and trade battles.

Trump also manipulates facts and the truth to sow the seeds of confusion. He does this to enhance his political capital with his base and ensure his political survival against the investigations into his conduct. He generates confusion by "flooding the zone" with so many assertions and allegations that most people cannot digest them all, leaving them bewildered as to the truth of even the most obvious among them. At the same time, he portrays himself and his administration as the ultimate arbiters of what constitutes truth. It is as if Trump were borrowing the Marx Brothers' famous line from *Duck Soup*: "Who ya gonna believe: me or your own eyes?"[29]

Sometimes, Trump's falsehoods are less complicated, with an entirely obvious motive. When confronted with a situation that he knows is damaging or embarrassing, he has been willing to just lie about it. On April 5, 2018, when reporters on Air Force One asked him about the payment that was made to Stormy Daniels in an attempt to cover up their affair, he simply said he didn't know about it. Months later, his attorney Michael Cohen asserted under oath that Trump authorized it from the start, and other sources corroborated that.[30] Trump may have lied about this to preserve domestic tranquility, or to avoid culpability for campaign finance violations.

Some of Trump's fabrications are blatantly and provably false, placing him and his associates in legal and political jeopardy. A very consequential example was Trump's assertion during the 2016 campaign that he had "nothing to do with Russia." In November 2018, court documents and Michael Cohen's guilty pleas revealed that Trump had a lot to do with Russia, showing that Trump's negotiations with Russians to build a hotel in Moscow continued throughout the primary elections, until June 2016.[31] Trump's lies about Russia may have altered voters' opinions, voting choices, and the ultimate outcome of the election.[32]

Trump offered an especially ludicrous lie after laughter interrupted his boastful speech at the 2018 United Nations General Assembly. As laughter rolled through the hall, Trump said, "(I) didn't expect that reaction, but that's okay."[33] Trump's spontaneous reaction confirmed his surprise and that he did not intend to provoke laughter. Yet, even though it was obvious to anyone who saw the leaders of the world laughing at him, when reporters asked him about it, Trump claimed, "Well, that was meant to get some laughter, but that was great." The next day at his press conference, Trump doubled down on his lie by blatantly falsifying his comments that prompted the laughter and then claiming, "They weren't laughing *at* me, they were laughing *with* me. We had fun. That was not laughing *at* me. . . . They didn't laugh *at* me. People had a good time with me. We were doing it together. We had a good time."[34]

Trump frequently refutes well-sourced news reports so stridently that he confirms their accuracy. He overdenies reports, becoming the king of "methinks" moments, as in Shakespeare's legendary assertion, "The lady doth protest too much, methinks." Trump has established a pattern of using this tactic to propagate falsehoods, which has become a convenient indicator of their falsity. In one instance, Maggie Haberman of the *New York Times* reported that Trump was displeased with his attorneys and was planning to make a change.[35] Trump vociferously condemned both the report and Haberman. As was later apparent, he put a hold on changes, briefly, to try to invalidate the report. A few weeks later, Trump made the exact changes that Haberman had previously foretold,[36] confirming that her reporting had been accurate.[37]

The penultimate example of Trump's "methinks" messaging occurs almost daily in his propaganda war against Special Counsel Mueller's investigation. Trump has been waging a campaign to convince his supporters of his innocence, discredit the investigation, and insulate himself from any consequences of Mueller's findings. At every opportunity, he claims that there was "no collusion" and that the investigation is a "witch hunt," even finding ways to inject those slogans in response to questions on unrelated issues. He accompanies these protestations with caustic, vituperative, fallacious allegations against Special Counsel Mueller, the FBI, the intelligence community, or anyone else he wants to target. But Trump provides no factual basis for his claims.

Trump applies his main skill set—branding and marketing—by repeating these overdenials as often as possible with the hope that audiences hearing them often enough will believe them. It brings to mind his comments after the Nevada primary: "We won with poorly educated. I love the poorly educated."[38] This is more enlightening than just an electoral assessment. It may be the most revealing indicator of what Trump thinks of the base voters that elected him, why he traffics in falsehoods, and who he believes is influenced by his repetitive claims. His branding of "no collusion" and "witch hunt" aims to manipulate the political marketplace in much the way that consumer markets are manipulated by slogans like "Just Do It," "Finger Lickin' Good," "Fly the Friendly Skies," and "Have It Your Way." He knows what effect branding has on his base.

Another explanation of Trump's propensity for falsehoods also merits consideration. Although he disseminates falsehoods on a routine basis, they may or may not constitute "lies." Oddly, Trump might be practicing the maxim made famous by the George Costanza character in *Seinfeld*, who said, "Just remember, it's not a lie if *you* believe it."[39] Trump might actually be so adept at self-deception that he converts delusions into facts. It is not comforting that someone serving as president might actually be living in his own alternative reality, since the consequences of that are horrifying. But, as Costanza points out, it could mean that his falsehoods and fabrications are technically not lies, for what that hairbreadth distinction is worth.

New tactics are urgently needed to counter Trump's falsifications. Although many Americans seek remedies to Trump's truth deficit, others are not interested. People among Trump's base take Trump's and his staff's deceptions on faith, out of loyalty. They willfully accept Trump's falsehoods as facts on the basis of their connection to him. Since he granted them his respect and validation, they reciprocate by accepting his reality, even when they know that it is not credible. His most committed supporters have shown that by respecting them it is possible to earn their loyalty and their belief. It is a matter of emotions, not empirical data or evidentiary support.

Thus, the real way to battle "fake news" from the White House is not just by education, but also by building a relationship with Trump's supporters. When their concerns, needs, and status are validated, they respond by offering their fidelity, and only then will they accept the authentic facts presented to them. It helps if they enjoy the messenger as that seems to be essential to earning their trust, which then dictates their beliefs. Gauging from their response to Trump, his supporters might be influenced less by what is being said than by who is saying it. They may be willing to take responsibility, reject "alternative facts," and believe the genuine substantiated facts, but that comes with preconditions that may exceed the media's mandate, which is to furnish the truth.

Trump's tactics pose challenges to media that have broad-based audiences, and journalists face a dilemma over how to respond to Trump's behavior. If they hold Trump and his staff accountable by asking questions that would expose his fabrications and falsehoods, it extends the conversation over an issue that Trump had chosen as a diversion or distraction from his personal vulnerabilities or from an important and sensitive policy issue. By calling his facts into question, the media inadvertently helps Trump achieve his underlying objective to hijack another media cycle. Conversely, if journalists do not ask questions about Trump's statements, so that they can instead focus attention on issues of policy importance, then Trump's falsities and deceptions go unchallenged and become accepted facts in the eyes of many Americans who are not given sufficient reason to believe otherwise.

Rather than choose between these two reportorial approaches, the professional media can do both by establishing a structure for journalistically responsible reporting. It would serve the dual purposes of providing insightful context to news reports and educating the populace about what is really going on, beyond the message that Trump or his spokespeople want to publicize. By systematically including an educational element in its reportage, the media can help readers and viewers become more sophisticated consumers of news, enabling the naive to gain understanding, equipping the gullible with the tools for critical thinking, and providing the ill-informed with the basis to discern between fact and fallacy.

On behalf of the interests of Americans, the media should adopt methods that contextualize Trump's and his administration's statements and announcements to promote their accuracy. First, statements and tweets that are false or deceptive should be characterized—when appropriate and accurate to do so—as allegations, deceptions, or distractions. For example, instead of "Trump tweeted, 'There was no collusion,'" his tweet should be reported as either "Trump alleged in a tweet, 'There was no collusion,'" or, more accurate still, "Trump exhibited his concern about Mueller's investigation and his desire to weaken public confidence in Mueller's findings by tweeting, 'There was no collusion.'" Similarly, instead of "Sarah Sanders said that the president's comments about Russian interference in our election speaks for itself," it should be reported as, "Sarah Sanders indicated, by her deflection of a reporter's question, that the administration is unwilling to resolve the president's contradictory comments on his belief about Russian interference with our election," or more simply, "Sarah Sanders declined to clarify the president's contradictory comments."

Second, to further assure that media reports convey facts, truth, reality, and accountability as much as possible, media coverage of any *issue du jour* can be improved through a three-part process, by assessing and reporting on:

1) the accuracy of the administration's position or claim;
2) their likely objective for taking that position or making that claim; and

3) from what other issue is the position or claim possibly aimed to distract or divert the nation's attention.

The benefits of this multipart approach include its ability to:

• promote accuracy, truth, accountability, and transparency;
• give attention to what the administration wants to present (which is
  necessary and fair to them); and
• effectuate the mandate of journalistic responsibility by illuminating
  hidden agendas, when they exist.

This methodology would enable responsible journalists to level the playing field against intentional falsehoods and Orwellian deceptions. The net
result is that all Americans who rely on the media for accurate, factual, and
informative reporting about their government would receive more honest
and insightful information.

For broadcast and cable TV reports, a complementary tool would add
value to the three-part process, particularly during live broadcasts of Trump
or his staff delivering a speech or comments. In the same way that the chyron,
which provides advisory comments at the bottom of the screen, is used to
provide "Breaking News" alerts or highlight the subject matter of a speech,
it can be used to flash a "Viewer Warning—Falsehood Alert" when someone
is saying something that is patently or demonstrably untrue. For example, following Trump's offensive comments about the Charlottesville incident, when
he deliberately misquoted his previous comments, a flashing chyron with that
warning would have been entirely justifiable. Standard use of such a tool
could deter deliberate fabrications.

For distortions of the truth that are easily foreseeable and even predictable, some shorthand responses should be prepared and ready for deploy-
ment. For example, the president's use of the term "fake news" follows an
unmistakable pattern. He invokes it when he is trying to deny or distract from
facts that have been reported, corroborated, and verified, but which he considers problematic. His assertions of "fake news" have routinely been found
to be untrue, and, in fact, they regularly signal the validity of the matter
being reported. So, rather than parsing the merits of each of his "fake news"
claims, each time that the president invokes that term, the media would be
justified in issuing a "Trump Deception" notice. It could be presented as a

chyron, a full screen banner, or oral introduction to the story about it. If his "fake news" comments were regularly greeted with that standard response, which is warranted due to his track record of its usage, then he might be discouraged from asserting it and eventually curtail the practice. These alerts would be entirely consistent with the media's mandate to illuminate the truth.

Solutions that fact-check Trump and his staff are, regrettably, necessary. Trump damages his credibility by his propensity to fabricate. But much worse, he also impairs the public's trust in government, which may be his intention. Media has a responsibility to provide truth in real time that counters Trump's falsehoods. Reflecting on a particularly difficult period during World War II, Winston Churchill wrote, "There is no worse mistake in public leadership than to hold out false hopes soon to be swept away. The British people can face peril or misfortune with fortitude and buoyancy, but they bitterly resent being deceived or finding that those responsible for their affairs are themselves dwelling in a fool's paradise." The American people have similar expectations that are disregarded by Trump, who routinely deceives both the people and himself.

IMPORTANCE DURING TRUMP'S TENURE AND THE POST-TRUMP ERA

Although the democratization of the media is an overwhelmingly constructive development and a cause for optimism, it brings with it new pitfalls, including disreputable click-bait media outlets, crowdsourced distortions, and perceptions of media bias. Ironically, the deluge of news and media outlets widens the choice of sources while narrowing the scope of viewpoints presented by each. Solutions can improve the reliability and truthfulness of information, and are necessary to legitimize new media technologies.

Ultimately, the responsibility lies with each consumer of news and information. No matter what is done at the corporate level, it is vital for everyone to become aware of suspicious practices. Americans should be educated to be astute consumers of news and that should begin in high school by teaching young Americans to distinguish between fact and fallacy, materiality and manipulation, dependability and duplicity, truth and trickery. A high school course in Media Consumer Protection would help students be mindful of pernicious practices, and promote critical thinking by teaching techniques that enable interpretation beyond the surface. It would prepare the next generation to discern authentic information and legitimate media reporting from deceptions and distractions fueled by ulterior motives. The course would align with the mandate of educators to provide youths with the skills that are essential to function in modern society, become judicious consumers, and develop into responsible adults. Aware consumers of media will generate a flight to quality that rewards reputable sources, which is the best defense against today's media abuses.

Beyond the media's own challenges, Trump has been waging war against them with his unrelenting flow of falsehoods, deceptions, and distortions. He poses great risk because he has the presidential bully pulpit. His disparagement and disavowal of the truth impairs public trust, damages our democratic institutions, and jeopardizes our social stability. He is an expert at manipulating the daily news cycle, and he even seems to keep newsworthy developments in his back pocket (e.g., firing a cabinet official, issuing a pardon, revoking a security clearance, declassifying documents) to spring on the media when he wants to distract them from something else. At best, he is creating confusion and preoccupying the media in order to keep voters bewildered so that popular opinion will not coalesce against him. At worst, he is conducting a full-scale assault on our democratic institutions by ushering in an Orwellian dystopia based on his delusional alternative reality and trying to co-opt the nation into adopting it as truth. It is incumbent upon all of us to be discerning consumers of news and the government's assertions in order to ferret out fact from fiction and hold him accountable.

Presidential historian Doris Kearns Goodwin, who has studied and written award-winning books about presidents Abraham Lincoln, Teddy Roosevelt, and Lyndon Johnson, has expressed her concerns about Trump's long-term impact on our treasured institutions. She cautions, "There is a terrible danger in growing accustomed to the erosion of meaning in our political discourse. Serious, perhaps lasting, damage is being done to our identity as Americans and to our democracy. We are moving in a direction in which trust will be vaporized and truth becomes a fugitive."[40]

Trump has pushed the boundaries, but that does not mean that his tactics will be deemed acceptable and normal in the post-Trump era. Although the tolerance for deviance will be wider after him than it was before him, his use of distortions, deceptions, "alternative facts," and falsehoods will probably be renounced. This is because his aberrant pathway to the presidency is not likely to be replicated, and any future president is likely to have cultivated support from a broad range of constituencies through many years and many elections before reaching the presidency. The usual vetting process based on a record of public service disqualifies someone who does what Trump does. A candidate will not succeed if they have a public track record of propagating egregious prevarications and obvious deceptions. It is very likely that falsehoods and deceptions will be repudiated, and there will be a return to fact-based conduct and appropriate discourse.

Republican legislators are sometimes a barometer of whether Trump receives fair and truthful media attention or unjustifiably negative bias. Elected officials often object to media coverage that they believe is unfairly biased. Some are willing to reinforce the media's credence by asserting its sacrosanct status in our social fabric. Since Trump's early days in office, some GOP legislators have voiced concerns about Trump's relationship with Russia and Putin; his comments on the violence in Charlottesville; his policy that separated immigrant children from their parents; his violations of the Constitution's Emoluments Clause and other ethical lapses; his possible culpability for obstruction of justice and collusion; and his vitriolic and narcissistic rants on social media. Although GOP legislators often defend Trump or decline to publicly respond to his offensive behavior, when they do voice concerns, they reaffirm the legitimacy of scrutiny by the media and the special counsel, and intensify the quest for full public awareness of Trump's conduct.

The issues surrounding the truth and accuracy of both media-generated and crowdsourced information are sure to intensify in the years ahead. Given the almost blinding pace of technological innovation, the preferred means to access news and media in 2020 and thereafter might be very different than it was in 2016, posing new issues along with it. The emergence of artificial intelligence, augmented reality, data analytics, and gaming technologies might be combined in new ways that reinvent the media experience. Younger voters, who rely heavily on their technology tools, will find new ways to stay informed. Increased use of new tools might inspire a higher percentage of younger Americans to vote. These technologies might even create shared experiences whereby groups can engage in political media together.

The ability to target particular demographic groups will be further enhanced through data analytics. Users might be able to select media content so specifically with AI and search tools that they can home in on issues of interest to them. However, in doing so, they might miss the big-picture message of an issue or debate, creating their own personal echo chamber that gives them only what they want to hear without any diversity of opinion. As exciting as the uses of new technologies will be, they might cause lapses in the authenticity of information that they transmit. Due to their complexity, technology tools are increasingly vulnerable to infiltrators who seek to capitalize on the tools' broad-scale usage. Technology tools might be diabolically used to alter political content, for example, by putting words in peoples' mouths that were not actually spoken, or by adding people into a photo even though they were not actually there.

Social media platforms are especially vulnerable to manipulation of facts and truth, since their content is user generated. Misuse, especially by foreign adversaries, like the Russians in 2016 who had nefarious intentions, is a virus that infects popular perceptions and therefore impacts our elections. Safeguards should be adopted to improve the veracity and reliability of posted information that appears in the feeds of American users.

- Social media users must have the right to limit their feeds to only US-based content, which should be the default, requiring users to opt in to allow content from foreign sources if they want to do so.
- Foreign-source opinion articles, when allowed, must cite a reputable US-based source that corroborates their opinion, which must be prominently cited in the posting's header or headline.
- Paid advertisements must disclose that they are paid advertisements.
- Opinion articles must disclose that they are opinion articles, or editorials, as opposed to fact-based news reports.
- Postings of news articles, or content that appears to be a news article, should present the name of the author and publication above the article's headline, in a font as large as the headline.
- A system should be developed that provides a seal of approval for news and opinion sources to validate their legitimacy and compliance with all content rules, so that users know that they are viewing content from a trusted source (possibly along the lines of NewsGuard,[41] created by Steven Brill in late 2017 to assess the general reliability of news websites and provide information about the websites' financial backing, awards, demerits, and track records).

The challenges of false information and media manipulation will persist, and may even become harder to thwart. The benefits of media proliferation will still outweigh the risks from its vulnerabilities, but steps must be taken to protect platforms and their users. Some legislators, executive branch officials, and expert commentators have voiced concerns about the inadequacy of attention to the prevention of malevolent media tampering and its potential impact on our elections in 2020 and beyond. The risks to our media and election systems are real and they compel our vigilance. The Trump administration has not acted against foreign intrusions, particularly from Russia, or domestic interference. This failure to act is likely intentional, as it mirrors Trump's denials of past interference by Russians. Current cabinet officials and intelligence chiefs also have not established vigorous protective solutions. Given the vital role of our media and the sanctity of our elections, this must be corrected.

As the need to distinguish between fact and fiction escalates, and the urgency for scrutiny of our governmental institutions intensifies, the media must be emboldened to fulfill its mandate as a vital pillar of our democracy. It is in times like these that the media's most essential responsibility—to apply transparency and accountability to governmental actions and officials—must flourish. Doing so is not the media's bias; it's their job.

CHAPTER 6

CONDUCT

THE ERA OF INCREASED TRANSPARENCY AND ACCOUNTABILITY

A "government of the people, by the people, for the people" must have solid mechanisms with which to hold their elected leaders accountable on a consistent, ongoing basis, rather than relegating that exclusively to the electoral process and the courts. In any democracy, accountability is essential to prevent government institutions from being debilitated by corruption, ethical abuses, and other toxic infections. Transparency is a key to accountability, although there is much room for debate over the degree and type of transparency that is sufficient.

In any presidential administration, as the appearance of impropriety escalates so too does the need for accountability and transparency. In the case of Donald Trump's presidency, the need for transparency and accountability is monumental, due to his surreptitious ties to Vladimir Putin and other Russians, his efforts to obstruct justice, and his infringements of the Constitution's Emoluments Clause, among other transgressions. The tone that he sets by his conduct also has had a ripple effect among his appointees who indulge in their own profligacy and other ethical abuses. Trump's flagrant misconduct will probably compel Congress to establish new standards for appropriate and ethical behavior to prevent extreme improprieties by future presidents and appointees.

THE NEED FOR ACCOUNTABILITY AND TRANSPARENCY

Ever since there has been government, there have been government improprieties. There are cases throughout human history of politicians and leaders who acted inappropriately or unscrupulously, using the power and privileges of their office for personal aggrandizement and/or unjustifiable benefit. It's something about human nature. Or, as British politician Lord Acton famously wrote in 1887, "Power tends to corrupt, and absolute power corrupts absolutely."

The United States is certainly not immune from human nature. Although corruption in the United States, both historically and recently, has been minimal compared to many other countries, we certainly have had our share of incidents, both large and small. A few of our presidents are remembered for rampant corruption in their administrations,[1] and a paucity of accomplishments during their tenures, with presidents Harding and Grant probably topping that list.[2] Sometimes corruption has offset accomplishments. That was especially evident with President Nixon, whose successes (e.g., détente with the Soviet Union, initiating relations with the People's Republic of China, creation of the EPA, National Environmental Policy Act of 1969, Clean Air Act of 1970, Clean Water Act of 1972, etc.) relinquished top billing in his legacy to his litany of ignominious endeavors, with Watergate overshadowing all else.

Over the years, handfuls of public officials at all levels have engaged in improprieties that jeopardized or even terminated their careers. Historically, those episodes came to light through traditional investigative methods and sources like eyewitness reports, phone call recordings, meetings, financial transactions, and bank records. In Congress, a variety of cases of corruption or unethical behavior have culminated in a member's retirement, resignation, or even imprisonment (e.g., Tom Delay, Jim Traficant, Duke Cunningham, Mark Foley, Dan Rostenkowski, Donald "Buz" Lukens, Bill Jefferson, Wilbur Mills, Wayne Hays, and the recent litany of sexual impropriety perpetrators). Some governors engaged in conduct that cut short their careers (e.g., Rod Blagojevich and George Ryan of Illinois, John Rowland of Connecticut, Edwin Edwards of Louisiana, and Bob McDonnell of Virginia). Presidential candidates have engaged in activities that have ended their candidacies, like Gary Hart, who denied an extramarital affair and challenged the press to prove otherwise, which they did.

More commonly, the inappropriate actions of public officials have either been sufficiently incidental that they received little or no public attention, or were deemed to be isolated instances that did not result in major consequences. For example, many Presidents engaged in nepotism to one degree or another, without it being prominent in their legacy. Other officials received public scrutiny (sometimes including rebukes) that did not end their careers (e.g., the "Keating Five" senators[3], and Senator David Vitter's involvement with prostitutes[4]).

Although this is just conjecture and speculation, it is likely that most public officials who have served for decades have done something minor that did not warrant public attention. Examples might include having a cup of coffee paid for by a lobbyist, having a pen from the office wind up at home at the end of the day, failing to report a small birthday gift, sharing a taxi ride with someone who paid the fare, using an office envelope to mail something home, or using campaign funds to purchase camera film for an event.

TRUMP'S CONDUCT AND THE TONE HE SETS FOR HIS ADMINISTRATION

On the spectrum of transgressions great and small, Donald Trump is setting a new stratospheric standard. Although one of his favorite slogans during both his campaign and his presidency has been "drain the swamp," his actions have worked to "stock the swamp." Exploration of Trump's relationship to "drain the swamp" begins by asking whether it is better characterized as irony or hypocrisy.

Trump never explained what the slogan actually meant or what he would do about it. If "drain the swamp" meant that government officials should not vacuum up campaign contributions from lobbyists, industries, and others who seek to influence policy and legislation, then Trump's fundraising from those targets makes him the principal offender.[5] If the slogan meant that he would prohibit the hiring of personnel who have conflicts of interest and financial holdings related to their policy decisions, then Trump has also been the perpetrator of what he assailed, given his hiring of secretaries Betsy DeVos,[6] Wilbur Ross,[7] Tom Price,[8] Steve Mnuchin,[9] and Alex Azar,[10] former CDC director Brenda Fitzgerald (who resigned the day after news broke about her conflicts of interest),[11] and former Economic Council chairman Gary Cohn.[12] If the slogan meant that people must not personally profit from government actions, then Trump is the ultimate swamp creature when he pursues tax reform that prioritizes his family's financial interests in his quest for elimination of the estate tax, shores up preferential tax rates for "pass through" family-owned businesses, and maintains the "carried interest" deduction that benefits real estate holders, despite his campaign promise to the contrary.

Even Trump's use of his executive powers compels ethical scrutiny. He has signed countless executive orders, many of which were on matters that ordinarily would be within Congress's jurisdiction to legislate. His frequent and eager use of executive orders, starting with his travel ban during his first days in office, has been criticized by many across the political spectrum, as they often financially benefit his allies and industries that support him, sometimes blatantly. He seems to enjoy executive orders, most likely because it provides instant gratification and helps him appear powerful to his base.

In 2017, he realized that his power to pardon people for their criminal conduct is extremely broad (virtually unlimited unless in exchange for a bribe or other flagrant offense). He wielded it like a royal scepter to pardon Arizona sheriff Joe Arpaio without the Justice Department first evaluating its propriety, and felt so empowered by doing so that he briefly went on a pardoning binge. Thereafter, he continually dangled the prospect of a pardon to encourage Paul Manafort and others not to divulge information to Special Counsel Mueller that would implicate him. Yet, if Trump were to pardon Manafort, Michael Cohen, or others who are central figures in Mueller's investigation, it is commonly believed that doing so would constitute *prima facie* evidence of obstruction of justice.

At the opposite end of the judicial process from pardons, Trump has sought to prosecute his political adversaries. In early 2018, he wanted to order the Department of Justice to prosecute Hillary Clinton and former FBI director James Comey.[13] Don McGahn, the White House counsel at the time, objected and drafted a memo detailing the potential consequences of such an order, including possible impeachment. Although Trump did not issue such a directive, he reportedly continued to discuss the matter, as well as the prospect of having a second special counsel investigate them.

In August 2018, Trump used his broad powers to revoke the security clearance of former CIA director John Brennan and threatened to revoke clearances from others who publicly criticized Trump, or whom he just didn't like. But the president's power to revoke a security clearance should only be utilized when there is good cause to do so, and exercising one's First Amendment rights to express an opinion is not good cause. When Trump threatened to revoke the security clearance of Bruce Ohr, a current Justice Department attorney who would be prevented from doing his job if he lost his clearance, it raised more serious concerns. Trump sought to revoke it because Ohr brought the Steele dossier about Trump to the FBI's attention, and Trump did not like the political activities of Ohr's wife. The prospect of revoking Mueller's clearance, which Trump was rumored to have considered in order to impair Mueller's ability to investigate Trump and his team again raised warnings that doing so could constitute obstruction of justice.

Trump has also engaged in blatant improprieties and indefensible conduct. By receiving payments from foreigners at his hotels and other businesses, he has violated the Constitution's Emoluments Clause since the moment that he took office and virtually every day since, epitomizing what he calls "the swamp." He engages in nepotism at the highest level by having his daughter and son-in-law as principal White House officials despite their lack of qualifications for the jobs (with Jared Kushner's expansive portfolio encroaching on the duties of the secretary of state). Trump's profligate extravagances, including his regular weekend jaunts to his resorts for personal pleasure, have cost taxpayers untold millions of dollars in Secret Service, Air Force One, and White House staff expenses. Trump's profiteering and unprecedented waste of taxpayer funds is an exponential growth of the swamp.

Following Trump's example, his cabinet officials and other senior appointees act as if they are at liberty to engage in unethical practices, multiplying the instances and cost of swamp-like conduct throughout the administration. Secretaries Tom Price, David Shulkin, and Steve Mnuchin engaged in air travel misuse, which eventually forced Price and Shulkin to resign. Administrator Scott Pruitt was forced out due to a litany of unethical actions, including travel extravagances, discounted housing from a lobbyist, using staff to find a job for his wife, building a soundproof meeting room, and multiple security sweeps of his office. Former secretary Ryan Zinke was investigated for benefiting from a Montana land deal, his wife's travel at government expense, misuse of security officers, reversing a decision to permit a casino after meeting with a competitor's lobbyist, redrawing the boundaries of two national monuments, and recklessly using $139,000 of government funds for an office door. Secretary Ben Carson came under fire for his lavish allocation of $31,000 for an office dining set. Secretary Wilbur Ross was exposed for conflicts of interest by failing to divest his investments and board positions with various companies, meeting with officials from at least one of those companies, and then taking action that advanced his, and the company's, interests.[14] Secretary Betsy DeVos was in the spotlight for a unique ethical controversy, having been appointed secretary of the Department of Education despite being totally uneducated about education issues, which was very apparent in her March 2018 interview on *60 Minutes*.[15]

Even Trump's allies in Congress seem to be emboldened by Trump's behavior, as if they had license to engage in similar activities. Actions against truly swamp-like conduct were initiated during Trump's tenure by his Justice Department against the first two congressmen who supported Trump: Chris Collins of New York for insider trading, and Duncan Hunter of California for misuse of campaign funds.[16] Despite the outrageous conduct that invited investigation and legal action, Trump castigated Jeff Sessions for bringing charges against them, referencing the impact that the charges will have on GOP control of Congress.[17]

Perhaps the vilest effect of Trump's swamp habits is that it welcomes, and even encourages, his staff and appointees to make policy decisions that serve the interests of the swamp's ultrarich beneficiaries, rather than serving the public interest by helping those who most need the government's help. Trump's deference to the swamp over the needs of the middle class and disadvantaged Americans is evident in:

- the EPA's decimation of environmental standards in favor of profiteering by major polluters;
- many provisions of the tax cuts legislation;
- the effort to eliminate Obamacare;
- Secretary DeVos's reduction of investigations into fraud and abuse by for-profit colleges and limitation of debt relief to students who were defrauded by those colleges;[18] and
- the policies of former attorney general Sessions that prioritized enforcement against disadvantaged communities rather than actions against white-collar criminals.

Trump's self-indulgent, reckless indifference to the law, and his conflicts of interest, are so expansive, ostentatious, and profound that whatever interpretation is assigned to the slogan "drain the swamp," it seems that he based the phrase on his own practices. Trump is the most extreme practitioner of swamp behavior in modern American political history. It is unlikely that he will be exempt from America's long tradition of accountability inculcated in our institutions.

Although Special Counsel Mueller's investigation did not result in criminal charges against Trump, it did not alleviate Trump's accountability for swamp-like conduct. Mueller's report provided considerable insight into Trump's interactions with Russians and apparent obstructions of justice that will help Congress hold Trump accountable, if it chooses to do so. But the president's financial practices were not addressed in the report (except with regard to Trump's ties to Russians), which conveyed the impression that Mueller considered those issues beyond the scope of his investigative authority. The report indicated that Mueller referred various matters to US prosecutors elsewhere in the country, resulting in fourteen ongoing investigations that could lead to prosecutions. Trump's finances, where swamp-infused conduct would be revealed, might be a subject of one or more of those actions, which could apply accountability to Trump and his close confidants in the future.

PRIVACY AND INSULATION GIVE WAY TO ACCOUNTABILITY AND TRANSPARENCY

Prior to twenty-four-hour cable news and the internet, there was often a gap between a public official's actions and the public's awareness of them. Not all governmental actions were able to be scrutinized. Some conduct flew below the radar. For senators and representatives, the distance between their state or district and Washington, DC, partially insulated them, at least from their local media that was, at that time, the principal watchdog over individual politicians. In effect, government officials were able to choose the standard of conduct to which they would adhere. While most opted for clean, "good government" practices, others did not. The ethics committees of the House and Senate have held many representatives and senators accountable over the years. Some officials engaged in practices that were deemed questionable, while others crossed the line into the realm of the unethical and even the illegal. In the latter cases, conduct might have stemmed from feelings of entitlement, empowerment, or arrogance, due to a politician believing that no one would ever find out what was happening behind the scenes.

In the pre-internet era, it was often difficult for local media to hold their DC representatives accountable. Scrutiny of legislators was especially challenging due to Congress exempting itself from Freedom of Information Act access to records (a similar approach was passed by Washington state's legislature in 2018 before being vetoed by the governor[19]). When the atmospherics of Washington, DC, alone did not provide sufficient privacy, the use of discretion often shielded legislators from publicity and exposure. Savvy politicians usually could steer clear of attention. Such discretion followed the maxim of Massachusetts politician Martin Lomasney, who is credited with the famous line, "Never write if you can speak; never speak if you can nod; never nod if you can wink."[20] The same sentiment was articulated with more granularity by Louisiana governor Earl Long who said, "Don't write anything you can phone. Don't phone anything you can talk. Don't talk anything you can whisper. Don't whisper anything you can smile. Don't smile anything you can nod. Don't nod anything you can wink."[21]

But those days are over, due to today's ubiquitous media and technology. Now, virtually anything that happens anywhere, even at private events, can easily and quickly become public. Smartphone video footage taken at campaign events killed Senator George Allen's run for the presidency in 2011 (the "macaca moment")[22] and damaged Governor Mitt Romney's bid in 2012 (when he dismissively spoke about 47 percent of the electorate)[23]. Even a timely wink can show up on video footage. Public officials at all levels—elected, appointed, and staff—and other public figures are on notice.

While email, scheduling software, calendar apps, security cameras, social networking apps, cell phones with location-based services, and other technologies are very useful business tools, they also provide an extraordinary amount of data, should such data ever be sought. These and other technology tools make it possible to search, find, track, sequence, compare, align, combine, compile, and aggregate all kinds of information and data. In some cases they can destructively cause embarrassment and reputational damage, while in other cases they can constructively illuminate behavior and truth. This has prompted an important update to Lomasney's and Long's cautionary notes, expressed in the maxim: "Never put anything in an email that you wouldn't want to see on the front page of the newspaper."[24]

Exposure can occur insidiously and nefariously, even illegally, through unauthorized hacking. The ultimate example of this was during the 2016 election, when the DNC's email server was hacked by Russian operatives, and the emails were posted on WikiLeaks. Although the hacking exposed unethical and unprofessional conduct by DNC chair Debbie Wasserman-Schultz and acting-chair Donna Brazile, it was still reprehensible. The ends do not justify the means. Even more offensive and chilling was the Russians hacking of the DNC email account belonging to John Podesta, the chairman of Hillary Clinton's campaign.[25] While the emails did not indicate any inappropriate campaign activity by Podesta or those with whom he communicated, the public revelation of his emails was an invasion of privacy that no one would want to endure (who would be happy about their risotto recipe, travel plans, and family dynamics being shared with the world?).

When accessed properly and ethically, technology can be purposeful, useful, reliable tools for unveiling mysteries and uncovering the truth about careless, duplicitous, or illegal conduct. Whether at the hands of the FBI, congressional investigators, or local law enforcement officials, these tools can help separate fact from fiction, identify the honorable and the deceivers, differentiate between sincerity and smokescreens, and, ultimately, distinguish truth from lies. Any digital tools may reveal insights and aid investigations. Data mining and cross-referencing between them multiplies the likelihood that revelations will emanate therefrom.

There are plenty of recent examples in which digital tools played a key role in ferreting out culpability and/or identifying culprits. For example, email played a major role in exposing David Petraeus for sharing classified information with his girlfriend/biographer,[26] use of Twitter exposed Anthony Weiner's sexting activity,[27] photos and video exposed John Edwards's sexual and financial relationship with his campaign contractor,[28] and emails exposed Chris Christie's staff for their role in "Bridgegate" (which may or may not have been undertaken with Christie's knowledge, approval, and/or command).[29] And, of course, Hillary Clinton's email server is an epic episode of unique magnitude: the day that the FBI acquired her server proved to be a pivotal moment in the 2016 election.

These days, while not everything is automatically scrutinized, almost anything can be, given a reason for scrutiny. There is a strong emphasis on transparency and accountability, partly because those objectives are much more achievable now, and partly because public skepticism compels the effort.

TRUMP'S UNFAMILIARITY WITH TRANSPARENCY

Incredibly, Donald Trump and his staff do not seem to be aware of this. On many occasions, Trump made comments that were televised, and thereafter falsely described what he had said, as if television cameras were unable to record his earlier comments for later playback. One of many outland-ish examples was in 2017, when he questioned the authenticity of the *Access Hollywood* recording, alleging that it was not his voice, even though he had acknowledged that it was in 2016, and even apologized for it.[30] Deliberate deceptions and mischaracterizations like that are also called lies,[31] and they are easily exposed by rolling the earlier video.

Emails can be more challenging to find, but they have similar effects. Trump's campaign and White House staff members have begun to discover that their emails reveal the truth that their spoken and tweeted words do not divulge. As Trump and his fellow "collusionists" (Donald Trump Jr., Jared Kushner, Paul Manafort, Michael Flynn, Roger Stone, Corey Lewandowski, Carter Page, and others) learned, the special counsel and congressional investigators are not obligated to accept their stories as gospel. Deceptions and smokescreens are no match for scheduling app data, video footage, records of electronic funds transfers with Russian banks, travel documents for meetings with WikiLeaks and Russian contacts, phone call logs, text messages, transcripts of Russian officials' phone calls, White House visi-tor lists, and cell phone location-tracking data. Trump's claim that he had "no business with Russia" seemed oblivious to the tools that can discover the truth. Sure enough, Mueller's report revealed that Trump continued negotiating with Russians through June 2016 in hopes of building a Trump Tower in Moscow.

Trump's extensive network of financial entanglements, opportunistic relationships, and overreaching communications provide fertile ground to investigators who are authorized to pursue transgressions. Fortified with a compendium of technological tools and data sources, the investigators will find answers. For Trump, who has profiteered throughout his life from the tools of branding and deception, it will be a rude awakening to discover that they wither when confronted by the tools of accountability.

Although the communications and interactions with Russians might not have directly involved Trump himself (probably intentionally, to preserve his plausible deniability), that veil could very well be pierced by investiga-tors' access to electronic records, emails, and even Trump's own tax returns. The US prosecutor in the Southern District of New York (to whom Mueller referred numerous matters he encountered) will also be able to access pri-mary source data that will then either corroborate or contradict the veracity of Trump's tax returns, which could open many other issues.

The decisions by Trump's attorney Michael Cohen, and *National Enquirer* publisher, David Pecker, to cooperate with federal prosecutors, and the immunity granted to Allen Weisselberg, the CFO of Trump's private businesses, are likely to yield a treasure trove of documents and other information that Trump had naively hoped would be insulated from transparency. The public releases of Cohen's and Omarosa Manigault Newman's secretly taped conversations with Trump are also likely to be very damaging to Trump, both politically and legally. Also significantly, Bob Woodward's well-sourced book *Fear*[32] exposes the behind-the-scenes machinations of Trump's appointees, backed up by Woodward's authorized audio recordings, with potential political and legal consequences.

Amazingly, Trump is so oblivious to the distinction between right and wrong, and so indiscreet about his oblivion, that many of his abuses are conducted in plain sight. His violation of the Emoluments Clause—by profiteering from foreigners who stay at his hotels—is obvious and ongoing. In May 2018, he expanded his disregard for accountability, despite the glare of the investigators' lights trained on him. After he tweeted that he would help China provide jobs for its people by easing sanctions on ZTE (the Chinese telecom company that sold equipment with American parts to Iran and North Korea), it came to light that China invested $500 million in an Indonesian resort development that features a Trump hotel and golf course.[33] A few days before Trump announced his decision to help ZTE, China granted many trademarks to Trump's daughter Ivanka for her products.[34] These actions create the appearance of conflicts of interest (quid-pro-quo or pay-to-play deals, or possibly worse) that Trump orchestrated in conflict with his duties as president. This may also explain why he proclaims that he and China's president are such good friends. Because Trump is so indiscreet, it wasn't even necessary to excavate his tax returns, phone records, or a surveillance source to learn about these transgressions.

Trump's acolytes have suggested that Trump is the most transparent president we have ever had. While his sloppy revelation of his conflict-laden ZTE-for-Indonesia deal might substantiate their point, that example is not what they had in mind. The fact that some of what he says is self-damaging does not satisfy his obligation for transparency. His advocates point to Trump's willingness to speak his mind in interviews and at press events, no matter how toxic his thoughts might be (like his "both sides" claim about the Charlottesville violence).

While this may be a clever twist for a commentator, it is dead wrong. It is either an intentional or unwitting attempt to validate Trump's cynicism. Transparency requires public access to all matters in the public interest. Trump offers transparency only to matters that are within *his* interest or willingness to provide. He has held few full press conferences because he would have to confront questions that he doesn't want to answer. He mainly takes questions in informal situations where he can pick and choose which ones to answer, and he doesn't even do that when he would likely be asked about Michael Cohen or Special Counsel Mueller. After meetings with foreign leaders, the media sometimes finds out what was discussed from the other government, not from the White House. If Trump were to honor his obligation for transparency, he would start by publicly revealing his ties to Russians, his reasons for being beholden to them, and his tax records. He hasn't done so, and it is clear that he will never do so willingly.

For most public officials, the call of public service, personal ethics, professional responsibility, and moral suasion are still the best reasons to adhere to responsible, "good government" practices. However, for others who are immune to those forces, the fear of getting caught may motivate them to maintain the high ground. The prevalence of first-rate sleuthing by investigative journalists, combined with new technology tools that reveal information, data, and insight, have created an awareness that eventually the truth of what transpired will become publicly known. The fear of the truth coming out is a great incentive to engage in governmental conduct and decision-making that is both appropriate and ethical. Although Trump's team did not abide by this practical reality during the campaign and the initial stage of his administration, they have probably come to recognize its value more recently.

Politicians and public figures are not the only players who are subject to higher standards of conduct, accountability for their actions, and scrutiny of their shortcomings. Emails and other digital data have also exposed many instances of corporate malfeasance. Examples include Enron's deliberate manipulation of energy markets and supply, Wells Fargo Bank's intentional overselling of unwanted products and falsification of sales numbers, Volkswagen's fraudulent air emission test results, Yahoo's disregard for security protections that resulted in major hacking and the company's slide into irrelevance, and many banks' lending and repossession practices that accelerated the mortgage crisis of 2008. As these and other companies have experienced, the expectations for accountability and transparency apply to virtually all sectors of society.

NEW SOURCES OF ACCOUNTABILITY AND TRANSPARENCY

Many governmental entities and nongovernmental organizations apply scrutiny to government activities. The ethics committees in Congress and inspector generals' offices within each executive branch department are among these, reviewing conduct by officials under their jurisdiction. Notably though, they become involved after the fact, through investigations into allegedly inappropriate activity. While an enforcement office that can levy justice can strike fear in the heart of a perpetrator, it does not have the same effect as the media, which can shine the light of public awareness onto ongoing activities. Both roles are necessary.

Governmental surveillance does have the capacity to identify malfeasance as it is occurring. Yet, surveillance has its own constraints, primarily legal, as authorization is necessary before efforts can be undertaken, and that usually requires court approval. Even though that may limit rapid response, our society would not tolerate procedures that are loosely applied, without due process and appropriate authorization. To do otherwise would resemble the activities of a police state.

Ironically, Congress established sweeping authority for the federal government to engage in surveillance when it first authorized the illusorily named Patriot Act in 2001.[35] When it was originally proposed and moving through Congress, the act's scope was represented in narrower terms than what became its actual scope. The Patriot Act and its reauthorization have led to many heated debates, both within and outside of Congress, over its intended effect, the reach of its activities, the circumstances that can trigger its use, and the thresholds of appropriate conduct under it. Senators Ron Wyden and Rand Paul have been especially vigilant against its overly zealous usage and injudicious management.[36]

The federal government constructed a massive facility in Utah to operate data collection and analysis activities under the Patriot Act and other authorities.[37] The staff at the facility has the tools, financial resources, and expertise to comb massive quantities of data and extract a wide range of information. Although government officials would suggest that the Patriot Act and the Utah facility are relevant only in the context of a discussion of homeland security issues, that is not necessarily accurate. Once the capacity for surveillance, data collection, and data analysis is established, the same operations could potentially be applied to other uses, for other purposes that would have been beyond the scope originally ordained for both.

The potential expanded usage has raised concern among public policy experts and some legislators who are focused on privacy and digital technology issues.[38] Just because the Utah facility has not been used for surveillance of domestic matters, and will principally be used for homeland security purposes, that doesn't mean that it couldn't be used for domestic purposes. It is quite possible that, over time, public sentiment will normalize the use of these resources for enforcement of government accountability and transparency. The fact that the Patriot Act's use would transcend homeland security objectives might be viewed as incidental when it could also be used to root out questionable governmental conduct. Identification of fraud, abuse, and public corruption might be considered a benefit that warrants use of the resources for these purposes.

Nonprofit organizations and public policy institutes also provide robust mechanisms for transparency and accountability. Their efforts focus on their research, accumulation, aggregation, and publication of government-related data sets. Common Cause, the Carnegie Endowment, Pew Research Center, and Public Citizen are among the groups that have a long track record of dedication to accountability of federal officials and the federal government (and, in some cases, state governments).

In recent years, many organizations developed initiatives, services, and programs that take transparency to a higher level, aided by digital technology. A small sampling includes the following organizations, as they are described on their websites:

- the Sunlight Foundation is a "nonpartisan, nonprofit organization that uses the tools of civic tech, open data, policy analysis, and journalism to make our government and politics more accountable and transparent to all. Our vision is for modern technology to enable more complete, equitable and effective democratic participation";[39]

- the Center for Responsive Politics is a "nonpartisan, independent, and nonprofit . . . research group tracking money in U.S. politics and its effect on elections and public policy," providing access through its OpenSecrets.org website that is a "comprehensive resource for federal campaign contributions, lobbying data, and analysis";[40]
- MapLight is a "nonpartisan . . . nonprofit organization that reveals the influence of money in politics, informs and empowers voters, and advances reforms that promote a more responsive democracy," whose "online tools and research bring transparency to government data and put a spotlight on the outsize influence of money in politics so that journalists and advocacy groups can hold lawmakers accountable";[41]
- "American Oversight is a non-partisan, nonprofit ethics watchdog and is the top Freedom of Information Act litigator investigating the Trump administration. Since our launch in March 2017, we have filed more than 100 public records lawsuits, uncovering and publishing tens of thousands of documents. . . . Relying on FOIA and other public records laws, we file requests to uncover misconduct that otherwise would not see daylight, and then we harness the independent power of the courts to force the administration to obey the law. . . . If the Trump administration tries to obstruct or ignore congressional subpoenas, we'll be going to court to compel the release of public documents and force transparency";[42]
- LegiStorm is a "non-partisan, for-profit company that researches, verifies and publishes information about Members of Congress and congressional staff";[43]
- the Scherman Foundation's Governmental Transparency and Accountability program "seeks to strengthen democracy in the US by increasing transparency and accountability and by promoting policies and practice. The Foundation believes that an informed, engaged citizenry with access to information is critical to sustain our democracy";[44]
- the Project On Government Oversight "is a nonpartisan independent watchdog that investigates and exposes waste, corruption, abuse of power, and when the government fails to serve the public or silences those who report wrongdoing. We champion reforms to achieve a more effective, ethical, and accountable federal government that safeguards constitutional principles";[45]

- Democracy Web, a project of the Albert Shanker Institute, provides "an overview of the essential principles and historical background on the basic architecture of democracy using the 12 categories of freedom measured by Freedom House . . . (and its) Study Guide then provides a framework for comparative analysis of the state of political rights and civil liberties around the world";[46]
- Transparency International is a nonprofit whose mission is to "stop corruption and promote transparency, accountability and integrity at all levels and across all sectors of society" to achieve "a world in which government, politics, business, civil society, and the daily lives of people are free of corruption";[47] and
- USAspending.gov "is the official source for spending data for the U.S. Government. Its mission is to show the American public what the federal government spends every year and how it spends the money . . . from the Congressional appropriations to the federal agencies and down to local communities and businesses." It displays "federal contract, grant, loan, and other financial assistance awards of more than $25,000" (as required by the Federal Funding Accountability and Transparency Act of 2006)."[48]

The federal government's internal accountability mechanisms and offices evolve slowly because, as products of laws or regulations, many steps and stakeholders are involved in their establishment or reform. However, nonprofits, research institutes, and other nongovernmental organizations are not subject to such restraints. They can be nimble, adaptive, expansive, and analytical to the extent that their mission, objectives, and creativity allow. In the Information Age, with digital everything, data is readily available on myriad issues that illuminate governmental conduct. Data mash-ups, in which multiple data sets are combined to produce especially revealing insights and correlations, will increasingly be a primary source of behavioral transparency and public accountability.

IMPORTANCE DURING TRUMP'S TENURE AND THE POST-TRUMP ERA

In the era of increased accountability and transparency, candidates should be discouraged from engaging in deliberately deceptive assertions that impair the electorate's faith in government. Clarity between what a candidate promised in prior campaigns and what they delivered may encourage disillusioned voters to participate. To supply this clarity, a nonpartisan Office of Consumer Protection in Politics (OCPP) could be created to generate disclosure statements about presidential candidates and candidates for other major offices. After being completed a few months before an election, statements would be updated monthly, posted on the internet, and included with voter information materials.

Statements would present side-by-side analyses of a candidate's previous campaign promises and their performance in fulfilling them, regardless of whether they are now running for the same office or a different one. Statements would assess the accuracy of the candidates' past and current assertions, and whether their estimates, projections, and analyses were/are supported by the facts. The OCPP would review economic and budget projections made in the candidate's previous executive or legislative speeches (e.g., did the budget deficit actually get cut in half in three years as promised?). The statements would also identify conflicting policies. For example, if a candidate advocated for personal responsibility and states' rights, and also advocated for federal law to impose government authority on personal life choices, the OCPP would highlight the conflicting positions. The statements would also analyze a candidate's claims of achievements in recent years, and other matters for which the candidate takes credit. The OCPP could compare the views of all the major candidates on certain pivotal issues of the day, with a side-by-side analysis.

An OCPP would be most helpful in dealing with career politicians and incumbent candidates. But Donald Trump had never run for office previously. Even if an OCPP had been in place, it would have been limited to assessing the assertions he made in his 2016 campaign. In absence of a governmental track record, the OCPP might have critiqued Trump's business background, including his projections for his companies' profitability alongside its actual results. In order to be as accurate as possible, it would have required Trump to submit his tax records for the most recent three or five years. If he failed to do so, then the OCPP would be empowered to make adverse conclusions.

Since Trump had no track record, the OCPP might also have been entitled to interpret Trump's "drain the swamp" mantra, pointing out that he never explained what he meant by it, and that the slogan itself gave no guidance. Rather than Trump invoking the common meaning of that phrase, suggesting that he would uproot corruption, stop pay-for-play profiteering, establish fiscal discipline, and/or require responsible behavior, the OCPP might have concluded that Trump simply meant that he would do things differently. He would then be held to account for each of his claims, criticisms, and promises regarding presidential conduct. Since Trump criticized Obama for playing too much golf, taking too many vacation days, and using teleprompters too often, the OCPP could compare Trump's record to Obama's on each of those metrics. It is unlikely that Trump would fare favorably on these criteria upon subsequent evaluations, just as his inadequacies on the usual "drain the swamp" criteria would be exposed. The conclusion from all of the criteria would likely have been that Trump was disingenuous, proud to be the Swamp Creature in Chief, and possibly even eager to challenge Warren Harding for the bottom rung on the ladder of presidential integrity.

Congress would be foolish not to respond to the American people's call for laws with new standards of ethics and accountability that would apply to subsequent presidents and administrations. Although Trump might veto such legislation, his doing so would still elevate the issues. It is also conceivable that the legislation could garner overwhelming support, even by veto-proof majorities, because his actions prompting the effort are so flagrant. Given what the public has witnessed throughout Trump's presidency, Congress should be willing to consider a comprehensive package of reforms that target Trump's offenses (fighting the previous battle) and offer other sensible restrictions on presidential activity (fighting the next battle).

Among the measures that Congress should consider are provisions that would:

- prohibit the president from maintaining any financial conflict of interest, and requiring divestiture prior to inauguration from any asset that an independent auditor determines has a reasonable likelihood of causing a conflict of interest;
- require any assets in a foreign-based or foreign-controlled company or other enterprise to be placed in a verified blind trust under the management of a genuinely independent and disinterested professional asset manager;
- prohibit the president from receiving even one dollar of income from a foreign government or official, regardless of the manner in which such income accrues to the president;

- prohibit the president from appointing anyone to a position as senior advisor to the president, departmental secretary, agency or bureau chief or director, or other senior level official who, in the previous ten years, had been a senior official in any entity that was regulated by the office in which they would be serving;
- prohibit any senior advisor to the president, departmental secretary, agency or bureau chief or director, or other senior level official from maintaining any financial conflict of interest, and requiring divestiture, prior to being sworn in, from any asset that an independent auditor determines has a reasonable likelihood of causing a conflict of interest;
- prohibit registered lobbyists from serving as senior advisors to the president, departmental secretaries, agency or bureau chiefs or directors, and other senior level officials (with an exemption for lobbyists who exclusively represent a 501c3 nonprofit, charitable foundation, governmental institution, and/or public interest entity);
- redefine campaign expenses so that congressional election-year mailings and other resources are characterized as campaign expenses to help level the playing field between incumbents and challengers, place a partial firewall between public resources and campaign resources, and minimize the advantage of incumbency; and
- prohibit legislators from discussing legislative issues with lobbyists who donate to their campaign. To ensure that everyone can express their opinions on issues while avoiding foul play and undue influence, Congress could create Congressional Interest Group Offices (CIGOs) for lobbyists and interest groups to share their opinions. Their views would be aggregated with those of others and given to legislators in balanced, nonpartisan analyses. CIGOs would produce briefing materials for each major issue coming up for a vote in committee or on the floor, and on other issues at the request of a legislator. Lobbyists could contact the CIGOs whenever they want to put forth facts, requests, and views. Analysts would be hired on the basis of their analytical abilities, not political ties. In addition to severing the link between lobbying, fundraising, and voting, CIGOs would ensure that members hear more than one side of an issue, which often does not happen today. Private citizens who are not lobbyists could still meet directly with their own representatives.

Stringent laws and guidelines to prevent the breach of public trust and the commission of offenses are designed to prevent problems from occurring. With rules in place, mechanisms that apply accountability and ethical standards on government officials would be relied upon to identify any violations and, more broadly, to inform the public about governmental conduct. Senator Elizabeth Warren's "Anti-Corruption and Public Integrity Act" is a laudable compilation of reforms that would go far in outlawing conflicts of interest and other abuses by lobbyists and government officials.[49]

Transparency is on the rise, due to new mechanisms and heightened expectations. It impacts the arena in which officials in government, business, and other sectors are operating. The advent of sophisticated tools and procedures has changed the privacy versus transparency balance in recent years. Although an Orwellian "Big Brother" is not constantly looking over our shoulders, new systems can be intrusive, and organizations that advance transparency can easily publish information that comes into their possession. The 2016 disclosure of the Panama Papers,[50] which publicized the previously secretive offshore investments of hundreds of billions of dollars, including those by 140 politicians worldwide, serves as a reminder that information that was thought to be closely held can become public very easily and quickly. That disclosure affected political careers and lives, and future disclosures could increasingly do the same, enhanced by new technology tools. Apparently the walls do have ears.

Donald Trump has not learned these lessons. Instead of being mindful of transparency, he focuses on the incessant leaks of documents and information from the White House and elsewhere in the Trump orbit. That is a problem of his own making. When Trump misrepresents facts or tells falsehoods, as he often does, people who know otherwise become motivated to disclose documents that demonstrate the fallacies. The truth almost always comes out, even if it takes a while. Eventually, historians gain access to documents and set the record straight.

When someone's stock in trade is misinformation, then the exposure of his falsehoods is his kryptonite. It is highly ironic that the person who begged WikiLeaks to publish someone else's emails when it would be advantageous to him is now stridently opposed to the public revelation of documents on the grounds that it is disadvantageous to him, as was the case with those referenced by Bob Woodward in *Fear*. The shoe is on the other foot, and Trump doesn't like the fit. Trump's disdain for leaks is consistent with his *modus operandi* in which he is governed by his own self-interests, rather than any consistent policy.

Trump is so hypersensitive about leaks that he directed the attorney general to initiate an investigation into the leaks that occurred early in his presidency, to identify the perpetrators. It is interesting that, after the investigation was announced, the public did not hear anything further. One has to wonder if that is because the investigation found that leaks originated from some people in the White House who are personally very close to Trump. Ronald Kessler echoed this suspicion in his 2018 book[51] in which he named Kellyanne Conway as the "number one leaker" in the White House and implied that there are other leakers in the president's inner circle.

Trump conflates the leak of classified information with the leak of information that can be influential in public policy debates, or damaging to his and other peoples' reputations. He is quite wrong about confusing the two, as a leak of classified information would be criminal, whereas a leak of the latter two types would just be embarrassing or uncomfortable. But he doesn't understand that, either out of an inability to differentiate or out of willful ignorance.

Following the *New York Times'* publication on September 5, 2018, of an anonymous op-ed from a senior official in the administration, Trump's response resembled his reaction to the earlier leaks. He declared "treason" in a tweet, and began a witch hunt among his appointees to identify the author, pressuring officials to disclaim authorship. Two days later, he called on the attorney general to conduct an investigation to find the author, and the White House floated the idea of all appointees submitting to polygraph tests. But this was appalling. The author did not commit a crime. The op-ed related to public policy and was damaging to Trump's reputation, but it did not leak or reveal any classified information. Justice Department action was unjustifiable. Subjecting appointees to polygraph tests would be a matter of Trump's personal vanity and emotional insecurity, not, as Trump claimed, national security. Trump's response again demonstrated his authoritarian, narcissistic belief that the government is his personal tool to do with as he pleases, erroneously conflating disloyalty to him with disloyalty to the country.

The leaks and the op-ed are certainly inconvenient for Trump. But, as long as they do not reveal classified information, they are useful in helping the public understand what is happening in the Trump administration, and why those things are happening. If Trump conducted himself in the way that previous presidents conducted themselves—with rationality, emotional restraint, professionalism, and integrity—then there probably wouldn't be many leaks. But because he doesn't, some people in Trump's universe are leaking information designed to keep Trump in check and protect the country. The leaks are also the result of the competitive and combative staff structure which Trump established. In that environment, leaks are a useful tool in policy battles.

It is a very good bet that documents will continue to be leaked to the media, private conversations and audio tapes will continue to become public, and compromising photographs will continue to be circulated, such as the ones of Trump with Russian officials in the White House that only came to light because the Russians released them. Leaks might also address the salacious activities in Russia that were included in the thirty-five-page dossier by British intelligence agent Christopher Steele. Revelation of other sexual improprieties—Trump's affairs with porn star Stormy Daniels and *Playboy* model Karen McDougal, and his campaign's payment of hush money to them—was yet another example of the treasure trove of information that eventually comes to light. Trump may wish that the modern day realities of transparency and accountability do not apply to him, but they do.

It is no longer possible to hide the truth under a cloak of invisibility. The facts will come out eventually. When they do, and Trump is looking for someone to blame for the leaks, rather than pointing fingers at all those surrounding him, he'd be better off buying a mirror, since the conditions that he created and maintains are the impetus for others to do what they feel they must.

CHAPTER 7

GLOBAL ECONOMY

THE EVOLVING CONCERNS OVER
TRADE AND GLOBALIZATION

D ebates over trade and globalization used to revolve around export imbalances, manufacturing sectors, trade barriers, and national economic growth. The focus has since widened as scrutiny shifted to labor standards, low wages, unsafe worksites, toxic air emissions, GMOs (genetically modified or engineered foods), waste generation, and other environmental and health impacts. Demonstrations and protests at the sites of World Trade Organization negotiations have become common, placing greater attention on the human costs of trade and globalization. These emerging issues have highlighted conditions in less developed economies that benefited from expanded trade relationships. Concerns have heightened about the flow of jobs outward from the United States and other developed countries, which have more worker and environmental protections, to less developed countries that have fewer protections.

Donald Trump tapped into this popular concern, stoked discord, and successfully rode the issue. It helped that a leading candidate in the Democratic primaries, Bernie Sanders, was also antagonistic toward trade, although his views were infused with concerns about global workers being oppressed while companies and owners profiteered. Trump's comments about trade and globalization went beyond policy, casting them as cultural issues. His language was often inflammatory and even spiteful. Trump demonized our trade partners, especially China, happily allowing xenophobia to energize his supporters. While the issues were worthy of debate, Trump's rhetoric conflicted with a sober conversation on the issues. Trade and globalization became punching bags, garnering animosity that ignored their important role in our domestic economy, and the realities of the global economy. Trump fanned the flames through his "America First" chant, together with his plan to cancel and renegotiate our trade agreements.

But doing that poses risks, since trade and globalization are, and will remain, important driving forces in our economy. Although Trump leveraged these issues for his electoral advantage, these concerns must be tempered so that our country can continue to harness trade and globalization to our advantage.

TRADE AND GLOBALIZATION IN THE 2016 CAMPAIGN

During the 2016 election, international trade became a major issue. Trump and Sanders placed it atop the agenda in their respective contests during the primaries. For Sanders, trade was central to his message, as it has been for decades, because it is closely linked with his mantra of economic egalitarianism that opposes policies benefiting millionaires and billionaires. In Trump's case, it was central to his appeal to blue-collar and working-class voters who lost jobs due to economic expansion in other countries. Trump used trade issues as a means to tap into resentment among voters who blamed foreigners for their economic challenges and were susceptible to a xenophobic message. Despite Trump's harsh tone, there was a rational basis for his position on trade. Most notably, China had been stealing American intellectual property and imposing unequal rules of engagement for many years, which the United States did not adequately counter due to the geopolitical and broader economic impacts of doing so. If Trump's rhetoric had led to sensible, thoughtful trade policy reforms, that may have been justifiable.

Trump also made these issues a central campaign theme because they were among the few about which he had firsthand knowledge. Of all the issues in the federal government's purview trade (in addition to taxes) was one with which Trump had actual experience by virtue of his international business transactions. Trump knew about trade, at least from the perspective of manufacturing ties and hats, as well as licensing rights for hotels and golf courses. Although his knowledge likely did not extend to the topics on the agenda of the US Trade Representatives, the World Trade Organization, the US-China Joint Commission on Commerce and Trade, the Export-Import Bank, and the International Monetary Fund, he was probably familiar with international lending and borrowing, currency fluctuations, royalty payments, and other subjects that had affected his businesses.

It is doubtful that trade would have been such a prominent issue if Trump and Sanders had not made it part of their daily messages. Prior to the primaries, the people who became energized by trade issues probably were not focused on them as the source of their predicament. Trade became a conduit to employment issues, triggering responses from those who felt economically disadvantaged or politically abandoned. Trump also capitalized on the nexus between the antitrade and anti-immigrant views of his base voters, who have a xenophobic predilection that makes it convenient to blame "the Other" for social ills, as is common among individualists who demonize those who impair their pursuits. For millions of voters, trade became the amorphous incarnation of all that was wrong with the economy, the distribution of wealth, and the lack of economic opportunity.

If Trump's campaign rhetoric embodied trade as the *Titanic*, then globalization was the iceberg. Trade was recognized, to some extent, as presenting both challenges and opportunities. But, according to Trump, there were no two sides to globalization. He excoriated globalization, presenting it as the problem, as if it produced only negative consequences.[1] He condemned it as something that had to be stopped, yet never defined "globalization" or explained what he meant by it. Doing so might have spoiled a useful rallying cry. Instead, globalization was treated as an elusive, rabid, all-encompassing virus that infected our economy and was metastasizing uncontrollably.

Maybe Trump's failure to explain what he meant was because antiglobalization had been his mantra for so long—since the late 1980s, when he joined others in assailing Japan[2] for flooding our markets with low-cost electronics—that he forgot the original impetus for his stance. Maybe Trump didn't explain globalization because he didn't know why Steve Bannon, whose mantra is nationalism and protectionism, told him to oppose it. Maybe Trump didn't explain it because his resentment was personal, rooted in his irritation with past foreign deals that didn't go his way even as globalization was on the rise.

Regardless of the reason for Trump's ambiguity, globalization served as an effective scapegoat for many of the economic ills afflicting Americans who still lived amidst the rubble of the 2008 Great Recession. That may have been good politics, but it wasn't good economics. Trump's harsh characterization of globalization was opportunistic and strategic, but it wasn't realistic, pragmatic, or true.

GLOBALIZATION'S BENEFICIAL IMPACT
ON THE US ECONOMY

Globalization has been one of the principal sources of America's wealth and prosperity throughout our history, going back to Alexander Hamilton's open trade policies to support domestic manufacturing.[3] While it has benefited America's wealthiest classes and big businesses that engage in global commerce, it has also benefited working-class Americans whose jobs depend on global markets and the flow of information within them. In a climate of economic interconnectedness, the United States predominates and is one of the biggest winners. American workers benefit through transnational outsourcing of goods and services contracts from companies based elsewhere to companies based in the United States. If Trump's America First policies were to prevail, globalization would be curtailed, revenues from contracts outsourced by foreign businesses to US companies would decrease, American workers' jobs and wages would be put at risk, and US companies would be vulnerable.[4]

In a globalized economy, many American jobs may require greater skill sets than they did a generation ago. But that's nothing new. When Henry Ford began building cars, there were probably complaints from blacksmiths who were asked to adapt from handling horses to handling machines. There were probably similar concerns among workers who were asked to build new-fangled jet engines in the 1950s, microwave ovens in the 1960s, transistors in the 1970s, and computers in the 1980s. The American economy always innovates, globalization increases the opportunity for innovation and the rewards for it, and increased trade translates to net job gains for Americans. To continue our heritage of innovation and economic leadership, we should make reforms, such as:

- high school curricula must be modernized to closely link education with jobs in today's economy;
- job skills training must be made available to people already in the workforce;
- access to capital must be expanded for prospective entrepreneurs;
- solutions must be prioritized for struggling localities, to narrow the income and wealth gaps between those who face entrenched obstacles and those who are thriving;

- policies must be crafted to foster the Maker Movement, which cultivates young innovators; and
- immigration policy must be modernized to attract people with skills and encourage foreigners who attend our colleges to remain and work in the United States.

Much attention has been placed on American manufacturing jobs lost to companies with lower operating costs in less developed countries, where wages and benefits are lower. Yet this is only part of the picture. A central element of a globalized marketplace is that it enables each region, country, and locality to focus on the goods and services that they can provide most efficiently and economically, to harness their own competitive advantages. It acknowledges that each country has a need, and a right, to stimulate their own domestic job growth through the development of locally based businesses. Countries are well advised to anticipate and address global demand for goods and services that are within their capacity to provide. Protectionist measures should not disrupt that by creating hurdles for a country's locally based companies to provide services to companies from other countries (outsourcing).

Outsourcing is distinct from the problematic practice of international offshoring, where a US-based company operates facilities in another country and diverts jobs to that site to lower operating costs. Offshoring is a greater threat to American jobs than outsourcing, and a more solvable problem since it is conducted by US companies that are subject to US law. Ironically, an America First policy would not affect offshoring. US companies that engage in offshoring could argue that they are, in fact, putting America First by lowering their operating costs internationally to increase their profits, even though they are doing that at the expense of American workers. This highlights the fact that America First might benefit some American companies, but not American workers.

While the concentration of some job functions has shifted to other countries, other job functions have flourished here, with commensurate job creation. America's greatest competitive advantages are our human capital, creativity, and structures that nurture innovation. Ultimately, the countries that can innovate best will prosper the most and thus control the job creation process. Between our educational institutions, intellectual property laws, access to capital, collaborative networks, entrepreneurial culture, and innovation ethos, we are ideally poised to leverage our advantages for prosperity and growth in the global economy. In essence, rather than ask for jobs, we can create them.

Around the world, globalization has opened markets for the sale of American goods and services. It has made the world receptive to American societal norms and standards, in addition to American products and preferences. It has opened minds to American ways of doing business, and even to democratic political systems. It has facilitated the free flow of information and knowledge from the United States to countries that have applied it to improve their sanitation systems, food production, public health, and resource conservation. It has facilitated the free flow of information and knowledge from other countries to the United States, where we have applied it to improve our systems and products, like medical research and products, alternative energy production, and environmental sustainability.

Globalization has showcased our capitalist economy, which has inspired countries such as Vietnam, Myanmar, Malaysia, and even the Peoples' Republic of China to emulate it and try to replicate it, albeit with their own adaptations. Globalization has incentivized the development of information technology experts and industries in countries such as India, Pakistan, Bulgaria, and Romania, each with their own focused areas of specialization in IT subsectors. It has inspired the establishment of policies and structures that encourage entrepreneurship in countries such as Kenya, South Africa, South Korea, and Taiwan.

POTENTIAL DAMAGE OF AMERICA FIRST TO THE AMERICAN ECONOMY

All of these and other benefits of enhanced trade, economic relations, and globalization are jeopardized by Trump's America First stance. By retracting from transnational business alliances and international trade agreements, the United States is gradually sacrificing its long-standing global leadership role in economic and business affairs. By disparaging globalism and multilateral action—which, according to Trump, restrain our sovereignty—while promoting unilateralism and nationalism (as he did at the UN General Assembly in 2018), Trump gives permission to autocrats and human rights abusers to do as they please. Our influence in international organizations, including those that set the rules for trade and business, has begun to diminish, hurting our economy. Our companies may be forced to forego international business opportunities and the profits and stock market returns that they generate. Our workers may no longer be widely welcomed. Our president may no longer be able to count on other countries' responsiveness to requests on economic matters. Consumer prices may escalate, and product choices may decline.

America First not only signifies that America is in decline, it also hastens the decline. Trump's failure to engage and lead on global matters, combined with his characteristic irascibility and unreliability with other world leaders, has diminished our standing as the leading voice on worldwide political, geopolitical, and security affairs. At the June 2018 G7 (Group of 7) meeting in Québec, Trump impaired relations with our closest allies by hurling nasty epithets at—incredibly—the prime minister of Canada, our neighbor and closest ally, and home to the nicest people on the planet. At the July 2018 NATO meeting and the next day in the UK, Trump further damaged our alliances by criticizing the leadership of Angela Merkel and Theresa May, moving the goalposts by calling for NATO members to spend 4 percent of their GDP on defense (beyond the policy of 2 percent that only three countries reached and others were working toward), and raising doubt about whether the United States would abide by Article 5 to come to the aid of Montenegro.[5] A few days later, at his summit with Putin in Helsinki, Trump's actions sharply conflicted with his America First mantra by undermining US policy and interests in favor of Russia's (e.g., validating Putin's denial of Russian interference in our elections, honoring Putin's outrageous proposal for Russians to question American officials and citizens, and criticizing the FBI and the US, saying, "I think the United States has been foolish").

America First has already caused the United States to forego leadership in a burgeoning economic zone by the US withdrawal from the Trans-Pacific Partnership, which also relinquishes our strategic geopolitical leadership in the region. America First has already resulted in a deliberate, self-inflicted depreciation of our global standing by the US withdrawal from the Paris Agreement. America First has already caused our allies to question our fidelity to the international order by Trump disparaging NATO and withdrawing from the United Nations Human Rights Council. America First could result in voluntarily ceding our economic advantages and facilitating the decline of the American-led era, by Trump engaging in a full-blown trade and tariff war. Concern over Trump's approach was aptly expressed by Donald Tusk, the president of the European Council (and leader of the European Union) who lamented, "The rules-based international order is being challenged, quite surprisingly, not by the usual suspects, but by its main architect and guarantor: the US."[6]

Contrary to the prideful, self-enamored nature of the slogan, America First has the opposite result, sliding us down the scale of relevance among players on the world stage. Russia, China, and other geopolitical forces probably sharpen their forks and knives every time that Trump utters those words, as they are ready to fill each vacuum created by an American retreat from leadership.[7] That has been Vladimir Putin's long-term objective, which benefited immeasurably from Trump's own words and his deference to Putin at their Helsinki meeting. Strategic adversaries such as North Korea, Syria, and Iran must be delighted at the prospect of being able to act against our interests with impunity, knowing that we would no longer be able to count on solid support from our longtime allies when disputes arise.

Americans have begun to realize that US preeminence in world affairs is not preordained, inevitable, or immutable. There is a growing national self-awareness of America's coveted status in global economics, geopolitics, security, international organizations, and socio-cultural affairs. As we relinquish our across-the-board global leadership, we will increasingly become just one of many players, even if we remain an economic leader in some industries. While it may be theoretically desirable to empower other countries, encourage shared responsibility, and promote partnerships without the United States dominating international interactions, that comes at a price. It is likely that, in the long run, most Americans would regret the reduced influence, power, and importance on the world stage that an America First policy would impose upon us. It begs the question: can we live with that?

Ironically, America First would produce two categories of economic winners, neither of which includes us. One would be the next largest global economies, which would compete among themselves to ascend into our traditional leadership role. The other category of winners would be the world's less developed economies, which would suddenly have more opportunities for which to compete without being constrained by our stringent labor, human rights, and environmental standards. Workers and marginalized populations in those countries might benefit more from these new opportunities than they ever could have benefited from any aid package or international development program. Although the business and financial elites in those countries do well under any circumstances, a diminished American presence would increase the prospects of lucrative employment for the masses that need jobs and job skill training. Our disengagement would bolster their pathways to prosperity and a higher quality of life. If Trump's real objective were to establish a beneficent international development strategy that assists less developed economies, it would have been nice if he had just said so.

The tool that Trump embraced in March 2018 to advance America First—his tariffs on imported steel (25 percent) and aluminum (10 percent)— will not produce a win for the United States. At best, the tariffs could only benefit the small number of US companies and workers that produce those materials.[8] Steel and aluminum production in the United States has diminished to a very small percent of what it used to be. Even in Pittsburgh, the "Steel City," the economy already transitioned in recent decades to high-tech industries and the arts. Imposition of a tariff to protect such a small slice of our economy has been denounced by the overwhelming majority of reputable economists.[9] Tariffs have a terrible track record, as they open a veritable Pandora's Box of economic woes.[10] Ironically, the tariffs that were intended to help American steel and aluminum producers could hurt them,[11] and there is no indication that the tariffs would enable the creation of new American steel or aluminum production companies.

Tariffs and other protectionist policies impose many consequences, calling into question the wisdom of this policy shift. First, the number of US companies that use steel and aluminum is far greater than the number of US companies that produce these materials.[12] US manufacturers will face increased costs, especially for specialized steel and aluminum that are available only from certain foreign suppliers.[13] These costs will be passed through to consumers, which may cause increases in inflation and/or the cost of living, and diminish sales, which would further impair manufacturers. Workers at these manufacturers may also be negatively impacted in terms of layoffs,[14] wages, benefits, and reductions in new hires.[15]

Second, other countries are responding with countermeasures that include retaliatory tariffs.[16] After Trump's announcement, the European Union and some of its member countries released plans to impose tariffs on Kentucky bourbon, Harley Davidson motorcycles, and Levi's jeans, followed by certain shirts and footwear, US steel, rice, and orange juice.[17] Trump responded by threatening a 25 percent tariff on European cars, making it likely that countries in the EU and elsewhere will apply tariffs to more US products. Then, the federal investigation into trade infringements on intellectual property (via Section 301 of the 1974 Trade Act) led to Trump's announcement of tariffs on Chinese goods, focusing on its technology sector. China responded with tariff plans for US products and agriculture, especially from "red states" that heavily favor Trump,[18] which led Trump to threaten more tariffs against China. As the salvos continue to spiral,[19] with more tariffs on more goods in more sectors, a full-blown tariff and trade war becomes more likely, with harsh impacts and no winners.[20] Even if Trump retreats from his threats of tariffs, the onset of protectionist rhetoric and policies triggered a dynamic that will not be easily reversed, as other countries are compelled to protect their interests.

Third, for a great many US manufacturers, a global multilateral imposition of tariffs would depress sales, revenues, and manufacturing.[21] Tariff costs would be passed on to end-users, causing consumer prices, layoffs, and inflation to rise.[22] These impacts would result in declines in our country's GDP, global economic growth, and both consumer and investor sentiment.[23] Decreased manufacturing and exports would increase America's global trade deficit and significantly decrease federal tax revenues. Ultimately, these effects could create a recession. If this economic environment were protracted or deep, the viability of some industries could be at risk. In the vernacular of macro-economists, imposing tariffs and starting a trade war is a really dumb idea.

Fourth, after Trump threatened not to make any exceptions to his tariffs, he reversed course, exempting Mexico and Canada,[24] along with temporary exemptions for other countries,[25] stating that it was for national security reasons. That minimizes the protectionist benefit to US steel and aluminum producers to such an extent that it illuminates the folly of imposing the tariffs at all.[26] By providing the loophole of national security, which is highly subjective and able to be asserted for virtually any country, the political nature of the tariffs became obvious.[27] Trump's approach is neither sufficiently protective of US producers nor sufficiently aimed at global overproducers to address the oversupply problem that he asserted. Ridiculously, Trump later imposed tariffs against Canada, supposedly for national security reasons, but really just to be punitive, out of personal pique against Prime Minister Justin Trudeau. Neither Trump's tariffs, nor his exceptions to them, make any economic or geopolitical sense.

So, since the imposition of tariffs is bad policy, and there is no wisdom to igniting a trade war, why did Trump do it? Why did he rush the process when his main economic advisors were hotly debating the issue and even they didn't know that he would be announcing the tariffs so quickly? It seems that there are a number of reasons.

First, while vilifying trade during the 2016 campaign, Trump told his base that he would enact protectionist policies. By announcing tariffs, he was simply trying to deliver on a promise, regardless of the economics, wisdom, and consequences of doing so. His agitation against trade began decades ago when Japan was "dumping" oversupplies of low-cost electronics. But Toshiba and Sony televisions are different from steel, aluminum, and the other targets of Trump's tariffs. Global economics have evolved since then, as has the role of US manufacturing in the global economy. Trump's decision to apply tariffs was political, to galvanize his supporters, rather than based on sound economics.

Second, Trump might have announced the tariffs just to improve his bargaining position for negotiations on bilateral trade agreements. It is possible that he never intended to actually impose the tariffs and didn't anticipate strong retaliatory actions from European countries and China. However, if Trump's plan had been to simply float the idea of tariffs to increase his negotiating leverage, it had to be done with temperance, discretion, and a sober tone to avoid reprisals from other countries. By announcing tariffs in a jingoistic, saber-rattling context, Trump sent a message of "game on." Even if it was intended as a ploy, once he announced his plan to impose tariffs, other countries took it seriously and responded in kind, setting the spiral in motion. Trump lost control of the process, discovering that a tariff or trade battle is easy to start but very difficult to stop. While Trump was able to unilaterally launch a tariff battle, the cessation of tariffs in multiple directions depends on a broad range of global actors and economic conditions.

Third, Trump rushed to announce the tariffs because he was scrambling to control the news cycle and distract the media from news that was damaging to him. Just prior to the tariffs being announced, the news of the day led with Special Counsel Mueller's intensified scrutiny of Jared Kushner, speculation about National Security Advisor H. R. McMaster being replaced, and Trump's reversal on gun control measures, which made Trump vulnerable to a sharp reaction from his base voters. These stories were politically injurious to Trump and likely motivated him to distract the media's attention. Trump might also have gotten word that the story about Stormy Daniels was on the way, giving him another reason to shore up his support among his base.

Fourth, the hasty announcement of tariffs might have resulted from Trump being rattled. The resignation of Hope Hicks the day before may have had the greatest impact. Earlier that week, she spent nine hours testifying to a congressional committee, and Trump may have been very worried about consequences from that. Hicks was known as a calming influence on Trump, with a unique ability to tamp down Trump's emotions. Losing her may have caused him emotional turbulence, leading to the impulsive and impetuous announcement of tariffs, even though the decision was premature. Although Trump was flailing, he surely knew that the tariff announcement would redirect media attention to the tariffs and away from Hicks and other sensitive topics.

Fifth, it has been widely reported that Trump's opinions are malleable, and that his decisions are often influenced by the opinions of the person who spoke to him last. On March 1, 2018, he had a meeting with his economic advisors at which they aired conflicting views, and the meeting concluded with the impression that Trump was going to postpone his decision. Soon after, he met with fifteen corporate executives from the steel and aluminum industries. It was during that meeting when he abruptly and unexpectedly announced the tariffs. Apparently he liked what he heard, or maybe he just liked the people who spoke.

Trump may have initiated and escalated the imposition of tariffs in 2018 with an eye toward his 2020 reelection. He may have gambled that there would be enough time for tariff wars to be resolved, and the economic pain that they cause to be abated, prior to 2020, when he would need a strong economy to bolster his campaign. He may reach an agreement with China that enables both sides to ratchet down the tension. He may agree not to increase tariffs from 10 to 25 percent, avoiding China's retaliation. But whatever the motive and the outcome, it is clear that Trump's decisions to both impose and limit tariffs, both instigate and then deescalate a trade war, were made to advance his own interests. He initiated the tariff and trade debacle for his personal political benefit (to fulfill a promise to his base and splash himself with the patina of a powerful leader). Once he needed trade combat to stop, he reversed direction, accommodated China, and did what he could to call off the tariff war (to curry favor with his base as Mueller's investigation intensified and neared its conclusion). The impacts of tariffs on American workers and consumers were mere afterthoughts.

Tariffs are risky bets, and there is no assurance that everything will work out as Trump hopes. Even if tariffs are abated with China and some other countries, that doesn't mean that all countries will reverse the process. The economic hardships that tariffs create are being felt in family finances across the country and are likely to get worse before they get better. If Trump were trying to level the international economic playing field, there were less drastic ways of doing so that would not have caused so much uncertainty, distress, rising costs, and loss of income. Trump had the power to start a tariff war, but he doesn't have the power to stop it.

IMPORTANCE DURING TRUMP'S TENURE AND THE POST-TRUMP ERA

Trade and globalization received such an elevated level of attention during the 2016 campaign that they became hot-button emotional issues. Skepticism about the global economy reached an outsized level and was inconsistent with our national inclination toward multilateral collaboration and international partnership. America First began as a rallying cry that signified the flexing of American economic muscle. But it puts us at risk of unilateralism and economic isolationism, which jeopardize our economic supremacy.

The politically fascinating aspect of Trump's proposed America First stance is that it would adversely impact the base voters who were most attracted to it. America First aimed to send a signal to aggrieved workers that their interests will be given priority over those of the global economy. The patriotic appeal of that slogan, combined with Trump's supporters' willingness to follow his lead and suspend critical reasoning, led them to embrace it. It had the sound of something that they should support, so they did. However, it may have been the product of Trump's desire to reverse policies that were disadvantageous to his own business interests. He wanted to win against US policies that caused him to feel victimized. Putting our country on the path of economic isolationism for the sake of chasing his personal demons will have the exact opposite result: hurting America's economy while benefiting the rest of the world.

What will happen when Trump's base truly understands the implications of America First? How will they react when America First costs them their jobs? Will they continue to support that slogan right up to the point they feel its economic fangs? Or will Trump's base gain clear vision into America First's impact on the next generation of our economy and forestall it from being fully implemented?

If Trump's supporters don't recognize the dangers of America First until it is institutionalized and hits them in the face, then it could get ugly. It might be one of the cleavers that ruptures their relationship with Trump and causes a massive backlash against him. If America First results in negative economic consequences for these voters, then the disenfranchisement, disillusionment, and anger that they expressed in the 2016 election might be just the tip of the iceberg compared to their reaction in 2020 and the post-Trump era. It seems likely that Trump was trying to insulate himself from a backlash when he departed from precedent in July 2018 by criticizing the Fed's interest rate hikes.[28] By saying, "I don't like all of this work that we're putting into the economy and then I see rates going up," Trump was signaling that he wants interest rates—not his tariffs—to get the blame if the economy suffers, even though his tariffs are the obvious catalyst of adversity. This appears to be especially important to him because of the disproportionately harsh impact that foreign tariffs are having on red states.

Trump's base may also become disenchanted with his America First rallying cry for a wholly unexpected reason. On May 13, 2018, Trump violated his own America First stance by tweeting, "President Xi of China, and I, are working together to give massive Chinese phone company, ZTE, a way to get back into business, fast. Too many jobs in China lost. Commerce Department has been instructed to get it done!" Despite promising to protect American jobs and combat China's trade practices, Trump switched, helping China's trade practices and protecting jobs . . . in China![29] It was diametrically opposed to what Trump said he would do, putting a spotlight on his transactional approach and his total lack of policy principles. The same week, it became apparent that Trump's decision to help ZTE was at least partly motivated by self-interest, as we learned that China's leader had directed a $500 million investment in an Indonesian infrastructure project that benefits a Trump property at the site.[30] ZTE had violated sanctions against Iran and North Korea, and ZTE's technology was cited for national security risks. Trump cast those concerns aside, as they apparently mattered less to him than China's investment in Indonesia.[31] The appearance of a conflict of interest was obvious. America First was reduced to nothing more than a slogan of convenience toward which Trump felt no allegiance, despite promising his base otherwise. This, too, may prove to be a test of his base's loyalty to him and to his protectionist rhetoric.

Trade and globalization issues generated so much antagonism in 2016 that the political pendulum on the issue may be poised to swing back in the near future, especially if Americans suffer from price hikes on imported consumer goods and are resentful of Trump violating his own mantra. It would not be the first time that the pendulum swung abruptly on the choice between globalism and isolationism. In November 1936, when the Gallup Poll (then the American Institute of Public Opinion) asked, "If another world war develops in Europe, should America take part again?" 95 percent said "no." But only four years and two months later, in January 1941 (before Lend-Lease, the Atlantic Charter, and Pearl Harbor), when the poll asked, "Should we . . . aid Britain even at the risk of war?" 68 percent said "yes."

Today's opinions on America First isolationism may be similarly fluid. When faced with the negative impacts of America First, most Americans are likely to reconnect with the value of the global economy and the US-based jobs that it enables. Political campaigns are likely to move on to other issues, deflating the volatility of the debate over globalization. Trade talks will probably revert to the domain of economists and currency watchers, as well as a few handfuls of ardent advocates, anti-GMO crusaders, and xenophobes. If trade and globalization return to the good graces of Americans, trade negotiations will command as much of our national attention as the World Badminton Championship match.

Trump's implementation of America First suffers from near-sighted vision into our country's role in the global economy. During the campaign and as president, Trump has continually assaulted our trade agreements as bad deals, claiming that he would negotiate much better deals. However, in his first two years in office, he didn't show any remarkable ability to improve trade relations or negotiate deals. Despite his stated intentions to negotiate a better NAFTA deal, he could only handle bilateral negotiations with Mexico, which he intensified in September 2018 to avoid more difficult negotiations with Mexico's incoming president. The revisions that were made amounted to a handful of fine-tuning adjustments that had been on the agenda for a while, rather than a comprehensive restructuring of the agreement. Trump got Canada to join the agreement afterward without accommodating many of their needs, which created doubts about the agreement being a sustainable, beneficial trade regime. He was more effusive about changing the name of the agreement than the substance of the new version. The tariff war that Trump initiated was an even less impressive display of his self-professed deal-making ability. Trump's regressive global tariffs continue to impair trade and ripple through global financial markets, helping only a narrow group of companies and workers while harming many more, and triggering retaliatory measures from many countries. The net result is that his tariffs are hurting the US economy.

Trump's trade efforts in his first two years were tantamount to doing business development for specific US corporations. During each visit to another country, he tried to make a sale of goods for one company or another, as if he were their VP of Sales. One notable example was when he lobbied Saudi Arabia's leaders in 2017 to purchase Boeing airplanes. That's nice, and it helped Boeing. But that is not a broad scale trade agreement that will boost American companies or industries over a sustained period of time. Plus, it diminishes the presidency, as other countries see him as just a traveling salesman. Maybe Tupperware and vacuum cleaners will be next.

Even when he spoke at the World Economic Forum in Davos, Switzerland, he was feckless. Rather than articulating a vision for global relations or espousing high-minded American principles, he presented global financial and business leaders with a simple sales pitch. Our national business development manager diminutively said, "America is open for business. . . . Now is the perfect time to bring your business, your jobs, and your investments to the United States." By crassly asking them to help us make money, he shrunk the stature of American business to that of a startup company that obsequiously contorts itself when requesting funding from venture capital investors.

Ironically, Trump's message at Davos conflicts with his America First mantra. By aggressively seeking their investment into our businesses, he invited financiers in other countries to own institutions and enterprises on which our economy is dependent. Rather than prioritizing America first, he welcomed their ownership, which would also give them control over decisions that affect millions of Americans, putting us at their mercy. In effect, by coaxing foreign investment to flow into in the United States, Trump was endorsing globalization, even though he putatively opposes it. Globalization has become an extension of his self-serving personality: he wants what he wants, when he wants it. His Davos pitch for international capital is a stark contrast to the harsh words he had for Palestinians a day or two earlier, when he said that the Palestinians were going to be denied US funding because they didn't support Trump's premature decision to move the American embassy to Jerusalem. The common thread between these two opposite edicts is that what Trump wants defines both.

When our country restores its visionary grasp of globalization and trade in the post-Trump era, we will benefit from multilateral trade pacts, improved trade relations, and long-term expansive trade strategies. These strategies should bolster our manufacturing, agriculture, and technology sectors, as well as support services industries in which we can establish or grow our competitive advantage. We could achieve this with a series of industry-wide initiatives pursued through a thoughtful methodology that:

- identifies industries with long-term high-growth potential that will be the focus of an initiative;
- engages multiple manufacturers that have relevant expertise and capabilities;
- engages family farms and large-scale agriculture interests that use advanced methods and IT tools;
- promotes US companies' intellectual property and expedites patent protection where appropriate;
- accesses venture capital, Export-Import Bank resources, and other funding sources, if needed;
- coordinates location and facility siting with local governments, along with zoning variances;
- provides telecom (high-speed broadband), transportation, and other infrastructure where needed;
- leverages the fulfillment, transport, and delivery infrastructure of companies and local governments;
- coordinates all of the stakeholders through a public-private partnership with federal leadership; and
- provides federal government support (e.g., enterprise zones, antitrust waivers, research, job skills training, technology transfer licensing, data sets, visas, expedited regulatory review, tax incentives) and advocacy on key trade issues (e.g., by the US Trade Representative, Commerce Department, and National Science Foundation working with the World Trade Organization to revise its rules, etc.).

An array of companies would benefit from participation in these joint initiatives by coordinating activities that are within their areas of proficiency. Companies would be welcomed to provide their expertise on product design and development, market research, manufacturing of component parts, assembly, marketing and communications, fulfillment, delivery, customer service, product servicing, etc. Additional elements could be brought into the picture to ensure each initiative's success and broaden the economic benefits to multiple companies and regions of the United States.

Trade is much more than just running around the world trying to sell a widget here and a gadget there. A coordinated, comprehensive, integrated approach would leverage our unparalleled capacity for innovation and production in the global economy and ensure the long-term growth and worldwide leadership of America's best-in-class manufacturing and services industries.

CHAPTER 8

FEDERALISM

THE TENSION BETWEEN FEDERAL AND STATE AUTHORITY

Since America's earliest days, the apportionment of power between the federal government and the states has been a dominant and recurring issue. It was among the major issues that led to the demise of the Articles of Confederation in the 1780s, and it was hotly contested during the development of our Constitution, as is well documented in the Federalist Papers. Since then, many legislative struggles and legal challenges have been impacted by the continuing debate over whether power should be concentrated in the centralized national government or dispersed to the state governments.

As a result of the 2016 election, this debate has surged forth again with extraordinary prominence and a new dynamic. Policies and actions by Trump and his administration have put this struggle front and center on the contemporary agenda, with broad implications for the balance of power. The federal and state roles that emerge will affect Americans for many years to come.

Very notably, the purposes for which the Trump administration has asserted federal authority has led many people across the ideological spectrum to abandon their long-held positions on the roles of federal and state government and instead support the position that they previously opposed. Many government officials have set aside their principle-based view of the apportionment of power in deference to policy outcomes on specific issues. In essence, many leaders have switched sides on the debate over the roles of state and federal government in order to win battles over important policies. Voters who are disillusioned by their elected leaders being unduly opportunistic at the expense of fundamental principles have one more reason to be dismayed.

TRADITIONAL FEDERAL AND STATE ROLES

Although it may seem antiquated, the legacy of the debate between the Federalists and the Anti-Federalists in the 1780s has never left us. Originally, the debate went to the heart of whether our country would be a loose affiliation of states bound together principally for international relations and defense or a cohesive union with a national identity that coordinates collective action on policy objectives.[1] It was a question of whether the state governments or the national government would predominate.

The Federalists believed that a strong national government would be more effective in stimulating economic growth and leveraging the consolidated power of the states to establish economic policy and other standards.[2] The Constitution (principally written by James Madison) embodied the notion of a predominant federal government.[3] For example, the Constitution's Interstate Commerce Clause gave broad latitude to the federal government to assert its jurisdiction whenever it determined that an issue impacts interstate commerce, which has been interpreted very expansively.[4] While concentrating power in a centralized government for many purposes, Federalists sought to limit the national government's power by preserving state authority on certain other matters, institutionalizing the separation of powers between the three coequal branches of government, and establishing a system of checks and balances.

The Anti-Federalists believed that the states were capable of functioning as the principal authorities and that a centralized national government would be too large and unwieldy and could be usurped and lead to tyranny.[5] They opposed the Federalists' proposals for authority to impose tariffs and establish a national banking system, as they felt that such structures could abridge the ability of states to respond to their own local priorities. The Bill of Rights emanated principally from the concerns of Anti-Federalists, who sought to ensure that a strong central government could not abridge certain fundamental rights.[6]

The Federalists were initially not in favor of creating a Bill of Rights because they felt that the enumeration of some rights might be misinterpreted to exclude other rights that were not explicitly stated. One of the ten amendments in the Bill of Rights directly addressed the key issue of the dividing line between federal and state authority. The Tenth Amendment states, "The powers not delegated to the United States by the Constitution, nor prohibited by it to the States, are reserved to the States respectively, or to the people."[7] As the articulation of the principle of states' rights, it is widely considered to be highly relevant in today's political, governmental, and legal landscapes. The Tenth Amendment and the Commerce Clause together offer bipolar guidance on questions of federal and state jurisdiction.

(These brief summations of the Federalists' and Anti-Federalists' orientations does a disservice to the extensive theories preserved in the writings of James Madison, Alexander Hamilton, and John Jay in the Federalist Papers, as well as those of George Clinton, Patrick Henry, Robert Yates, and others in the Anti-Federalist Papers. The attenuated characterizations of the two sides of the debate are offered merely as a reference point back to our nation's origins, from which some of today's issues extend.)

The continuing relevance of this debate was recently featured in popular culture. The philosophies of both sides were showcased in a contemporary context by the play *Hamilton*, which has had tremendous box office success. Lin-Manuel Miranda gave the country a wonderful gift by reawakening the history of these issues, presenting them in a form with popular appeal, and introducing them to another few generations of voters. *Hamilton* made the point that many divisive issues in today's America are echoes from our roots in the 1700s.

In the 1790s, the Federalists, an informal ideological group during the development of the Constitution, evolved into the Federalist Party, and the Anti-Federalists evolved into the Democratic-Republican Party (probably realizing that a political party named "Anti-"anything would not be starting off on a positive note). They continued to represent their respective sides on the debate between a strong national government and states' rights.

Over the years and centuries, our governmental structure, based on a centralized federal government, has proven to be immensely beneficial. The prescience and wisdom of our Founding Fathers provided us with a mechanism to set national standards that serve all Americans regardless of where they reside. The federal government's role has been especially vital in protecting lives and livelihoods, preserving rights, preventing harm, improving safety, and assuring responsible commercial conduct, among other things.[8]

In contrast, historically, the states' rights rationale was often used by those who were trying to shield their state or localities from federal laws that imposed higher standards of conduct or accountability. The nullification crisis[9] of the 1830s—in which South Carolina and other states asserted that they could decide which federal laws would apply within their jurisdictions and which laws they would nullify—was the quintessence of states' rights. Federal laws, regulations, and enforcement have provided basic protections that state governments often were not willing to confer.

The protection of civil rights highlights the importance of action by the federal government, first by its failure to act, and then through (eventual) decisive action. Prior to the Civil War, the federal government failed to take meaningful action on what today we call civil rights. In the few instances where the government did something, its gestures ranged from paltry to pathetic. Although the landmark Thirteenth, Fourteenth, and Fifteenth Amendments to the Constitution were established between 1865 and 1870, Congress did not effectuate them or otherwise protect civil rights. What little it did was incidental.

In the early-1900s, the federal government did not protect civil rights. That era was typified by the 1906 Brownsville Affair, in which African American soldiers were framed for the killing of a white man. During World War I, black soldiers were mainly relegated to menial tasks. When France welcomed African Americans into their fighting ranks, Colonel Linard of the American Expeditionary Force (under General John J. Pershing) issued a deplorably racist warning to the French that included degrading instructions that sought to perpetuate the adverse treatment of black soldiers.[10] From the early 1900s through the 1940s, when African Americans were being lynched with appalling frequency,[11] Congress unconscionably and inexcusably failed to pass a law prohibiting lynching.[12] It was not until 2005 that Congress acted, at which point it passed a bill apologizing for its failure to pass an antilynching law for over a century.[13] Efforts to make lynching a federal hate crime are now, finally, moving forward, as the Justice for Victims of Lynching Act passed the Senate in February 2019 and is slated for action in the House.[14]

In the late 1940s, President Truman's desegregation of the military and nascent enforcement efforts were the first major steps in the federal government's evolution toward being proactive on civil rights. In the 1950s, the Supreme Court took incremental action. Despite its historic verdict in *Brown v. Board of Education*, the Court stated that reform should occur "with all deliberate speed," another term for "slowly." Wholesale change did not occur until the 1960s, when the Civil Rights Acts, Voting Rights Act, Fair Housing Act, and many other laws were established and enforced. States that thought they could perpetuate their previous iniquities were disabused of their misconception, even though it was a painstaking process in the states that stridently resisted change. But there was no room for a states' rights argument that would allow a state to perpetuate inequality and discrimination.

As the transformation continued, elevating civil rights to the top echelon of American values, again there were echoes from the debates between the Federalists and Anti-Federalists. The legislators and states that resisted the new laws in the 1960s and beyond were the progeny of the mindset that had previously objected to the federal government imposing its will. Yet, the nationwide approach prevailed because the new laws reflected the values of the country's emerging consensus that recognized the injustice of the old ways and asserted new ones. Our Constitution made that possible in ways that would not have been possible under the structure set forth in the Articles of Confederation.

Environmental laws began a similar process in the 1970s. Until then, the federal government had largely failed to act, other than to create national parks and preserve some federal lands. Yet, it had the power to act, and when it began doing so—creating the EPA, Clean Air Act, and Clean Water Act— it acted assertively. Prior to national standards, some states were responsible stewards, while others did little or nothing to protect natural resources and prevent environmental offenses from jeopardizing human health. Initially, recalcitrant states opposed the concept of national laws and regulations with baseline requirements for appropriate environmental conduct. It is now accepted that the federal government has the authority to act, and today's debates usually center on the scope, specifics, and costs of standards and regulations. While some states and industries still argue that certain standards are too stringent or don't consider economic impacts, and Trump's EPA is reversing regulations, the federal government's right to set national standards is clear. Madison, Hamilton, and Jay would be happy about that.

SWITCHING OF ROLES: TRUMP EMBRACES THE FEDERALISTS' VIEW

Traditionally, conservatives embraced a states' rights posture, calling for the federal government's role to recede, and the states' authority to be predominant.[15] Their view is characterized by calls for limited government or a reduction in the size and scope of the federal government. Typical examples include the localization of civil rights, the GOP's long-held desire to eliminate the Department of Education (which would transfer federal authority to the states, along with the funds that it allocates), the elimination of routine scrutiny of states to ensure compliance with the Voting Rights Act, and the conversion of Medicaid and other federal programs to a block grant program that would be administered by the states, with funding increases being limited to the rate of inflation.

The Trump administration presents a clear contrast to that traditional stance. During the campaign, and especially since becoming president, Trump has expressed his disdain for many federal regulations and laws. His administration has trumpeted its intention to uproot an array of standards that were developed over many years to protect America's land and people. In most cases, rather than shift power to the states, Trump aims to consolidate authority at the federal level, retaining control in order to decimate the programs or the standards that they set.[16] This attitude was expressed by former Trump advisor Steve Bannon, who starkly stated that his overarching goal was the "deconstruction of the administrative state."[17] Rather than shift responsibilities to the states, Bannon and Trump aimed to achieve their policy goals by making the federal government as ineffective as possible. They planned to neuter federal policies and regulations, immobilize its functions, and dismantle it from within.

In general, federal law provides certainty and clarity through uniform national standards, establishing the level of protection or conduct that is acceptable and usually at a higher standard of conduct or protection than what previously existed in the states. For example, when the federal government first enacted laws against hate crimes with enhanced criminal sentences, some states did not have hate crimes laws. The federal hate crime law became the baseline standard for protection against hate crimes in all fifty states. The same dynamic has occurred countless times throughout our history through federal laws on factory safety, mining operations, pollution reduction, minimum wage levels, remediation of toxic lands, and myriad other issues. Usually, federal preemption is not applied, which means that states are allowed to exceed federal baseline requirements, for example, in the case of water quality, minimum wages, and air pollution laws.

Unfortunately, however, federal law can also lower the national baseline of acceptable protection or conduct. Although it may appear as though the federal government is taking constructive action, it can jeopardize health, safety, and/or fairness when it achieves uniformity and clarity by imposing standards that are lower than those that previously existed in the states. This can be done through regulations, executive orders, and legislation that preempt state law. All of these are among the tools that the Trump administration has used in its first two years for "deconstruction of the administrative state."

Many Trump administration actions would lower standards, reverse progress, and harm both human health and the environment. Former EPA administrator Pruitt, with a prior history of implementing the wish lists of polluters and fossil-fuel interests, reversed many regulations that protect the environment, and stopped enforcement of environmental laws.[18] The EPA's degenerative process is well underway, as Pruitt halted rules that limit toxic discharges from coal-fueled plants, establish emission standards for heavy-duty trucks, increase fuel efficiency standards for automobiles, and require the coal industry to monitor and report toxic mining waste in waterways.[19] Pruitt discarded President Obama's Clean Power Plan, and the EPA replaced it with a cynically named Affordable Clean Energy Rule that favors fossil fuels over renewable energy and abandons sharp cutbacks in carbon emissions. The shift is environmentally indefensible and baldly hypocritical. The new policy lets states decide what fuels to allow, whether to regulate emissions, and what the acceptable level of emissions is. But months earlier, Pruitt took issue with the Clean Air Act's California standards for vehicle emissions on the basis that states should *not* be able to decide what level of emissions to allow. He insisted on a single national standard. The administration's hypocrisy was transparent, as they gave opposite rationales for these policies. The only consistency between them was that both benefited fossil-fuel interests and were environmentally disastrous.

Interior secretary Zinke has also made many environmentally damaging decisions. He halted a study (by the National Academies of Science, Engineering, and Medicine) that was evaluating the correlation of mountain top coal mining (by explosions) to cancer and other diseases among nearby residents.[20] In 2018, Zinke's plan to severely curtail the Endangered Species Act was opposed by a wide range of interest groups and communities, igniting a major political firestorm.

In addition to these departmental decisions, Trump has signed an array of anti-environmental executive orders, for example, to reopen federal lands to new coal leases, allow off-shore oil drilling in territorial waters (except where it would affect his hotels[21]), revoke flood-risk standards, and withdraw the United States from the Paris Agreement.[22] To mitigate the damage and embarrassment of being the only country that rejected the Paris Agreement's strategy to counter environmental impacts that could destabilize the entire world, many of our subnational governments (states and cities) pledged participation in the global effort to minimize climate change. In September 2018, the Global Climate Action Summit in San Francisco demonstrated the chasm between Americans and the president on the urgency of effective measures against climate change—which puts cities, homes, and hundreds of millions of lives at risk, and could cost trillions of dollars worldwide during this century—while also optimistically illuminating some constructive developments and potential solutions.

Other reversals of well-accepted national standards are being undertaken at the Department of Justice, Department of Labor, Department of Energy, Department of Health and Human Services, the Consumer Financial Protection Bureau, and elsewhere. The common thread between their actions is the reversal of protections and rights that were established in recent decades. These actions reflect Trump's dedication to fulfilling the dreams of his base voters by reestablishing 1950s America and all of its inequities, injustices, improprieties, irresponsibility, and instability.

Trump's aggressive reduction of protections, and reversal of Obama-era policy, is on vivid display with his policies on Deferred Action for Childhood Arrivals (DACA) and Sanctuary Cities.[23] While immigration is squarely within federal jurisdiction, his use of an executive order to put almost two million "Dreamers" (DACA beneficiaries) in jeopardy of being deported to countries that are foreign to them is indefensible. His order gave Congress six months to forestall his action. It was broadly opposed in public opinion polls and challenged by legislators of both parties. Some asserted that the policy is inadvisable, while others declared that it is outright unconscionable, amoral, and offensive to American values.

Trump's antipathy toward Sanctuary Cities impairs public safety and puts Americans at risk. He wants local police to enforce immigration laws by detaining people who cannot readily demonstrate their legal immigration status and turning them over to federal officials for deportation. But law enforcement statistics show that when people fear that calling the police could lead to their own deportation, they often do not report domestic abuse and other crimes. This allows crimes to proliferate against both immigrants and citizens. Time and money spent by police on immigration screening—which is beyond their mandate and in conflict with it—minimizes the police's ability to ensure safe communities. In March 2018, AG Sessions went to Sacramento to castigate California and some of its mayors for their Sanctuary Cities laws. He implied that those laws harkened back to nullification and announced a lawsuit against the state.[24] The irony of Sessions, a lifelong states' rights advocate, suing a state to impose the federal government's will is profound yet unsurprising in light of the shift of positions that Trump has caused. In response to Sessions's comments and lawsuit, Governor Jerry Brown fiercely objected to "these political stunts"[25] while especially taking umbrage at the comparison to nullification.[26]

The Trump administration is extending federal authority even further by asserting jurisdiction on matters that are principally within states' jurisdiction but that the federal government also can affect. Federal authority can be asserted by virtue of the Constitution's Interstate Commerce Clause, various federal laws, or a nexus to a federal program. For example, in January 2018, Sessions announced his directive to prosecute possession and distribution of cannabis even in states where it has been legalized. This reversal of an Obama-era policy is setting up a head-to-head conflict between federal and state authority as eight states and the District of Columbia have legalized marijuana for recreational use, and twenty-nine states have legalized it for medical use.[27]

There are other examples of the Trump administration trying to usurp state authority and create lower national standards. Prior to his ouster, former health and human services secretary Tom Price was eager to limit medical malpractice lawsuits by overriding state statutes that govern judicial decisions on damages for medical errors.[28] The longtime wish of many Republicans for tort reform in medical malpractice cases, which would standardize damages at a level that is lower than currently allowed in most states, was on Price's agenda, even though patient protection would suffer.

Trump has even gone so far as to assert a federal role where none exists. Even though elections are operated by each state, without a federal role in voting operations, Trump created a Presidential Advisory Commission on Election Integrity (i.e., his voter fraud investigation). The commission directed states to provide detailed information about their voters, even though the federal government has no authority to do so, since the logistics of elections are exclusively within the states' domain.[29] If the requested data had been furnished by the states, it could easily have been used to intimidate voters, suppress election participation by certain groups of voters, or enable election meddlers (such as the Russian hackers who are still interfering in US politics, according to intelligence experts) to easily access states' information about voters through a unitary access point. The commission also aimed to purge voters from voter rolls if they hadn't voted in recent elections. That process would have erroneously purged many people with common last names, which would have disproportionately impacted African Americans, Latinos/Hispanics, and some groups of Asian Americans, among whom there is a prevalence of common last names.[30] As is evident from the comments and backgrounds of the commission's instigators and supporters, it was no accident or coincidence that minorities would have been the primary targets of the purge.

It makes sense that this makes no sense. Trump created this commission to corroborate his delusional claim that three million votes were illegally cast for his opponent in the 2016 election. Trump's usurpation of state authority was unjustifiable, and the commission itself, which was created to justify a falsehood, was a baseless farce. With lawsuits challenging its validity, and so many state election officials—both Republicans and Democrats—refusing to cooperate, the commission was disbanded.[31]

Trump is also deconstructing the federal government through his choice not to hire people for many vital positions. Two years into Trump's tenure, an extraordinary number of senior departmental positions remain vacant, including high-ranking subcabinet officers, subject-matter experts, and ambassadors to many countries where vital US interests are at stake. The White House alleges that the Republican-led Senate is delaying action on nominees, but that is rarely the case. Far more often, the administration has simply not forwarded nominees. For many key positions, there is no nominee for the Senate to consider. Many positions also remain vacant for which Senate confirmation is not even necessary. Some commentators suggest that the administration has left positions unfilled to lower costs; in light of Bannon's comments, it is more likely being done to disable the government and make it ineffective.

Although Trump takes a federal-centric approach, which is unusual for a Republican president, he is doing so for a nefarious reason. Rather than make the federal government effective, he is trying to centralize authority at the federal level and then emasculate it. His policies consistently aim to lower the standards or requirements on activities and industries that Trump wants to assist. At the same time, the Trump administration supports states' rights when doing so is the clearer path to instituting a particular policy or carving an exemption from a federal rule.[32] If the administration succeeds in neutralizing the federal government with the assistance of the GOP-controlled Congress, then they would put us on a path toward the "deconstruction of the administrative state."

SWITCHING OF ROLES: DEMOCRATS EMBRACE THE ANTI-FEDERALISTS' VIEW

Trump's plan endangers much of the progress that has been made in the past eighty-five years. Federal regulations have been dismantled. Decisions are being made to stop enforcing some statutes, and begin strictly enforcing other ones that had been widely considered unjust or unwise. Funding is being withheld from some agencies in an intentional attempt to starve them of the means with which to carry out their mandate and immobilize them. Programs on which many Americans rely are being threatened with severe budget cuts, and in some cases, outright elimination. Republicans in Congress are proposing legislation to lower national standards that protect rights, safety, and opportunity for all Americans.

These tools are being used like a wrecking ball on American values and society through a wide variety of dystopian measures and objectives, including:

- imposing a travel ban aimed at countries with predominantly Islamic populations;
- relaxing rules that limit companies' emissions of chemical, particulate, and toxic air pollutants, even though their adverse effects pose hazards to human health in local communities;
- adding a question to the 2020 national Census form that asks whether respondents and others in their household are US citizens;
- threatening to withhold federal funds from cities and states that do not direct local police resources to function as federal immigration agents (Sanctuary Cities);
- redirecting civil rights resources to protect white Americans against discrimination, turning the concept of civil rights upside-down;

- imposing harsh mandatory sentencing guidelines with maximum prison terms in criminal cases that disproportionately impact communities of color;
- reducing or removing restrictions on mineral and fossil-fuel mining or extraction;
- allowing gun dealers, payday lenders, and other predatory lenders to access credit through the banking system;
- reducing labor rights (wages and working conditions) and job-site safety protections for workers;
- freezing climate change research and environmental disaster response scenario planning;
- withholding federal funds from Planned Parenthood programs; and
- defunding foreign aid assistance and international development programs on which the people of many countries rely for basic sustenance and support.

If allowed to continue, the combined effect of these and other infringements against our long-held national values would result in a society with lower standards, fewer protections, and less equality. The rich would become richer while the poor become poorer; the empowered would flourish while the marginalized scramble; business decisions would prioritize financial costs ahead of environmental costs; corporate welfare would continue to flourish through the tax code while programs that support individuals' quality of life would be curtailed; criminal justice would be applied gently to some and severely to others; and opportunity would be extended to the type of Americans that Trump likes but not to those who he doesn't.

These developments cause consternation in many states, sometimes among Republicans as well as Democrats. For example, during the 2017 deliberations over repealing Obamacare, the Republican governors of Ohio, Nevada, and Arizona vocally opposed efforts to curtail Medicaid or turn it into a block grant program.[33] Many Republican state officials recognize the potential harm that Trump's deconstruction crusade could inflict on the people of their state, as well as the pressure that it would exert on their states' finances.

When Jeff Sessions announced his plan to enforce federal laws against marijuana—even in states where it has been legalized—one of the most vocal critics was Republican senator Cory Gardner of Colorado.[34] Gardner objected to the move as a vitiation of states' rights. He retaliated by placing a hold on the confirmation of nominees and struck a narrowly tailored deal with Trump so that the policy would "not impact Colorado's legal marijuana industry"[35] (which apparently applies only to his state and is only based on a verbal assurance from Trump). When Secretary DeVos reversed a policy that gave students relief from debts incurred at for-profit colleges, one of the most vocal critics was the Republican attorney general of Colorado, Cynthia Coffman (among other Republican state attorneys general), who similarly objected on the basis of states' rights being offended.[36]

Some states have resorted to unorthodox actions, such as joining together as subnational participants in international agreements to demonstrate their compliance with important global efforts that the Trump administration has renounced, such as the Paris Agreement.[37] States have also invited collaboration from corporations that would further bolster the prospects of subnational compliance to maintain our country's standing as a reliable partner for international business.

Lawsuits are increasingly being initiated to prevent the Trump administration from dismantling key federal policies and protections. During Trump's first two years, California alone filed over forty lawsuits against the Trump administration.[38] For example, in March 2018, California filed a lawsuit in federal court that opposes, on constitutional grounds, a question about each person's citizenship being added to the 2020 Census form.[39] In April 2018, New York filed a similar lawsuit in federal court on behalf of eighteen states and sixteen cities (six of the states are led by Republican governors, although all of the states' attorneys general are Democrats).[40] In January 2019, the district court decided the New York case in favor of the states and cities that challenged the inclusion of the citizenship question, and in February 2019, the US Supreme Court took the unusual step of bypassing the court of appeals and agreeing to decide the case on an expedited basis during the term that ends in June 2019.[41]

Some state attorneys general—mostly but not exclusively Democrats—are looking at a new, creative, and ironic use of the Tenth Amendment. States' rights arguments were traditionally used by conservatives who wanted to shield their state from federal laws, particularly those laws that sought to protect the rights of residents in every state. Now, liberal and progressive state leaders are leveraging the Tenth Amendment to insulate their residents from federal actions that would abridge protections and rights and to preserve their state's ability to exceed federal standards.[42]

In August 2017, California became the first state to file a lawsuit challenging the ability of the federal government to impose its will against Sanctuary Cities.[43] This followed Jeff Sessions's announcement that cities and states would lose funding if they did not direct their police officers to screen and detain people based on their immigration status (prior to Sessions's the March 2018 announcement that he would sue the state). Sessions's policy would be tantamount to local police officers functioning as federal immigration officials, forcing police to detain law-abiding residents solely based on their immigration status and hand them over to federal officials for mass deportations.

In suing the federal government, joining lawsuits by San Francisco and Chicago, California attorney general Xavier Becerra invoked the Tenth Amendment. Becerra explained, "We're not asking our police and sheriffs' deputies to violate the rights of the people they're sworn to protect. There's a very different use of the Tenth Amendment and the states' rights argument today. . . . We're trying to protect people, not to harm them."[44] He further detailed his position in 2018, stating, "I believe anytime the federal government tries to violate the Tenth Amendment, and the rights of the states to decide how to do general welfare and public safety for their citizens, that we have a great chance of winning in court. In this particular case, where the Trump administration has decided to sue California, they're essentially trying to coerce us into doing the federal government's job. . . . We don't believe the federal government can get in the way of the way California wants to do its public safety."[45]

While the courts are deliberating over these lawsuits, politicians should take the opportunity to rebrand Sanctuary Cities with another moniker that would more accurately and effectively express the issue. By rebranding the issue as "Community Policing Rights" or "Local Police Management," the emphasis would be placed on the right of states and cities to administer their local police activities and protect the public in the way that they deem appropriate. Reframing the issue would clarify that states and cities simply do not want to be forced to act like immigration officers on behalf of the federal government, since doing so would conflict with their mandate and exceed their authority.

To maintain quality-of-life standards and federal funding levels, some states are taking action to preserve policies that are codified in federal law or regulations and are at risk of being dismantled. For example, ten states and the District of Columbia collaborated on a 2017 lawsuit against the EPA and the Army Corps of Engineers to enforce the 2015 Clean Water Rule protecting lakes, rivers, and streams from pollutants.[46] States could also counteract the Trump administration's reduction of federal standards by invoking the Tenth Amendment when defending state laws that enhance federal laws with more meaningful protections. States may assert the Tenth Amendment when opposing federal preemption of their ability to enact laws that preserve the overall well-being of their residents. This approach could be used to promote equality (civil rights, LGBTQ rights, pay equity, voting rights, immigrants' rights, and DACA for the "Dreamers"), environmental protection (air, water, lands, climate change), justice (police conduct, criminal procedures, sentencing guidelines, white-collar crimes), security (privacy, government surveillance), and safety (workplace, communities, consumer protections, protection from predatory financial practices).

Many conservatives embrace Trump's assertion of federal authority because the shift of stance on states' rights serves their ideological interests on particular issues.[47] Yet, some conservatives who are traditional advocates for states' rights continue adhering to that position as a matter of principle. For them, the issue is not whether new federal laws would impose a lower or higher threshold of conduct, based on conservative or progressive ideology (even though they are inclined toward a lighter federal touch, as states' rights advocates historically sought to minimize the federal government's role). These officials and advocates are more concerned about the structural integrity of, and division of authority between, the state and federal governments' respective roles. This was Senator Gardner's rationale in strongly opposing Sessions's plan to enforce laws against the legal marijuana industry in Colorado.

For many Americans within and outside of government, the shift of positions by liberals/progressives and conservatives on states' rights is noticeable and fascinating. Because of the Trump administration's actions in its first two years, and its plans for other policies, both Democrats[48] and Republicans[49] are switching sides on the debate over the Tenth Amendment. Ironically, the mantra of states' rights has a new constituency and a new critic.

SUPREME COURT JUSTICES ARE LIKELY TO SWITCH SIDES

The realignment of conservatives and progressives on Tenth Amendment and states' rights issues is likely to be accompanied by a similar shift among

Supreme Court justices and judges at other levels. If a case on these issues reaches them, it will raise a dilemma between legal principles and policy ramifications. Justices who normally hew toward states' rights and are aligned with conservative policy ideologies will have to choose which to sacrifice in favor of the other. Justices who normally hew toward federal primacy and embrace liberal policy ideologies will face the same choice.

It is unclear how the dilemma will be resolved, and different justices may resolve it differently. One might suggest that a justice or judge who favors a states' rights philosophy will continue to do so regardless of the policy implications of the decision and vice versa for those who favor federal supremacy. That might happen, particularly among those who are especially committed to their philosophy. However, the track record suggests that, when principle and policy on a major consequential issue have a head-on collision at the Court, policy prevails more often than not, even if only covertly.

As we have seen before on many issues, these alignments are malleable. Often, policy ramifications and politics seep in, even if that is not readily acknowledged. The well-known maxim "where you sit is where you stand" is operative here, signifying that the ideology with which a justice sits is likely to determine where they will stand on a decision. Justices and judges are often influenced by the practical consequences of their decisions, and Tenth Amendment situations are ideally positioned for that, since the potential consequences are extensive.

The ultimate example of justices blatantly realigning their jurisprudential views to fit the political and practical consequences of their decision was in the *Bush v. Gore* case[50] that, in effect, resolved the presidential election of 2000. Without excavating that entire drama, the principle was similar to the Tenth Amendment issue: it was a question of the roles and responsibilities of the federal and state governments. The justices who normally favored states' rights abandoned that position to embrace federal authority and vice versa. The shift was transparent and, to many Americans, troublesome.

A similar shift in positions occurred in the Supreme Court's decision on *District of Columbia v. Heller*,[51] which involved the question of whether the Second Amendment creates individual rights, specifically the right of an individual to own a firearm. That case was decided on a 5–4 vote by the justices who usually embraced a strict interpretation of the Constitution's language and its original intent and who contorted their interpretation of the

Second Amendment to fit that narrative. Although they invoked the 1700s when framing their rationale, they transcended the Second Amendment's language and interpreted it in a contemporary context, which offends both textualism and originalism. Conversely, the minority opinion was held by the justices who usually favor a contemporary or loose interpretation of "the living Constitution." The lead dissenting opinion, written by Justice John Paul Stevens, interpreted the Second Amendment in terms of its original meaning and a strict interpretation of its language. It is obvious that the nine justices did not simply base their opinions on the facts of the case and the constitutional interpretations that they long professed. Their positions derogated from their stated philosophies and instead aligned with their beliefs about the subject matter at stake.

A battle is brewing between the Trump administration, which is infringing on the rights of states and individuals, and some state legislatures and attorneys general, whose reactions aim to protect and defend those rights. This collision course is likely to present another landmark case to the US Supreme Court. Justices will, once again, have to decide which matters more to them: their jurisprudential principles or their personal political ideology on the topic.

IMPORTANCE DURING TRUMP'S TENURE AND THE POST-TRUMP ERA

In the Trump era, the Tenth Amendment and states' rights arguments will become increasingly vital tools to protect the rights of individuals and preserve the high quality-of-life standards that have been made possible by decades of federal law. Ironically, states will sometimes find themselves asserting their rights to maintain federal standards, and in other instances will argue against federal preemption so that they can exceed the levels of protection or conduct that are specified by new federal dictates. The states will surely invoke these tools to defend their own authority to act on many issues into which the Trump administration has been injecting itself. The federal-state division of authorities and a contemporary interpretation of the Constitution that embraces its spirit beyond its textual language are vital for fair and equitable assertion of rights, protections, and safety.

Trump's appointment of conservatives to federal courts—over eighty in his first two years—will result in a pronounced and prolonged shift in judicial opinions. As these jurists tend to apply strict constructionist principles of constitutional interpretation (i.e., textualism, originalism), the demarcation between federal and state authority will be fought for years after Trump's presidency. States' regulation of technology, business, products, and services may give rise to contentious litigation. When Trump-appointed jurists hear cases about harm resulting from asbestos, will they rule against the victim because there was no mention in the Constitution about state regulation of asbestos? Will state laws be invalidated because strict constructionists don't find anything in the Constitution's text about a state's right to enact safety measures for cars and computers, chemicals and chainsaws, clean air and clean water? Despite the need for a contemporary, loose interpretation of the spirit of "the living Constitution"—not just the "four corners" of its literal language—Trump has been appointing people to the bench who may rule harshly against the states' authority to ensure rights and protections for their people. As the features of modern life evolve rapidly, if the courts do not adapt along with them through a contemporary interpretation of "the living Constitution," then they will increasingly be viewed as archaic and antiquated.

Although these dynamics will be vitally important to the Department of Justice and highly consequential to the policymaking at other federal departments and agencies, it is doubtful that Donald Trump will be interested in any of these machinations. As someone who is notoriously disinterested in the details of policy and is bereft of guiding principles, these debates are trivial to Trump. He is driven by two forces, neither of which will be deterred by any action taken by the states or the balance of power between the federal and state governments.

First, he acts according to what he wants to do, according to his own opinions and best interests, and assumes that the rest of humankind should bend to his will. When others do not fall in line with his dictates, he views their dissent as aberrant behavior, dismisses it derisively, and doubles-down in trying to exert his will. If this seems irrelevant to federal-state dynamics, that's for a good reason: it is. Trump neither understands nor cares about legal constructs such as federal and state jurisdiction, even though they are fundamental to our country and Constitution. He acts as though he will eventually win every argument, not necessarily on the legal merits, but rather as his privilege.

He guards his personal financial and business interests closely, so that they are not vulnerable to what a state or other entity could do. This explains why he is so unnerved by Special Counsel Mueller's investigation. It is one of few situations involving his financial and business activities where Trump has no control over the outcome.

Second, Trump acts according to what he believes his base wants him to do. He does this to solidify their support, reward their loyalty, and court their gratifying applause at his next rally. While he desperately wants to win anything there is to win, he is also very concerned about his brand and the appearance of winning. The next best thing to winning is to wage an aggressive fight and convince his supporters that he won. When states object to his executive orders or the administration's actions, he dismisses that by saying that he will win the matter in court. When he loses in court, he proclaims that he will eventually win at the Supreme Court, believing, perversely, that they will do whatever he wants. Even if he loses at the Supreme Court, that doesn't matter much to him because he can assert to his base that he did everything that he could do and fought the good fight all the way to the Supreme Court. Since Trump has no attachment to policy or its underlying principles, he is insulated from the details of the Court's decision. As long as he has no financial interests at stake, he can explain away his loss at the Court and distract his audience toward some other manufactured crisis.

On the other hand, these issues mean a great deal to the states, especially those whose leaders are ideologically opposed to Trump's plans. As the Trump administration peels away the rights, protections, and policies that have created America's high quality-of-life standards, many states will take the field and carry the ball on behalf of their denizens. Some states go to court to make Tenth Amendment arguments that protect federal funds or prevent the dismantling of programs and protections. Some states may enact legislation that fills the void created by a federal retreat or establishes higher standards when federal standards are unacceptably low. If the federal government sues them, then states can make Tenth Amendment states' rights arguments to assert their right to legislate.

Some states may become accustomed to using the Tenth Amendment to defend their rights and those of their residents. It will become a backstop against Trump's use of federal authority to pursue his interests and thrill his base. After states have used it a few times, they may become psychologically comfortable with doing so, and the attorneys general that make a practice of it might create a unit in their offices that are dedicated to this, as watchdogs of the state's interests. With units that are dedicated to these Tenth Amendment lawsuits, and budgetary resources to facilitate them, states' practice of defending against the Trump administration's diminution of rights and protections will become institutionalized and sustainable.

In the post-Trump era, the use of Tenth Amendment states' rights arguments in this way might accelerate, becoming a standard operating procedure that continues to be used by both Republican and Democratic state attorneys general. Collaboration among the attorneys general of various states might become a common practice, even across partisan lines. Use of these mechanisms may also be replicated by other states that witness the benefits secured by early adopters of this approach. The result might be a new era of intensified battles, on myriad issues, between the federal and state governments over their authority to act and the standards that they seek to establish.

CHAPTER 9

BIPARTISANSHIP

THE CONCURRENT RISE OF PARTISANSHIP AND BIPARTISANSHIP

By all measures, we are witnessing a period of extreme partisanship, particularly in Congress, that has been festering and even intensifying for years. It infects the operations of our government and impairs the development of policy and legislation that is vital to serving the needs of Americans in all geographic regions and socioeconomic strata. It also sends a bleak message to young Americans that discourages them from aspiring to public service, and a discordant message to other countries that must wonder whether they can collaborate with us when we can't seem to collaborate with each other.

At the same time, our government, including Congress, conducts much of its daily work on a bipartisan basis. Departmental appropriations bills, debt limit adjustments, reauthorizations of many programs and offices, and even some policy issues are managed by members of both parties working together. These efforts typically fly below the radar and do not receive much attention from the media, which is much more focused on the high-profile contentious issues that generate partisanship. Yet, bipartisan teamwork often keeps the legislative trains running on time. Many senators and House members from opposing parties appreciate and enjoy each other, and some are even close friends. While it is unlikely that many members will share a car for a ride halfway across the country from their districts to Washington, DC, the road trip that Will Hurd (R-TX) and Beto O'Rourke (D-TX) famously took together in 2017 sent a very positive message that earned plaudits from voters on both sides of the aisle.[1]

Ironically, both partisanship and bipartisanship are flourishing at the same time, though in different ways, and on some matters more than others. Even more notably, as the rift widens between Trump and Republicans in

Congress, the Democrats are standing by, surveying the landscape for legis-lative opportunities. Trump has alienated many Republicans in the Senate and House, giving rise to scenarios in which Democrats may collaborate with Trump for pragmatic reasons, to achieve specific objectives. It is also increasingly plausible that Democrats and Republicans in Congress might collaborate on legislation without presidential involvement, out of necessity. The ultimate irony would be if Trump causes bipartisanship to proliferate, even if only because he forced congressional Republicans to divorce him on the grounds of irreconcilable differences.

THE NATURE AND IMPORTANCE OF BIPARTISANSHIP

Although there is no official handbook for what bipartisanship looks like in practice, it is basically the willingness of people to communicate, collaborate, compromise, and find common ground to act across ideological lines in good faith, on the merits, toward "win-win" policies and decisions. A cornerstone of bipartisanship is the identification of shared values and principles on which officials with diverse interests are willing to work together. Supreme Court Justice Sonia Sotomayor's March 2017 comments about working together across ideological lines at the Court are equally applicable to collaborating across party lines in Congress:

> I start always . . . with respect for the passion and good intentions of each other. . . . If it is a person of goodwill talking to you, there is something in what they're saying to you—about their views, their needs, what is worri-some to them—that has justification. And if you can look at someone else's position and understand what's motivating them, what they're afraid of, what they think they need to give them comfort to get them closer to your point of view; if you can address those things, you can persuade and move people. . . . For me, that sense of engaging people on their terms, on their needs, and moving those things closer to what I need has always been a suc-cessful way of negotiating. . . . There's always a reason for peoples' feelings. . . . If you can spend the time figuring out what that is, you can use that information to come to a fairer answer.[2]

Ideally, bipartisanship continues on a sustained basis, encouraging offi-cials from opposing political parties to deliberate on diverse and creative solutions, as long-term vested partners. Theoretically, it can displace the traditional dialectic between political parties and ideologies by instituting a standard operating procedure of constructive engagement. It enables issues of mutual concern to be addressed, tensions to be mollified, legislative processes to be made more efficient, and sustainable policies to be produced with support from a broad range of stakeholders. It is the antithesis of a short-term transactional approach in which each party tries to squeeze all that they can from their opponent, assuming that it will be the last time that they would need to negotiate with them.

Bipartisanship does not mean equality or parity between political parties. It does not mandate the abdication of principles and values, or the relinquishment of power, to reach consensus for its own sake. Bipartisanship does not require that positions receive near-unanimous support—a "lowest common denominator" among all officials—as a price for progress. It does not mean that elected officials should capitulate to ultimatums issued under the guise of bipartisanship from other lawmakers who threaten to forestall progress on key initiatives.

Bipartisanship is necessary for our government to respond promptly and effectively to social, economic, security, and other problems. It enables government to craft and implement a vision for long-term national prosperity, and it is vital for our democracy to flourish. Legislation that is enacted into law with broad bipartisan support is much more likely to gain permanence, whereas legislation that is passed with only partisan support is much more likely to be severely altered or even repealed when the opposing party gains control of the process.

Unfortunately, however, partisanship has become virulent in American politics. It gridlocks government and sets a tone of intransigence that aggravates cultural fragmentation. It disenfranchises the electorate, causing disillusionment and animosity. Laws that are passed with only partisan support become the focus of the other party's ire and campaign slogans.

Though elections are designed to be competitive and even combative, there is no need—nor justification—for continuing that tenor once an election has determined the composition of our government. That is the time for bipartisanship, to enact sound policies, respect our elected leaders, ensure our nation's moral high ground, and reassert our global leadership. We do not need to abandon our party affiliations or principles when legislating or governing together. Instead, we just need to commit to collaborate for effective government and relegate combative partisanship to the few months preceding the next general election.

Bipartisan efforts are actually undertaken on a fairly routine basis in Washington, DC. While the public spotlight is riveted on ideological or emotional issues that trigger partisan passions, lawmakers of both parties work together on many operational issues, to maintain consistent, efficient, and effective governmental functions. Although challenging, bipartisan collaboration occurs in many forms between officials with diverse political views and philosophies. Among the specific actions and ongoing processes that are conducted in a bipartisan manner are:

- joint sponsorship of legislation: bills and amendments are frequently sponsored by a Republican and a Democrat together, as coequal partners;
- cosponsors of legislation: legislation commonly gains the support of many legislators from both parties who sign on as cosponsors;
- working groups: some complex, contentious issues are negotiated by small groups of legislators from both parties, producing solutions that appeal to legislators with diverse priorities;
- coalitions: occasionally, a group of legislators from both parties form a voting bloc to address an ongoing contentious concern (e.g., the "Gang of 14," in which seven Republican and seven Democratic senators collaborated on judicial appointments); and
- votes: in its most basic form, bipartisanship is exhibited by votes across party lines.

EFFORTS TOWARD BIPARTISANSHIP BY PRESIDENT OBAMA

During his 2008 campaign, candidate Barack Obama expressed his commitment to bipartisanship.[3] He sought to promote an overarching tone based on mutual respect, receptivity to diverse opinions, openness to innovative yet practical solutions, and debate that enhances understanding. He started down that path[4] and characterized objectives in terms of collaboration on shared goals for the greater good and decision-making based on facts rather than ideology.

Despite hurdles, President Obama crossed party lines and transcended partisan boundaries on many issues.[5] For example, during the drafting of the Dodd-Frank Wall Street Reform and Consumer Protection Act of 2010, he accepted many compromises that accommodated the views of Republicans, while accepting others that addressed those of Democrats. His bipartisan consensus building efforts were also evident during deliberations over increasing the US troop presence in Afghanistan, his education reform proposal's plan to increase teacher accountability, the tax-cut extensions of December 2010, and the infamous 2011 budget "sequester," each of which appealed to Republicans to one degree or another. In assessing Obama's track record on bipartisanship from the perspectives of both the left and the right, Bill Scher concluded, "Both narratives overlook Obama's unsung bipartisan legacy. Almost everything he did accomplish on the domestic front was due to his tenacious pursuit of Republican votes."[6]

Most notably, President Obama began the development of the ACA as a bipartisan effort, although that fact seems to have been forgotten in the partisan morass that followed its passage. In the early stages of the process, President Obama convened bipartisan "summits" with a broad range of stakeholders and met with Republican lawmakers (at the White House and at the Republicans' policy retreat) to hear their views.[7] He also continued to adjust his reform proposal during the bill's drafting and legislative proceedings, to accommodate the positions of Republicans.

Although Obama made a solid effort to develop his healthcare bill in a bipartisan process, it was not tailored to the dynamics of congressional legislating. His approach to drafting the bill conformed to his beliefs about bipartisanship, as he discussed it during the campaign. He treated Republicans and their views with respect; he was receptive to their diverse opinions; he was open to practical solutions; he listened in debates to understand their needs; he collaborated on their shared objectives; and he made decisions based on facts rather than ideology. As a result, the overall structure of the healthcare system in his proposal reflected the views expressed by Republicans.[8] He even based his overall plan on Governor Mitt Romney's health reform law in Massachusetts, which was rooted in the Heritage Foundation's principle of an individual mandate.[9] Obama chose a market-based approach that provided health insurance through private sector health insurance companies. He did not propose a single-payer approach, even though that would have pleased Democrats.

But the problem was that in order for the minority party to feel that they got something that they wanted, they had to fight and win it in battle. President Obama gave them major victories by accommodating their primary policy needs within his proposal. After hearing their views, Obama structured the ACA in a way that he believed would achieve a balance to the satisfaction of both parties. The Republicans did not have to secure their needs through tough negotiations at the eleventh-hour stage of the process. By addressing their most essential needs up front and embedding them in the structure of his proposal, Obama enabled them to shift their opening bid. In other words, he made it convenient for the Republicans to move the goalposts.

Since the Republicans did not have to fight against a single-payer plan, and since the proposal reflected the Heritage/Romney approach, they fought against the bill on other grounds. The bill was based on an individual mandate, so the Republicans objected to the individual mandate. They fought against mandatory coverage of essential benefits and many other provisions. Instead of mandatory benefits, they wanted insurance companies to be able to sell meager policies that covered very little, accompanied by a government financed high-risk pool that would irresponsibly put the cost of serious illnesses on the federal government. In effect, the Republican plan would have privatized insurance companies' profits while socializing their costs. Republicans advocated for provisions that Democrats stridently opposed, such as tort reform, caps on punitive damages, medical malpractice insurance reform, and the elimination of the McCarran-Ferguson Act (which prohibits interstate selling of insurance). Democrats considered them intolerable because of their chilling effect on consumer protection.

During the bill's "markup" in two Senate committees with jurisdiction, over 150 Republican amendments were adopted. By incorporating so many Republican amendments, in addition to the adjustments that Obama made to accommodate the GOP's key concerns that they raised in meetings with him, the bill was a fairly bipartisan product.[10] Still, the Republicans continued to oppose the bill, largely to deny Obama a win.[11] They just shifted their grounds for opposition. Basically, they opposed any meaningful reform of the health system, continued their decades-long fight against expansion of the social safety net, and refused to regard healthcare as a right for all Americans.

As a result, the legislation moved through the House and Senate without support from Republicans, except for one vote in committee by Senator Olympia Snowe (R-Maine). Essentially, the Republicans were committed to denying President Obama the appearance of a bipartisan victory, regardless of what was in the bill.[12] When Scott Brown won the Senate seat in Massachusetts, it was clear that there would be no chance of passing a final bill in the Senate following a conference committee, so the House approved the Senate's bill to avoid that. That left a lingering flavor of partisanship even though Obama had tried hard to make it a bipartisan effort but was thwarted by the opposition's recalcitrance.

To achieve bipartisanship, a hand that is extended must be reciprocated. Since President Obama extended his hand, the assessment of bipartisanship in the ACA's development should focus on his efforts and the compromises that were inherent in his proposals. The final vote is only one of many relevant metrics. The way that the process ended has dimmed the memory of all the steps that led up to it, especially its origins as a bipartisan effort.

Obama's bipartisan intentions on healthcare reform, and the Republicans' stalwart opposition to it, must also be viewed in the context of the broader Republican strategy against Obama. It was widely reported that a group of senior Republican leaders in the House and Senate, as well as other Republican power brokers, convened a strategy meeting on Obama's 2009 inauguration day.[13] The main decision from that meeting was that, even though the country was facing economic peril, they would oppose Obama every step of the way in order to prevent him from being re-elected in 2012.[14] They planned to oppose legislation even when they supported the policy, in an effort to deny Obama any successes. In light of this, it is clear why the Republicans moved the goalposts on healthcare reform and refused to support any of his efforts. Faulting Obama for failing to be bipartisan, when the opposition committed to consistently oppose him regardless of his proposals, is an injustice and factually inaccurate.

Obama's bipartisan efforts on other issues were also not well recognized by the public. That is certainly not to say that he acted in a bipartisan way on everything across the board. But typically, bipartisanship was his preference and his intention. There was a popular misconception that characterized his efforts as being highly partisan. Even though inaccurate, that impression gained traction and became solidified, particularly among people who did not pay close attention to news from Washington and filled their informational void with the venomous rants against Obama that regularly aired on conservative talk radio shows and a cable TV network whose calling card was its anti-Obama bias.[15]

Even though President Obama was constantly and unfairly castigated by these overtly biased media outlets, one aspect of their assertions was true, even though many of his legislative efforts aimed for bipartisan balance. During the 2008 campaign, Obama had expressed his desire to change the culture of Washington by improving cross-party collaboration, reducing the acrimonious rhetoric, introducing a new style of politics, and making bipartisanship the norm instead of the exception. He set his sights very high. It could be said that he overpromised. Changing the culture of DC may have simply been a much heavier lift than he anticipated, since that change depended on others as much as on him. So, it may have been predictable that he would fall short of his ambitious objective.

STATUS OF BIPARTISANSHIP UNDER DONALD TRUMP

That set the stage for Donald Trump. During the 2016 election, the goal of bipartisanship resurfaced. Many voters were overtly disillusioned and upset that President Obama did not change the Washington culture in the ways that he had aimed to improve it. In 2008, they wanted the atmosphere to change, and they wanted that even more in 2016. They blamed Obama—fairly or unfairly—for failing to deliver on his promise for greater multi-party collaboration and a new bipartisan way of doing governmental business. As a result, many of these voters lost faith and confidence in politicians and other entrenched political players and were mindful of that when they went to the polls.

Between the two main candidates in the election, Hillary Clinton was obviously the only one who was part of the political establishment, with a long history in Washington politics. That became a liability. Although it was by no means the only reason, the biggest reason, or even a major reason why Hillary lost, it was a factor. Many Americans thought they'd give Trump a try, since he wasn't part of the Washington establishment that had let them down. As Trump rhetorically suggested on the campaign trail in various contexts, "What do you have to lose?"[16] Many Americans were complacent about their choice. Because Trump won, aided by many protest votes cast by voters venting their anger against establishment elites, now he is the one with a lot to lose. Specifically, he risks the support of many voters if he does not change the culture of Washington by facilitating effective bipartisan working relationships.

Trump's victory, together with the Republicans' control of both the House and the Senate, gave the GOP control over both the executive and legislative branches of the federal government during Trump's first two years. Suddenly, they were in the proverbial put-up-or-shut-up situation, as they controlled all the levers of lawmaking. During Obama's tenure, the GOP had been the opposition party and came to be known as "the party of 'no.'" Their principal objective was to be obstreperous, acting as a partisan check on the president's power, challenging and defeating him at every opportunity.

Because of their success, the GOP became the party of governance. With Trump at the helm, they have to make decisions that enable the government to operate in an effective and efficient manner. To achieve that, common sense dictates that Republicans should abandon the more extreme positions that had been used to motivate their voters and leverage their bargaining power. They would be well served by adopting a pragmatic stance that would broaden the range of issues on the legislative agenda, unify their caucus, attract support from across the political aisle, and enable Congress to operate efficiently. This pragmatic approach would position Republicans to pass legislation that benefits millions of Americans (for example, on job creation and infrastructure improvement) and is sustainable over the long term. This approach is also necessary to show the American people that the Republicans can govern.

But during the first two years of the Trump administration's tenure, the Republicans in Congress have only rarely been able to do that. The healthcare fiasco showcased their shortcomings, especially the infighting between the factions of their own party—the Freedom Caucus conservatives and the Tuesday Group moderates—that put the bill at the precipice of defeat in the House before it surprisingly passed, and over the precipice in the Senate, where it was defeated.

Another of the GOP's major shortcomings was its adherence to hardline conservative policy that alienated Democrats and prevented them from participating in the process. Senator Mitch McConnell is often touted as a masterful legislator because he can usually twist enough arms to get the votes to hold his caucus together and pass legislation. But, if he had pursued a bipartisan policy approach, he would not have had to do all that arm twisting. He could have gotten an easy victory.

Instead, all of McConnell's policy options on Obamacare were fractious, accompanied by a highly partisan strategy to cobble together the votes, on which he then failed. Repeal of Obamacare was a rallying cry or slogan, not a sensible policy: great for campaigns but lousy for governing. As experienced as McConnell is, he should have known that. He, of all people, should have known that taking benefits away from Americans is politically dangerous and very different from opposing their creation.

Even if the Republicans had succeeded in passing a repeal of Obamacare, by pursuing such a strictly partisan policy, they would have ensured that the Democrats would mount an equally fierce counterresponse the next time that they regain control. The Democrats might have pushed for a single-payer solution the next time they take control of Congress and the presidency, and that assuredly would have been on the table if Obamacare had been repealed. The Republicans could have forestalled that scenario and improved the healthcare system by collaborating with Democrats to solve Obamacare's technical and operational problems.

In contrast with the ACA repeal, the Republicans notched a major victory when they passed tax cut legislation on a strictly partisan basis. Aided by the budget reconciliation rules that allowed passage by a simple majority, they successfully enacted the deepest cuts to corporate, individual, estate, and other taxes in a generation, along with the elimination of the ACA's individual mandate, and restrictions on oil drilling in the Arctic Wildlife Reserve, among other policy changes.[17] Although tax cuts are central to the Republicans' brand and ideology, the GOP leadership still had to work hard to secure the support of all Republicans in the Senate and a sufficient number for passage in the House. It was a victory in that they got the tax cuts that they wanted. However, by doing it on a strictly and *harshly* partisan basis with very inequitable tax relief that principally benefits the wealthiest Americans and residents in states where the GOP prevails, they practically invited the Democrats to revise the law when they regain control.[18]

A more sustainable approach was briefly pursued to resolve the issues surrounding DACA. In that instance, three Republican and three Democratic senators collaborated as the "gang of six" to work out a bipartisan solution, and other bipartisan teams also formed to generate possible compromises.[19] Because it was being addressed as part of the legislation to keep the government funded and could not pass with a simple majority, votes from some Democrats would have been needed. Despite being slated for passage on a bipartisan basis, which would also have secured its long-term viability, Trump unceremoniously torpedoed the deal.[20]

Bipartisanship is perhaps even more vital in foreign affairs, especially during the Trump era, due to the potential national security ramifications. Trump's unrelenting penchant for irascible rhetoric, verbally and via Twitter, causes consternation among both allies and adversaries. His fractious remonstrations can deplete America's credibility as a reliable global actor and give the impression that the United States would be unable to respond to urgent circumstances due to our internal divisions. Bipartisan support and collaboration can play an invaluable role in alleviating fears and maintaining stability by showing that our country is unified in its foreign policy pursuits.

Amid ominous circumstances, Trump's contentious comments on global issues can spur foreign leaders to react, rhetorically or kinetically, in aggressive, exploitative, and adventuresome ways that put Americans at risk. The threats that Trump hurled toward North Korea in August and September of 2017 could easily have gotten out of control, with tragic consequences. Although we dodged a bullet (or much worse) that time, White House officials must find a way to prevent Trump from engaging in ego-driven bellicose bluster that antagonizes an adversary at a time when finely tuned diplomacy is needed.

Bipartisanship is critical in contentious global situations in order to galvanize allies and partners in support of a synchronized response. Without our government being unified, we can't ask other countries to unify with us. Of course, the better solution is for Trump not to escalate rhetoric in the first place.

THE CHALLENGE THAT PARTISANSHIP IMPOSES

The Obamacare repeal-and-replace morass of 2017 was the quintessence of partisanship. The drama at every step of the way, the final collapse, and the anticipated political fallout exposed the dangers and costs of partisanship. Even with that stark experience, many legislators of both parties continue clinging to partisan pathways, like a preprogrammed default mechanism, as if they are ineluctably drawn to it.

However, it is a matter of choice. The Republicans, by virtue of being in control of Congress, could have recalibrated and worked with Democrats to gain some positive results, rather than holding on to absolutist positions and ending up with very little. Those who reject bipartisan collaboration apparently have not understood the value of the time-tested maxim "don't let the perfect be the enemy of the good."

Morality also plays an important role in the choice to collaborate and compromise, according to one of the planet's most esteemed practitioners of moral conduct. During Pope Francis's visit to the United States in 2015, he spoke about the philosophical and psychological roots of partisanship and bipartisanship, linking it with a worldview that is dominated by a "good versus evil" dichotomy. In his address to Congress, Pope Francis discussed these issues in his own unique, poignant, and unimpeachable manner:

> There is another temptation which we must especially guard against: the simplistic reductionism which sees only good or evil; or, if you will, the righteous and sinners. The contemporary world, with its open wounds which affect so many of our brothers and sisters, demands that we confront every form of polarization which would divide it into these two camps. We know that in the attempt to be freed of the enemy without, we can be tempted to feed the enemy within. To imitate the hatred and violence of tyrants and murderers is the best way to take their place.[21]

"Simplistic reductionism," as Pope Francis stated it, is the cornerstone of partisanship, fed by a "good versus evil" mentality that creates an us-versus-them conflict. This mentality is tempting because it reinforces self-righteousness and provides comforting self-affirmation. It is very easy and convenient since it rejects the need to reach beyond oneself, asserts alignment with all that is good, insulates officials from criticism and opposition, and obviates the need to understand or accommodate other perspectives. It provides an emotional justification for refusing to cooperate and collaborate, and thus, it is a natural predicate for partisanship.

Legislators who embrace hard-line partisanship might object to this characterization of their approach on the grounds that they are merely voicing the political preferences of their districts. They might insist that pragmatic realities compel their intransigence. But that is a fallacy that provides refuge for the unwilling. No one ever voted for a senator or representative thinking they were getting a king or queen. Voters know that their senators will be 2 among 100, and their congressperson will be 1 among 435. Voters understand that no one serving in Congress will get 100 percent of what they want, and that they will have to cooperate and compromise with others. There is no expectation that the officials whom they elect will triumph over all efforts that do not mirror their wish lists. Since cooperation, collaboration, and compromise are the currency of a multi-stakeholder deliberative body, by with-holding good faith participation in that process, legislators fail to do their job. Although "simplistic reductionism" may be a crutch for self-interested politi-cal expediency, it is inconsistent with leadership and responsibility.

Even as Congress engages in high-profile partisan struggles, many issues are addressed in a bipartisan manner, both in Congress and in the adminis-tration. Many senators and House members feel that needless partisanship does not serve their constituents' interests. Some legislators have teamed up with a colleague across the aisle to develop solutions with shared priorities (e.g., senators Lamar Alexander and Patty Murray on improvements to the healthcare system, senators James Lankford and Amy Klobuchar on secur-ing our elections from foreign interference, senators Ron Wyden and Rand Paul on data privacy, senators Lindsey Graham and Dick Durbin leading the "gang of six" proposal on DACA reform). Many House members have joined the bipartisan Problem Solvers Caucus[22], which develops mutually agreeable solutions to thorny policy issues. In so doing, participants improve working relations, the benefits of which carry over to other issues. Over time, exhaus-tion from constant combat and the futility of inaction are likely to inspire more legislators to partner with one or more colleagues from the other party.

Similarly, many issues and programs managed by the executive branch advance under the guidance and professionalism of career staff and even some appointees. While high-visibility issues are often polarized, the imple-mentation of many laws, regulations, and programs are not. This is often the case, for example, with issues concerning transportation, broadband, health research, infrastructure, technology, small business, and food safety. These efforts are often fueled by input and collaboration based on expertise, insights, and operational capacity, regardless of a stakeholder's ideology or political affiliation.

During a discussion at the 2018 StartUp Health conference, the former chief technology officer of the federal government illuminated the pragmatic bipartisanship that regularly occurs in the executive branch. Aneesh Chopra, who served in the Obama administration, described the two tracks on which the government operates:

> There are two Washingtons. There's the Washington we see in the cable news shows . . . everyone hates each other, battle royale, fight to the death, who's up/who's down. That's what's perceived, and I acknowledge that

there is a great deal of that still in aspects of Washington. The agenda that we just described (the shift from closed to open data, the migration of medical records from manila folders to electronic folders that can talk to each other, and the shift in payments to reward value), that's part of the quiet Washington where people on both sides of the aisle actually want to sit together and make things work. But they don't want to say it too loudly because then it's a partisan thing where, if you're for it, then someone has to be against it. Let's get people in the room and talking about the things that need to be done. . . . Whether you're a partisan on the left or a partisan on the right, you can still see the benefits of this activity.[23]

Chopra's assessment demonstrates the practical reality that bipartisan collaboration is the standard operating procedure on which the federal government functions. In Congress, too, beyond the glare of the spotlight that transfixes the nation's attention on contentious issues, bipartisanship is central to the management and resolution of many problems that require legislative action. The national media's focus on disputes that are driven by partisanship—which are important and must be covered—comes at the expense of highlighting the progress driven by bipartisanship.

MECHANISMS TO OVERCOME PARTISANSHIP AND WELCOME BIPARTISANSHIP

In today's highly charged political atmosphere, most legislation is handled without the constant attention of media coverage. These efforts advance through collaborative negotiations, joint development and sponsorship of legislation, productive committee proceedings, and orderly floor action. It is an example of the "80/20 rule," meaning that most legislation—perhaps 80 percent—is handled in a bipartisan manner, while the other 20 percent, which generates partisan tension, is the focus of media scrutiny. That leaves the public with the false impression that everything is stuck in a constant quagmire of intense conflict.

More needs to be done to make bipartisanship the norm, especially for controversial issues. The means for achieving this are, however, elusive. There is no definitive methodology to promote bipartisanship, since it requires a good faith process rather than a singular product or transactional outcome. While it is difficult to get elected officials to agree to reforms and ground rules, let alone adhere to them, establishing some mechanisms and guidelines would help to foster a collaborative, congenial environment for legislating. The following tactics and ground rules can help to stimulate a bipartisan spirit, which could materialize into constructive progress:

- Working Groups and Relationship Building: Congressional leaders could establish informal working groups for legislators who hold differing philosophies to meet weekly to collaboratively develop solutions on key issues. Each group would combine senators and representatives (both parties, both chambers) who don't already spend time with each other and might not otherwise have reason to do so. The groups would foster cross-party relationships and build understanding of each other's positions. Participants would candidly discuss the explanations and rationales for their views, offer honest critiques of one's own positions, and find innovative solutions that transcend entrenched party positions. Groups would seek consensus on specific issues that are delegated to them by the leadership.
- District Tours: To elevate understanding of the conditions, concerns, and needs of each other's districts that impact decision-making, legislators from opposite parties and different states would be paired for reciprocal tours of each other's districts (or states, for senators). By proverbially "walking a mile in each other's shoes," participants would gain insight into their colleagues' policy concerns and legislative priorities. Legislators who sit on the same committee should be paired together so that committees and legislation can benefit from the mutual understanding that is achieved. Pairings from different states and social structures (e.g., rural vs. urban) would increase understanding of different lifestyles in locations that are not already familiar to them.
- Elimination of the Hastert Rule: Since the 1990s, Speakers of the House often permitted or prevented floor votes on legislation according to whether it had the support of "the majority of the majority" party. Although this practice began prior to Dennis Hastert's speakership, it became known as the "Hastert Rule" because of his adherence to it. In effect, this rule limits the minority party's influence on the legislative agenda. Even when a bill could pass by getting enough votes from a combination of Republicans and Democrats, the Hastert Rule does not allow a bill to reach the House floor if a majority of the party

in control does not support it. Elimination of this rule would enable legislators of both parties to collaborate in advancing legislation, thus incentivizing bipartisan efforts.

- Objective Analyses: To enhance transparency, accountability, and consistency, each bill that comes to the House or Senate floor for a vote should be accompanied by an analysis from a nonpartisan, objective office, like the Congressional Research Service. The analyses would include the qualitative impacts on various demographic groups (e.g., by income, geographic region, and other factors where relevant, such as age, race/ethnicity, gender, and sexual orientation). Analyses would state a bill's fiscal impact and evaluate its long-term effects to encourage focus on long-term policy impacts, which tend to deflate emotionally driven, short-term issues. (This approach is not needed for the budget and departmental appropriations bills, which are annual in scope and duration.)

- Lobbying Reform: The nexus of money and policy is where many abuses occur. Thus, lobbyists should not deliver both campaign contributions and legislative requests. Partisanship is intensified when talks about fundraising and policy coexist, due to promises being made. The elimination of earmarks responded to this but did not go far enough. Although lobbyists should be prohibited from directly discussing legislation with members and senators, they are still entitled to communicate their views. To provide a channel for their input, Congress could create Congressional Interest Group Offices (CIGOs) with which lobbyists could interact. CIGOs would relay information to those who prepare objective analyses on bills that are slated for committee or floor action, and on other issues requested by a legislator. Legislators would receive balanced analyses that include the views of lobbyists and others, and a critique of them, without the foul play or undue influence of lobbyists who advocate for their clients, irrespective of the public interest. CIGOs would be nonpartisan, with staff hired for their objective analytical abilities and expertise rather than their political ties.

- Collaborative Win-Win Negotiations: At the start of each Congress, lawmakers would take a seminar on mediation and dispute resolution, to help set a constructive tenor. The seminars would promote cooperation and collaboration. Topics would include "benevolent negotiations" that build trusted, reliable, long-term partnerships for sustained bipartisanship. Benevolent negotiations would encourage legislators to negotiate with good faith offers that accommodate each other's main needs, rather than staking out hard-line positions and nickel-and-diming each other toward a middle-ground settlement. Once essential needs are satisfied, parties could voluntarily sweeten the pot by offering additional benefits to the other side. This would advance a climate of respect, accommodation, and trust, like mediation without a mediator, nurturing long-term relationships and hurdling obstacles.

- Issue Selection: The Speaker of the House and Senate Majority Leader determine the legislative agenda, with little or no accommodation of the minority party's priorities. Establishing criteria for issues to receive legislative action would boost cooperation and collegiality by ensuring bipartisan input into the process, even when Republicans and Democrats have different rationales for action. Criteria should favor action on exigent problems with widespread adverse effects. The influence of the minority party would remain limited, since disputes would still be resolved by the majority party.

- Agree First on Values: Consensus on policy solutions can be enhanced by first identifying the beliefs, aims, principles, and emotions that underlie legislative proposals, since fundamental values are often mutually shared. Agreement on unified values fosters mutual respect and understanding, paving the way for action. After identifying the values that are at stake, it is easier for legislators to agree to protect or preserve them, at which point it is easier to craft policy options. With bipartisan shared values, it becomes easier to reach agreement on policy options, rather than trying to convince each other to adopt an opposing view based on values that are not mutually held.

- Fact-Based Dialogue: When debating policy on contentious issues, legislators should substantiate their assertions through verifiable facts and studies, provided by reliable sources. Restrictions should be placed on anecdotes, metaphors, opinions, emotions, or recriminations against opposing views. The reliability of sources may be disputed, which can be resolved by questioning the methodologies used by those sources. Requiring a factual basis will usually provide enough accountability to improve the accuracy of each party's arguments, and narrow the scope of disputes.

- Data-Driven Policy: Use of data collection, aggregation, and analysis is increasingly common in the legislative process, as well as in the resulting policy solutions. Data is available on virtually any public policy topic and can be useful in informing legislative and administrative decision-making. Proposals should include a data component to monitor implementation progress, measure effectiveness, and provide transparency. Multiple data sets from government and other sources can be aggregated in creative ways to produce robust displays that reveal informative insights into conditions, needs, resources, metrics, impacts, and outcomes of any program or policy solution.

- Achieve Consensus: Legislators in leadership roles, including committee chairpersons, have an institutional responsibility to prioritize consensus over their personal or political ideology. Although many have strident views, imposing them increases fractiousness, entrenchment, and partisanship. By not exerting their ideology, they are able to lead with equanimity, as honest brokers, and produce legislation that achieves consensus. Some lawmakers have employed this practice, providing a template that deserves plaudits and replication, as it promotes legislative productivity.

Although this is by no means an exhaustive compilation of all the mechanisms that can increase cooperation, collaboration, collegiality, and compromise, these measures can have a beneficial impact. They can cultivate bipartisan relations and operations, enabling greater effectiveness, efficiency, productivity, and responsiveness of government, with win-win results.

IMPORTANCE DURING TRUMP'S TENURE AND THE POST-TRUMP ERA

Partisanship was already at a fever pitch prior to the Trump era. During the Trump administration's first two years, the divide between the parties has widened. The divide is sure to further expand as Trump pushes Republicans to support draconian legislation such as the repeal of Obamacare and other efforts, and as he imposes countless ill-conceived executive branch policies.

"Kakistocracy" is a fun word, but there is nothing funny about a government that is under the control of the worst or least qualified people. Trumpism celebrates inexperience, intemperance, and incivility in its policies, pabulum, and procedures, and hallows the "kakistocrocrats" who embody it. The incompetence embodied in a kakistocracy is sometimes intentional, like when migrant families were separated without proper recordkeeping to enable reunification. At the same time that Thailand's government heroically found children trapped in a cave, the Trump administration was ignominiously losing track of children by not doing paperwork. Trump's personal incompetence is often publicly displayed, epitomized by his July 2018 summit with Putin. The entire world witnessed Trump's feckless and narcissistic press conference performance, his subservience, lack of preparation, and infidelity to his own country.

Trumpism has become the catalyst to a counterreaction. Americans who are disillusioned or offended by Trumpism are embracing its antitheses: sagacious experience, discretion, respectfulness, knowledge, and sound professional judgment, all of which flourish in a meritocracy. Ironically, while the person in power subverts the principles underlying our democracy, he has also reinvigorated many sectors of society who want to see our government operating effectively and efficiently. The separation of families, the Trump-Putin press conference, and Trump's comments following the Charlottesville violence did more to boost bipartisanship than anything that Trump could have planned. All three incidents compelled Republicans and Democrats—legislators, officials, and experts—to unify in voicing their objections and displeasure.

The electorate has a strong appetite for enhanced bipartisanship to improve the functionality and responsiveness of our government. Throughout successive elections, culminating in the 2016 election, voters have expressed a desire to see a change in the culture of Washington that makes our government less confrontational, more productive, and pragmatically effective. Bipartisanship is a key benchmark for that transformation. Through collaboration and cooperation based on mutual respect among officials with diverse ideologies, legislators can generate constructive compromises for government to effectively serve the populace.

Some partisans may assail bipartisanship as being impossible, impractical, or simply naive. Such assertions are usually made out of a lack of effort, creativity, or willingness to abandon cynical and malevolent perceptions of political advantage. Bipartisan action is distinct from naive notions of harmony because it enables practical progress, and confers pragmatic electoral advantages. The first step to enabling bipartisanship is having the desire to do so. If both sides are willing, then it can happen.

At the same time that partisanship is increasing, bipartisanship is increasing, too, and the trend is likely to continue in the post-Trump era. Bipartisanship could gain further traction during Trump's tenure and beyond, and become a consistent practice in Congress, interspersed amidst partisan clashes.

There's also a scenario in which bipartisanship could soar while Trump is in office and carry forward into the post-Trump era. It involves Trump *inadvertently* changing the culture of Washington and creating the atmosphere for bipartisanship to flourish. This scenario began when Trump criticized and ridiculed GOP lawmakers including senators Mitch McConnell, Dean Heller, the late John McCain, Jeff Flake, Lisa Murkowski, Bob Corker, and others in both chambers. Even when the senators who are still serving make nice and work with Trump thereafter, neither they nor their colleagues forget what he said about them. When Steve Bannon left the White House, he signaled that he would intensify the battle between Trump and Republicans in Congress. He has been doing that, and the epithets could eventually escalate into a veritable war between the Republican White House and the Republicans in Congress. Trump's animosity toward Congress could become so intense that he would be unwilling to work with Republicans on legislation and refuse to sign any bills.

Republicans could become so demoralized that they resort to extreme solutions. They are likely to become acutely aware of the need to find a way to govern, even if only to do the bare minimum to keep the government afloat—for example, raise the ceiling on the federal debt, pass appropriations bills to fund the government, reauthorize programs when they near their expiration, and pass urgent or time-sensitive legislation. In this critical, albeit unlikely, situation, the Republican leadership just might bite the bullet and engage Democrats in a delicate, pragmatic, institutional alliance to enable Congress to function. Legislation essential for the government to operate could be addressed in a straightforward, nonideological manner, and pass with overwhelming, veto-proof majorities. Any bills that Trump vetoes would be returned to Congress for votes to override the veto, and Congress would have the votes to do so. This alliance of necessity could accelerate if the Mueller report's evidence of obstruction of justice causes concerns to escalate, and if Trump impedes congressional investigations to the point that Republicans acknowledge that impeachment is the only solution.

Once Republicans and Democrats collaborate a few times on critical, time-sensitive matters, it will become easier to continue that process, and they might act on a broader range of policy issues while they're in the flow of collaboration. It could usher in a new era of pragmatic bipartisanship, and establish a template that could continue in the post-Trump era.

As polls about Congress indicate, legislators who lead cross-party initiatives receive a positive response from most of the electorate. The aura of leadership will surround those who are bold enough to collaborate across traditional barriers, enabling them to govern effectively and achieve results. Voters in many districts hunger for leaders who recognize that, despite their differences, all lawmakers can, should, and must work together toward mutually agreeable policies that benefit an extensive majority of Americans.

CHAPTER 10

VOTER SHIFTS

EXPOSURE OF THE REAL TRUMP AND THE IMPACT ON KEY TRUMP VOTERS

T hroughout American history, strong sentiments have dictated the direction of our politics, elections, and government. At the time that they are dominant, they seem unalterable, as if bound for permanence. A quintessential example was when President George W. Bush was at the crest of his popularity, benefiting from post-September 11 national unity and the initial phase of the Iraq War. His senior advisor, Karl Rove, envisioned the creation of a "permanent Republican majority."[1] But, of course, Rove's desired dominance was no more enduring than many other waves of popular opinion. The air of permanence dissipates when a countervailing sentiment sweeps in, dislodging the one preceding it.

Just as the pendulum of voter sentiment had swung so far during the Bush-Cheney days that Barack Obama was able to grab it and swing in the opposite direction, Donald Trump caught it at the end of Obama's ride and steered it in an altogether new path. The question for 2020 will be whether the pendulum will swing fiercely again. In politics as in physics, will the maxim that "for every action there is an equal and opposite reaction" hold true?

That will depend, in large part, on the public's perception and assessment of the incumbent. Americans are gaining new insights into Trump's character and conduct virtually every day. Revelation of the real Donald Trump may cause different reactions among different segments of his supporters. Trump's base voters strongly approve of him personally, support him fully, are deeply committed, and would not even consider defecting. His hardcore base will probably always stick with him, even if he were to, as he said, "stand in the middle of Fifth Avenue and shoot somebody," or even if he were proven to be functioning as an unwitting agent of Vladimir Putin, as some people have hypothesized.[2]

But not all people who voted for Trump, or who express their support to public opinion pollsters, are among his base. Many of his 2016 voters and current supporters generally approve of him while also expressing discontent with his personal conduct, tweets, or policies. These nonbase supporters support him conditionally and might consider embracing another candidate. Some pundits erroneously fail to differentiate between Trump's base and nonbase supporters. But the distinction is important because the two groups might respond differently to the truth about Donald Trump as more information about him and his activities comes to light.

Among those whose support for Trump is lukewarm, how receptive will they be to an alternative candidate? Among those who voted for Trump but are not among his devoted base (especially independents, crossover Democrats, and even many Republicans), knowing what they know now, and with more to come in the days ahead, will they happily buckle up for another ride on Trump's roller coaster? Or will they become disheartened and want to swap the roller coaster for a pleasure cruise, with a stable, sanguine captain at the wheel, charting a serene course? The 2020 election will answer those and other questions. The outcome will show either that the political pendulum is ready to swing in a new direction or that Trumpism has sufficient momentum to continue its trajectory for a while.

Currently, our country is inundated with all things Trump, all the time. Although there is no precise parallel in US history to Donald Trump's tactics and immersive presence, it is useful to compare the smothering ubiquity of Senator Joe McCarthy's fabricated anticommunist crusade that framed the American political climate in the 1950s.[3] The obsession with McCarthy's baseless accusations dominated American politics and culture. Many people struggled and failed to curtail and transcend McCarthyism.[4] But, at a certain point, the falsity of McCarthy's claims was exposed, people doubted both the message and the messenger, and rationality was restored.[5] The American people saw it for what it was, had enough, outgrew it, and rejected it. That sequence of sentiments is one possible template for the country's near future.

Leading up to the 2020 election, Americans will likely learn who Trump really is. He will surely retain the loyalty and support of his most dedicated base voters, as the success of some candidates whom he endorsed in the 2018 midterm election indicates. But Trump's true nature and objectives will alienate a key group of swing voters who account for a sizeable percentage of his 2016 vote and his ongoing approval numbers. If Trump's support among them wanes, it will not be possible for him to win reelection, although there is one implausible scenario that could work in his favor. If swing voters defect, or abstain from voting, there will be major implications for Republican candidates running for other offices. The loss of enthusiasm among many of Trump's 2016 voters will affect the electoral prospects of down-ticket Republican candidates even if Trump is not on the ballot (which is also a distinct possibility). Even more importantly, the consequences could have a profound impact on the future of the Republican Party.

TRUMP'S SKILLS AND THE REAL DONALD TRUMP

Donald Trump definitely has a politically useful skill set, albeit not the usual skills that we've seen in our past presidents. He doesn't have the legislative prowess of FDR and LBJ, the vision of Kennedy and Teddy Roosevelt, or the foreign affairs understanding of Wilson and Nixon. He doesn't have the communication skills of Reagan and Bill Clinton, the managerial skills of Truman and George H. W. Bush, or the moral fiber of Carter and Eisenhower. And he doesn't have the decision-making judgment, thirst for knowledge, or intellect of any of them.

Trump's assets are concentrated in marketing, branding, sales, and media manipulation, which are valuable in politics just as they are in real estate and reality TV. The Moniker Man has branded many people with derogatory nicknames to influence his audience's opinions of each person who he names. His ability to energize his audience, emotionally connect with his preferred demographic groups, and craft messages that appeal to his target market is undeniable. He is skilled at provoking the media so that they cover what he says and does, which amplifies his message. It could be argued that these skills are just as important as a candidate's policy positions because they enable the candidate to form a bond with the voters and maintain his presence in their consciousness.

The way that he used his skills both helped and hurt his 2016 campaign, since that which ingratiated him to some voters repelled others, and energized both. Either way, he leveraged his skills well enough to cross the finish line in first place. Whether one approves of him or not, enough Americans did vote for him to win the presidency. As president, he has continued to leverage these skills to maintain his relationship with his base and project his message practically whenever he wants. The results of the 2018 midterm election showed that he can still motivate a sizeable share of the electorate to follow his lead, albeit only in certain states and mainly in rural communities. Whether one likes him or not, everyone should be willing to recognize that his talents earned him a devoted following.

The Trump administration has many accomplishments, depending on one's point of view. Many of his policies and actions both excite his supporters and enrage his opponents. These include his travel ban, judicial appointments, withdrawal from international agreements, tax cuts, reversal of many environmental regulations, and reductions in civil rights and equal justice enforcement. Voters whose ideology comports with these actions have plenty to cheer about. If Trump's meeting with Kim Jong-un produces positive results with North Korea in the near future, and if tariffs lead to advantageous trade agreements, then a broader swath of voters may respond positively, even if they still object to Trump's tactics in reaching them (e.g., first risking war through dangerous saber-rattling rhetoric, and first risking a trade war by imposing ill-advised tariffs). However, voters who are demoralized or offended by the bulk of Trump's policies, comments, tenor, values, and personal conduct will not be swayed by a few positive outcomes.

With regard to Trump's tone and tenor, his comments are plainspoken, direct, self-serving, and calibrated to both excite his base and manipulate others. He speaks publicly on matters that all other presidents relegated to private meetings, ignoring the political and policy consequences of public comments on evolving positions and national security issues. For example, when speaking about North Korea at his September 2018 press conference in New York, Trump may have either lied or recklessly impaired national security and declassified sensitive information by saying, "President Obama thought you had to go to war. You know how close he was to pressing the trigger for war? . . . And he said to me that he was very close to going into war." Trump's rhetoric is often inflammatory, bombastic, politically incorrect, counterproductive, juvenile, and completely false. His oratory—especially at his rallies—and his tweets are intended to give him instant gratification from the applause of his base regardless of how many people he offends.[6] He has shown himself to be eager to champion white identity politics and ethnic nationalism, both of which appeal to his loyal supporters, even though these themes alienate most other voters. It's as if he heard only the first half of the old expression "you have to break some eggs . . . to make an omelet."

Trump's personal shortcomings were summarized by former House Speaker John Boehner's former spokesman, Michael Steele, who said, "I haven't spoken to anyone who is involved with this White House who fundamentally disputes the idea that the President is often disengaged, very emotional, and relatively impervious to the facts a lot of the time."[7] Trump doesn't speak specifically, factually, or accurately about issues, preferring instead to arouse his audience's emotional reactions with cultural markers, and he eagerly engages in baseless vilifications and adolescent name-calling to do that.

In a moment of exuberance after he won Nevada's primary, Trump inadvertently revealed one of the main reasons for his incessant falsehoods, deceptions, and repetitive branding. In his impulsive victory speech, he exulted, "We won with poorly educated. I love the poorly educated." While he cited other groups whose vote he won that day, "love" was accorded only to "the poorly educated" and evangelicals. As Alec MacDonald observed, "Now, there is certainly nothing wrong with being uneducated. Being uneducated sucks. You know what also sucks? A political leader's campaign depending on the fact most people voting for him are uneducated."[8]

It appears that Trump's comments, tweets, and positions cynically aim to bolster support from "the poorly educated" for his political benefit and survival. If Trump believes that he is highly educated and the bulk of his supporters are "poorly educated," then his falsehoods and deceptions that confuse and manipulate their opinions amount to predatory behavior, beyond mere political utilitarianism. While many in Trump's base might not care about this, it probably matters to others. Usually, people who are disparaged, demeaned, manipulated, or subjected to condescension resent the perpetrator. If Trump's base feels that he discounts them as "poorly educated" and takes advantage of them, there could be consequences.

Trump cynically propagates falsehoods for his base's consumption, such as when he attempted to repair the damage that he created at his 2018 press conference with Vladimir Putin in Helsinki. When a reporter asked Trump whether he believed that it was Russia that meddled in the 2016 election, he said, "I don't see any reason why it would be."[9] The next day, he claimed that he meant to say "would not" instead of "would," even though the change would make that statement inconsistent with his other comments during and after the press conference.[10] His condescending attempt to add "not" to mollify the debacle reveals his low regard for the intellect of the supporters for whom he made that revision (there was no chance of his skeptics believing that claim). It's hard to imagine that his "not" excuse would convince anyone, although some GOP legislators, who sought a reason not to criticize Trump further, pretended to accept it to give themselves cover and avoid the issue. Trump's revisionism was juvenile and ludicrous, at best.

A similar example occurred two days after Trump appointed Matthew Whitaker as acting attorney general. The selection appeared to be fueled by Whitaker's antagonism toward Mueller's investigation and the tactics that Whitaker proposed to neutralize it, both of which he stated on television before joining the administration.[11] When trying to create the impression that he did not choose Whitaker for those reasons, Trump said, "I don't know Matt Whitaker." But, the previous month, he told an interviewer, "I know Matt Whitaker."[12] Trump's blatant contradiction was an obvious falsehood. It is difficult to imagine that he thought that this would fool anyone. It fits his pattern of erroneous statements that are designed to manipulate the views of his base, with no chance of anyone else being convinced.

An alternative explanation of why Trump caters to "the poorly educated" is that he identifies with them due to what he perceives as his own intellectual deficiency. Although he attended college, doing so does not necessarily confer knowledge, wisdom, or competence, especially when coupled with a lack of intellectual curiosity and an aversion to reading (even a briefing book in preparation for a high-stakes summit). For example, at his September 2018 press conference, he talked about a supporter briefing him on events in Syria, saying, "I didn't hear of Idlib Province." He went on to say that he realized that the supporter was right when he saw something about the Idlib events in the *New York Times*, even though his intelligence briefings surely had addressed the tragedy in Idlib. Either Trump did not pay attention to the briefings, did not understand them, or refused to even read or listen to them. Not smart (in his parlance).

Even Trump's staff has noted his dearth of intellect. In *Fear*, Bob Woodward wrote that former secretary Rex Tillerson called Trump a "f—-ing moron." Secretary Jim Mattis said that Trump "acted like—and had the understanding of—'a fifth- or sixth-grader.'" Chief of Staff John Kelly said, "He's an idiot. It's pointless to try to convince him of anything. He's gone off the rails. We're in Crazytown."[13] Despite claiming to be "like, really smart" and a "very stable genius,"[14] facts substantiate the opposite. Trump's contradictory comments, poor judgment, policy reversals, inability to understand the details of his own policies, and mangled language are not signs of genius.

Trump's shortcomings were displayed in multiple ways when he made his pitch for "would not" instead of "would." He was trying to claim that he trusted the opinion of his intelligence agencies over that of Putin. Yet, while grudgingly accepting the conclusion that Russia interfered in our election, he added, "Could be other people also," which was the opposite of their conclusion.[15] Moments earlier, while trying to show solidarity with the intelligence agencies, he negated that, too. After saying, "I have a full faith in our intelligence agencies," the lights in the room briefly went out, and he said, "Whoops, they just turned out the lights. That must be the intelligence agencies." Right after he expressed his faith in them, he negated it by blaming them, albeit jokingly, with an improvised comment. A genuine "stable genius" would not impair their own objective or diminish their message, and definitely would not do it in consecutive sentences.

Many of Trump's comments and tweets are calculated to provoke the media, distract them from more consequential issues and his personal shortcomings, and weaken the public's trust in them. Trump also demonizes politicians—legislators, governors, foreign leaders—and the media to pressure them to do what he wants. By manipulating the media's coverage and the public's attention, he controls the daily news cycle. His incessant repetition of deceptions, falsehoods, and fabrications aims to ingrain his assertions as facts, shift public opinion toward his false narratives, and confuse the public to degrade their confidence in legitimate news. This seems to be both a branding ploy, so that his preferred reality will take root as accepted truth, and a defense mechanism, to build a firewall of support against the political and legal consequences of Special Counsel Mueller's findings.

Trump's actions, words, and tweets reveal his profound worry about public exposure of facts regarding collusion with Russians, and obstruction of justice to conceal it, that congressional committees plan to illuminate with the aid of information in Mueller's report.[16] Trump is probably also concerned about the investigations into his financial and business affairs, including violations of the Constitution's Emoluments Clause (which are likely referenced in the report, although redacted from it), by the Southern District of New York and other prosecutors. Trump's protestations convey the impression that he knows the truth about all of these matters and has a guilty conscience about them, recognizing that they taint the legitimacy of his election and his self-acclaimed business prowess.

Based on what is publicly known about Trump's interactions with Putin and Russians, it seems that the ongoing investigations may reveal three aspects of the kompromat that Putin might have on Trump:

- existence of kompromat: the possibility that Trump's finances (e.g., loans from Russians and Russian banks), business interests (e.g., building a hotel in Moscow), personal behavior (described in the Steele dossier), and coordination of campaign assistance (e.g., WikiLeaks and social media manipulation) were the sources of Russia's leverage over him;
- actions because of kompromat: Trump complying with Russian requests due to leverage on him (e.g., the Trump Tower meeting about relief from sanctions, Michael Flynn's activities with Russians, withholding criticism of Putin despite his interference in our 2016 election and his military incursions against Ukraine); and
- concealing the kompromat: Trump's efforts to obstruct justice, which aimed to hide all of this from public disclosure, insulate him and his family from legal jeopardy, and evade political consequences (e.g., falsehoods and media manipulation, encouraging others to lie or withhold information, firing FBI director Comey, attempting to fire Mueller and limit the scope of his investigation, and threatening Michael Cohen).

By siding with Putin about Russian interference with our elections and disregarding the findings of our intelligence agencies at the Helsinki summit, Trump exacerbated his political problems in addition to adding fuel to Mueller's investigation. Many officials, both Republicans and Democrats, objected to his failure to defend our democracy. Some believed that his patriotism was put in question, and others went further to suggest that it constituted "high crimes and misdemeanors" (the constitutional standard for impeachment) by his obeisance to a foreign adversary.[17] If concerns about Trump's patriotism remain—which impact the most fundamental presidential responsibilities— then his presidency could be vulnerable on that front, too. That might be a bridge too far even for some in his base.

Trump is still seeking insulation from the outcome of Mueller's investigation. Trump incessantly alleges his innocence in comments and tweets like "there was no collusion and there was no crime."[18] The frequency of that assertion was rivaled only by the constant fallacious claim of a "witch hunt."

Although Mueller determined that there was not enough evidence to substantiate charges of criminal conspiracy, which would have required specific elements to be proven beyond a reasonable doubt, his report documented many instances of collusion between Russians and Trump campaign officials, which may or may not have involved Trump himself.[19]

Trump acts as if he wants the public to suspend common sense and simply accept as truth everything that he says, just because he says it. His actions demonstrate his desire to uproot public confidence in the principles, procedures, and precedents of constitutional justice that evolved over the past 230 years. Even if Trump says "no collusion" every day, that doesn't make it true. Even if he convinces his devotees to adopt his alternative reality and false narrative, that cannot shield him from the law. Even if he is merely naive, the maxim that "ignorance of the law is no excuse" still applies. Not only is Trump trying to rewrite history and invalidate the laws that could place him in legal jeopardy, he is also trying to rewrite the fundamental values, standards, perceptions, and laws that are the foundation of our society.

These and other well-documented mendacities (e.g., misogyny, bigotry, racism, profligacy, profiteering) call into question Trump's character.[20] Prior to Trump, inquiries into the character of candidates mainly looked at their honesty and their policies. Aside from catching a candidate lying, character issues were often a surrogate for the degree to which a candidate harbored conservative views on reproductive rights, family values, religion, sexual mores, education, and similar matters. But Trump's conduct and comments have changed that. In his case, character issues revert to a more traditional interpretation. Attention has focused on his moral fiber, ethical compass, habitual dishonesty, and temperament, as well as his lack of empathy, compassion, humility, respectfulness, aptitude, and other elements of one's humanity and capacity.[21] His deficiencies of character have concerned Republicans, Democrats, independents, and others, including many people who generally support him.[22] Trump's choice of advisors reinforces skepticism about his judgment and values, as embodied by his saying of disgraced casino owner Steve Wynn, "Steve is always calling. He's always got advice, right Steve? 'Donald, I think you should do this and that.' His advice I like to listen to, I'll be honest."[23]

Despite Trump's character issues, most people in his base continue to support him,[24] although many would prefer that he develop some self-control and tamp down his aggressive, impulsive rhetoric. At the same time, many within his base support him *because* of these behaviors, celebrating his character traits and the image that he projects.[25] Both of these groups within his base identify with him and didn't feel like they were fooled or misled into supporting him, even though the image that he branded of himself is oxymoronic: the blue-collar billionaire. On election night 2016, his base must have felt like they had a winning lottery ticket. They wanted his rebellion against the establishment.[26] They had lost confidence in both parties after years of promises not being kept. They waited in vain without seeing sufficient results. They were upset and so was Trump. They share his psychology of victimization. When Trump feels slighted and slashes back, his base feels empowered, as if they are being personally disparaged by the entire political establishment and they get to punch it back. During the campaign, he bore their burdens, spoke their language, and paternalistically assured them that "I alone can fix it."

Trump projects himself as a counterpoint to Obama.[27] Whereas Obama is a cerebral, articulate, nuanced, erudite communicator, Trump's speech is brash, blustery, banal, bellicose, and brutish. Whereas Obama navigated complex policy issues, Trump dispenses myopic platitudes, substituting cultural markers and his cult-of-personality style for wise policy. Whereas Obama was so balanced that he was known as "no-drama Obama," Trump cultivates an atmosphere of constant chaos and unabashedly thrives on drama. Whereas Obama aligned himself with Lincoln's words, "With malice toward none, with charity for all," Trump is a purveyor of retribution and punition. Whereas Obama was an egalitarian who sought empowerment of all Americans for their success, Trump is an authoritarian who caters to privileged elites while plying his base with tokens and rhetoric, for which they praise and follow him as they would a father figure. Whereas Obama treated people with respect, dignity, and congeniality, Trump eagerly engages in disparagement, ridicule, and condemnation. Whereas Obama engaged foreign leaders (except hostile nations and terrorists) with partnership and equanimity, Trump fabricates a false air of personal dominance and superiority (e.g., pushing Montenegro's prime minister out of the way at a NATO Summit).[28] Where Obama offered a carrot, Trump uses a stick.

During the campaign, Trump's criticism of Obama was not limited to policy, principles, persona, and performance. For example, Trump repeatedly criticized Obama for playing golf and taking time for vacation. Hypocritically, Trump has spent an exorbitant amount of his presidency doing both, far in excess of any previous president. He ridiculed Obama for using a teleprompter, tweeting "Why does @BarackObama always have to rely on teleprompters?"[29] and boasting "I don't use teleprompters."[30] Yet, Trump is wedded to them, using teleprompters both during the campaign and then increasingly as president.[31] He especially relies on a teleprompter, and even sticks to the script, when he is speaking on sensitive issues or in high-stakes situations that demand accuracy and/or decorum,[32] which is so unlike his usual tone that his persona in those instances has been dubbed "Teleprompter Trump."[33]

Maybe Trump executed a shrewd branding campaign, with a calculated strategy to run as the antithesis of Obama. He may have positioned himself as Obama's polar opposite to capitalize on resentment that Trump saw fomenting within some demographics. With Trump's main skills as a marketing and branding expert, his anti-Obama campaign might just have been his latest project. Maybe Trump repudiates Obama at every opportunity because of Trump's character deficiencies, fueled by his deep-seated inferiority complex and racist orientation. Or maybe Trump positioned himself against Obama during the campaign—and continues to do so as president—as retribution for Obama ridiculing him at the White House Correspondents' Dinner in 2011, which permanently pierced Trump's thin skin.

After Trump's election victory, he made the customary (obligatory) visit to the White House to meet with President Obama, during which the two reportedly had a civil discourse. They also appeared to speak congenially on Inauguration Day. In an interview with Fox News a few days after the inauguration, Trump claimed, "We get along. I don't know if he'll admit this, but he likes me. I like him." When the interviewer asked, "How do you know he (likes you)?" Trump replied, "Because I can feel it. That's what I do in life—it's called like, I understand."[34] Those interactions led many observers to believe that the relationship might be on a new, positive course. Some were still baffled by the incongruity a year later.

But actually, that is not surprising for three reasons. First, Trump hungers for approbation and praise,[35] such as what he receives from his adoring crowds at rallies. His need for validation is why he often agrees with attendees at meetings, conveying the impression of a good meeting, before meeting with someone who holds the opposite view (whose approval Trump also seeks), leading him to reverse course and contradict himself. In his two encounters with Obama, Trump courted Obama's favor, hoping to be rewarded with it. Second, just as Trump is highly influenced by his most recent conversation on policy matters (like when the pope urged him to remain in the Paris Agreement), he is equally pliant with recent personal interactions.[36] But after the glow of an encounter fades, Trump reverts to his prior emotional impulses. Once Obama was gone, Trump's engrained hostility toward him resurfaced. Third, Trump probably hears the name "Obama" often during his national security briefings and other meetings in which the continuity of policy is at issue. It is likely that these constant reminders regularly renew—and even intensify—Trump's antipathy for the man who made a couple of jokes at his expense.[37]

The likelihood that Trump intentionally decided to countermand all things Obama was bolstered when we learned about the contents of the note that Obama left for Trump in the presidential desk.[38] It seems as though Trump has deliberately contravened each of the points of advice that Obama offered (other than the personal one about valuing friends and family).

- Obama's advice to "build more ladders of success for every child and family that's willing to work hard" was offended by Trump's reversal on the DACA program that put all of the Dreamers (children of undocumented immigrants) at risk of deportation, his budget cuts to education, his personnel reductions for civil rights programs at schools and elsewhere, and his departments' discriminatory actions against transgendered Americans in schools and the military.
- Obama's advice to "sustain the international order that's expanded steadily since the end of the Cold War, and upon which our own wealth and safety depend" was rejected when Trump withdrew from the COP21 Paris Agreement, the Trans-Pacific Partnership, and the Iran Nuclear Agreement, contentiously moved our embassy to Jerusalem, denigrated Haiti and African countries, hesitated to support NATO's Article 5, provoked North Korea, offended our G7 and NATO allies, initiated a tariff and trade war, and eagerly supported autocratic rulers, especially Vladimir Putin.
- Obama's advice that, as "guardians of . . . democratic institutions and traditions—like rule of law, separation of powers, equal protection and civil liberties—that our forebears fought and bled for . . . it's up to us to leave those instruments of our democracy at least as strong as we found them," has been repeatedly and completely eviscerated by Trump in his apparent obstructions of justice, Charlottesville and

NFL/NBA comments, disparagement of Congress and the courts, pardon of Joe Arpaio, the travel ban, the Election Integrity Commission, encouraging rough treatment of potential criminals during arrests, etc.; and by his appointees, as in Jeff Sessions's actions against Affirmative Action, termination of consent decrees and policing reforms, disenfranchisement of voters by supporting efforts to purge voter registration rolls, etc.

Trump has sought to convey an image of himself as a confident, knowledgeable, cavalier, authoritative, strong leader. This lifelong branding campaign has been among his most essential pet projects. It took root with his base voters, many of whom formed opinions of him by watching his show, *The Apprentice*, in which he acted out that manufactured image.

But with the presidency comes transparency and scrutiny. Now that a microscope is on Trump like never before, his true self is being exposed, evident even to people who averted their eyes in 2016. It reveals that the real Donald Trump is unlike the image that Trump portrays.[39] This is clear from:

- his disloyalty to, and savage disparagement of, his staff, including Jeff Sessions, Rex Tillerson, David Shulkin, Kirstjen Nielsen, Wilbur Ross, and Omarosa Manigault-Newman;
- comments by his staff that have been widely reported, as when John Kelly called him an "idiot" and Rex Tillerson called him a "moron";
- his aggressive use of the presidency to generate personal wealth for his Washington, DC, hotel, the use of his resorts (which necessitates government activity and spending at them in serving the president), the ZTE deal with China, and his daughter's patents from China;
- his support for, and warm relations with, foreign authoritarians such as Vladimir Putin, Xi Jinping, Abdel Fattah el-Sisi, Recep Tayyip Erdogan, Kim Jong-un, King Salman, and Rodrigo Duterte;
- his unjustified antagonism toward some of America's closest allies, including Angela Merkel, Justin Trudeau, Theresa May, NATO, and the European Union; and
- his demonization of anyone who doesn't do what he likes or wants, from legislators, judges, Hillary Clinton, and LeBron James, to James Comey, Robert Mueller, Mika Brzezinski and Joe Scarborough of MSNBC, and the media as a whole.

The media provides transparency and scrutiny regardless of who is president. In addition to their reporting, Trump's tweets and ubiquitous presence reveal his character, while the facts emanating from Special Counsel Mueller's and Congress's investigations expose his true nature. His self-branded persona has already been contradicted by much of what has become known, with more to come in the months ahead. It is increasingly evident that, in spite of what he wants people to believe, some might say that he is actually a weak, insecure, self-obsessed, delusional, disloyal, emotionally diminutive figure who hyperextends himself to overcompensate for his personal faults, ineptitude, and intellectual impotence. His reckless disregard for the truth and his willingness to lie his way around it are probably the most obvious indicators that the image that he branded is his safe harbor from reality. As the truth takes root in the national conscience, there will be political and electoral consequences.

THE REAL DONALD TRUMP IS ALIENATING 2016'S RELUCTANT TRUMP VOTERS

In 2016, Trump could craft whatever image he wanted, claiming to be whoever he wanted to be, because he had no record as a public official. But he won't have that luxury after four years as president, if he is still in position to run for reelection in 2020. He will be well defined by his actions and statements. No longer will he have the benefit of the "green screen" effect, on which impressions and phony images can be projected. Most voters will easily recognize his falsehoods because they will conflict with his record and the evidence that has been discovered by the investigations. Exposure of Trump's true nature, which continues to be illuminated through daily dramas, revelations, and self-disclosures, is likely to be a game-changer in 2020 since the election will largely be a referendum on the real Donald Trump, regardless of who else is on the ballot.

Trump's temperament, style, policies, and incessant insults have alienated countless Republicans. Many have left the party, switching their registration to independent or a third-party.[40] As a result, Trump's high level of support among Republicans in opinion polls is deceptive, since it reflects his support among a smaller number of people—those who remain registered as Republicans—and does not reflect those who have left the party. His job approval among Republicans is typically over 80 percent; although high, it is the opinion of a smaller share of the electorate and not as meaningful as it would be if GOP registrants were still close to parity with Democrats. A Pew Research Center study of registered voters in March 2018 showed that 37 percent identify as independents, 33 percent as Democrats, and 26 percent as Republicans.[41] The wave of Republicans who have left their party might also be an early indicator of party realignment. Many former Republicans might be looking for a new political home, while those who remain within the GOP might identify more with Trump than with traditional Republican values, policies, and candidates.[42]

Most of Trump's loyal base voters will probably choose to see the image-crafted, branded Trump that he wants them to see. To his most committed supporters, Trump will always be the renegade, authoritarian leader to whom they are devoted.[43] They love the way he says whatever he wants, regardless of the consequences. They love the way he pokes his finger in the eyes of both political parties. They love the way he gives voice to their xenophobic, white grievance mentality, which spawns their "build the wall" chant. They love the way he shakes up the global order without concern for economic or geopolitical impacts. Out of loyalty, they might even continue to faithfully accept his "alternative facts." But even if their passion for Trump is as intense in 2020 as it was in 2016, it might not matter much.

Trump's base was just one of the significant voting blocs that contributed to his vote total. There were also Trump's reluctant voters, who have been characterized as predominantly white and older, like his base voters but with higher levels of education.[44] Altogether, Trump got 46.1 percent of the popular vote, comprised of both his base and others who voted for him due to other reasons. With support now gauged by opinion polls, it is important to emphasize that Trump's base is a subset of those who support him in the opinion polls. His job approval numbers include both his hardcore base and others who are not within his base, but who still approve of his job performance to one degree or another.

In 2017, expert analysts estimated that Trump's highly committed base is approximately 18 to 24 percent of the electorate. If Trump is on the ballot in the 2020 election, these are the voters who will most reliably support him. He will probably retain them with very few defections. The 2017 figures are instructive because they reflect the share of the electorate that held steady in support of Trump even when his job approval numbers were waning and reached their nadir. Those numbers fluctuated thereafter, influenced by daily news, combining the opinions of both loyal and transient supporters.

- In a May 2017 report, Nate Silver of FiveThirtyEight determined that Trump's base amounted to 21 or 22 percent of the electorate.[45]
- In August 2017, Steven Shepard reported that a poll by *Politico* and *Morning Consult* showed that Trump's base constituted 18 percent of the electorate.[46] Shepard noted that Trump's base was a smaller share of the electorate than previously thought, citing contemporary polls by CNN/SSRS (24 percent), Quinnipiac University (23 percent), CBS News, Gallup, and Investor's Business Daily/TIPP.
- In an August 2017 *Washington Examiner* article, Kristen Soltis Anderson determined that Trump's base constituted 24 percent of the electorate (citing data from polls by Monmouth University, CNN, Gallup, and *Morning Consult/Politico*).[47]
- In August 2017, former DNC chair Howard Dean corroborated these figures when he said, "This battle is the battle for the 10 or 15 percent of the people who voted for Donald Trump who are basically decent people who wanted change and now are disgusted by what's going on."[48] (Dean's 10 or 15 percent figure is reached by subtracting the percent that is Trump's base from the percent of all voters who approve of Trump's job performance.)
- Other experts have confirmed those numbers for the Trump base's share of the electorate[49] and the decrease of his base since polls taken in the first half of 2017.[50]

In 2018, a study by Real Clear Opinion Research (an arm of *Real Clear Politics*) confirmed the point that Trump's hardcore base is a subset of his overall supporters. The September 2018 public opinion survey categorized the electorate into five "tribes."[51] The survey determined that Trump's base (the MAGA tribe) amounted to just 12 percent of the electorate, and that traditional Republicans (the Mainline GOP tribe) are 14 percent of the electorate, for a combined total of 26 percent favoring the GOP. The other three tribes are Independent Blues (24 percent), The Detached (24 percent), and The Resistance (26 percent). Trump can count on support from the MAGA tribe's 12 percent. Even if he secures the Mainline GOP tribe's 14 percent, that combined 26 percent still falls far short of his job approval numbers. He needs support from the other tribes.

Trump voters in 2016 who were not among his diehard base will be a much more fluid voting bloc in the 2020 election and a pivotal factor in the outcome. Loosely applying the numbers, if the roughly 21 to 24 percent who are seen as constituting Trump's base (excluding the low-end figures: 12 percent by Real Clear Opinion Research and 18 percent by Shepard) are subtracted from Trump's 46.1 percent share of the 2016 popular vote, one can infer that approximately 22 to 25 percent of votes cast for Trump were from voters not among his base. Whether Trump's nonbase voters amounted to 26, 24, 22, or 20 percent of the 2016 electorate, the point remains the same. A large share of his support came from voters who were not within his hardcore base, and were not highly committed to him. Since the support of his nonbase voters was tepid, their opinions will have a major impact on the 2020 election's outcome.

The distinction between Trump's base and nonbase voters was reconfirmed by an ABC News/*Washington Post* poll taken in April 2019. In that poll, only 28 percent said that they would definitely vote for Trump (akin to base voters), while an additional 14 percent said that they would consider voting for him (akin to nonbase voters).[52] The poll also found that Trump's support was not solid among groups that would have been expected to overwhelmingly support him: only 63 percent of Republicans said that they would definitely vote for him and among conservatives that number dropped to 51 percent.[53]

Job approval ratings are also insightful. Polls taken in the latter half of 2017 had Trump's job approval ranging from 32 to 40 percent of those polled (excluding the Rasmussen poll, which is widely seen as lacking credibility). In early and mid-2018, the *Real Clear Politics* averages of the preceding months' polls hovered around 40 percent, inching higher shortly before the 2018 midterm election and back down to 40/41 percent in January 2019. Assuming that job approval numbers in polls correlate to support, these numbers reflect a clear decline in his support from his 46 percent share of the 2016 vote. By subtracting the percentage of Trump's hardcore base (21 to 24 percent) from those who most consistently approve of his job performance (40 percent), his nonbase supporters have declined to 16 to 19 percent of the electorate (from 22 to 25 percent in the 2016 election). That translates to 16 to 19 percent of the population supporting Trump without being highly committed to him.

(The Real Clear Opinion Research survey's 12 percent in the MAGA tribe indicates that 28 to 30 percent of people who approve of his job performance in most polls are nonbase supporters who are not highly committed to him.)

At 16 to 19 percent, Trump's nonbase supporters would be a large and influential voting bloc. Since their support is soft, they would be "reachable" by other candidates and could sway both the popular vote and the Electoral College vote. In a general election head-to-head matchup against one Democrat, it would be crucial for Trump to get the votes of that entire 16 to 19 percent bloc to bring his vote total up to his polling numbers. Even if the *Real Clear Politics* average of job approval numbers ticks upward a few percent, votes from all of his nonbase supporters would remain critical to Trump's electoral viability.

Even if Trump solidifies his nonbase support, it is difficult to see how he would attract the votes of many people beyond this group. If they were not even willing to say that they approved of his job performance, then they would be unlikely to vote for him, unless, perhaps, they feel that they are pressed to vote for the lesser of two evils. If he gets a full 40 percent of the popular vote, his numbers would still be far short of what he needs to win (except in one scenario, discussed below). If Trump's nonbase supporters see past the branded veneer to the real Donald Trump and don't like the misogyny, racism, xenophobia, unpatriotic conduct, and unethical profiteering that they find, then their votes might drift to another candidate, and Trump's total share of the popular vote might sink into the thirties.

That stark reality would force most candidates to throw in the towel. If Trump pursues reelection with such low and lukewarm support, his only potential route to victory would be to effectively disqualify his opponent. That would result in another vitriolic and venomous campaign that might even make his 2016 campaign against Hillary Clinton seem quaint and friendly by comparison, as he desperately tries to hold onto the office that he didn't think he would actually win in 2016.

Holding onto his nonbase supporters to reach the 40 percent mark will be a stretch for Trump. A September 2017 analysis by FiveThirtyEight found that the largest decline in his support was in some of the states where he had large margins of victory in 2016: Wyoming, West Virginia, North Dakota, Oklahoma, and Idaho.[54] If that trend continues, it would seriously decay Trump's prospects in states where he had solid wins in 2016, not just in blue states. That decay could swing votes in the Electoral College. The 2018 midterm election only hints at guidelines for the 2020 election. Trump only campaigned in states where he believed he was popular, with approval ratings higher than his national average. In most, his candidates won, although usually with smaller margins of victory than Trump had in 2016. Whether his candidates won or lost their elections, the characteristics of the candidates mattered more than Trump's imprimatur, and the outcomes, therefore, provide only minimal insight.

Trump also faces challenges among demographic groups on which he has relied. An August 2017 Quinnipiac University poll found that Trump was losing support among whites without a college degree.[55] An October 2017 report by Reuters showed his loss of support in rural communities, including among men, whites, and people who did not attend college.[56] CNN reported in December 2017 that Trump's support has declined among men, whites, people over fifty years old, white evangelical Protestants, and whites who did not attend college.[57] These reports corroborate the decline in Trump's support among segments of his most committed base, including white and older voters,[58] in addition to declines among women, nonwhite, and young voters (ages eighteen to thirty-four) who typically register lower levels of support for Trump than the overall population. Even if his support within his key voter groups rebounds upward, the fact that they dipped shows that they are fluid, and not a sure bet for Trump.

The 2018 midterm showcased these challenges to Trump's 2020 reelection prospects. The groundswell of support for Democratic Party candidates that led to forty seats in the House of Representatives "flipping" to the Democrats was largely attributed to suburban voters, notably including white women and college-educated voters. This change from recent years reflects a shift among Trump's nonbase voters, and it does not bode well for Republicans in 2020. While energizing his base in some (but not all) of the places where he held rallies, the Senate candidates whom he supported and who won their elections were in largely rural states where white, older, evangelical, and non-college-educated voters constitute a higher percentage of the electorate than most states. Even if Trump maintains the support of these voters in 2020, their impact will be muted in most other states due to their lesser share of the population. The GOP's success in 2018, by which they retained control of the Senate, had more to do with which states had Senate races in 2018 (every two years, one-third of Senate seats are up for election, and the outcome is tied to which seats are on the ballot). In most cases, their margins of victory were smaller than Trump's in 2016, which could be an indicator of Trump's (or the GOP's) erosion of support. The outcome in the House is, therefore, a much more accurate indicator of the national mood. The midterm showed that Trump continues to solidify his base, but has not extended it.

Subgroups of Trump's voters were drawn to him for different reasons.[59] Many of his 2016 nonbase voters cast their votes for him begrudgingly and are not among his ardent loyalists. Some of them voted for Trump due to allegiance to the Republican Party, GOP economic policies, or conservative ideology, despite their distaste for the candidate. Some voted for him because they disliked Hillary Clinton even more than they disliked Trump. Others voted for him because he was a celebrity whom they recognized. Although it is unclear what percentage of his nonbase voters voted for him reluctantly, it is certainly a substantial percentage, and it will be a key group of swing voters in 2020.

Many voters who reluctantly voted for Trump likely did so to send a message to Washington. Many were angry, disillusioned, or resentful about being neglected or marginalized for years. They were upset with the political status quo in Washington and the perception of insulated, unconcerned elites controlling both parties. They may have considered their votes to be largely symbolic since they believed, as most Americans did, that Hillary Clinton would surely win. This was their chance to voice their discontent. They mistakenly thought that they could just vote their anger away without impacting the outcome.

After Trump won, focus groups and interviews indicated that many Trump voters felt a combination of satisfaction and buyer's remorse.[60] Many who had been resigned to accept Hillary Clinton as president were glad that Trump won, or that Hillary lost.[61] They were gratified to witness the power of their vote after the unimaginable actually happened. Voting for Trump was largely a cathartic act, disgorging some of the anger that they harbored against the political establishment. But, as the gravity of the outcome set in, many of his nonbase voters shifted their thoughts to the new president, confronting the reality that they had given the presidency to someone about whom they had grave concerns.[62] Buyer's remorse took hold when these voters were sobered by the real world consequences of their action. After sending a message and getting their anger out of their systems, they began confronting the impact of their choice and their responsibility going forward.[63]

The reluctant Trump voters were the proverbial dog that caught the car. It was like the closing scene in the film *The Candidate*[64] after Robert Redford's character wins a Senate seat and asks his campaign manager, "What do we do now?" While reluctant Trump voters may be inspired to remain engaged in the political process, they are likely to approach voting with much more seriousness and responsibility in the future. The Trump administration's antics and ethics have already triggered discussions about how long to support Trump among many voters, as well as the circumstances and rationales that would shift their support to opposition. Among those who voted for Trump simply to try something different, beyond the norm, some might now be appreciating the value of norms. It is reasonable to anticipate that many who voted for him in 2016 as a protest vote will not vote for him a second time.

Most of Trump's 2016 nonbase voters were Republicans, as well as independents and third-party registrants. There was also a crossover of Democrats, most notably in the three states that surprisingly went for Trump and determined the outcome (Pennsylvania, Michigan, and Wisconsin).[65] If Trump's Republican nonbase voters feel that he deceived them (e.g., revelations about his true nature, false promises to "drain the swamp," excessive waste of time [golf] and money [constant trips to his resorts]) or worse, lied to them (his negotiations to build a hotel in Moscow and other business deals in Russia, ties to Saudis, loans from foreign sources), and are upset that they voted for him on false pretenses, then a GOP primary opponent can make a compelling case that Trump is unelectable in 2020. Despite Trump's high job approval numbers among Republicans in 2018, he could be vulnerable in contested primaries when nonbase supporters will be able to vote for a different Republican who better represents their personal values and political ideology. Howard Dean acknowledged that Democrats will be targeting this group when he said, "This battle is the battle for the 10 or 15 percent of the people who voted for Donald Trump who are basically decent people who wanted change and now are disgusted by what's going on."

As exposure of the real Donald Trump continues daily, 2016's nonvoters and reluctant Trump voters are recognizing that Trump is impairing the presidency itself. Although Trump's hardcore devotees see it differently, many people across the ideological and political spectrum have expressed concern that Trump is disgracing the office of the president. The lack of patriotism that he exhibited at his Helsinki summit with Putin exemplifies this. A growing chorus believes that he lacks the dignity, character, civility, ethics, judgment, intellect, discipline, and composure to lead a conga line, let alone lead the greatest nation on the planet. When Americans cast their votes in the 2020 election, it is likely that the revelation of Trump's nature will guide their votes as much or more than any single issue or invective.

The electorate's emerging hunger for a president who embodies the best of us and works to improve the lives of the least well off among us will not augur well for Trump in 2020.

IMPACT OF TRUMP'S NON-BASE SUPPORTERS ON THE 2020 ELECTION

Crystal balls, tea leaves, and Vegas odds-makers would all be hard-pressed to predict whether Donald Trump will be on the ballot in November 2020. He might look at his polling numbers, see their decline, and decide that one term was enough. His cabinet might invoke the Twenty-Fifth Amendment and remove him from office. He might be defeated by another Republican in the primaries. He might lose the nomination at the Republican Convention. He might be impeached and convicted by Congress. Or, he just might be on the ballot, after having become disciplined and judicious, apologized to the groups and individuals whom he has offended, brokered peace in the Middle East, established bipartisan tranquility in Congress, racked up historically high job approval numbers, and swept the primary elections. (Even though that seems implausible, anything can happen. After all, the Chicago Cubs did win the World Series.)

If Trump is on the ballot, he will continue bonding with his base voters through his personality-centric politics, partly because that's his style, and partly because he doesn't have the policy chops that it takes to impress voters. Trump will do what he does best, and his base will love it. He will surely be able to count on the enthusiastic, vocal, and engaged support of the 21 to 24 percent of voters who are his ardent loyalists.

Trump's nonbase supporters are different, and their voting choices might be mixed. Many will support him because they celebrate his selections of conservatives Neil Gorsuch and Brett Kavanaugh to become Supreme Court justices. Others may vote for Trump because they like his tax cuts and are benefiting from the economy (regardless of whether the strong economy is mainly due to the groundwork laid by Obama or to Trump's deregulation). Some may vote for Trump because they like some of the policy changes undertaken by the EPA or the Justice Department. And still others may vote for Trump out of basic party loyalty, once their choices are reduced to him or a Democrat.

But Trump is vulnerable to attrition among his 2016 nonbase voters. Those who were not enthusiastic about voting for him the first time will probably be less enamored with him in 2020 after all that has come to light since 2016. The approximate 16 to 19 percent of the population that now constitutes Trump's soft, nonbase supporters probably have a breaking point, at which they will abandon him. It is unclear what would trigger that, but the answer might be provided by the evidence in Mueller's report, financial hardships from Trump's tariffs, concern about his patriotism, or evidence provided by Michael Cohen through his guilty pleas and cooperation with Mueller. Trump's nonbase voters might shift their support to a candidate in the primaries who is a true conservative or one who is considered to be more electable in the general election. If he makes it to the general election, then some of his nonbase supporters—many of whom are independents—might support the Democratic candidate, swaying the outcome in some states and thereby in the Electoral College tally.

Trump faces additional challenges in 2020. For one thing, Trump's opponent will be someone other than Hillary Clinton, which deflates one of the main reasons why many nonbase supporters and swing voters floated to Trump. It is highly doubtful that many people who voted for Hillary Clinton will change course and support Trump. There just isn't any reason for a Hillary supporter to approve of Trump more in 2020 that they did in 2016. In light of everything that has happened and become publicly known during his presidency (with more sure to come), if a voter did not like Trump the first time around, then they will only find more reasons to dislike him as time goes on. So, in effect, there are many votes that Trump could lose in 2020, but not many that he could gain.

New voters in 2020 are also likely to have a major impact. The tsunami of activism that followed the 2016 election shows that many more votes against Trump will be available next time around. Many eligible voters did not vote in 2016, either out of complacency, indifference, the belief that a Hillary Clinton victory was a *fait accompli*, or a false sense that everything will be fine.[66] Those who preferred Hillary but didn't vote were jolted from complacency and indifference. Since then, there has been a surge in voter registration, beyond what normally occurs before a midterm election. Voter turnout during the 2018 primaries rose dramatically compared to other midterm election years, with a small increase among Republicans and an enormous increase among Democrats. It seems likely that there will be an unprecedented level of purposeful engagement and activism in the run-up to the 2020 election.

Demographic factors will also play a key role among both Trump's base and nonbase supporters. Older voters were among Trump's strongest supporters in 2016 and younger voters were among his weakest, with his numbers among eighteen to thirty-five-year-olds declining further since then. The natural progression of older voters matriculating out of the electorate and younger voters entering the electorate bodes ill for Trump based on the number of voters in each age cohort and each cohort's voting propensity.

Many of Trump's 2016 voters had high hopes for him and gave him the benefit of the doubt, figuring that they would give him a chance since establishment candidates had let them down in previous years. Now that he has an extensive track record, in 2020 he will not be able to ask for the benefit of the doubt, since there is none. Every voter will have an opinion about whether he fulfilled their hopes or let them down. As his manufactured image peels away and reveals that much of what Trump said in 2016 was untrue, many of these people may feel that they were deceived and react to that.

Trump's nonbase supporters may also be heavily influenced by economic conditions. In 2017, it seemed that the economy's rising tide was lifting all boats and that a strong economy would be a significant asset to Trump. However, the tariff and trade battles that Trump initiated in early 2018 may have turned that dynamic upside-down. After Trump initiated tariffs on Chinese goods, China's government retaliated by announcing its plan to impose tariffs, particularly on agricultural products from red states that heavily favored Trump in 2016.[67] It is likely that his support among his nonbase supporters whose finances suffer from the tariffs will weaken by 2020, and he could lose many of their votes.[68]

Trump apparently realized that tariffs could also impact the 2018 midterm election and impair the GOP's standing. To hedge against that, in July 2018, Trump began publicly criticizing Fed chairman Jay Powell's plans to hike interest rates. It appeared that Trump recognized that the economy would be hurt by the tariffs and sought to shift the blame to interest rates. Despite his diversionary tactic, increasingly painful effects of the tariffs in

2019 and 2020 could have a devastating impact on Trump's prospects in states that he won in 2016 and consequently on the 2020 Electoral College outcome.

But the biggest hurdle to Trump's reelection is Trump himself.[69] His regressive and destructive executive orders, regulatory actions, legislation, and policies have enraged opponents and created new ones. His vilification of countless constituencies (other than his base) has inflamed the ire of an enormous share of the electorate. He continually initiates fights—with the media, Gold Star families, NFL and NBA players, everyone who is upset by the separation of migrant children from their parents, etc.—that alienate more potential voters at every turn. He reads a script from a teleprompter, painstakingly stifling his instincts and personality to please his staff, yet invariably reverts to bombastic form in the next hour or day, throwing off the yoke of temperance and good judgment. He tweets opinions and recriminations that should never even be thought, let alone communicated.

If Trump is on the ballot in 2020, much attention will be placed on the fate of Republicans running for House and Senate seats (and state races). With Trump at the top of the ticket, his loyalists and opponents alike will be highly motivated to vote. In "deep red" locales, he would be an asset; elsewhere, his irascibility and alienation of constituencies would be a liability. The GOP's 2020 losses could exceed those of the 2018 midterm election. If Trump continues to vilify both Democrats and Republicans in his tweets and at his rallies while pursuing his own personal agenda, then GOP party dynamics could be jumbled. If he forces another government shutdown over border wall funding or another controversial issue, then voters will likely blame Republicans in addition to Trump. Republican candidates might not be able to count on his support and might need to distance themselves from him.[70] Trump's nonbase voters might be unsure of which direction to turn and be confused about the party's internal friction. They might feel abandoned without a political home. This may cause reverberations down-ballot. If Trump's lukewarm nonbase supporters are alienated and disenchanted, many might even abstain from voting. Their diminished presence in the election would virtually assure massive Republican losses in Senate and House races beyond the impact of the 2018 midterm.

This could result in a realignment of the GOP that could be a one-cycle deviation or have a lasting effect that impairs the party in future elections.

IMPORTANCE DURING TRUMP'S TENURE
AND THE POST-TRUMP ERA

There are far too many factors and unforeseeable twists and turns to be able to make well-founded prognostications about the presidential and legislative outcomes of the 2020 election. Yet, a few points about the run-up to the election and its underlying climate seem clear.

- Most Republican elected officials have been loath to publicly criticize or oppose Trump too soon (e.g., on Charlottesville, racism, misogyny, maligning of Haiti and African countries, his interactions with Russians, obstruction of justice, etc.) for fear of alienating Trump's base voters who are central to their own electoral calculations. If Trump's job approval percentage among GOP voters declines into the low 70s, then many will voice opposition to Trump for sake of their own electability, and if it reaches the 60s, then they will likely jump ship *en masse*.
- Trump's support within the GOP will deteriorate if someone picks up where Steve Bannon left off in effectively stoking a GOP internecine battle over a purist Trumpian worldview. If someone galvanizes the nativist, protectionist, ethnocentric, racist forces, it could divide the GOP and imperil its chances of success up and down the ballot.
- Special Counsel Mueller's findings might reverberate throughout the campaign and be a major factor in the 2020 election. Although technicalities and Justice Department policy kept Mueller from taking action against Trump and his family members, Mueller's report detailed ten instances of obstruction of justice.[71] It is likely that the evidence of Trump's and his family's transgressions will be engrained in the national consciousness due to congressional hearings, prosecutions by the Southern District of New York, and the campaign tactics of other candidates. Although this would not deplete Trump's support with his devoted base voters, it could erode confidence among his nonbase supporters, which could impair his electoral prospects. It may also encourage other Republicans to challenge Trump in the primaries, which could further hamper Trump if he eventually gains his party's nomination.
- Republican legislators wanted to stick with Trump long enough to fulfill some of their legislative dreams (e.g., tax cuts and the repeal of

Obamacare). Since they already got the tax cuts and they know that a future President Pence would sign into law the other reforms that are on their wish list, they don't really need Trump. Thus, if Republicans believe that having Trump at the top of the ticket will doom everyone else (especially if Mueller's findings of improprieties gain traction), and they don't want their campaigns to be consumed with defending Trump, then they may cooperate with Democrats and commence impeachment proceedings. By running in 2020 with President Pence, the reelection chances of House and Senate Republicans would dramatically improve.

The first of these four points has already weighed heavily on GOP thinking. If Republican officials oppose Trump too early, either while his job approval numbers remain high or at the first sign of a dip, they might lose their reelection by offending Trump's base of voters. But, being beholden to poll numbers has risks. If Republican lawmakers stand idly by, watching Trump's job approval numbers among GOP voters and waiting too long before taking a stand against Trump, they might lose both their reelection and their party. If Republican officeholders remain silent amidst Trump's many flagrant offenses, then voters may conclude that the GOP is complicit. Trump's non-base supporters would have reason to question the GOP's principles and purpose, prompting many to defect. The Republican Party might either morph into the Trumpian Party or separate from Trump, either of which would devastate the party. Down-ticket GOP candidates might be without a party structure to support them. Rather than being captive to the polls, Republican lawmakers may be more successful if they justify their actions on the basis of principles, policy, and Special Counsel Mueller's conclusions.

If Trump wins in 2020 under these circumstances, the traditional GOP would either be neutered or restructured. Many Republican officeholders would lose their races, the party would be redefined, and most Republican voters would not know where to turn in the aftermath. The more that the GOP's longtime intramural battles between moderates and conservatives are replaced by battles between pluralists and nativists, the more likely it is that there will be upheaval within the party. The GOP could splinter into two parties, separating Trumpians and those with traditional Republican values and aims.

If Trump runs and loses in 2020, then the postmortem assessment could be expected to point to Trump's shortcomings, transgressions, policies, and decisions. If the GOP is perceived as being complicit with Trump's offenses, bereft of cogent policy ideas, devoid of principles, or unable to inject them into the vacuum that Trump created, then there may be no rationale remaining for a GOP (with emphasis on the "O" in "GOP," as in "Outdated, Outcast, and Ousted"). If the 2020 election causes Republicans to lose faith and feel estranged, then the Republican Party might splinter in two: the Trumpian Party and the "Republican't Party," splitting their membership. Both sides would be too disheveled to agree on anything and too numerically inconsequential to be effective or compete for control. It would almost be as if the party handed the baton back to their Whig predecessors, awaiting a similar fate. Even more dramatically, the GOP could dissolve into many parties, with each component of the Republican coalition creating its own party, none of which would be electorally viable.

Hopefully, Republicans will not play timid during their, and the nation's, hour of urgency. Even most Democrats would probably acknowledge that they want the GOP to remain a viable party, albeit not in the White House and only in the minority in Congress. Having two major parties at parity, plus or minus, is good for our democracy and useful to our system of checks and balances. The Democrats would not be the same without the Republicans. It would be like Magic without Bird, or Wilt without Russell. Those legends needed each other to bring out the best in them, and the two parties also benefit from competing with each other over ideas and influence.

If the Republican Party were mortally wounded, we would all fret together over what would fill the void. Some new force would soon arise, partly because nature abhors a vacuum and partly because human nature does not long endure tranquility. Since the Democrats would not be empowered by our diverse split-personality national identity to singularly fill the void for long, fear would be rampant over the three-headed monster that might show up to take over where the Republicans leave off. We would all have plenty to lose, from the stability of our democratic institutions, to our leadership in global affairs; from our political processes and civility, to the advances that have been made in recent decades toward a more inclusive, just, and equitable society. And, speaking of lots to lose, just imagine what it would do to the charts of the Dow Jones, S&P 500, and Nasdaq, not to mention our nation's credit rating!

As mentioned, there is one scenario in which Trump stands a reasonable chance of reelection, and it might even be the scenario for which he has been preparing. During his first two years in office, most of his actions and communications have been designed to appeal to his base. Almost every time that he had the opportunity to broaden his appeal, he opted instead to reinforce the support of his base, even though it is already solid. As a result, he has the ironclad support of 21 to 24 percent of the electorate. Some of his nonbase supporters will vote for him, as will some independents, since voters make their choices for myriad reasons. His vote total could conceivably reach the 40 percent mark.

A crowded field of candidates would be Trump's dream scenario. It is highly implausible that he could match his 46 percent vote share from 2016, and a 40 percent share would fall short of what he would need for victory in a two-person head-to-head race against a Democrat. So, the situation in which he could still succeed is if there are three major viable candidates on the ballot, or, ideally for him, four viable candidates. Although the Republican Party has shown some fissures, a full-fledged separation is unlikely at this point, and the four-candidate scenario with a split among Democrats is an extremely unlikely long-shot. Yet, there are signs of growing pains in both parties and it is not inconceivable that internal party divisions could spur realignment. A crowded field could split the vote in unprecedented ways and introduce multidimensional mayhem into party dynamics.[72] A 30 or 35 percent share could win in a crowded field, and Trump could even draw support from independents and some disenchanted Democrats. There is reason to believe that Trump has been facilitating this type of transformation.

Since Trump's obsession with pleasing his base has been obvious, some observers and strategists have recognized that Trump may be preparing for the possibility of a crowded general election field to increase his chances. Doug Sosnik, who served in President Clinton's White House, opined that Trump's base-centric strategy is bolstered by polling methodologies that tend to undercount his support, and some people not wanting to admit to pollsters that they support Trump. Sosnik points out that "the continued decline in support for both political parties works to Trump's advantage. The lack of voters' faith in both parties increases the probability that there will be a major third-party candidate on the 2020 ballot. It will also lead to other minor-party candidates joining the presidential race. The multi-candidate field will further divide the anti-Trump vote, making it possible for him to get reelected simply by holding on to his current level of support."[73]

Trump would run either as: (a) the nominee of the GOP, in which case other Republicans would branch off into a new party, or (b) as an independent—perhaps the nominee of a new Trumpian Party—in which case other Republicans would field their own nominee. Veteran political operative Tad Devine believes that the latter is Trump's preferred path, saying, "I think he's positioned himself from the beginning to run outside the Republican Party, and frankly I think that's his best option."[74]

A split in the Republican Party might reflect the division in the House between the Freedom Caucus (conservatives and spending hardliners) and the Tuesday Group (moderates and globalists) or a new division between the pluralists and the Trumpian nativists. The party that is not led by Trump would embrace the ideology that felt most marginalized by Trump's candidacy. With a split on the Republican side, Trump's vote would fall short of 40 percent, and would probably be closer to 30 percent (his loyal base plus 6 to 8 percent more, from among his nonbase supporters). But, in a multicandidate race, 30 percent might be the largest share. Trump's actions and communications convey that he hopes that his loyal base, plus some independents, could get him an Electoral College win by targeting states where he has strong support, like how he campaigned in the months leading up to the 2018 midterm election. If he doesn't win outright in that way, he could hope for no one to get 270 electoral votes, in which case the election would be decided by a free-for-all in the House of Representatives (although that would no longer be advantageous for Trump, since the Democrats won control in the 2018 midterm).

Although Trump cannot control the process on the Democratic side, he has been provoking an internal division, and the Democrats have exposed their divergent philosophies. On one side are progressives and social justice populists. While it is risky to categorize candidates, and they might characterize themselves differently, this group might be said to include senators Cory Booker, and Kamala Harris, Mayor Pete Buttigieg, former representative Beto O'Rourke, and former HUD secretary Julián Castro. On the other side are moderates who offer an economic message that also encompasses working-class whites and lagging communities (as depicted in J. D. Vance's book, *Hillbilly Elegy*[75]) in which the opioid crisis is a visible symptom of frustration and futility. This group might be said to include former vice president Joe Biden, representatives Tim Ryan and Seth Moulton, former governor John Hickenlooper, and Senator Kirsten Gillibrand (most of her record places her in this group, with a notable exception being her staunch advocacy for women). Senators Elizabeth Warren and Bernie Sanders might fit in both categories, as they are progressives whose policies focus on economic populism to benefit the working class, which could give them crossover appeal.

The Democrats would benefit by offering a candidate who is not only Trump's polar opposite on policy but is also a stylistic opposite in terms of humility, temperament, composure, professionalism, dignity, and being a bipartisan unifier. A candidate with that tone would have a broader appeal than a candidate who takes on Trump with a campaign that is equally combative, harsh, shrill, and flamboyant. The nominee can differentiate their message and policies from his by espousing empathetic, egalitarian, and constructive values to heal the nation. The Democrats have the moral high ground, and that is a valuable asset that will attract many voters in the 2020 election. If they squander it by responding to Trump on his terms, then they would lose that advantage and lose the mud wrestling contest in which Trump is proficient. Candidates who combine policy pragmatism with a temperate tone, and who could leverage the moral high ground, include Governor Jay Inslee of Washington, Congresswoman Tulsi Gabbard, Congressman Eric Swalwell, Senator Amy Klobuchar, and, here too, Mayor Pete Buttigieg. Each could also deliver the themes of the party's two main wings.

The Democrats must also be mindful of not fighting the last war, which is to say, not relitigating the 2016 election. Campaign tactics change; policy priorities change; voter sensibilities change. Any Democrat who approaches the 2020 election as if it were a do-over of 2016, and a chance to show that they can fight Trump the way that Hillary Clinton should have, might have an uphill climb if they win the nomination and then find Trump with an updated strategy. The video that Joe Biden released when he announced his candidacy certainly pulled some emotional heartstrings. But it also characterized Biden fighting Trump with somewhat of a 2016 flavor, and made the case for a return to the better days of the pre-Trump era. Biden also asserted that Pennsylvania, which turned out to be pivotal in 2016, will be the ultimate 2020 battleground, and that his strength there will enable him to defeat Trump. Yet, these assumptions about the 2020 race deserve reconsideration because some segments of the electorate might prefer to leave the past behind, and Trump might be scaling up his forces in other battleground states.

That doesn't mean that Democrats should pull their punches, be docile, and settle for moral victories, restraining themselves from responding to Trump's name calling, spurious allegations, and other attacks. There is space to fight Trump when necessary, while consistently articulating a forward-looking message. Democratic candidates should respond forcefully and factually on the merits, while illuminating Trump's divisive tactics and his effort to inject fear and anger into the American psyche. Since countering Trump's fallacies inadvertently frames the discussion, Democrats should instead focus on the venom, incivility, divisiveness, and falsity that produced them. In short, when Trump attacks, the Democrats should elevate.

Party unity is essential for the Democrats as the first step to blunt Trump's divide-and-conquer approach to muting the force of a singular opponent. It is not likely that the Democratic Party coalition would splinter into two (or more) parties, fielding separate candidates for a presidential election that is theirs to lose. Theoretically, that could happen if the various adherents of the two strategies cannot coalesce. But they have every reason to reach consensus. If Trump continues along the trajectory of his first years in office, then as long as the Democrats don't nominate Bart Simpson or someone of similar caliber, they will have the clear advantage . . . at least until their candidate utters the word "deplorables."

In light of the intensified congressional investigations, prosecutions of Trump associates (Michael Cohen, Paul Manafort, Roger Stone, and others), malfeasance detailed in Mueller's report, and other developments, it also bears considering that the GOP candidate for president on the November 2020 ballot might be Mike Pence. He would provide some familiar stability and a return to the rule of law, while at the same time wreaking havoc of a different sort.

With Pence, some GOP dynamics and strategies would revert back to how things were before the 2016 "politiquake" that made the political ground shake, the House buckle (the Senate, too), and Republicans duck and cover. Although the GOP might still be in jeopardy of losing many seats in 2020, with Pence in charge, the party itself would remain intact without dividing, suffering realignment, or being marginalized. The party would live to fight another day. The GOP factions that were benched by Coach Trump would resume their spots on the playing field, reengaging all factions (about five) that comprise the GOP coalition (which is analogous to the Democratic Party's coalition). The Republican Party would have to endure some turmoil, but that would be a small price to pay for avoiding a full-scale existential crisis.

As for the possibility of havoc, that would depend on the circumstances that give rise to Pence becoming the presidential candidate on the 2020 ballot. If it were the result of Trump withdrawing from the race or resigning from office, then Pence and the GOP would be totally off the hook, with no ill feelings or adverse consequences from the base. Trump would have made the decision to withdraw or resign, so Trump's base would find a way to adjust to that, and their ire would be directed elsewhere.

In the incredibly implausible scenario where Pence challenges Trump and defeats him in the primaries, or engineers a takeover at the Republican Convention by lobbying delegates to nominate him after Trump won many primaries, then havoc would be an understatement. It would be a full-fledged crisis and all-out political warfare. In these highly unlikely situations, the Trumpians would view Pence's actions as a disloyal and unforgivable betrayal, and they would do all they could to retaliate against Pence and other establishment Republicans.

In the middle ground between those scenarios, it becomes murky. If the ongoing scrutiny of Mueller's findings causes Trump's support among GOP voters to decline significantly in the months following the report's release, then Republicans in Congress may feel compelled to join with Democrats to act on charges in accordance with their constitutional role, their patriotic duty to place country over party, and their own political survival (distancing themselves from such conduct). If Republicans perceive Mueller's allegations about Trump to be highly condemnatory and fully evidenced, then many of them might even reluctantly support the conclusion that the evidence compels impeachment. If concerns within the GOP escalate to that level, then even many loyal Trumpians might recognize that it is unavoidable. The same dynamics would apply if Trump were removed from office, however unlikely, by his own cabinet invoking the Twenty-Fifth Amendment. The expression "if you see something, say something" applies to politics just as to terrorism, and solid evidence of obstruction of justice could inspire leaders and voters to "say something."

Congressional Republicans would have to handle Trump's hardcore base delicately, convincing as many of them as possible that Mueller's findings require action. Even though the Democrats would initiate impeachment (since the 2018 midterm results gave them control of the House, where the impeachment process begins), Republicans would need to reassure Trump's base that they would remain a priority constituency for the GOP even without Trump at the helm. Many Trumpians would recognize that sticking with Trump would lead to disaster in the Electoral College and congressional races. The GOP would have to mitigate the damage that the base could do in down-ballot contests by convincing Trumpians that their own interests are at stake. The GOP could hope for a sizeable share of Trump's base to grudgingly accept the necessity of impeachment, even though many Trump loyalists would still oppose it. Since Trump's base amounts to about 21 to 24 percent of the electorate, if impeachment alienated only half of them—about 10 to 12 percent of all voters—then the GOP could survive that loss, be competitive in many 2020 congressional races, and remain intact for subsequent elections.

Pence's standing with Trump's base and nonbase supporters would be mixed, although he probably would gain the support of many of them if he conducts himself in a statesmanlike manner during the process and keeps his distance from both Congress's and the Justice Department's handling of the matter. His harshly conservative social and fiscal policies would ingratiate him with many Trump supporters, and Pence is a skilled politician who could leverage that dynamic. Democrats could be counted on to fiercely and passionately oppose Pence for his consistent fealty to hard-line conservative policies,[76] as they did with Pence's extreme positions against LGBTQ rights when he was governor of Indiana,[77] which would further reinforce Pence's popularity among Trumpians.

If impeachment is managed in a responsible and dignified manner, then Pence would gain the support of many "never Trump" GOP voters. Their return to active participation with the GOP would bolster Republicans' 2020 prospects. With temperance in a time of national crisis, the GOP would raise their standing with independents and maybe even some Democrats, in addition to the "never Trump" Republicans. Many Republicans have been itching to get back into the mix, and Pence would create a climate for their reengagement. He could galvanize their support and expand the pool of potential supporters. Even if the GOP suffers losses in 2020, the party would remain sufficiently intact to mount a comeback.

Republicans who worry about Trump's temperament, willingness to engage in nuclear warfare, and marginalization of our global leadership would eagerly welcome Pence at the top of the ticket. Activating those voters would compensate for the loss of Trumpians in some states and districts, although there might still be fallout in some congressional districts where Trump's support is concentrated. Pence would have an upside potential that Trump does not, since he can inspire GOP factions that feel excluded from Trump's political calculations. Although there are too many unknowns to see how Pence would fare in an election, it does seem clear that he would do much better than Trump, in light of the Mueller report's findings that Trump engaged in serious wrongdoing. The financial markets would also respond favorably to Pence since, with him, they would get all the things that they like best about Trump (less regulation and favorable taxation) without the negatives (tariffs, uncertainty, and daily drama, which would be replaced by steady predictability).

If Pence were on the ballot in 2020 as the presidential candidate, the Republican Party would have a credible candidate at the top of the ticket, which would help down-ballot candidates even if Pence faced headwinds in his race. The GOP would probably pull through without wholesale party fragmentation, realignment, or long-term devastation, as long as Pence didn't win the nomination by challenging Trump. Democrats would be mobilized by Pence's candidacy, while the LGBTQ community and its supporters in both parties would be downright terrified of him winning, due to his history of actions antithetical to LGBTQ interests and equality.[78] But his LGBTQ antipathy would primarily impact the general election and would likely not hinder his success in the GOP primaries. The internal party politics of a Pence candidacy may still get ugly, and it would certainly require some delicate maneuvering with Trump's base. But that shouldn't be surprising or daunting for an experienced politician, especially one playing for the highest stakes in politics.

Under Pence, the Republican Party would likely be able to transition out of its Pitchfork Populism phase and refocus on the long term policies and objectives that define its identity.

A MESSAGE TO FELLOW
PATRIOTS WHO SUPPORT TRUMP

T he ten dynamics featured in this book are some of the important ways in which Donald Trump is impacting our country. They provide a framework to identify, categorize, and characterize the daily deluge of issues, actions, and utterances that collectively impose the Trump Effect on our politics, government, culture, and society. They are by no means an exhaustive roster of the ramifications of Trump's presidency, as there surely are others. But these ten are among the most salient and consequential areas of his impact.

For people concerned about Trump's and his administration's impact, hopefully this book has been a constructive, comprehensible, and user-friendly critique that applies structure and insight to the ocean of elements comprising Trump and his governance. The ten dynamics provide some guideposts for action that will be useful now and in the post-Trump era, as we strive to reassert the norms, decorum, processes, principles, and mutual respect that are hallmarks of modern America's greatness.

For people who support Trump—including those among his base who passionately support him—it is important to start with a hearty Thank You. If you are reading this after reading all that preceded it, having endured an analysis that is sometimes critical of the man you admire and the administration that you celebrate, you deserve kudos and appreciation. It may have been a difficult journey and you may have taken issue with a number of passages, despite best efforts to fairly address your perspectives and interests. Hopefully the book sheds light on matters that you, too, found useful and edifying as you evaluate the impact that Trump and his administration will have on your life for years to come.

Even Trump's opponents recognize that, during the campaign, he listened to his supporters, recognized your situation and struggles, validated your concerns and opinions, and served your interests. It is clear that many Trump supporters felt disregarded and disrespected by both political parties for many years—as well as discounted and disenfranchised from the political process—without your needs being met and your requests receiving the attention they deserved. That was understandably disheartening. It was surely gratifying that Trump recognized what others had not, promised to serve your interests, and spoke your language. It must also be satisfying that, as president, he takes your views into account and often makes decisions on the basis of what he promised you or what he thinks you would like.

In return, hopefully Trump supporters would acknowledge that what he is doing, and the way he is doing it, has put our nation in a historically precarious position. Many of his actions offend principles and beliefs that his base, too, holds dear. As a businessman, Trump notoriously reneged on contracts without justification. He eagerly sued people who had strong legal positions but not the financial means for lengthy litigation against him. He has insulted so many groups that even his voters have reason to be offended, since they, too, have ties to Gold Star families, descendants of non-European people, people with disabilities, veterans, and, yes, women. Special Counsel Mueller's court filings and final report provided evidence about a broad range of nefarious activities. Trump has used his office to personally profit from foreigners who patronize his hotels and businesses in clear violation of the Constitution's Emoluments Clause. He created the appearance of a conflict of interest when he eased sanctions against ZTE after China invested $500 million that benefited his Indonesian property (and granted trademarks to his daughter). And the list goes on.

Just prior to the 2016 Republican Convention, Adam Gopnik expressed his concerns about Trump. Based on historical precedents in other countries, Gopnik warned of the governing tactics that he feared Trump would employ, including "the glorification of the nation, and the exaggeration of its humiliations, with violence promised to its enemies, at home and abroad; the worship of power wherever it appears and whoever holds it; contempt for the rule of law and for reason; unashamed employment of repeated lies as a rhetorical strategy; and a promise of vengeance for those who feel themselves disempowered by history. It promises to turn back time and take no prisoners. That it can appeal to those who do not understand its consequences is doubtless true. But the first job of those who do understand is to state what those consequences invariably are. Those who think that the underlying institutions of

American government are immunized against it fail to understand history. In every historical situation where a leader of Trump's kind comes to power, normal safeguards collapse."[1]

Sadly, Gopnik was prescient. Each of his concerns materialized during Trump's first two years in office. Trump has used each tactic multiple times, and in some cases, incessantly. Taken together, these tactics describe a style of government that is unacceptable in America, as it is unlike and in conflict with the previous 240 years of our national experience. It offends the ethos of our constitutional democracy. And there's no sign of abatement. Trump's problematic behavior is incurable, as it is very likely intertwined with the five factors underlying his decision-making described in chapter 3: narcissism, anger, retribution by deconstruction, retribution by replacement, and authoritarianism.

Although some of the concerns might not cause Trump's supporters much anxiety, some certainly should, and it is difficult to comprehend why they wouldn't. Even Trump's most loyal, devoted fans surely recognize that he fabricates . . . or tells falsehoods . . . or lies. Even his attorneys have acknowledged that reality in their public discussion about whether Trump should meet with Mueller. Trump's supporters might respond by saying that all politicians lie. But in Trump's case, the problem is the frequency, brazenness, scope, incredulity, shamelessness, and purpose of his lies. If he were to occasionally tell a lie, especially if it were to prevent sensitive national security information from becoming known to our adversaries, it would be excusable. But when his comments, and those made on his behalf by his staff, are demonstrably and factually false, self-serving, consequential, and recurring daily, then it should matter to everyone. A few lies become a pattern, which becomes a practice, which becomes a propensity, which becomes a predilection, which becomes pathological, which becomes predictable. Trump has been predictably lying for quite some time.

This should be problematic to Trump's supporters for multiple reasons. First, most people would not accept someone in their daily life lying to them on a regular basis. If someone objects to their children, friends, and neighbors lying to them even occasionally, why should they accept the president lying to them routinely? Second, when one person lies to another routinely, that is a clear sign of disrespect. Why support a president who clearly disrespects you? Third, when someone in whom trust has been placed lies routinely, including about important matters, that usually breaks the bond of trust. If the president, whom supporters trust to treat them well and honorably, lies to them, how can those supporters trust him to prioritize their interests and not harm them on issues that matter? Fourth, if someone asserts that they care about what you care about and promises to deliver on it, a track record of lies calls all of that into question. Why support a president who might be lying about sharing your concerns and could be acting against the things that you care about?

All of these actions, concerns, and offenses are behaviors that Trump's supporters surely would not tolerate from any other president. Like most Americans, Trump's supporters have principles and beliefs about basic proper conduct, dislike being fed falsehoods, and are law-abiding Americans who strongly support the Constitution and the rule of law. The Constitution, more than anything else, is what unites all groups of Americans, defines our national identity, holds us together as a country, and makes us a beacon of democracy in the eyes of the international community. Trump's supporters and opponents are equally committed to upholding it.

With so many controversies and challenges being introduced and even invited by Trump, his supporters have a special role in determining how events will unfold. In light of recent developments, there are some tough and urgent questions that all Americans—including all Trump supporters—need to ask and answer honestly:

- At what point has someone gone too far in defying principles that are vital to our social fabric?
- At what point has a president become a liability and a danger to the nation, even though he gave you recognition and a seat at the table?
- At what point have a president's undignified comments, capricious actions, and disdain for hundreds of years of valued precedents diminished the presidency and jeopardized our global stature?
- At what point has Trump offended our laws so much that it cannot be overlooked, even if he is doing things you like?
- At what point has Trump's demonization of the investigations into his conduct been exposed as just a desperate, cynical, and false attempt to avoid justice by discrediting an honest and honorable process, despite his repeated assertions of "witch hunt" and "no collusion"?
- At what point have Trump's violations of the Constitution, having taken an oath to "preserve, protect and defend the Constitution of the United States," disqualified him from serving as president?

These questions compel consideration of whether one man is more important than the country as a whole. Trump's supporters should ask themselves whether they have more faith in him or in everything they were taught about our country. All Americans should recall that the Constitution provides a stable, fair, law-based system of governance that aspires to treat all people with dignity, protect their rights, and enable them to thrive. Anyone who believes in the importance of the Constitution has a duty to support the Constitution and the rule of law when those protections are challenged and consider the lengths to which they will go to do that. Standing up for principle is not a partisan effort. It is an inherently American action and part of our heritage.

Mickey Edwards, a vice president at the Aspen Institute and a former Republican congressman, wrote, "The founders gave us a great blessing, but they also gave us a great curse. The constitutional system they left us can survive only if it maintains the trust of its citizens and only if those citizens are capable of wisely using the power the Constitution places in their hands. The success of democracy therefore rests on performance of the government, on the wisdom of citizens, and on a public trust that the system works—for all the people."[2] As he implores, all Americans must rise to the moment, assert our rights and responsibilities, and demand that our elected officials enforce our system of government and the system of checks and balances within it. It is as if the citizenry has taken the oath that each of us "will to the best of (our) ability, preserve, protect and defend the Constitution of the United States."

Now that Mueller's report has been released, it is clear that Donald Trump, and people acting on his behalf, engaged in contemptuous activities that fit into three categories:

1. Collaboration with Russians: Mueller provided detailed evidence of conduct that is fair to characterize as collaboration or collusion (although not criminal conspiracy) between Americans and the Russians who he determined had interfered with our 2016 election.[3]
2. Obstruction of Justice: Mueller identified ten actions that gave rise to concerns that Trump obstructed justice and that Mueller implied would have constituted obstruction of justice if the person engaged in such actions was someone other than a sitting US president.[4]
3. Financial and Business Improprieties: Although Mueller's report did not address these issues (other than Trump's efforts to build a hotel

in Moscow), references to twelve ongoing cases or investigations were redacted from the report, some of which might relate to Trump's financial, business, and/or other affairs.

This compendium of conduct is at best troubling, and could be construed as reprehensible or worse. By providing detailed evidence, yet declining to seek indictments, Mueller in essence referred these matters to Congress for it to determine their severity and consequences. The shift from the judicial to the legislative arena invites all Americans to express their views about the path forward. As the public began digesting the evidence in Mueller's report, opinions ran the gamut. Some people declared scrutiny into Trump's actions to be completed, insisting it's time to move on. Some proclaimed Mueller's report to be the basis for impeachment, insisting it's time to begin the process. Others opted for a middle-ground approach, invoking principles and precedents, and calling for actions such as hearings, a rebuke, congressional censure of the president, and enactment of laws that prohibit certain activities in the future.

While no solution will satisfy everyone, it would be consistent with American values, the pursuit of truth, and principles of fairness to initiate a comprehensive, informative national discussion that applies transparency and context to the issues. An informed public will then be able to choose the next steps. Congressional hearings are necessary to inform the nation and bring the facts into full view. Hearings would focus on Trump's conduct that Mueller found problematic, conduct that comes to light from prosecutions (that were redacted from Mueller's report) and congressional investigations, and the ongoing risks to the country that are posed by that conduct. Resistance to illumination and transparency would be tantamount to urging Americans to avoid the truth and bury their heads in the sand.

Professor Lawrence Tribe is often recognized as the penultimate expert on constitutional law. In April 2019, he said, "The Mueller report is written as an essential invitation for the House to take up its constitutional responsibility. They need to expose to the American people what a corrupt, dangerously criminal presidency we now have. It seems to me vital that that begin as soon as possible. If this isn't enough to establish the need to put every Senator on record as to whether they take their oath to uphold the Constitution seriously, I can't image what would be. Keep in mind the dangerous precedent that would be set if the House basically says, 'well, we've heard the evidence;

never mind.' That would really mean that Donald Trump, in a potential second term, or any future president, would know that there is essentially no limit to what that president could get away with. I think it's time to stand up for principle and not focus entirely on the political fallout."[5]

It is now incumbent upon all Americans—Republicans, Democrats, and even Trump's most loyal supporters—to fulfill the people's role in the constitutional process by supporting Congress's oversight responsibility, transparency, and the right of the nation to be fully informed about our president's conduct. Once that is achieved, the country will be well prepared to decide what should happen thereafter, which may involve enacting new laws, passing a resolution rebuking the president for minor infringements of his duties, or impeaching the president for major violations of ethics, laws, or his oath of office.

It certainly takes courage and strength of character to stand up for what is right when doing so means chastising or holding accountable someone who has been an ally and a source of validation. Ironically enough, Trump himself provided a template for doing so during his February 2018 meeting with senators about gun control, following the school massacre in Florida. Trump spoke in favor of gun control and against the NRA's position, even though the NRA strongly supported his candidacy, when he criticized some senators for not doing enough, saying, "You're afraid of the NRA."[6] When faced with Trump's constitutional, legal, and ethical abuses, his supporters should realize that he gave them a green light to be courageous and not afraid of him.

Trump's opponents are also obliged to summon the courage to do what is right, since many of them are even more opposed to Pence becoming president, which would be the natural result of impeachment process. In that precarious predicament, principles must prevail over party politics. In a crisis, both Trump's supporters and opponents would be called upon to be courageous and do what is consistent with our national values, instead of acquiescing to a vast and historic series of transgressions.

If people were to retreat from the challenge, ignoring the truth and becoming entrenched in their own ideological camps, it would hasten fragmentation of our society, animus toward our vital institutions, and distrust of each other that would exacerbate divisions and take a very long time to repair. If Americans are pitted against each other at a time when action on such unmistakably problematic circumstances is needed, then all of us and our national identity would be vulnerable. This divide-and-conquer approach would debilitate our government, diminish our economic prosperity, and impair our ability to lead in the global arena. Anyone struggling with the decision to step up and meet the challenge would be well served to consider the wise maxim: "If you're not part of the solution, you're part of the problem."[7]

If all Americans join together, in concerted collaboration across ideological lines, to take action based on facts emanating from Mueller's report, prosecutions that were redacted from his report (when information about them becomes known), and congressional investigations, the country will become stronger and benefit from the process. We need to act together, as one nation, so that the country can move in the direction of healing our divisions and ushering in a constructive, participatory next chapter in the American experience.

"We the People of the United States, in Order to form a more perfect Union" must jointly commit ourselves to reversing the antagonism, dissension, and fragmentation that tears the fabric of our social structure and cohesion. We are strongest, most effective, most prosperous, most gratified, and most successful when we are unified by a shared purpose and mutual respect. When we look beyond one person to the needs, beliefs, and ambitions of all communities and cultures, we find what each group needs for achievement of its version of the American Dream. Once identified, we can address those needs and return to a path toward sustained, broad-based accomplishments, success, and fulfillment.

ACKNOWLEDGMENTS

W hen I was about thirteen, a great man gave me vital advice that has remained with me ever since, and that was an inspiration for this book. That great man, my father, Joseph Kane, taught me, "Don't share in other people's delusions." In my father's career as a psychiatric social worker and in other roles—including as the head of a division at a mental institution—he dealt with many people who were driven to destructive and self-destructive behavior due to their delusions (about themselves or the world around them). Through his insights about these cases (which he discussed anonymously), he taught me to focus on verifiable reality, isolate fiction from fact, and pursue the truth.

That lesson helped me countless times in my career, although never more so than now. My father's admonishment is especially pertinent amid the daily deluge of dystopian and Orwellian deceptions from the nation's loudest megaphone. Today's incessant dissemination of delusions seeks to gain buy-in from people who suspend critical reasoning, and thus do not recognize these delusions for what they are. My father's experience and words of wisdom are an underlying message of this book, and they would be his advice to all Americans.

Both of my parents instilled within me core values of egalitarianism, empathy, and respect for all people, which steer my life and are cornerstones of this book. Their worldview was crafted by the Great Depression, World War II (my father dodged bullets in combat), McCarthyism, and other true tests of national character. My wonderful mother, Rosalyn Kane, took the lead in shaping my political sensibilities (hers stemmed from her job in the 1940s at the Women's Bureau of the US Department of Labor, led by Secretary Frances Perkins). They infused me with foundational tenets, such as Dr. Martin Luther King Jr.'s moral guidepost, "Injustice anywhere is a threat to justice everywhere," President Kennedy's "Ask not . . ." call to public service, and Senator Robert F. Kennedy's hallmark of visionary idealism, "Some [people] see things as they are and ask why. I dream of things that never were and ask why not."

My mother was also my principal writing coach for decades, starting with word games in the car, and later always being available to critique and revise my syntax, structure, and punctuation toward better self-expression.

So, when it comes to acknowledgments, my parents, Rozie and Joey, are first and foremost. In a sense, both of them wrote this book, even though they were no longer here to do so.

Two wonderful, dear friends were monumentally helpful and influential throughout every stage of the process that culminated in this book. Robert Goldman and Bill Funderburk recognized my capacity to write, commiserated with me about the direction in which the country was going, and validated my determination to reenter the arena. They repeatedly urged me to write, virtually igniting a flame under the seat of my pants and turning it up until I did so. They stood with me at every step along the way, offering encouragement, discussing governmental developments and their implications, reading drafts of my chapters, and providing extremely valuable feedback and advice. I am profoundly grateful to Brother Rob (I write but you're right) and Brother Billy (*Bold Metrics Work*).

The realization that I should write also stems from Linda Bloom, of the acclaimed Linda and Charlie Bloom writing duo. Although their books are of a different genre, and the book she urged me to write is on a different and apolitical topic, she challenged me—even dared me—to write it. Linda's support and offer of assistance inspired me to begin writing. I set that project aside to write this book, but I hope to revive it eventually. Thanks, Linda, for lighting the path.

A special friend and a special cousin also contributed in important ways. I am indebted to Jules Radcliff for his uniquely vital assistance, and I always benefit from his acute insights into political dynamics that were cultivated through his decades of work in and around the political and governmental arenas. Whether there is a need for keys to knowledge or the car, Jules always has them. And, while my conversations with Amy Kane always make my day, our talks in spring 2017 helped me envision the book and played a key role in one of the chapters. Amy's sensibilities informed my work, and she's a great teammate (the Dodgers should take notice and let her go to work in the dugout!).

I am grateful to many professionals in the publishing community whose efforts were pivotal in bringing this book to fruition. My literary agent, Nancy Rosenfeld, believed in my book and the importance of bringing it to market. Nancy's assiduous efforts to place the book with the right publisher were crucial. I am profoundly grateful to Steven Mitchell, the recently retired editor in chief of Prometheus Books, both for deciding to publish this book, and for his impact on my work. Steven reviewed an early draft, provided valuable feedback, and advised me about the roadmap to publishing. Steven's indispensable guidance and support helped me refine the book and navigate the process. My book also benefited greatly from the skillful production and professional attention of the staff at Prometheus Books, the guidance of associate editor Sheila Stewart who oversaw the editing process, and the dedicated diligence of my copyeditor, Lauren Humphries-Brooks, whose edits, explanations, and suggestions were enormously helpful.

Over the years, I have had innumerable conversations with elected and appointed officials, coworkers, and colleagues about issues and observations, all of which informed the writing of this book. I greatly appreciate each of them, and my book benefited from their perspectives. I also gained valuable insights and information at many conferences, conventions, forums, and industry-specific events. They include programs and events convened by the Aspen Institute, the Bipartisan Policy Center, the Milken Institute, the Center for American Progress, the Commonwealth Club, Town Hall Los Angeles, Business for Social Responsibility, the Brookings Institution, Verde Exchange, Renaissance Week, the Clinton Global Initiative, the Global Climate Action Summit, AlwaysOn, Health 2.0, StartUp Health, the U.S. Conference of Mayors, New America, Social Capital Markets, Digital Hollywood, Silicon Valley Leadership Group, and the Public Policy Institute of California.

Finally yet vitally, friends and family provided support that kept me conscientiously and eagerly attached to my laptop during many writing marathons. Some also provided a valuable sounding board for ideas. You know who you are, and there are too many to thank. On second thought—and quickly, before the orchestra starts to play—I'd like to give a shout-out with thanks to Richard and Wendy, Julia, Domini, Francine and Bill, Tara, Valerie, Daniel, Juliette, Jeffrey (JBD), Flora, Deborah, David (DAC), Craig, Cheryl, Joan, Kevin, Asad, Barbara, Gregory, Sandra, Bradley, Stephen, Nancy and David, Jon, and Dennis (with apologies to those who I forgot to mention).

NOTES

PREFACE

1. Tom Liddy, "Trump Said He Felt He Was Going to Lose the Election, despite Denying It," ABC News, January 2, 2017, https://abcnews.go.com/Politics/trump-felt-lose-election-denying/story?id=44517236.

2. Eugene Volokh, "Liberty, Safety, and Benjamin Franklin," *Washington Post*, November 11, 2014, https://www.washingtonpost.com/news/volokh-conspiracy/wp/2014/11/11/liberty-safety-and-benjamin-franklin/?noredirect=on&utm_term=.bfcdba826128.

CHAPTER 1

1. *Oxford Living Dictionary*, s.v. "nation (*n.*)," https://en.oxforddictionaries.com/definition/nation. "A large body of people united by common descent, history, culture, or language, inhabiting a particular state or territory."

2. *Black's Law Dictionary*, s.v. "What Is Nation?," https://thelawdictionary.org/nation/. "A people . . . existing in the form of an organized jural society, inhabiting a distinct portion of the earth, speaking the same language, using the same customs, possessing historic continuity, and distinguished from other like groups by their racial origin and characteristics. . . . See Montoya v. U.S., 180 U.S. 201."

3. Ayodele Gansallo and Judith Bernstein-Baker, *Understanding Immigration Law and Practice* (New York: Wolters Kluwer, 2017), p. 570. US law governing natural-born citizenship is based on two deep-rooted legal principles: *jus soli*, which is based on being born on United States territory, and *jus sanguinis*, which is based on one or both parents being US citizens.

4. "What Is a 'Nation'?," Global Policy Forum, https://www.globalpolicy.org/nations-a-states/what-is-a-nation.html. "A nation is a large group of people with strong bonds of identity—an 'imagined community,' a tribe on a grand scale."

5. Paul James, *Nation Formation: Towards a Theory of Abstract Community* (Thousand Oaks, CA: SAGE, 1996).

6. Ernest Renan, *What Is a Nation? and Other Political Writings* (New York: Columbia University Press, 2018), p. 261.

7. Alexis de Tocqueville, *Democracy in America, Volume II*, trans. Henry Reeve (New York: Colonial Press, 1899), p. 104. "Individualism . . . disposes each member of the community to sever himself from the mass of his fellow-creatures; and to draw apart with his family and

friends; so that, after he has thus formed a little circle of his own, he willingly leaves society at large to itself."

8. *Merriam-Webster Dictionary*, s.v. "rugged individualism (*n.*)," https://www.merriam-webster.com/dictionary/rugged%20individualism. "The practice or advocacy of individualism in social and economic relations emphasizing personal liberty and independence, self-reliance, resourcefulness, self-direction of the individual, and free competition in enterprise."

9. John Dewey, *Individualism Old and New* (Amherst, NY: Prometheus Books, 1999), pp. 44–45. "The virtues that are supposed to attend rugged individualism may be vocally proclaimed, but it takes no great insight to see that what is cherished is measured by its connection with those activities that make for success in business conducted for personal gain."

10. Herbert Hoover, "Principles and Ideals of the United States Government" (speech, Madison Square Garden, New York, NY, October 22, 1928), Miller Center, University of Virginia, https://millercenter.org/the-presidency/presidential-speeches/october-22-1928-principles-and-ideals-united-states-government.

11. Herbert Hoover, *The Challenge to Liberty* (New York: C. Scribner's Sons, 1934), pp. 54–55.

12. Jean-Jacques Rousseau, *On the Social Contract: or Principles of Political Right*, trans. Ian Johnston (Arlington, VA: Richer Resources, 2014). "Each one of us puts his person and all his power in common under the supreme direction of the general will, and as a body we receive each member as an indivisible part of the totality. This act of association immediately replaces the individual personality of each member of the contract with a moral and collective body composed of as many members as there are voices in the assembly. And from this same act, the assembly acquires its unity, its communal self, its life, and its will."

13. Birol Akkus, Tom Postmes, and Katherine Stroebe, "Community Collectivism: A Social Dynamic Approach to Conceptualizing Culture," *PLOS One* 12, no. 9 (September 28, 2017), https://journals.plos.org/plosone/article?id=10.1371/journal.pone.0185725. "Community collectivism is shaped by prevalent values and practices within the community. . . . Abiding by these values would be a prerequisite not just for the community to live harmoniously, but also for the individual to fit in and be accepted."

14. George Lakoff and Glenn Smith, "Why Democracy Is Public: The American Dream Beats the Nightmare," *Huffington Post*, July 28, 2011, https://www.huffingtonpost.com/george-lakoff/why-democracy-is-public-t_b_911205.html.

15. Denny Coates, "Ralph Waldo Emerson—An Intellectual Giant," Building Personal Strength, February 5, 2010, http://www.buildingpersonalstrength.com/2010/02/ralph-waldo-emerson-intellectual-giant.html.

16. Julie Fenster, "The Greatest Rallying Cry: Give Me Liberty or Give Me Death," *American Heritage*, https://www.americanheritage.com/content/greatest-rallying-cry-give-me-liberty-or-give-me-death.

17. George Washington, "Why the British Continue to Fight, December 18, 1778," letter to Benjamin Harrison, *Revolutionary War: The Turning Point, 1777–1778*, Library of Congress American Memory Timeline Classroom Materials, http://www.loc.gov/teachers/classroommaterials/presentationsandactivities/presentations/timeline/amrev/turning/continue.html.

18. Craig Biddle, "Individualism vs. Collectivism: Our Future, Our Choice," *Objective Standard* 7, no. 1 (Spring 2012), https://www.theobjectivestandard.com/issues/2012-spring/individualism-collectivism/.

19. Paul Ryan, speech for "Celebration of Ayn Rand" event, Atlas Society, February 2, 2005, quoted in Jane Mayer, "Ayn Rand Joins the Ticket," *New Yorker*, August 11, 2012, https://www.newyorker.com/news/news-desk/ayn-rand-joins-the-ticket.

20. "New Survey Reveals Americans Believe Country Has 'Lost Its Identity,'" *VOA News*, April 6, 2016, https://www.voanews.com/a/mht-quinnipiac-survey-reveals-americans-believe-country-has-lost-identity/3273301.html.

21. Matt Sedensky, "AP-NORC Poll: Divided Americans Fret Country Losing Identity," AP-NORC Center for Public Affairs Research, March 5, 2017, http://www.apnorc.org/news-media/Pages/AP-NORC-Poll-Divided-Americans-fret-country-losing-identity.aspx.

22. Laurie Kellman and Emily Swanson, "Poll: Americans Divided on Admitting Refugees," AP-NORC Center for Public Affairs Research, March 6, 2017, http://www.apnorc.org/news-media/Pages/Poll-Americans-divided-on-admitting-refugees.aspx.

23. Marc Hetherington and Jonathan Weiler, *Prius or Pickup? How the Answers to Four Simple Questions Explain America's Great Divide* (New York: Houghton Mifflin Harcourt, 2018).

24. Krishnadev Calamur, "A Short History of 'America First,'" *Atlantic*, January 21, 2017, https://www.theatlantic.com/politics/archive/2017/01/trump-america-first/514037/.

25. *American Experience*, season 30, episode 3, "The Gilded Age," directed by Sarah Colt, produced by Helen Dobrowski and Sarah Colt for WGBH Educational Foundation, aired on PBS, February 6, 2018, https://www.pbs.org/wgbh/americanexperience/films/gilded-age/.

26. Hillary Clinton, *It Takes a Village* (New York: Simon & Schuster, 1996).

27. Robert Dole, nomination acceptance speech, Republican National Convention, August 15, 1996, quoted in Mo Barrett, "First Lady Defends Views on Raising Children," CNN AllPolitics, August 27, 1996, http://www.cnn.com/ALLPOLITICS/1996/news/9608/27/hillary.speech/index.shtml.

28. E. J. Dionne Jr., "Biden Joins Campaign for the Presidency," *New York Times*, June 10, 1987, https://www.nytimes.com/1987/06/10/us/biden-joins-campaign-for-the-presidency.html.

29. Ashley Parker, "'Corporations Are People,' Romney Tells Iowa Hecklers Angry over His Tax Policy," *New York Times*, August 11, 2011, https://www.nytimes.com/2011/08/12/us/politics/12romney.html.

30. *Burwell v. Hobby Lobby*, 573 U.S. ___ (2014). The US Supreme Court, in a 5 to 4 decision, allowed a closely held company to exempt itself from certain provisions of the ACA on the basis of the Religious Freedom Restoration Act, but it didn't apply to publicly owned corporations.

31. Grover Cleveland, "Second Inaugural Address of Grover Cleveland, Saturday, March 4, 1893," Avalon Project, Yale Law School, http://avalon.law.yale.edu/19th_century/cleve2.asp.

32. Alfred Johnson, ed., *Cyclopedic Review of Current History*, vol. 6, no. 2 (Buffalo: Garretson Cox & Co., 1897), p. 270, quoting Rep. William McKinley in a campaign speech supporting the gold standard when running for Governor of Ohio (August 20, 1891).

33. H. Wayne Morgan, *William McKinley and His America* (Kent, Ohio: Kent State University Press, 2003), quoting Gov. William McKinley's speech to supporters while campaigning for the presidency (July 1896).

34. Gillespie, Metzgar, and Kelley, *Our Home Defenders* (William McKinley presidential campaign poster), 1896, lithograph, Library of Congress Prints and Photographs Division, https://www.loc.gov/pictures/item/94513583/.

35. Ira Katznelson, review of *The Triumph of William McKinley*, by Karl Rove, *New York Times*, January 20, 2016, https://www.nytimes.com/2016/01/24/books/review/the-tri umph-of-william-mckinley-by-karl-rove.html.

36. D. L. Chandler, "Little Known Black History Fact: The Brownsville Affair," BlackAmericaWeb.com, https://blackamericaweb.com/2016/09/07/little-known-black -history-fact-the-brownsville-affair/.

37. "Progressive Party Platform of 1912," August 7, 1912, Teaching American History, https://teachingamericanhistory.org/library/document/progressive-platform-of-1912/.

38. Calvin Coolidge, speech to the Society of American Newspaper Editors, January 17, 1925, quoted in Ellen Terrell, "When a Quote Is Not (Exactly) a Quote: The Business of America Is Business Edition," *Inside Adams* (blog), Library of Congress, January 17, 2019, https://blogs.loc.gov/inside_adams/2019/01/when-a-quote-is-not-exactly-a-quote-the -business-of-america-is-business-edition/.

39. Howard Quint and Robert Farrell, *The Talkative President: The Off-the-Record Press Conferences of Calvin Coolidge* (Cambridge: University of Massachusetts Press, 1964), quoting President Calvin Coolidge from his final press conference, March 1, 1929.

40. Kevin Ballen, "What You Can Do for Your Country," *Harvard Political Review*, March 12, 2019, quoting President John F. Kennedy's Inaugural Address (January 20, 1961), http://harvardpolitics.com/united-states/what-you-can-do-for-your-country/.

41. Gov. Ronald Reagan, in "The Image of America and the Youth of the World," debate with Sen. Robert Kennedy, moderated by Charles Collingwood, *Town Meeting of the World*, CBS, May 15, 1967, transcript available at https://www.jfklibrary.org/learn/about -jfk/the-kennedy-family/robert-f-kennedy/robert-f-kennedy-speeches/the-image-of-america -and-the-youth-of-the-world-with-gov-ronald-reagan-cbs-television-and-radio-may.

42. "What Does '1,000 Points of Light' Mean (Think First President Bush)?" Quora website with crowdsourced responses interpreting the phrase coined by Vice President George H. W. Bush during his presidential nomination acceptance speech at the Republican National Convention (August 18, 1988), https://www.quora.com/What-does-1000-points-of -light-mean-think-first-President-Bush.

43. Jill Lawrence, "Republicans Learned All the Wrong Lessons from Bush's 'Read My Lips' Snafu," *The Week*, April 7, 2014, https://theweek.com/articles/448193/republicans -learned-all-wrong-lessons-from-bushs-read-lips-snafu.

44. Ben Smith, "The End of the DLC era," *Politico*, February 7, 2011, https://www .politico.com/story/2011/02/the-end-of-the-dlc-era-049041.

45. E. J. Dionne, "Governing in an Age of No Majorities: Bill Clinton's Mission for a Second Term," Brookings, December 1, 1997, https://www.brookings.edu/articles/ governing-in-an-age-of-no-majorities-bill-clintons-mission-for-a-second-term/.

46. Michael Tanner and Tad DeHaven, "TANF and Federal Welfare," Downsizing the Federal Government (a project of CATO Institute), September 1, 2010, https://www.down sizinggovernment.org/hhs/welfare-spending.

47. Arthur Wilmarth, "The Road to Repeal of the Glass-Steagall Act," George Washington University Law School Public Law Research Paper No. 2017-61, July 2017, https://papers.ssrn.com/sol3/papers.cfm?abstract_id=3026287.

48. Dana Milbank, "Country Before Ideology, and Other Quaint Ideas from GOP History," *Washington Post*, November 11, 2010, http://www.washingtonpost.com/wp-dyn/ content/article/2010/11/10/AR2010111007441.html?nav=E8.

49. Ron Fournier, LeadingQuotes.win, December 16, 2010, http://leadingquotes.win/9348/best/at-his-best-obama-promised-to-work/.

50. Andrew Rosenthal, "You Didn't Build That," *Taking Note* (blog), *New York Times*, July 27, 2012, https://takingnote.blogs.nytimes.com/2012/07/27/you-didnt-build-that/.

51. Eugene Kiely, "'You Didn't Build That,' Uncut and Unedited," FactCheck.org, July 24, 2012, quoting President Barack Obama's speech at Roanoke, Virginia, campaign event, July 13, 2012, https://www.factcheck.org/2012/07/you-didnt-build-that-uncut-and-unedited/.

52. David Graham, "The President Who Doesn't Read," *Atlantic*, January 5, 2018, https://www.theatlantic.com/politics/archive/2018/01/americas-first-post-text-president/549794/.

53. Jana Heigl, "A Timeline of Donald Trump's False Wiretapping Charge," PolitiFact, March 21, 2017, https://www.politifact.com/truth-o-meter/article/2017/mar/21/timeline-donald-trumps-false-wiretapping-charge/.

54. Adam Goldman, Mark Mazzetti, and Matthew Rosenberg, "F.B.I. Used Informant to Investigate Russia Ties to Campaign, Not to Spy, as Trump Claims," *New York Times*, May 18, 2018, https://www.nytimes.com/2018/05/18/us/politics/trump-fbi-informant-russia-investigation.html.

55. Christina Wilkie, "Here's How Trump Stands to Benefit from the Republican Tax Bill," CNBC, December 1, 2017, https://www.cnbc.com/2017/12/01/heres-how-trump-stands-to-benefit-from-the-republican-tax-bill.html.

56. David Morgan, "Republican ObamaCare Repeal Would Benefit Wealthiest: Study," Reuters, March 13, 2017, https://www.reuters.com/article/us-usa-obamacare-taxes-idUSKBN16K2G6.

57. Timothy A. Kohler et al., "Greater Post-Neolithic Wealth Disparities in Eurasia than in North America and Mesoamerica," *Nature* 551, no. 7682 (November 30, 2017): 619–22.

58. Eric Sorenson, "Researchers Chart Rising Wealth Inequality Across Millennia," *Washington State University News*, November 15, 2017, https://news.wsu.edu/2017/11/15/researchers-chart-rising-inequality-across-millennia/.

59. Julie Hirschfeld-Davis, "Trump to Cap Refugees Allowed into U.S. at 30,000, a Record Low," *New York Times*, September 17, 2018, https://www.nytimes.com/2018/09/17/us/politics/trump-refugees-historic-cuts.html.

60. Salvador Rizzo, "The Facts about Trump's Policy of Separating Families at the Border," *Washington Post*, June 19, 2018, https://www.washingtonpost.com/news/fact-checker/wp/2018/06/19/the-facts-about-trumps-policy-of-separating-families-at-the-border/?noredirect=on&utm_term=.b548578deedb.

61. Julie Hirschfeld-Davis and Michael Shear, "How Trump Came to Enforce a Practice of Separating Migrant Families," *New York Times*, June 16, 2018, https://www.nytimes.com/2018/06/16/us/politics/family-separation-trump.html.

62. Louis Nelson, "Trump's Solution for Reunifying Migrant Families: 'Don't Come to Our Country Illegally,'" *Politico*, July 10, 2018, https://www.politico.com/story/2018/07/10/trump-migrant-families-separated-706144.

63. Jamiles Lartey, "Trump Blames Missed Reunification Deadline on Families: 'Don't Come to Our Country Illegally,'" *Guardian*, July 10, 2018, https://www.theguardian.com/us-news/2018/jul/10/donald-trump-family-reunification-deadline-border-separations.

64. Jenna Johnson, "Trump Lavishes Praise on Rob Porter, Former Top Aide Accused of Domestic Violence," *Washington Post*, February 9, 2018, https://www.washingtonpost

.com/news/post-politics/wp/2018/02/09/trump-lavishes-praise-on-rob-porter-former-top -aide-accused-of-domestic-violence/?utm_term=.9890225ec28a.

65. Bess Levin, "Trump Hires Sexual Harassment Facilitator Bill Shine as Comms Director," *Vanity Fair*, June 28, 2018, https://www.vanityfair.com/news/2018/06/bill-shine -white-house-fox-news.

66. Eliza Relman, "Trump Says Kavanaugh Is 'Under Assault,' Blames Christine Blasey Ford for Not Going to the FBI When She Was in High School," *Business Insider*, September 21, 2018, https://www.businessinsider.in/trump-says-kavanaugh-is-under -assault-blames-christine-blasey-ford-for-not-going-to-the-fbi-when-she-was-in-high-school/ articleshow/65903402.cms.

67. Jonathan Allen, "Trump Mocks Kavanaugh Accuser Christine Blasey Ford at Campaign Rally," NBC News, October 3, 2018, https://www.nbcnews.com/politics/ politics-news/trump-mocks-christine-blasey-ford-mississippi-campaign-rally-n916061.

68. Tovia Smith, "Education Dept. Proposes Enhanced Protection for Students Accused of Sexual Assault," NPR News, November 16, 2018, https://www.npr.org/ 2018/11/16/668556728/education-dept-proposes-enhanced-protection-for-students -accused-of-sexual-assau.

69. Matt Ford, "The 19 Women Who Accused Donald Trump of Sexual Misconduct," *Atlantic*, December 7, 2017, https://www.theatlantic.com/politics/archive/2017/12/what -about-the-19-women-who-accused-trump/547724/.

70. Aaron Levin, "Goldwater Rule's Origins Based on Long-Ago Controversy," *Psychiatric News* (American Psychiatric Association), August 25, 2016, https://doi.org/ 10.1176/appi.pn.2016.9a19. The article cites Section 7.3 of the APA's *Principles of Medical Ethics*: "[I]t is unethical for a psychiatrist to offer a professional opinion unless he or she has conducted an examination and been granted proper authorization for such a statement" (adopted 1973).

71. Claire Pouncey, "Trump's Mental Health—Is It Morally Permissible for Psychiatrists to Comment?" *New England Journal of Medicine*, February 1, 2018, https:// www.nejm.org/doi/10.1056/NEJMp1714828.

72. David Shields, *Nobody Hates Trump More Than Trump: An Intervention* (New York: Thought Catalog Books, 2018).

73. Yoni Appelbaum, "'I Alone Can Fix It,'" *Atlantic*, July 21, 2016, https://www .theatlantic.com/politics/archive/2016/07/trump-rnc-speech-alone-fix-it/492557/.

74. Donald Trump, interview by Laura Ingraham, *The Ingraham Angle*, Fox News, November 2, 2017, video available at https://www.youtube.com/watch?v=EA2pH3CD5Ns (at 8:05–8:08, in response to question about understaffing at the State Department).

75. Monique Judge, "Very Unstable Genius Says If You Impeach Him 'Everybody Would Be Very Poor,'" *The Root*, August 23, 2018, https://www.theroot.com/very-unstable -genius-says-if-you-impeach-him-everybody-1828564687.

76. Aaron Blake, "19 Things Donald Trump Knows Better Than Anyone Else, According to Donald Trump," *Washington Post*, October 4, 2016, https://www.washing tonpost.com/news/the-fix/wp/2016/10/04/17-issues-that-donald-trump-knows-better -than-anyone-else-according-to-donald-trump/?utm_term=.746f915bc4b2.

77. Oliver Noble, "24 Things Trump Does Better Than Anybody (According to Trump)," *Vice News*, February 22, 2017, https://news.vice.com/en_us/article/nedxnm/ 24-things-nobody-does-better-than-trump-according-to-trump.

78. Kevin Mathews, "20 Things Trump Says He's the Best At—And Why He's Wrong," Care2, November 2, 2016, https://www.care2.com/causes/20-things-trump-says-hes-the-best-at-and-why-hes-wrong.html.

79. Donald Trump (@realDonaldTrump), "Can you believe Mitch McConnell, who screamed Repeal & Replace for 7 years, couldn't get it done," Twitter, August 10, 2017, 3:54 a.m., https://twitter.com/realdonaldtrump/status/895599179522650112?lang=en.

80. Chris Cillizza, "This Is the Most Donald Trump Interview Donald Trump Has Ever Given," *Washington Post*, December 9, 2015, https://www.washingtonpost.com/news/the-fix/wp/2015/12/09/this-is-the-most-donald-trump-interview-donald-trump-has-ever-given/?utm_term=.b4b1549c239b.

81. Morgan Gstalter, "Trump Again Labels Himself a 'Very Stable Genius,'" *The Hill*, July 12, 2018, https://thehill.com/homenews/administration/396628-trump-calls-himself-a-stable-genius.

82. Jennie Neufeld, "Read the Full Transcript of the Helsinki Press Conference," *Vox*, July 17, 2018, https://www.vox.com/2018/7/16/17576956/transcript-putin-trump-russia-helsinki-press-conference.

83. Bandy Lee and Leonard Glass, "We're Psychiatrists. It's Our Duty to Question the President's Mental State," *Politico*, January 10, 2018, https://www.politico.com/magazine/story/2018/01/10/were-psychiatrists-its-perfectly-healthy-to-question-the-presidents-mental-state-216266.

84. Bandy Lee et al., *The Dangerous Case of Donald Trump: 27 Psychiatrists and Mental Health Experts Assess a President* (New York: Thomas Dunne Books, 2017).

85. Julie Hirschfeld-Davis, "Trump's Cabinet, with a Prod, Extols the 'Blessing' of Serving Him," *New York Times*, June 12, 2017, https://www.nytimes.com/2017/06/12/us/politics/trump-boasts-of-record-setting-pace-of-activity.html.

86. Eddie Glaude Jr., "Trump's Cabinet of Worship Is a Scary Sign of American Collapse," *Time*, June 13, 2017, http://time.com/4816374/trump-cabinet-praise-scary/.

87. Jessica Taylor, "Another Reversal: Trump Now Says Counterprotesters Also to Blame for Charlottesville," NPR, August 15, 2017, https://www.npr.org/2017/08/15/543743845/another-reversal-trump-now-says-counterprotesters-also-to-blame-for-charlottesvi.

88. Noble, "24 Things Trump Does Better Than Anybody."

89. Conor Friedersdorf, "Trump's Brazen, Effective Lie," *Atlantic*, May 2, 2018, https://www.theatlantic.com/politics/archive/2018/05/revisiting-a-brazen-effective-lie/559433/.

90. Ken Meyer, "Trump Appeals for Border Wall in New Year's Eve Fox Interview: 'It Is Not Old Fashioned,' It's like the Wheel," *Mediaite*, December 31, 2018, https://www.mediaite.com/tv/trump-appeals-for-border-wall-in-new-years-eve-fox-interview-it-is-not-old-fashioned-its-like-the-wheel/.

91. "Day 701: Trump, Who Can't Use a Computer, Brags about Knowing Technology 'Better Than Anyone,'" *Medium*, December 21, 2018, https://medium.com/@Trump Timer/day-701-trump-who-cant-use-a-computer-brags-about-knowing-technology-better-than-anyone-ef66aeaaf587.

92. Donald Trump, "I Was Going to Fire Comey Anyway, Trump Tells Lester Holt in Interview," NBC News, May 11, 2017: https://www.nbcnews.com/nightly-news/video/i-was-going-to-fire-comey-anyway-trump-tells-lester-holt-in-interview-941538371971?v=railb&.

93. Burgess Everett, Sarah Ferris, and Caitlin Oprysko, "Trump Says He's 'Proud' to Shut Down Government during Fight with Pelosi and Schumer," *Politico*, December 11, 2018, https://www.politico.com/story/2018/12/11/trump-border-wall-congress-budget-1055433.

94. Omarosa Manigault Newman, *Unhinged: An Insider's Account of the Trump White House* (New York: Gallery Books, 2018).

95. Martina Stewart, "Trump Orders Declassification of FBI Documents Sought by House Republicans," NPR, September 17, 2018, https://www.npr.org/2018/09/17/648883919/trump-orders-declassification-of-documents-about-fbi-sought-by-house -republicans.

96. Zack Beauchamp, "'This Is a Constitutional Crisis': A Legal Expert on Trump's Emergency Declaration," *Vox*, February 15, 2019, https://www.vox.com/policy-and -politics/2019/2/15/18226315/trump-emergency-national-wall-border-illegal.

97. Charlie Savage and Robert Pear, "16 States Sue to Stop Trump's Use of Emergency Powers to Build Border Wall," *New York Times*, February 18, 2019, https://www.nytimes.com/2019/02/18/us/politics/national-emergency-lawsuits-trump.html.

98. Emily Zaumer, "Trump Complains about Having a 'Bad Hair Day' Hours after 11 People Die in Synagogue Shooting," *People*, Oct. 28, 2018, https://people.com/politics/trump-says-bad-hair-day-hours-after-synagogue-shooting/.

99. Tess Koman, "Here's Donald Trump Throwing Paper Towel Rolls like Basketballs at Hurricane Survivors," *Cosmopolitan*, October 4, 2017, https://www.cosmopolitan.com/politics/a12778809/donald-trump-puerto-rico-paper-towels/.

100. Marisa Schultz, "Trump: 'I Was Having Fun' Throwing Paper Towels in Puerto Rico," *New York Post*, October 8, 2017, https://nypost.com/2017/10/08/trump-i-was-hav ing-fun-throwing-paper-towels-in-puerto-rico/.

101. Desire Thompson, "Apparently, Trump Wanted to Throw Cans of Chicken at Hurricane Victims," *Vibe*, October 6, 2017, https://www.vibe.com/amp/2017/10/trump -wanted-to-throw-cans-of-chicken-at-hurricane-victims.

102. Jonathan Easley and Jordan Fabian, "White House Official Mocked 'Dying' McCain at Internal Meeting," *The Hill*, May 10, 2018, https://thehill.com/homenews/administration/387182-white-house-official-mocked-dying-mccain-at-internal-meeting.

103. William P. Davis, "'Enemy of the People': Trump Breaks Out This Phrase during Moments of Peak Criticism," *New York Times*, July 19, 2018, https://www.nytimes.com/2018/07/19/business/media/trump-media-enemy-of-the-people.html.

104. Michael Calderone, "Trump Takes Authoritarian Stance in Portraying Journalists as Anti-American Enemy," *Huffington Post*, August 23, 2017, https://www.huffpost.com/entry/donald-trump-portrays-journalists-as-anti-american_n_599da653e4b0d8dde99a844c.

105. Caitlin Yilek, "Trump Didn't Want to Win the Election Because He Thought Losing Could Offer 'Untold Opportunities,'" *Washington Examiner*, January 3, 2018, https://www.washingtonexaminer.com/trump-didnt-want-to-win-the-election-because-he-thought -losing-could-offer-untold-opportunities-book.

106. David Fahrenthold and Jonathan O'Connell, "DC, Maryland Can Proceed with Lawsuit Alleging Trump Violated Emoluments Clause," *Washington Post*, March 28, 2018, https://www.washingtonpost.com/politics/dc-maryland-may-proceed-with-lawsuit-alleging -trump-violated-emoluments-clause/2018/03/28/0514d816-32ae-11e8-8bdd-cdb33a5eef 83_story.html?noredirect=on&utm_term=.ac37a648d091.

107. Brett Samuels, "Trump Lashes Out at Mueller for Alleged Conflicts of Interest," *The Hill*, July 29, 2018, https://thehill.com/homenews/administration/399427-trump-says -he-and-mueller-had-nasty-business-relationship.

108. Ezra Klein, "Donald Trump's Corrupt Firing of Andrew McCabe," *Vox*, March 17, 2018, https://www.vox.com/policy-and-politics/2018/3/17/17133284/donald-trump-andrew-mccabe-jeff-sessions-fired-former-fbi-director.

109. Chas Danner, "Mueller Removed FBI Agent from Russia Investigation over Anti-Trump Texts," *Intelligencer* (blog), *New York Magazine*, December 2, 2017, http://nymag.com/intelligencer/2017/12/mueller-removed-investigator-over-possible-anti-trump-texts.html.

110. Jonathan Easley, "GOP Fuels 'Secret Society' Talk with FBI Text Messages," *The Hill*, January 24, 2018, https://thehill.com/homenews/house/370571-gop-fuels-secret-society-talk-with-fbi-text-messages.

111. Howard Fineman, in panel discussion led by Chuck Todd, *MTP Daily*, MSNBC, January 24, 2018, transcript available at http://www.msnbc.com/transcripts/mtp-daily/2018-01-24.

112. Peter Overby, "Trump's Cabinet Scandals: Is Abuse of Office Contagious?" NPR, March 8, 2018, https://www.npr.org/2018/03/08/591524460/trumps-cabinet-scandals-is-abuse-of-office-contagious.

113. Jonathan Chait, "The Michael Cohen Bribery Scandal Is Now a Trump Bribery Scandal," *Intelligencer* (blog), *New York Magazine*, May 16, 2018, http://nymag.com/intelligencer/2018/05/michael-cohen-bribery-scandal-is-now-a-trump-bribery-scandal.html?gtm=top&gtm=bottom.

114. Dustin Racioppi, "Sen. Cory Booker Calls for Unity in Prime-Time DNC speech," *USA Today News*, July 26, 2016, https://amp.usatoday.com/story/news/politics/elections/2016/07/25/sen-cory-booker-unity-dnc/87555212/.

115. Marc Benioff and Karen Southwick, *Compassionate Capitalism: How Corporations Can Make Doing Good an Integral Part of Doing Well* (Wayne, NJ: Career Press, 2004).

CHAPTER 2

1. Frank Hobbs and Nicole Stoops, *Demographic Trends in the 20th Century*, Census 2000 Special Reports, Series CENSR-4, US Census Bureau (Washington, DC: US Government Printing Office, 2002), https://www.census.gov/prod/2002pubs/censr-4.pdf; Thomas L. Mesenbourg, "A Look at the 1940 Census," US Census Bureau on *Washington Journal*, C-SPAN, March 30, 2012, https://www.census.gov/newsroom/cspan/1940census/.

2. Campbell Gibson and Kay Jung, "Historical Census Statistics on Population Totals by Race (1790 to 1990) and by Hispanic Origin (1970 to 1990) for Large Cities and Urban Places" (working paper POP-WP056, US Census Bureau, Population Division, September 2002), https://www.census.gov/library/working-papers/2002/demo/POP-twps0056.html; "Decennial Census of Population and Housing, by Decade: 1940," US Census Bureau, https://www.census.gov/programs-surveys/decennial-census/decade.1940.html; Census of Population and Housing, US Census Bureau, https://www.census.gov/prod/www/decennial.html.

3. Karen R. Humes, Nicholas A. Jones, and Roberto R. Ramirez, "Overview of Race and Hispanic Origin: 2010," 2010 Census Briefs, C2010BR-02, US Census Bureau, March 2011, https://www.census.gov/prod/cen2010/briefs/c2010br-02.pdf.

4. Humes, Jones, and Ramirez, "Overview of Race and Hispanic Origin"; Mesenbourg, "Look at the 1940 Census."

5. Ibid.

6. Grayson K. Vincent and Victoria A. Velkoff, *The Next Four Decades: The Older Population in the United States, 2010 to 2050*, Current Population Reports, P25-1138, US Census Bureau, May 2010, https://www.census.gov/prod/2010pubs/p25-1138.pdf; Mesenbourg, "Look at the 1940 Census," slide 11.

7. Ibid.

8. Bernadette Proctor, Jessica Semega, and Melissa Kollar, "Income and Poverty in the United States: 2015," Current Population Reports, P60-256(RV), US Census Bureau, September 2016, https://www.census.gov/content/dam/Census/library/publications/2016/demo/p60-256.pdf.

9. Colin Peterson, Matthew Snipp, and Sin Yi Cheung, "Earnings," in "State of the Union: The Poverty and Inequality Report," ed. Stanford Center on Poverty and Inequality, special issue, *Pathways Magazine*, 2017, https://inequality.stanford.edu/sites/default/files/Pathways_SOTU_2017_earnings.pdf.

10. Janelle Jones, "Black Unemployment Is at Least Twice as High as White Unemployment at the National Level and in 12 States and D.C.," Economic Policy Institute, October 30, 2018, https://www.epi.org/publication/2018q3_unemployment_state_race_ethnicity/.

11. Devah Pager, Bruce Western, and Bart Bonikowski, "Discrimination in a Low-Wage Labor Market: A Field Experiment," *American Sociological Review* 74, no. 5 (2009): 777–99, https://www.ncbi.nlm.nih.gov/pmc/articles/PMC2915472/.

12. Regents of the University of California v. Bakke, 438 U.S. 265 (1978).

13. Nicki Lisa Cole, "Meet the People behind Donald Trump's Popularity," ThoughtCo., June 14, 2018, https://www.thoughtco.com/meet-the-people-behind-donald-trumps-popularity-4068073.

14. Josh Lowe, "Why the 'Poorly Educated' Love Donald Trump Back," *Newsweek*, November 25, 2016, https://www.newsweek.com/donald-trump-brexit-austria-french-presidential-election-national-front-525281.

15. Isaac Chotiner, "Why White Evangelicals Abandoned Their Principles for Donald Trump," *Slate*, March 13, 2018, https://slate.com/news-and-politics/2018/03/why-white-evangelicals-abandoned-their-principles-for-trump.html.

16. Sean McElwee, "Data for Politics #14: Who Is Trump's Base?" *Data For Progress* (blog), August 23, 2018, https://www.dataforprogress.org/blog/2018/8/21/data-for-politics-14-who-is-trumps-base.

17. Steven Rosenfeld, "12 Features of White Working-Class Trump Voters Confirm Depressed and Traumatized Multitudes Voted for Him," *Salon*, May 19, 2017, https://www.salon.com/2017/05/19/12-features-of-white-working-class-trump-voters-confirm-depressed-and-traumatized-multitudes-voted-for-him_partner/.

18. Alison Durkee, "Trump Inauguration Transcript 2017: Read the President's Full Speech and Remarks," *Mic*, January 20, 2017, https://mic.com/articles/166134/trump-inauguration-transcript-2017-read-the-president-s-full-speech-and-remarks#.KTGqq9oQ2.

19. David Brooks, "Revolt of the Masses," *New York Times*, June 28, 2016, https://www.nytimes.com/2016/06/28/opinion/revolt-of-the-masses.html.

20. The distinction between Trump's base and nonbase voters is discussed in chapter 10.

21. Steve Holland and Ginger Gibson, "Confident Trump Says Could 'Shoot Somebody' and Not Lose Voters," Reuters, January 23, 2016, https://www.reuters.com/article/us-usa-election-idUSMTZSAPEC1NFEQLYN.

22. Bobby Azarian, "An Analysis of Trump Voters Has Identified 5 Key Traits: A New Report Sheds Light on the Psychological Basis for Trump's Support," *Psychology Today*, December 31, 2017, https://www.psychologytoday.com/us/blog/mind-in-the-machine/201712/analysis-trump-supporters-has-identified-5-key-traits.

23. Graham Vyse, "How Trump Wins Reelection," *New Republic*, February 26, 2018, https://newrepublic.com/article/147119/trump-wins-reelection.

24. Hallie Jackson and Frank Thorp, "Trump and Judge Curiel: What Republicans Are Saying," NBC News, June 9, 2016, https://www.nbcnews.com/politics/2016-election/trump-judge-curiel-what-republicans-are-saying-n588801.

25. Jill Duerr Berrick, "What Have They Got to Lose? When Will Black Americans Win?," *San Francisco Chronicle*, August 28, 2016, https://www.sfchronicle.com/opinion/openforum/article/What-have-they-got-to-lose-When-will-black-9189465.php.

26. Sean McElwee and Jason McDaniel, "Economic Anxiety Didn't Make People Vote Trump, Racism Did," *Nation*, May 8, 2017, https://www.thenation.com/article/economic-anxiety-didnt-make-people-vote-trump-racism-did/.

27. German Lopez, "The Past Year of Research Has Made It Very Clear: Trump Won because of Racial Resentment," *Vox*, December 15, 2017, https://www.vox.com/identities/2017/12/15/16781222/trump-racism-economic-anxiety-study.

28. Vann Newkirk, "Trump's White-Nationalist Pipeline," *Atlantic*, August 23, 2018, https://www.theatlantic.com/politics/archive/2018/08/trump-white-nationalism/568393/.

29. William Saletan, "What Trump Supporters Really Believe: The President's Racist Base, by the Numbers," *Slate*, August 29, 2017, https://slate.com/news-and-politics/2017/08/trumps-bigoted-base-by-the-numbers.html.

30. Melissa Ryan, "How the President and Neo-Nazis Work Hand in Hand," *The Progressive*, January 31, 2018, https://progressive.org/magazine/trump-s-army-how-the-president-and-neo-nazis-work-hand-in-ha/.

31. W. E. B. Du Bois, *Black Reconstruction in America: 1860–1880* (New York: Free Press, 1998), p. 700.

32. Sean Illing, "Why This Professor Sees Trump as 'An Opportunity to Imagine a New Kind of Politics': Professor Eddie Glaude Jr. on Trump's Victory and the Future of Race and Politics in America," *Vox*, January 26, 2017, https://www.vox.com/conversations/2017/1/26/14310054/obama-donald-trump-race-relations-america-election-2016-eddie-glaude.

33. Nicole Karlis, "After Calling Her 'Low IQ,' Trump Lectures Maxine Waters on Civility: 'Be Careful,'" *Salon*, June 25, 2018, https://www.salon.com/2018/06/25/after-calling-her-low-iq-trump-lectures-maxine-waters-on-civility-be-careful/.

34. Sheryl Estrada, "Trump at GOP Rally: Maxine Waters Has 'Very Low IQ,'" DiversityInc, March 12, 2018, https://www.diversityinc.com/trump-gop-rally-maxine-waters-low-iq/.

35. Emily Stewart, "Trump Is Insulting LeBron James's Intelligence—and Don Lemon's—on Twitter," *Vox*, August 4, 2018, https://www.vox.com/2018/8/4/17650982/trump-lebron-james-tweet-don-lemon.

36. David Smith, "Trump's Tactic to Attack Black People and Women: Insult Their Intelligence," *Guardian*, August 10, 2018, https://www.theguardian.com/us-news/2018/aug/10/trump-attacks-twitter-black-people-women.

37. Laignee Barron, "'A New Low.' The World Is Furious at Trump for His Remark about 'Shithole Countries,'" *Time*, January 12, 2018, http://time.com/5100328/shithole -countries-trump-reactions/.

38. Adam Lusher, "Neo-Nazis Say Donald Trump's 'Shithole Countries' Comments Show He Thinks Like Them," *Independent*, January 13, 2018, https://www.independent.co .uk/news/world/americas/us-politics/donald-trump-shithole-countries-neo-nazis-white -supremacists-celebrate-more-or-less-same-page-racist-a8157796.html.

39. Emily Swanson and Russell Contreras, "AP-NORC Poll: Most Americans Say Trump Is Racist," Associated Press, February 28, 2018, https://apnews.com/9961ee5b 3c3b42d29aebdee837c17a11, citing February 2018 AP-NORC Center for Public Affairs Research Poll, http://apnorc.org/PDFs/AP-NORC%20Omnibus%20February%202018/ February%202018%20Custom%20Poll%20Topline_Second%20AP%20Story.pdf, p. 14.

40. "Our View: Donald Trump Just Resurrected Joe Arpaio from Irrelevance," editorial, *Arizona Republic*, August 25, 2018, https://www.azcentral.com/story/opinion/ editorial/2017/08/25/donald-trump-resurrects-joe-arpaio-irrelevance/604067001/.

41. Doug Saunders, "The Real Reason Donald Trump Got Elected? We Have a White Extremism Problem," *Globe and Mail*, November 12, 2017, https://www.theglobeandmail .com/news/world/us-politics/the-real-reason-donald-trump-got-elected-we-have-a-white -extremism-problem/article32817625/.

42. Ta-Nehisi Coates, *We Were Eight Years in Power: An American Tragedy* (New York: Penguin Random House, 2017), p. 342.

43. Preston Mitchum, "Donald Trump, Racist-in-Chief: Here Are the 10 Most Racist Things He's Done So Far," *The Root*, December 19, 2016, https://www.theroot.com/donald -trump-racist-in-chief-here-are-the-10-most-rac-1790858151.

44. Rob Garver, "5 Times Donald Trump Condoned Violence against Protesters," *Fiscal Times*, March 10, 2016, http://www.thefiscaltimes.com/2016/03/10/5-Times -Donald-Trump-Condoned-Violence-Against-Protesters.

45. Niraj Chokshi, "Assaults Increased When Cities Hosted Trump Rallies, Study Finds," *New York Times*, March 16, 2018, https://www.nytimes.com/2018/03/16/us/trump-rally-vio lence.html.

46. Feroze Dhanoa, "Acts of Hatred, Racism Come in Immediate Aftermath of Donald Trump's Election," Patch, November 14, 2016, https://patch.com/us/across -america/incidents-hatred-racism-come-immediate-aftermath-donald-trumps-election.

47. John Mitchell, "How Trump Manipulates His Base's Fear of Black Men," *Philadelphia Tribune*, November 21, 2017, https://www.phillytrib.com/commentary/how -trump-manipulates-his-base-s-fear-of-black-men/article_55bac494-7866-5c79-b095 -b4ed4ce59033.html.

48. German Lopez, "How Trump Both Stokes and Obscures His Supporters' Racial Resentment," *Vox*, August 31, 2017, https://www.vox.com/policy-and-politics/2017/8/ 31/16226488/trump-identity-politics-racism.

49. Michael Finnegan and Mark Barabak, "'Shithole' and Other Racist Things Trump Has Said—So Far," *Los Angeles Times*, January 12, 2018, https://www.latimes.com/politics/ la-na-trump-racism-remarks-20180111-htmlstory.html.

50. John Meacham, interviewed by Andrea Mitchell, *Andrea Mitchell Reports*, MSNBC, August 2017 [transcription by the author].

51. Diana Mutz, "Status Threat, Not Economic Hardship, Explains the 2016 Presidential Vote," *PNAS* 115, no. 19 (May 8, 2018), http://www.pnas.org/content/115/19/E4330.

52. Jennifer Rubin, "The Demographic Change Fueling the Angst of Trump's Base," *Washington Post*, September 6, 2017, https://www.washingtonpost.com/blogs/right-turn/wp/2017/09/06/the-demographic-change-fueling-the-angst-of-trumps-base/?utm_term=.1b0cff7117d3.

53. Candace Smith, "Some White Trump Supporters Fear Becoming Minority," ABC News, November 2, 2016, https://abcnews.go.com/Politics/white-trump-supporters-fear-minority/story?id=43229203.

54. Ryan Beckwith, "Donald Trump Weaponized Conspiracy Theories: QAnon Shows We're Now in an Arms Race," *Time*, August 2, 2018, http://time.com/5356443/trump-conspiracy-theories-qanon/.

55. Rosenfeld, "12 Features of White Working-Class Trump Voters."

56. Michael Eric Dyson, *Tears We Cannot Stop: A Sermon to White America* (New York: St. Martin's, 2017), p. 44.

57. Ibid., pp. 46, 98.

58. Ibid., p. 86.

59. "Implicit Association Test," Harvard's Project Implicit, https://implicit.harvard.edu/implicit/education.html.

60. Jason Stanley, *How Fascism Works: The Politics of Us and Them* (New York: Random House, 2018), pp. 3–4.

61. Ibid., p. 26.

62. The contrast between the experiences of whites and nonwhites harkened back to the aftermath of World War I, when African Americans returned home to outright racial hostility and violence, about which Presidents Harding, Coolidge, and Hoover did virtually nothing to abate.

63. Nancy Isenberg, *White Trash: The 400-Year Untold Story of Class in America* (New York: Penguin Books, 2016), pp. 206–30.

64. Ben Cosgrove, "'The Luckiest Generation': LIFE with Teenagers in 1950s America," *Time*, November 29, 2014, http://time.com/3544391/the-luckiest-generation-life-with-teenagers-in-1950s-america/.

65. Louis Wirth, "The Problem of Minority Groups," in *The Science of Man in the World Crisis*, ed. Ralph Linton (New York: Columbia University Press, 1945), p. 347.

66. Marisa Hotchkiss and Jessica Phelan, "Uses of Census Bureau Data in Federal Funds Distribution," US Census Bureau, September 2017, https://www2.census.gov/programs-surveys/decennial/2020/program-management/working-papers/Uses-of-Census-Bureau-Data-in-Federal-Funds-Distribution.pdf.

67. Tyler Huckabee, "The Problem with Saying 'All Lives Matter,'" *Relevant Magazine*, July 6, 2016, https://relevantmagazine.com/current16/problem-saying-all-lives-matter/.

68. German Lopez, "Why You Should Stop Saying 'All Lives Matter,' Explained in 9 Different Ways," *Vox*, July 11, 2016, https://www.vox.com/2016/7/11/12136140/black-all-lives-matter.

69. See, for example, the Equity Metrics program at UC Berkeley's Haas Institute for a Fair and Inclusive Society (https://haasinstitute.berkeley.edu/equitymetrics).

70. Los Angeles Department of Water and Power's Equity Metrics Data Initiative, www.ladwp.com/ladwp/faces/wcnav_externalId/au-fr-corporateperformance-emdi.

71. Wirth, "Problem of Minority Groups," p. 347.

72. Richa Chaturvedi, "A Closer Look at the Gender Gap in Presidential Voting," Fact Tank, Pew Research Center, July 28, 2016, http://www.pewresearch.org/fact-tank/2016/07/28/a-closer-look-at-the-gender-gap-in-presidential-voting/.

73. Jamelle Bouie, "The Next Consensus: Young Voters' Strong Belief in Racial Egalitarianism May Triumph over Trump's Politics," *Slate*, March 6, 2018, https://slate.com/news-and-politics/2018/03/young-voters-will-provide-a-counterweight-to-trumps-racism.html.

74. Nancy Wadsworth, "The Racial Demons That Help Explain Evangelical Support for Trump," *Vox*, April 30, 2018, https://www.vox.com/the-big-idea/2018/4/30/17301282/race-evangelicals-trump-support-gerson-atlantic-sexism-segregation-south.

75. Dyson, *Tears We Cannot Stop*, p. 222.

76. "Jeff Sessions' Record on Civil Rights, Race Revisited after Trump's Attorney General Tap," *Fortune*, November 19, 2016, http://fortune.com/2016/11/19/jeff-sessions-race-civil-rights/.

77. Jay Willis, "Attorney General Sessions Is Using His Job to Purge America of People Who Don't Look like Him," *GQ*, April 12, 2017, https://www.gq.com/story/jeff-sessions-immigration-crackdown.

78. David Graham, "Why the Justice Department Is Targeting Affirmative Action," *Atlantic*, August 2, 2017, https://www.theatlantic.com/politics/archive/2017/08/the-justice-department-embraces-white-grievance/535683/.

79. Lawrence Hurley, Julia Ainsley, "Rights Groups Assail Justice Department over College Race Probe," Reuters, August 2, 2017, https://in.reuters.com/article/us-usa-justice-discrimination/rights-groups-assail-justice-department-over-college-race-probe-idUSKBN1AI2SE.

80. Camila Domonoske, "Trump Administration Rescinds Obama-Era Guidance Encouraging Affirmative Action," NPR, July 3, 2018, https://www.npr.org/2018/07/03/625750918/trump-administration-rescinds-obama-era-guidance-encouraging-affirmative-action.

81. Jeannie Suk Gersen, "At Trial, Harvard's Asian Problem and a Preference for White Students from 'Sparse Country,'" *New Yorker*, Oct. 23, 2018, https://www.newyorker.com/news/our-columnists/at-trial-harvards-asian-problem-and-a-preference-for-white-students-from-sparse-country.

82. Adam Shaw, "Sessions Ends Obama-Era Leniency on Sentencing, Infuriating Civil Rights Groups," Fox News, May 24, 2017, https://www.foxnews.com/politics/sessions-ends-obama-era-leniency-on-sentencing-infuriating-civil-rights-groups.

83. James Peterson, "Jeff Sessions Is Slowly but Surely Undoing America's Criminal Justice Progress," *Think* (blog), NBC News, November 23, 2017, https://www.nbcnews.com/think/opinion/jeff-sessions-slowly-surely-undoing-america-s-criminal-justice-progress-ncna823126.

84. Jasmine Tyler, "Trump Administration Threatens 'Sanctuary Cities,'" Human Rights Watch, February 2, 2018, https://www.hrw.org/news/2018/02/02/trump-administration-threatens-sanctuary-cities.

85. Charles Stewart, "Trump's Controversial Election Integrity Commission Is Gone. Here's What Comes Next," *Washington Post*, January 4, 2018, https://www.washingtonpost.com/news/monkey-cage/wp/2018/01/04/trumps-controversial-election-integrity-commission-is-gone-heres-what-comes-next/?utm_term=.6405aaa8de08.

86. Benjamin Wermund, "DeVos Rewrites Rules for School Civil Rights Probes," *Politico*, March 1, 2018, https://www.politico.com/story/2018/03/01/betsy-devos-school-civil-rights-rules-711790.

87. Moriah Balingit, "'Astounding Ignorance of the Law': Civil Rights Groups Slam DeVos for Saying Schools Can Report Undocumented Students," *Washington Post*, May 23, 2018, https://www.washingtonpost.com/news/education/wp/2018/05/23/astounding-ignorance-of-the-law-civil-rights-groups-slam-devos-for-saying-schools-can-report-undocumented-students/?utm_term=.daacf2c65b33.

88. Matthew Rozsa, "Jeff Sessions Is Reviving the War on Drugs, and It's Going to Hurt Minorities," *Salon*, April 10, 2017, https://www.salon.com/2017/04/10/jeff-sessions-is-reviving-the-war-on-drugs-and-its-going-to-hurt-minorities/.

89. Marybeth Gasman, "DeVos Needs History Lesson after HBCU School Choice Comment," *The Hill*, March 1, 2017, https://thehill.com/blogs/pundits-blog/education/321851-devos-needs-history-lesson-after-hbcu-school-choice-comment.

90. Emma Brown, "U.S. Commission on Civil Rights to Investigate Civil Rights Enforcement Under Trump," *Washington Post*, June 16, 2017, https://www.washingtonpost.com/news/education/wp/2017/06/16/u-s-commission-on-civil-rights-to-investigate-civil-rights-enforcement-under-trump/?utm_term=.511c27ef83c7.

91. Elise Boddie, "The Arc of the Moral Universe," *ACS Blog*, American Constitution Society, January 19, 2015, https://www.acslaw.org/?post_type=acsblog&p=10657.

CHAPTER 3

1. Matt Welch, "What John McCain Taught Us about Torture," *New York Times*, August 27, 2018, https://www.nytimes.com/2018/08/27/opinion/john-mccain-torture-.html.

2. Scott Shackford, "Sens. Rand Paul and Ron Wyden Unveil Long-Awaited, Privacy-Protecting Surveillance Reform Bill," *Reason*, October 24, 2017, https://reason.com/2017/10/24/sens-rand-paul-ron-wyden-unveil-long-awa.

3. Alan Rappeport, "Corker Says He Faced 'Tough' Decision in Supporting Republican Tax Bill," *New York Times*, December 18, 2017, https://www.nytimes.com/2017/12/18/us/politics/tax-bill-republicans.html.

4. Sarah Trumble and Lanae Erickson, "The Manchin-Toomey Background Check Compromise," Third Way, April 17, 2013, https://www.thirdway.org/one-pager/the-manchin-toomey-background-check-compromise.

5. Mark Memmott, "Son's Coming Out Leads Sen. Portman to Reverse on Same-Sex Marriage," NPR, March 15, 2013, https://www.npr.org/sections/thetwo-way/2013/03/15/174390242/sons-coming-out-leads-sen-portman-to-reverse-on-same-sex-marriage.

6. The "nuclear triad" refers to the military readiness of land-based, sea-based, and air-based nuclear missiles.

7. Senator Marco Rubio, responding to questioner Hugh Hewitt, Republican Party primary debate, December 15, 2015 [transcribed by the author].

8. David Lloyd Roberts, "Introduction to the Law of Armed Conflict: Basic Knowledge," Lesson 1 in *The Law of Armed Conflict*, International Committee of the Red Cross, June 2002, https://www.icrc.org/eng/assets/files/other/law1_final.pdf, pp. 12–13.

9. Oliver Noble, "24 Things Trump Does Better Than Anybody (according to Trump)," *Vice News*, February 22, 2017, https://news.vice.com/en_us/article/nedxnm/24-things-no body-does-better-than-trump-according-to-trump.

10. David Cay Johnston, *The Making of Donald Trump* (Brooklyn, NY: Melville House, 2016).

11. Steve Reilly, "Hundreds Allege Donald Trump Doesn't Pay His Bills," *USA Today*, June 9, 2016, updated April 25, 2018, https://www.usatoday.com/story/news/politics/elections/2016/06/09/donald-trump-unpaid-bills-republican-president-laswuits/85297274/.

12. Emily Flitter, "Trump's Art of the Deal—Dispute Your Bills," Reuters, November 13, 2015, https://www.reuters.com/article/us-usa-election-trump-bills-specialrepor-idUS KCN0T214Q20151113.

13. Jessica Stillman, "Meet the (Many) Small Business Owners Stiffed by Donald Trump," *Inc. Magazine*, September 26, 2016, https://www.inc.com/jessica-stillman/meet -the-many-small-business-owners-stiffed-by-donald-trump.html.

14. Roger Parloff, "Why U.S. Law Makes It Easy for Donald Trump to Stiff Contractors," *Fortune*, September 30, 2016, http://fortune.com/2016/09/30/donald-trump -stiff-contractors/.

15. Alexandra Berzon, "Donald Trump's Business Plan Left a Trail of Unpaid Bills," *Wall Street Journal*, June 9, 2016, https://www.wsj.com/articles/donald-trumps-business-plan -left-a-trail-of-unpaid-bills-1465504454.

16. David Barstow, Susanne Craig, and Russ Buettner, "Trump Engaged in Suspect Tax Schemes as He Reaped Riches from His Father," *New York Times*, October 2, 2018, https://www.nytimes.com/interactive/2018/10/02/us/politics/donald-trump-tax-schemes -fred-trump.html.

17. Mark Shields and David Brooks, in discussion with Judy Woodruff, "Shields and Brooks on North Korea Summit Takeaways," *PBS NewsHour*, June 15, 2018, video, 11:40, https://www.pbs.org/video/shields-and-brooks-1529097653/, at 3:20–3:42.

18. Amanda Taub, "The Rise of American Authoritarianism," *Vox*, March 1, 2016, https://www.vox.com/2016/3/1/11127424/trump-authoritarianism.

19. David Frum, "How to Build an Autocracy," *Atlantic*, March 2017, https://www .theatlantic.com/magazine/archive/2017/03/how-to-build-an-autocracy/513872/.

20. Michael Schmidt and Michael Shear, "Trump Says Russia Inquiry Makes U.S. 'Look Very Bad,'" *New York Times*, December 28, 2017, https://www.nytimes.com/2017/12/28/us/politics/trump-interview-mueller-russia-china-north-korea.html.

21. Sonam Sheth, "Trump Is Venturing into Uncharted Legal Territory as He Muses about Pardoning Himself," *Business Insider*, June 4, 2018, https://www.businessinsider.my/can-trump-pardon-himself-analysis-2018-6/.

22. Ken Gormley, "If Trump Pardons Himself, He's Admitting He's Guilty of Impeachable Crimes," *Washington Post*, June 8, 2018, https://www.washingtonpost.com/opinions/if-trump-pardons-himself-hes-admitting-hes-guilty-of-impeachable-crimes/2018/06/08/da96d98a-6a94-11e8-9e38-24e693b38637_story.html?utm_term= .e003e5017bb9.

23. Helen Dewar, "President Isn't Above the Law, Nixon Insists," *Washington Post*, June 5, 1977, https://www.washingtonpost.com/archive/politics/1977/06/05/president-isnt -above-the-law-nixon-insists/71923838-492f-49d7-921f-0add6743501e/?utm_term=. 9a146b01439b.

24. "Trump to U.N.: 'Honor Our Sovereignty,'" *New York Sun*, September 25, 2018, https://www.nysun.com/foreign/trump-at-the-un-honor-our-sovereignty/90398/.

25. Adil Najam, "Is America a 'Sovereign' Nation? A Look at Trump's New Favorite Word," *The Hill*, September 23, 2017, https://thehill.com/opinion/white-house/352028-is-america-a-sovereign-nation-a-look-at-trumps-new-favorite-word.

26. Spencer Ackerman, "No Laughing Matter: U.N. Speech Shows Trump Thinks He's the Boss of Everyone," *Daily Beast*, September 25, 2018, https://www.thedailybeast.com/at-the-un-trump-treats-global-cooperation-as-a-threat.

27. Stewart Patrick, "Narcissistic Nationalism: Trump's Second UN General Assembly Address," *Council on Foreign Relations* (blog), September 25, 2018, https://www.cfr.org/blog/narcissistic-nationalism-trumps-second-un-general-assembly-address.

28. Matt Kwong, "Trump's 'Sovereignty' Pitch at UN Could Be Good News for Autocrats," CBC/Radio Canada, September 19, 2017, https://www.cbc.ca/news/world/trump-united-nations-general-assembly-north-korea-1.4297589.

29. Steve Berman, "Mueller? Trump Is Just Getting Started, from a Certain Perspective," Resurgent, March 19, 2018, https://theresurgent.com/2018/03/19/mueller-trump-is-just-getting-started-from-a-certain-perspective/.

30. Tom McCarthy, "Trump Decries 'Attack on Our Country' after FBI Raids His Lawyer's Office," *Guardian*, April 10, 2018, https://www.theguardian.com/us-news/2018/apr/09/michael-cohen-raid-trump-lawyer-fbi-mueller-documents.

31. Zachary Fryer-Biggs, "Trump's Attacks on Mueller's Investigation Are Getting Way More Personal," *Vox*, April 11, 2018, https://www.vox.com/2018/4/11/17224268/trump-mueller-attacks-tweets-rosenstein-crazy.

32. Charlie Savage and Eric Lichtblau, "Trump Directs Justice Department to Investigate 'Criminal Leaks,'" *New York Times*, February 16, 2017, https://www.nytimes.com/2017/02/16/us/politics/justice-department-leak-investigation-trump.html.

33. Natasha Bertrand, "Trump Wants Sessions to Investigate 'Anonymous.' But There Was No Crime," *Atlantic*, September 7, 2018, https://www.theatlantic.com/politics/archive/2018/09/trump-sessions-investigate-anonymous-official-times-op-ed/569671/.

34. Brett Samuels, "Trump Blasts Sessions over Criminal Charges against GOP Lawmakers," *The Hill*, September 3, 2018, https://thehill.com/homenews/administration/404837-trump-blasts-sessions-over-investigations-into-gop-lawmakers.

35. Jonathan Chait, "Donald Trump: L'état, C'est Moi," *Intelligencer* (blog), *New York Magazine*, July 20, 2017, http://nymag.com/intelligencer/2017/07/donald-trump-ltat-cest-moi.html.

36. Stephan Lesher, "Stephan Lesher: L'état, C'est Moi," The Hour, May 3, 2018, https://www.thehour.com/opinion/article/Stephan-Lesher-L-etat-c-est-moi-12885609.php.

37. Roger Cohen, "L'état, C'est Trump!" *New York Times*, May 19, 2017, https://www.nytimes.com/2017/05/19/opinion/donald-trump-investigation-roger-cohen.html.

38. Robert Costa, Amy Goldstein, "Trump Vows 'Insurance for Everybody' in Obamacare Replacement Plan," *Washington Post*, January 15, 2017, https://www.washingtonpost.com/politics/trump-vows-insurance-for-everybody-in-obamacare-replacement-plan/2017/01/15/5f2b1e18-db5d-11e6-ad42-f3375f271c9c_story.html?utm_term=.b50b78365a85.

39. Henry Jackson, "6 Promises Trump Has Made about Health Care," *Politico*, March 13, 2017, https://www.politico.com/story/2017/03/trump-obamacare-promises-236021.

40. Caroline Kenny, "Trump Confirms He Called Health Care Bill 'Mean,'" CNN, June 26, 2017, https://www.cnn.com/2017/06/25/politics/donald-trump-confirms-mean -health-care/index.html.

41. Trade, globalization, and the tariffs are further discussed in chapter 7.

42. Exec. Order No. 13769, "Protecting the Nation from Foreign Terrorist Entry into the United States," 82 Fed. Reg. 8977 (January 27, 2017), https://www.federalregister.gov/ documents/2017/02/01/2017-02281/protecting-the-nation-from-foreign-terrorist-entry -into-the-united-states.

43. "Timeline of the Muslim Ban," American Civil Liberties Union of Washington, https://www.aclu-wa.org/pages/timeline-muslim-ban.

44. Alex Altman, Joseph Hincks, and Tara John, "Donald Trump's Many, Many Business Dealings in 1 Map," *Time*, January 10, 2017, http://time.com/4629308/donald -trump-business-deals-world-map/.

45. Dan Mangan, "Trump Brags about Not Paying Taxes: 'That Makes Me Smart,'" CNBC, September 26, 2016, https://www.cnbc.com/2016/09/26/trump-brags-about-not -paying-taxes-that-makes-me-smart.html.

46. Jean Murray, "Pass-Through Taxes and Business Owners," The Balance: Small Business, https://www.thebalancesmb.com/pass-through-taxes-and-business-owners-398390.

47. Sahil Kapur, Jennifer Jacobs, and Saleha Mohsin, "How the Carried Interest Break Survived the Tax Bill," *Bloomberg*, December 22, 2017, https://www.bloomberg.com/news/ articles/2017-12-22/cohn-mnuchin-split-helped-break-trump-s-carried-interest-pledge.

48. Jesse Byrnes, "Trump on Lack of Nominees: 'I Am the Only One That Matters,'" *The Hill*, November 2, 2017, https://thehill.com/blogs/blog-briefing-room/news/358573 -trump-on-lack-of-nominees-i-am-the-only-one-that-matters.

49. Steven Cook, "Jamal Khashoggi's Disappearance Is Even Stranger Than It Seems," *Foreign Policy*, October 9, 2018, https://foreignpolicy.com/2018/10/09/jamal-khashoggis -disappearance-is-even-stranger-than-it-seems/.

50. "Saudi Arabia's Mohammed bin Salman: 'I Love Working with Trump,'" Al Jazeera News, October 5, 2018, https://www.aljazeera.com/news/2018/10/saudi-crown -prince-loves-working-trump-181005193430836.html.

51. Raf Sanchez, "Turkey 'Has Recordings of Jamal Khashoggi's Torture and Murder in Saudi Consulate,'" *Telegraph*, October 12, 2018, https://www.telegraph.co.uk/ news/2018/10/12/turkey-has-recordings-jamal-khashoggis-torture-murder-saudi/.

52. Elliot Hannon, "CIA Concludes Saudi Crown Prince Mohammed Bin Salman Ordered Khashoggi Murder in Istanbul Consulate," *Slate*, November 17, 2018, https://slate. com/news-and-politics/2018/11/cia-saudi-crown-prince-mohammed-bin-salman-ordered -khashoggi-murder-istanbul-turkey-consulate.html.

53. James McAuley, "The Broken Bromance? The Trump-Macron Relationship Is on the Rocks," *Washington Post*, November 10, 2018, https://www.washingtonpost.com/world/ 2018/11/10/broken-bromance-trump-macron-relationship-is-rocks/?utm_term= .59706de2d602.

54. Laura Carlsen, "Trump and Mexico's Next President Are on Honeymoon. But It Won't Last," *Fortune*, August 1, 2018, http://fortune.com/2018/08/01/amlo-mexico-trump -elections-2018/.

55. Rebecca Kheel, "Trump Extends Indefinite Syria Strategy: Report," *The Hill*, September 7, 2018, https://thehill.com/policy/defense/405532-trump-extends-indefinite -syria-strategy-report.

56. Jeremy Diamond and Elise Labott, "Trump Told Turkey's Erdogan in Dec. 14 Call about Syria, 'It's All Yours. We Are Done,'" CNN, December 24, 2018, https://www.cnn .com/2018/12/23/politics/donald-trump-erdogan-turkey/index.html.

57. Mark Landler and Helene Cooper, "In Latest Shift, Trump Agrees to Leave 400 Troops in Syria," *New York Times*, February 22, 2019, https://www.nytimes.com/2019/02/ 22/world/middleeast/trump-troops-syria-.html.

58. John Haltiwanger, "Trump Claims to Have a 'Very, Very Good Relationship' with Merkel after He Insulted Germany to Its Face and Said Russia Controlled It," *Business Insider*, July 11, 2018, https://www.businessinsider.my/trump-insults-germany-then-says-he-has -good-relationship-with-merkel-2018-7/.

59. Alex Ward, "Trump Just Committed to NATO's Article 5. Finally," *Vox*, June 9, 2018, https://www.vox.com/world/2017/6/9/15772292/trump-article-5-nato-commit.

60. Terrance Mintner, "Is Trump's Plan Promoting Peace or Alienating Palestinians?" *Jerusalem Post*, September 20, 2018, https://www.jpost.com/Arab-Israeli-Conflict/Is-Trumps -plan-promoting-peace-or-alienating-Palestinians-567569.

61. Heather Stewart and David Smith, "Donald Trump Cancels London Visit Amid Protest Fears," *Guardian*, January 12, 2018, https://www.theguardian.com/us-news/2018/ jan/12/donald-trump-visit-to-london-called-off-amid-fears-of-mass-protests.

62. Jonathan Lemire and Matthew Pennington, "In Big Shift, Trump Assesses Kim Jong Un as 'Very Honorable,'" AP News, April 24, 2018, https://www.apnews.com/20384f0 6fd0c4c468349b43f7a55d896.

63. Roberta Rampton, "'We Fell in Love:' Trump Swoons over Letters from North Korea's Kim," Reuters, September 30, 2018, https://www.reuters.com/article/us-north korea-usa-trump/we-fell-in-love-trump-swoons-over-letters-from-north-koreas-kim-idUS KCN1MA03Q.

64. Shields and Brooks, "North Korea Summit Takeaways," at 1:20–1:23.

65. Adam Davidson, "A Theory of Trump Kompromat," *New Yorker*, July 19, 2018, https://www.newyorker.com/news/swamp-chronicles/a-theory-of-trump-kompromat.

66. S. A. Miller and Dave Boyer, "Trump Sides with Putin over U.S. Intel," *Washington Times*, July 16, 2018, https://www.washingtontimes.com/news/2018/jul/16/donald-trump -sides-vladimir-putin-over-us-intellig/.

67. Charles Sykes, "A New Servility: Donald Trump's Atrocious Performance in Helsinki Shows That Nothing Positive He Might Do Is Worth the Downside," *Weekly Standard*, July 16, 2018, https://www.weeklystandard.com/charles-j-sykes/trump-helsinki -summit-his-servility-to-vladimir-putin-is-unbecoming-of-a-president.

68. Jennifer Jett, "Right and Left React to Trump-Putin Meeting," *New York Times*, July 17, 2018, https://www.nytimes.com/2018/07/17/us/politics/trump-putin-meeting-reac tions.html.

69. Matt Viser, "At Helsinki Summit, Trump Leaps to Putin's Defense," *Boston Globe*, July 16, 2018, https://www.bostonglobe.com/news/politics/2018/07/16/ republicans-call-trump-helsinki-performance-shameful-and-putin-calls-meeting-success/ G9uRwJSaYCuIW0Z4CVKdUK/story.html.

70. Jen Kirby, "GOP Lawmakers React to Trump-Putin Summit: Lots of Condemnation, Few Concrete Plans," *Vox*, July 16, 2018, https://www.vox.com/2018/ 7/16/17577244/trump-putin-summit-mccain-paul-ryan-republican-lawmakers-react.

71. David Herszenhorn, "Putin Preens While Trump Settles Old Scores," *Politico*, July 16, 2018, https://www.politico.com/story/2018/07/17/putin-trump-agenda-summit-725964.

72. Julia Ioffe, "Now We All Know What Putin Has on Trump," *GQ*, July 17, 2018, https://www.gq.com/story/what-putin-has-on-trump.

73. Aaron Blake, "The Growing Trump-Putin Kompromat Question," *Washington Post*, July 17, 2018, https://www.washingtonpost.com/news/the-fix/wp/2018/07/17/does-putin-have-kompromat-on-trump-suddenly-its-no-longer-such-a-taboo-question-thanks-to-trump/?utm_term=.197607b25720.

74. Jeremy Bash, interview by Hallie Jackson, *MSNBC Live with Hallie Jackson*, MSNBC, July 20, 2018 [transcription by the author].

75. Tara Golshan, "Trump's Bizarre and Confusing DACA Meeting with Congress, Explained," *Vox*, January 9, 2018, https://www.vox.com/2018/1/9/16870060/trumps-immigration-meeting-congress-daca-explained.

76. Jim Newell, "Conservatives Persuade Trump to Trash Spending Deal, Making Government Shutdown More Likely," *Slate*, December 20, 2018, https://slate.com/news-and-politics/2018/12/government-shutdown-trump-veto-spending-bill-wall-funding-border-security.html.

77. Burgess Everett, "McConnell, Ryan Pitch Trump on Plan to Avoid Shutdown: The President Seemed Receptive to Delaying a Fight over Border Wall Funding until after the Election," *Politico*, July 25, 2018, https://www.politico.com/story/2018/07/25/mcconnell-ryan-trump-shutdown-741266.

78. Igor Bobic, "Trump Again Threatens to Shut Down His Own Government over Wall Funding," *Huffington Post*, July 29, 2018, https://www.huffingtonpost.ca/entry/trump-shut-down-government-wall_n_5b5dbf11e4b0b15aba999a7e.

79. Michael Shear, "Trump Stuns Lawmakers with Seeming Embrace of Comprehensive Gun Control," *New York Times*, February 28, 2018, https://www.nytimes.com/2018/02/28/us/politics/trump-gun-control.html.

80. Emily Stewart, "Trump's New Position on Gun Control Is Starting to Look a Lot like the NRA's," *Vox*, March 12, 2018, https://www.vox.com/policy-and-politics/2018/3/12/17109798/trump-gun-control-proposal-betsy-devos-parkland-nra.

81. Thomas Kaplan and Sheryl Gay Stolberg, "Will He or Won't He? Conflicting Trump Messages Sow Immigration Confusion," *New York Times*, June 15, 2018, https://www.nytimes.com/2018/06/15/us/politics/trump-immigration-compromise.html.

82. Mallory Shelbourne, "Trump Tells Republicans to 'Stop Wasting Their Time' on Immigration," *The Hill*, June 22, 2018, https://thehill.com/homenews/administration/393595-trump-tells-republicans-to-stop-wasting-their-time-on-immigration.

83. Benjamin Siegel and John Parkinson, "House Rejects Republican Compromise Immigration Bill," ABC News, June 27, 2018, https://abcnews.go.com/Politics/house-rejects-republican-compromise-immigration-bill/story?id=56200199.

84. Brent Griffiths, "Trump Falsely Claims He Never Told House Republicans to Vote for Immigration Bill," *Politico*, June 30, 2018, https://www.politico.com/story/2018/06/30/donald-trump-immigration-vote-tweets-689501.

85. Mary Bottari, "ALEC Embraces Trumpism," The Center for Media and Democracy's PR Watch, February 14, 2017, https://www.prwatch.org/news/2017/02/13213/alec-embraces-trumpism.

86. Katha Pollitt, "Why Evangelicals—Still!—Support Trump," *Nation*, March 22, 2018, https://www.thenation.com/article/why-evangelicals-still-support-trump/.

87. David Dayen, "Trump's Judicial Picks Are Keeping Republicans Happy—And Quiet," *New Republic*, June 9, 2017, https://newrepublic.com/article/143227/trumps -judicial-picks-keeping-republicans-happyand-quiet.

88. Sarah Pulliam Bailey, "Dozens of Evangelical Leaders Meet to Discuss How Trump Era Has Unleashed 'Grotesque Caricature' of Their Faith," *Washington Post*, April 16, 2018, https://www.washingtonpost.com/news/acts-of-faith/wp/2018/04/12/when-you -google-evangelicals-you-get-trump-high-profile-evangelicals-will-meet-privately-to-discuss -their-future/?utm_term=.7e5e23625511.

89. Jonathan Chait, "Trump Says in Interview He Is the Sole Arbiter of Truth," *Intelligencer* (blog), *New York Magazine*, November 19, 2018, http://nymag.com/intelligencer/ 2018/11/trump-chris-wallace-interview-enemy-of-the-people-fake-news.html.

90. Makiko Yamazaki and Steve Holland, "Japan's PM Nominated Trump for Nobel Peace Prize on U.S. Request: Asahi," Reuters, February 16, 2019, https://www.reuters.com/ article/us-northkorea-usa-trump-japan/japans-pm-nominated-trump-for-nobel-peace-prize -on-us-request-asahi-idUSKCN1Q6041.

91. David Morris, "Donald Trump Fought the NFL Once Before. He Got Crushed," *Fortune*, September 24, 2017, http://fortune.com/2017/09/24/donald-trump-nfl-usfl/.

92. William Cohan, "Donald Trump Is Irrelevant to Corporate America," *New Yorker*, September 9, 2017, https://www.newyorker.com/news/news-desk/donald-trump-is-irrele vant-to-corporate-america.

93. Daniel Hemel, "What Americans Should Learn from the Trump Tax Story— and One Way to Help Stop Further Trickery," *Time*, October 5, 2018, http://time.com/ 5416649/trump-tax-lessons/.

94. Tom McCarthy, "Why Is Donald Trump Attacking the US Intelligence Community?" *Guardian*, August 19, 2018, https://www.theguardian.com/us-news/ 2018/aug/18/why-is-donald-trump-attacking-the-us-intelligence-community.

95. Nash Riggins, "Donald Trump Might Hate the Establishment—But That's What's Saving His Presidency," *Independent*, September 6, 2018, https://www.independent.co.uk/ voices/trump-white-house-us-president-bob-woodward-new-york-times-gary-cohn-a8525401 .html.

96. Charles Pierce, "The Only Thing Trump Knows Is That He Hates Obama," *Esquire*, August 2, 2018, https://www.esquire.com/news-politics/politics/a22627175/trump -administration-emissions-rules-rollback-obamacare/.

97. Jeff Goodell, "Scott Pruitt's Crimes against Nature: Trump's EPA Chief Is Gutting the Agency, Defunding Science, and Serving the Fossil-Fuel Industry," *Rolling Stone*, July 27, 2017, https://www.rollingstone.com/politics/politics-features/scott-pruitts-crimes-against -nature-195720/.

98. Katie Benner, "Trump's Justice Department Redefines Whose Civil Rights to Protect," *New York Times*, September 3, 2018, https://www.nytimes.com/2018/09/03/us/ politics/civil-rights-justice-department.html.

99. Emily Weitz, "After Decades of Civil Rights Advances, Trump's DOJ Sets the US Backwards," *Vice Impact*, January 12, 2018, https://impact.vice.com/en_us/article/ev5q8j/ after-decades-of-civil-rights-advances-trumps-doj-sets-the-us-backwards.

100. Jack Moore, "The Trump Administration Plans to Sue Colleges for Affirmative Action Policies That 'Discriminate' against White People," *GQ Online*, August 2, 2017, https://www.gq.com/story/trump-college-admissions.

101. Elliot Mincberg, "Report Card on One Year of Jeff Sessions as Attorney General: 'An Insult to Justice,'" People For the American Way, February 2018, http://www.pfaw.org/report/report-card-on-one-year-of-jeff-sessions-as-attorney-general-an-insult-to-justice/.

102. Masood Farivar, "How US Attorney General Jeff Sessions Has Rolled Back Obama-Era Policies," *VOA News*, December 30, 2017, https://www.voanews.com/a/us-attorney-general-jeff-sessions-roll-back-obama-policies/4185452.html.

103. Lydia Wheeler, "Federal Judge Rules against Sessions's Effort to Hit Sanctuary Cities," *The Hill*, October 5, 2018, https://thehill.com/regulation/court-battles/410149-california-judge-rules-against-sessionss-effort-to-hit-sanctuary.

104. Erik Larson et al., "Gay Workers Get Win over Trump with U.S. Anti-Bias Ruling," *Bloomberg*, February 26, 2018, https://www.bloomberg.com/news/articles/2018-02-26/sexual-orientation-bias-violates-u-s-law-appeals-court-says.

105. Mark Stern, "Supreme Court, in 5–4 Decision, Allows States to Purge Voters for Their Failure to Vote," *Slate*, June 11, 2018, https://slate.com/news-and-politics/2018/06/supreme-court-greenlights-ohio-voter-purges-in-husted-v-randolph.html.

106. Leon Neyfakh, "The Shadow Civil Rights Division," *Slate*, August 3, 2017, https://slate.com/news-and-politics/2017/08/the-department-of-justice-is-building-a-shadow-civil-rights-division.html.

107. Alex Swoyer, "Trump Sets Record, Appoints the Most Federal Appeals Judges in First Two Years," *Washington Times*, October 16, 2018, https://www.washingtontimes.com/news/2018/oct/16/donald-trump-appoints-conservative-judges-federal-/.

108. Katherine Foley, "It's Very Weird That Trump Is Recruiting for His Appointees on Job Boards," Quartz, November 7, 2018, https://qz.com/1454056/trump-is-recruiting-presidential-appointees-on-job-boards/.

109. Sonam Sheth, "The Russia Controversy May Be Scaring Political Appointees from Joining the Trump Administration," *Business Insider*, May 31, 2017, https://www.businessinsider.com/trump-russia-controversy-prevents-appointees-from-joining-administration-2017-5.

110. Michelle Cheng, "Trump Still Hasn't Filled Top Jobs, and He Has (Mostly) Himself to Blame," FiveThirtyEight, July 3, 2017, https://fivethirtyeight.com/features/trump-still-hasnt-filled-top-jobs-and-he-has-mostly-himself-to-blame/.

111. James Prince, interview with the author, April 25, 2018.

112. Altman, Hincks, and John, "Donald Trump's Many, Many Business Dealings."

113. Ben Rhodes, interview in *The Final Year*, directed by Greg Barker (New York: HBO, 2017).

114. Ali Vitali, "Is Trump (Finally) Ready for a 'Pivot' to Presidential?" NBC News, August 1, 2017, https://www.nbcnews.com/politics/white-house/shake-smoke-clears-finally-trump-s-chance-pivot-n788501.

115. Ramesh Ponnuru, "Parsing Trump's Pivot," *National Review*, September 8, 2017, https://www.nationalreview.com/2017/09/trump-pivot-debt-limit-daca-choosing-democrats-moving-left/.

116. Ezra Klein, "There Is No Trump Pivot, and There Never Will Be," *Vox*, September 22, 2017, https://www.vox.com/policy-and-politics/2017/9/22/16346904/there-is-no-trump-pivot-there-never-will-be.

117. David Frum, interview by Fareed Zakaria, *Fareed Zakaria GPS*, CNN, January 21, 2018 [transcription by the author].

118. Roger Cohen, "L'État, C'est Trump!" *New York Times*, May 19, 2017, https://www.nytimes.com/2017/05/19/opinion/donald-trump-investigation-roger-cohen.html.

119. Kathleen Hunter, "Trump's Patriotism Questioned after Helsinki," *Bloomberg*, July 17, 2018, https://www.bloomberg.com/news/articles/2018-07-17/trump-s-patriotism-questioned-after-helsinki.

120. Wolf Blitzer, *The Situation Room*, CNN, March 13, 2018.

121. Evan Osnos, "Trump vs. the 'Deep State': How the Administration's Loyalists Are Quietly Reshaping American Governance," *New Yorker*, May 14, 2018, https://www.newyorker.com/magazine/2018/05/21/trump-vs-the-deep-state.

122. Michael Crowley and Bryan Bender, "Bolton Pick Underscores Trump's Foreign Policy Confusion," *Politico*, March 22, 2018, https://www.politico.com/story/2018/03/22/bolton-trump-foreign-policy-confusion-482168.

123. Jules Witcover, "Just When You Thought Trump's Foreign Policy Couldn't Get More Chaotic, Enter John Bolton," *Baltimore Sun*, March 26, 2018, https://www.baltimoresun.com/news/opinion/oped/bs-ed-op-0327-witcover-trump-bolton-20180326-story.html.

124. James Hohmann, "Trump Has No Nominees for 245 Important Jobs, Including Ambassador to South Korea," *Washington Post*, January 12, 2018, https://www.washingtonpost.com/news/powerpost/paloma/daily-202/2018/01/12/daily-202-trump-has-no-nominees-for-245-important-jobs-including-an-ambassador-to-south-korea/5a57cce830fb0469e8840085/?utm_term=.72ef8662391d.

125. Ashley Parker, Philip Rucker, and Josh Dawsey, "Trump's Loyalty Tests Cause Hiring Headaches," *Chicago Tribune*, April 29, 2018, https://www.chicagotribune.com/news/nationworld/politics/ct-trump-loyalty-tests-20180429-story.html.

126. Lisa Rein and Abby Phillip, "Help Wanted: Why Republicans Won't Work for the Trump Administration," *Washington Post*, June 17, 2017, https://www.washingtonpost.com/politics/help-wanted-why-republicans-wont-work-for-the-trump-administration/2017/06/17/61e3d33e-506a-11e7-b064-828ba60fbb98_story.html?utm_term=.bba157e9ab2d.

127. Jonathan Karl and Jordyn Phelps, "Trump's Empty Administration: What's behind the High Number of Vacant Government Jobs," ABC News, June 16, 2017, https://abcnews.go.com/Politics/trumps-empty-administration-whats-high-number-vacant-government/story?id=47851403.

128. Tal Kopan, "Trump's Cabinet Woes Could Cripple Administration, Ex-WH Staffers Say," CNN, July 28, 2017, https://www.cnn.com/2017/07/27/politics/trump-cabinet-ripple-effects/index.html.

129. Sarah Westwood and Pamela Brown, "White House Struggles to Replace Departing Staff," CNN, June 15, 2018, https://www.cnn.com/2018/06/15/politics/white-house-staffing-marc-short/index.html.

130. Abigail Tracy, "Will Anyone in Washington Still Work For Donald Trump? With Staffers Facing the Prospect of Subpoenas and Legal Bills, the White House Is Struggling to Attract Much-Needed Talent," *Vanity Fair*, May 31, 2017, https://www.vanityfair.com/news/2017/05/donald-trump-white-house-staffing.

131. Ruth Marcus, interview by Chuck Todd, *MTP Daily*, MSNBC, January 31, 2018 [transcription by the author].

132. Jacqui Fatka, "Argentina Now Open to U.S. Pork Imports," Feedstuffs, April 13, 2018, https://www.feedstuffs.com/news/argentina-now-open-us-pork-imports.

133. Mike Pomranz, "Colombian Avocados Approved for U.S. Import," *Food & Wine*, August 14, 2017, https://www.foodandwine.com/news/us-import-colombian-avocados.

134. Ezra Klein, "This Is What Makes Republicans and Democrats So Different," *Vox*, January 13, 2016, https://www.vox.com/2016/1/13/10759874/republicans-democrats-different.

CHAPTER 4

1. Scott Detrow, "Clinton Campaign Had Additional Signed Agreement with DNC in 2015," NPR, November 3, 2017, https://www.npr.org/2017/11/03/561976645/clinton-campaign-had-additional-signed-agreement-with-dnc-in-2015.

2. Eddie Scarry, "Donna Brazile Finally Admits She Shared Debate Questions with Clinton Campaign," *Washington Examiner*, March 17, 2017, https://www.washingtonexaminer.com/donna-brazile-finally-admits-she-shared-debate-questions-with-clinton-campaign.

3. Danielle Kurtzleben, "Here's How Many Bernie Sanders Supporters Ultimately Voted for Trump," NPR, August 24, 2017, https://www.npr.org/2017/08/24/545812242/1-in-10-sanders-primary-voters-ended-up-supporting-trump-survey-finds.

4. Shawn Griffiths, "Sanders Supporters Get Their Day in Court against Wasserman Schultz," Independent Voter Network, April 24, 2017, https://ivn.us/2017/04/24/sanders-supporters-get-day-court-dnc/.

5. Ida A. Brudnick and Jennifer E. Manning, *African American Members of the United States Congress: 1870–2018*, Congressional Research Service, report RL30378, updated April 26, 2018, https://fas.org/sgp/crs/misc/RL30378.pdf.

6. "Membership," Congressional Black Caucus, https://cbc.house.gov/membership/.

7. Jennifer E. Manning, *Membership of the 115th Congress: A Profile*, Congressional Research Service, report R44762, February 17, 2017, https://digitalcommons.ilr.cornell.edu/key_workplace/1911/.

8. Herbert White, "Congressional Black Caucus Grows in Size and Clout after Blue Wave," *Charlotte Post*, December 5, 2018, http://www.thecharlottepost.com/news/2018/12/05/national/congressional-black-caucus-grows-in-size-and-clout-after-blue-wave/.

9. "The Congressional Hispanic Caucus and Conference," United States House of Representatives website, http://history.house.gov/Exhibitions-and-Publications/HAIC/Historical-Essays/Strength-Numbers/Caucus-Conference/.

10. "Members," Congressional Hispanic Caucus, https://congressionalhispaniccaucus-lujangrisham.house.gov/members.

11. "Members," Congressional Hispanic Conference, https://hispanicconference-mariodiazbalart.house.gov/membership.

12. Camilo Montoya-Galvez, "Diverse Freshman Class Will Bolster Record Number of Latinos in Congress," CBS News, November 27, 2018, https://www.cbsnews.com/news/diverse-freshman-class-will-bolster-record-number-of-latinos-in-congress/.

13. "115th Congress Membership," Congressional Asian Pacific American Caucus, https://capac-chu.house.gov/members.

14. "CAPAC Applauds Historic Asian Pacific American Representation in the 116th Congress," Congressional Asian Pacific American Caucus, November 29, 2018, https://capac-chu.house.gov/press-release/capac-applauds-historic-asian-pacific-american-representation-116th-congress.

15. "Caucus History," Women's Congressional Policy Institute, www.womenspolicy.org/our-work/the-womens-caucus/caucus-history/.

16. "Congressional Caucus for Women's Issues," Women's Congressional Policy Institute, www.womenspolicy.org/our-work/the-womens-caucus/.

17. Drew DeSilver, "A Record Number of Women Will Be Serving in the New Congress," Fact Tank, Pew Research Center, December 18, 2018, https://www.pew research.org/fact-tank/2018/12/18/record-number-women-in-congress/.

18. Lizzy Spangler, "8 Political Organizations That Help Women Run for Office," StudyBreaks, November 21, 2017, https://studybreaks.com/news-politics/women-political -organizations-run-office/.

19. Danielle Kurtzleben, "More Than Twice as Many Women Are Running for Congress in 2018 Compared with 2016," NPR, February 20, 2018, https://www.npr.org/2018/02/20/585542531/more-than-twice-as-many-women-are-running-for-congress-in -2018-compared-to-2016.

20. Emma Symons, "Surge of Women Clamoring to Run for Office in Wake of 2016 Election Outcome," Women in the World, May 5, 2017, https://womenintheworld.com/2017/05/05/surge-of-women-clamoring-to-run-for-public-office-in-wake-of-2016-election -outcome/.

21. Joanna Walters, "This Group Trains Women to Run for Office. Here's How One Outraged Post-Trump Class Fared," *Washington Post*, February 13, 2018, https://www.wash ingtonpost.com/lifestyle/magazine/this-group-trains-women-to-run-for-office-heres -how-one-outraged-post-trump-class-fared/2018/02/12/d9de3d02-020d-11e8-bb03 -722769454f82_story.html?utm_term=.6408b46346c6.

22. Emily Stewart, "Grassley Explains All-Male, All-White Senate Republican Judiciary Panel: Women Don't Want to Do the Work," *Vox*, October 6, 2018, https://www.vox.com/policy-and-politics/2018/10/6/17945182/grassley-republican-women-senators-judiciary -committee.

23. Katherine Tully-McManus, "Lawmakers Reach Deal to Tackle Sexual Harassment on Capitol Hill," *Roll Call*, December 12, 2018, https://www.rollcall.com/news/politics/lawmakers-reach-deal-tackle-sexual-harassment-capitol-hill.

24. Katherine Tully-McManus, "Jackie Speier and Bradley Byrne Aim to End Taxpayer Settlements for Discrimination," *Roll Call*, December 14, 2018, https://www .rollcall.com/news/politics/jackie-speier-bradley-byrne-aim-end-taxpayer-settlements -discrimination.

25. "'Cracking and Packing': Tame the Gerrymander," *Baltimore Sun*, October 3, 2017, https://www.baltimoresun.com/news/opinion/editorial/bs-ed-1004-wisconsin-gerrmander -20171003-story.html.

26. Exec. Order No. 11365, "Establishing a National Commission on Civil Disorders," 32 Fed. Reg. 11111 (July 29, 1967), https://connecting4communities.files.wordpress. com/2013/10/executive-order-11365.pdf.

27. "Report" (NCJ 08073), National Advisory Commission on Civil Disorders (Washington, DC: Government Printing Office, 1968), https://www.ncjrs.gov/pdffiles1/Digitization/8073NCJRS.pdf.

28. Civil Rights Digital Library, "Poor People's Campaign," http://crdl.usg.edu/events/poor_peoples_campaign/?Welcome.

29. H. L. Mencken, "Bayard vs. Lionheart," *Evening Sun* (Baltimore), July 26, 1920, https://www.newspapers.com/clip/21831908/hl_mencken_article_26_jul_1920_the/.

30. Dahlia Lithwick, "Husted v. (A.) Philip Randolph Institute: Ohio's Legal Justification for Its Massive Voter Purge Is Complete Gobbledygook," *Slate*, January 10, 2018, https://slate.com/news-and-politics/2018/01/ohios-legal-justification-for-its-massive-voter-purge-is-complete-gobbledygook.html.

31. Max de Haldevang, "The US Supreme Court Just Made It Easier for States to Prevent Citizens from Voting," Quartz, June 11, 2018, https://qz.com/1302254/the-us-supreme-court-decision-in-the-ohio-voting-case-made-it-easier-for-states-prevent-citizens-from-casting-a-ballot/.

32. Matt Lewis, "Donald Trump Is Turning Young Voters Off the GOP—and Maybe Forever," *Daily Beast*, June 13, 2017, https://www.thedailybeast.com/donald-trump-is-turning-young-voters-off-the-gopand-maybe-forever.

33. Nick McGillivray, "What Are the Effects of Social Media on Youth?" Turbo Future, October 12, 2015, https://turbofuture.com/internet/effects-of-social-media-on-our-youth.

34. Suren Ramasubbu, "Influence of Social Media on Teenagers," *Huffington Post*, September 6, 2017, https://www.huffpost.com/entry/influence-of-social-media-on-teenagers_n_7427740.

35. Jeffrey Gottfried and Elisa Shearer, "News Use across Social Media Platforms 2016," Journalism and Media, Pew Research Center, May 26, 2016, https://www.journalism.org/2016/05/26/news-use-across-social-media-platforms-2016/.

36. John Wihbey, "How Does Social Media Use Influence Political Participation and Civic Engagement? A Meta-Analysis," Journalist's Resource, October 18, 2015, https://journalistsresource.org/studies/politics/digital-democracy/social-media-influence-politics-participation-engagement-meta-analysis/.

37. Joseph Kahne and Benjamin Bowyer, "The Political Significance of Social Media Activity and Social Networks," *Political Communication* 35, no. 3 (February 2018): 470–93, https://www.tandfonline.com/doi/full/10.1080/10584609.2018.1426662.

38. Monica Anderson, "Social Media Causes Some Users to Rethink Their Views on an Issue," Fact Tank, Pew Research Center, November 7, 2016, https://www.pewresearch.org/fact-tank/2016/11/07/social-media-causes-some-users-to-rethink-their-views-on-an-issue/.

CHAPTER 5

1. Sam Meredith, "Facebook-Cambridge Analytica: A Timeline of the Data Hijacking Scandal," CNBC, April 10, 2018, https://www.cnbc.com/2018/04/10/facebook-cambridge-analytica-a-timeline-of-the-data-hijacking-scandal.html.

2. Green Seal, https://www.greenseal.org/about/. "Green Seal® is the nation's premier ecolabel, symbolizing transparency, integrity and proven environmental leadership. We develop life-cycle-based, multi-attribute standards and certify products and services that can prove they meet our strict criteria for human health, reduced environmental impact and excellent performance. Operating as a nonprofit since its founding in 1989, Green Seal has certified thousands of products and services in over 450 categories, and is specified by countless schools, government agencies, businesses and institutions."

3. Jeffrey Jones and Zacc Ritter, "Americans See More News Bias; Most Can't Name Neutral Source," Gallup, January 17, 2018, https://news.gallup.com/poll/225755/americans-news-bias-name-neutral-source.aspx; Knight Foundation, "Public Trust in the Media

Is at an All-Time Low. Results from a Major New Knight-Gallup Report Can Help Us Understand Why," *Medium*, January 15, 2018, https://medium.com/trust-media-and -democracy/10-reasons-why-americans-dont-trust-the-media-d0630c125b9e.

4. "Liberal Media Bias? Facts and Myths Regarding the Liberal Media," Fact and Myth, July 30, 2018, http://www.factandmyth.com/liberal-media/liberal-msm-bias.

5. Marvin Kalb, *Enemy of the People: Trump's War on the Press* (Washington, DC: Brookings Institution, 2018).

6. Kristen Bellstrom, "What Is Donald Trump's Beef with NBC Reporter Katy Tur? Here's the Backstory," *Fortune*, November 3, 2016, http://fortune.com/2016/11/03/donald -trump-katy-tur/.

7. Irin Carmon, "Donald Trump's Worst Offense? Mocking Disabled Reporter, Poll Finds," NBC News, August 11, 2016, https://www.nbcnews.com/politics/2016-election/ trump-s-worst-offense-mocking-disabled-reporter-poll-finds-n627736.

8. Margaret Hartmann, "23 Outrageous Moments from Trump's Rally in Phoenix," *Intelligencer* (blog), *New York Magazine*, August 23, 2017, http://nymag.com/ intelligencer/2017/08/23-outrageous-moments-from-trumps-rally-in-phoenix.html.

9. Joe Concha, "Shep Smith: Journalists Are Not the Enemy of the People," *The Hill*, July 26, 2018, https://thehill.com/homenews/media/399074-shep-smith-journalists-are -not-the-enemy-of-the-people.

10. Yaron Steinbuch, "Fox News Backs CNN Lawsuit over Jim Acosta's Suspended Press Pass," *New York Post*, November 14, 2018, https://nypost.com/2018/11/14/fox-news -backs-cnn-lawsuit-over-jim-acostas-suspended-press-pass/.

11. United States v. New York Times Co., 328 F.Supp. 324, 331 (S.D.N.Y. 1971).

12. Martin Barron, "Shining a Light in Dark Corners," interview by Jeffrey Goldberg, *Ideas: The Magazine of the Aspen Institute*, December 1, 2017, https://www.aspeninstitute.org/ longform/aspen-ideas-winter-2017/shining-a-light-in-dark-corners/.

13. Ted Johnson, "Trump: AT&T-TimeWarner Deal 'Not Good for the Country,'" *Variety*, November 21, 2017, https://variety.com/2017/politics/news/donald-trump-att -time-warner-2-1202621063/.

14. Joseph Weber, "Trump Attacks 'Garbage' Washington Post; Calls Kelly Story 'Hit Job,'" Fox News, April 8, 2018, https://www.foxnews.com/politics/trump-attacks-garbage -washington-post-calls-kelly-story-hit-job.

15. Lloyd Grove, "Sinclair/Tribune Merger Has Left & Right United to Fight Terrifying Pro-Trump TV Cartel," *Daily Beast*, April 13, 2018, https://www.thedaily beast.com/media-foes-on-left-and-right-team-up-to-fight-the-sinclairtribune-merger.

16. Glenn Kessler, "Trump Fact Checker Says President Averages 22 Lies and Inaccuracies Every Day," *Independent*, April 1, 2019, https://www.independent.co.uk/news/ world/americas/trump-fact-check-lies-claims-first-year-office-a8849661.html.

17. Dan Balz, "Trump and Truth: Another Difficult Week," *Washington Post*, April 7, 2018, https://www.washingtonpost.com/politics/president-trump-and-truth-another -difficult-week/2018/04/07/cf73f642-39e7-11e8-8fd2-49fe3c675a89_story.html?utm_ term=.717104794199.

18. George Orwell, "Politics and the English Language," in *Politics and the English Language and Other Essays* (Garsington, UK: Benediction Classics, 2010), p. 22.

19. George Orwell, *Nineteen Eighty-Four /1984* (New York: Harcourt Brace & Co., 1949), pp. 3, 14, 23, 92.

20. Daniel Dale and Tanya Talaga, "Donald Trump: The Unauthorized Database of False Things," *Toronto Star*, November 4, 2016, https://www.thestar.com/news/world/uselection/2016/11/04/donald-trump-the-unauthorized-database-of-false-things.html.

21. Sean Lavery et al., "Trump and the Truth," *New Yorker*, September–November 2016, https://www.newyorker.com/topics/trump-truth-fact-checking-investigation.

22. Maria Konnikova, "Trump's Lies vs. Your Brain," *Politico Magazine*, January/February 2017, https://www.politico.com/magazine/story/2017/01/donald-trump-lies-liar-effect-brain-214658.

23. David Leonhardt and Stuart Thompson, "Trump's Lies," *New York Times*, December 14, 2017, https://www.nytimes.com/interactive/2017/06/23/opinion/trumps-lies.html?mtrref=www.google.com&gwh=52C0DDB40698532EFD28F63A8F798C9F&gwt=pay.

24. Eugene Kiely, "The Whoppers of 2017: Trump Monopolizes Our List of the Year's Worst Falsehoods and Bogus Claims," FactCheck.org, December 20, 2017, https://www.factcheck.org/2017/12/the-whoppers-of-2017/.

25. Rebecca Sinderbrand, "How Kellyanne Conway Ushered In the Era of 'Alternative Facts,'" *Washington Post*, January 22, 2017, https://www.washingtonpost.com/news/the-fix/wp/2017/01/22/how-kellyanne-conway-ushered-in-the-era-of-alternative-facts/?utm_term=.e84516414179.

26. "A President's Credibility," *Wall Street Journal*, March 21, 2017, https://www.wsj.com/articles/a-presidents-credibility-1490138920.

27. Brian Flood, "NBC's Andrea Mitchell Rips Trump Administration: 'People Just Flat-Out Lie,'" *The Wrap*, April 10, 2017, https://www.thewrap.com/nbcs-andrea-mitchell-rips-trump-administration-people-just-flat-lie/.

28. Paul Waldman, "Trump's Transubstantiation of Falsehood into Truth," *The Week*, March 1, 2018, https://theweek.com/articles/758186/trumps-transubstantiation-falsehood-into-truth.

29. John Beckett, "Who Ya Gonna Believe, Me or Your Lying Eyes?" *Patheos* (blog), June 20, 2017, https://www.patheos.com/blogs/johnbeckett/2017/06/ya-gonna-believe-lying-eyes.html.

30. Eric Levitz, "Trump Definitely Directed the (Probably Illegal) Hush Payment to Stormy Daniels," *Intelligencer* (blog), *New York Magazine*, November 9, 2018, http://nymag.com/intelligencer/2018/11/trump-micahel-cohen-hush-payment-stormy-daniels-karen-mcdougal-campagin-finance-wsj.html.

31. Nicole Hong, Rebecca Ballhaus, and Michael Rothfeld, "Cohen Says Trump Remained Involved in Moscow Tower Project during Campaign," *Wall Street Journal*, November 29, 2018, https://www.wsj.com/articles/cohen-says-trump-stayed-involved-in-moscow-tower-project-during-campaign-1543539269.

32. Alex Ward, "Trump Tower Moscow, and Michael Cohen's Lies about It, Explained," *Vox*, February 27, 2019, https://www.vox.com/world/2018/11/29/18117910/cohen-trump-tower-moscow-mueller-testimony.

33. Renae Reints, "UN General Assembly Laughs as Trump Brags about His Administration," *Fortune*, September 25, 2018, http://fortune.com/2018/09/25/trump-un-speech-laugh/.

34. Emily Tamkin, "Diplomats Say They Were Definitely Laughing at Trump at the UN," *BuzzFeed News*, September 26, 2018, https://www.buzzfeednews.com/article/emilytamkin/diplomats-un-laughed-donald-trump.

35. Maggie Haberman, "Clinton Impeachment Lawyer May Aid Trump in Mueller Response," *New York Times*, March 10, 2018, https://www.nytimes.com/2018/03/10/us/politics/trump-mueller-flood.html.

36. Jeremy Diamond and Pamela Brown, "Dowd Resigns as Trump's Lawyer Amid Disagreements on Strategy," CNN, March 22, 2018, https://www.cnn.com/2018/03/22/politics/john-dowd-white-house/index.html.

37. Rebecca Ballhaus and Peter Nicholas, "Emmet Flood to Replace Ty Cobb on Trump's Legal Team," *Wall Street Journal*, May 2, 2018, https://www.wsj.com/articles/ty-cobb-leaving-donald-trumps-legal-team-1525280088.

38. Josh Hafner, "Donald Trump Loves the 'Poorly Educated'—and They Love Him," *USA Today*, February 24, 2016, https://www.usatoday.com/story/news/politics/onpolitics/2016/02/24/donald-trump-nevada-poorly-educated/80860078/.

39. Matt Gertz, "Donald Trump, Sean Spicer, and the George Costanza Rule of Lying," *Media Matters* (blog), January 24, 2017, https://www.mediamatters.org/blog/2017/01/24/donald-trump-sean-spicer-and-george-costanza-rule-lying/215108.

40. Doris Kearns Goodwin, "Teddy vs. Trump: The Art of the Square Deal," *Vanity Fair*, September 17, 2018, https://www.vanityfair.com/news/2018/09/teddy-vs-trump-the-art-of-the-square-deal.

41. Mathew Ingram, "NewsGuard Wants to Rank the News Based on Credibility," *Columbia Journalism Review*, March 4, 2018, https://www.cjr.org/the_new_gatekeepers/newsguard-news-ranking-credibility.php.

CHAPTER 6

1. Jess Bolluyt, "These Are the Presidents Who Had the Most Corrupt Cabinets (And How Donald Trump Compares)," Culture Cheat Sheet, January 14, 2019, https://www.cheatsheet.com/culture/presidents-with-corrupt-cabinets-and-how-donald-trump-compares.html/.

2. Sean Illing, "'The Fish Rots from the Head': A Historian on the Unique Corruption of Trump's White House," *Vox*, December 21, 2018, https://www.vox.com/2017/11/16/16643614/trump-administration-corruption-russia-investigation.

3. *Herold's Financial Dictionary*, "What Was the Keating Five?" https://www.financial-dictionary.info/terms/keating-five/.

4. Colley Charpentier et al., "Vitter Re-Emerges and Asks Again for Forgiveness," *Times-Picayune* (New Orleans), July 16, 2007, http://blog.nola.com/times-picayune/2007/07/vitter_reemerges_and_again_ask.html.

5. Carrie Levine and Michael Beckel, "Billionaires and Corporations Helped Fund Donald Trump's Transition," Center for Public Integrity, February 23, 2017, https://publicintegrity.org/federal-politics/billionaires-and-corporations-helped-fund-donald-trumps-transition/.

6. Michael Stratford, "DeVos Review Identifies 102 Financial Interests with Potential Conflicts," *Politico*, January 20, 2017, https://www.politico.com/story/2017/01/betsy-devos-potential-conflicts-financial-review-233906.

7. John Nichols, "The Time Has Come for the Extreme Vetting of Wilbur Ross: New Revelations about the Commerce Secretary's Sordid Financial Arrangements Demand the

Scrutiny He Has Avoided Up to Now," *Nation*, November 6, 2017, https://www.thenation.com/article/the-time-has-come-to-for-the-extreme-vetting-of-wilbur-ross/.

8. Jayne O'Donnell, "HHS Nominee Tom Price Bought Stock, Then Authored Bill Benefiting Company," *USA Today*, February 2, 2017, https://www.usatoday.com/story/news/politics/2017/02/02/hhs-nominee-tom-price-bought-stock-then-authored-bill-benefiting-company/97337838/.

9. Jeff Hauser, "Steven Mnuchin's Stealth Conflict of Interest," *CEPR Blog*, Center for Economic and Policy Research, December 18, 2017, http://cepr.net/blogs/cepr-blog/steven-mnuchin-s-stealth-conflict-of-interest.

10. Derrick Jackson, "Conflicts of Interest in the Trump Administration: The Cases of Alex Azar and Brenda Fitzgerald," *Union of Concerned Scientists Blog*, Union of Concerned Scientists, February 5, 2018, https://blog.ucsusa.org/derrick-jackson/conflicts-of-interest-in-the-trump-administration-the-cases-of-alex-azar-and-brenda-fitzgerald.

11. Sarah Karlin-Smith and Brianna Ehley, "Trump's Top Health Official Traded Tobacco Stock While Leading Anti-Smoking Efforts," *Politico*, January 30, 2018, https://www.politico.com/story/2018/01/30/cdc-director-tobacco-stocks-after-appointment-316245.

12. Josh Keefe, "Trump Administration Conflicts of Interest: How Gary Cohn Could Sell US Infrastructure to Goldman Sachs," *International Business Times*, May 26, 2017, https://www.ibtimes.com/political-capital/trump-administration-conflicts-interest-how-gary-cohn-could-sell-us-infrastructure.

13. Michael Schmidt, Maggie Haberman, "Trump Wanted to Order Justice Dept. to Prosecute Comey and Clinton," *New York Times*, November 20, 2018, https://www.nytimes.com/2018/11/20/us/politics/president-trump-justice-department.html.

14. Dan Alexander, "Wilbur Ross' Calendar Reveals Dozens of Meetings with Companies Tied to His Personal Fortune," *Forbes*, July 13, 2018, https://www.forbes.com/sites/forbesdigitalcovers/2018/07/12/wilbur-ross-calendar-reveals-dozens-of-meetings-with-companies-tied-to-his-personal-fortune/#6fc86138526a.

15. Alia Wong, "DeVos Digs Herself Deeper," *Atlantic*, March 14, 2018, https://www.theatlantic.com/education/archive/2018/03/betsy-devos-60-minutes/555566/.

16. Seth McLaughlin, "Early Trump Backers Now Facing Federal Criminal Charges," *Washington Times*, August 22, 2018, https://www.washingtontimes.com/news/2018/aug/22/chris-collins-duncan-hunter-facing-federal-crimina/.

17. John Gizzi, "US Prosecutors Slammed by Trump Have Republican Credentials," *Newsmax*, September 3, 2018, https://www.newsmax.com/john-gizzi/republican-prosecutors-chris-collins-duncan-hunter/2018/09/03/id/880028/.

18. Danielle Ivory, Erica Green, and Steve Eder, "Education Department Unwinds Unit Investigating Fraud at For-Profits," *New York Times*, May 13, 2018, https://www.nytimes.com/2018/05/13/business/education-department-for-profit-colleges.html.

19. Ranji Sinha, "Gov. Inslee Vetoes Bill That Would Keep Legislative Records Secret," KIRO7.com, March 2, 2018, https://www.kiro7.com/news/local/thousands-urge-inslee-to-veto-bill-that-would-keep-legislative-records-secret/708047016.

20. Steve Poftak, "Don't Nod If You Can Wink," Pioneer Institute Public Policy Research, March 10, 2008, https://pioneerinstitute.org/news/dont-nod-if-you-can-wink/.

21. Mark Jacobson, "Edwin Edwards Will Live Forever," *New York Magazine*, July 16, 2014, http://nymag.com/nymag/features/edwin-edwards-2014-7/index5.html.

22. James Hohmann, "Allen Apologizes for 'Macaca' Moment," *Politico*, June 3, 2011, https://www.politico.com/story/2011/06/allen-apologizes-for-macaca-moment-056212.

23. Tim Carmody, "Mitt Romney's Damning '47 Percent' Video and the New Politics of Privacy," *Verge*, March 14, 2013, https://www.theverge.com/2013/3/14/4103184/romney-prouty-47-percent-video-new-politics-of-privacy.

24. David Carr, "Same Gaffes, but Now on Twitter," *New York Times*, June 12, 2011, https://www.nytimes.com/2011/06/13/business/media/13carr.html?mtrref=www.google.com&gwh=7297DCF72AD2F9A9C21CF64B72F381AC&gwt=pay.

25. Raphael Satter, "Inside Story: How Russians Hacked the Democrats' Emails," AP News, November 4, 2017, https://www.apnews.com/dea73efc01594839957c3c9a6c962b8a.

26. Adi Robertson, "Behind the Email Trail That Brought Down General Petraeus," *Verge*, November 12, 2012, https://www.theverge.com/2012/11/12/3636992/fbi-petraeus-email-investigation.

27. Ed Pilkington, "Anthony Weiner Resigns over Twitter Photo Scandal," *Guardian*, June 16, 2011, https://www.theguardian.com/world/2011/jun/16/anthony-weiner-resigns-twitter-scandal.

28. Russell Goldman, "Rielle Hunter Reveals John Edwards' Multiple Mistresses in Tell-All," ABC News, June 18, 2012, https://abcnews.go.com/Politics/rielle-hunter-memoir-happened-reveals-john-edwards-affair/story?id=16589982.

29. Ted Sherman and Matt Arco, "A Closer Look at the Emails and Evidence the Bridgegate Jury Is Reviewing," NJ.com, October 4, 2016, https://www.nj.com/news/2016/10/the_bridgegate_trial_exhibits_building_a_case.html.

30. Lauren Gambino, "Denying Accuracy of Access Hollywood Tape Would Be Trump's Biggest Lie," *Guardian*, November 29, 2017, https://www.theguardian.com/us-news/2017/nov/29/denying-accuracy-of-access-hollywood-tape-would-be-trumps-biggest-lie.

31. Jacqueline Thomsen, "'Access Hollywood' Fires Back at Trump: 'The Tape Is Very Real,'" *The Hill*, November 27, 2017, https://thehill.com/homenews/administration/362070-access-hollywood-fires-back-at-trump-the-tape-is-very-real.

32. Bob Woodward, *Fear: Trump in the White House* (New York: Simon & Schuster, 2018).

33. Matthew Yglesias, "Trump Helps Sanctioned Chinese Phone Maker after China Delivers a Big Loan to a Trump Project," *Vox*, May 15, 2018, https://www.vox.com/policy-and-politics/2018/5/15/17355202/trump-zte-indonesia-lido-city.

34. Edward Helmore, "Ivanka Trump Won China Trademarks Days before Her Father's Reversal on ZTE,'" *Guardian*, May 28, 2018, https://www.theguardian.com/us-news/2018/may/28/ivanka-trump-won-china-trademarks-donald-trump-zte-reversal.

35. Uniting and Strengthening America by Providing Appropriate Tools Required to Intercept and Obstruct Terrorism (USA PATRIOT Act) Act of 2001, Pub. L. No. 107-56, 115 Stat. 272 (2001), available online at https://www.govinfo.gov/content/pkg/PLAW-107publ56/pdf/PLAW-107publ56.pdf.

36. Kate Nocera, "Rand Paul and Ron Wyden Will Fight the Reauthorization of the Patriot Act Together," *BuzzFeed News*, May 11, 2015, https://www.buzzfeednews.com/article/katenocera/rand-paul-and-ron-wyden-will-fight-the-reauthorization-of-th.

37. James Bamford, "The NSA Is Building the Country's Biggest Spy Center (Watch What You Say)," *Wired*, March 15, 2012, https://www.wired.com/2012/03/ff-nsadatacenter/.

38. John Hollenhorst, "Safety or Surveillance: What Is the NSA's Utah Data Center?" KSL.com, October 25, 2012, https://www.ksl.com/article/22705217/safety-or-surveillance-what-is-the-nsas-utah-data-center.

39. "Our Mission," Sunlight Foundation, https://sunlightfoundation.com/.

40. "Our Vision and Mission: Inform, Empower and Advocate," Center for Responsive Politics, https://www.opensecrets.org/about/.

41. "About Us" and "What We Do," MapLight, https://maplight.org/about/ and https://maplight.org/what-we-do/.

42. "About," American Oversight, https://www.americanoversight.org/about.

43. "About Us: Our Company," LegiStorm, https://www.legistorm.com/index/about.html.

44. "Core Fund—Governmental Transparency and Accountability," Scherman Foundation, http://scherman.org/programs/government-transparency-and-accountability/.

45. "About: Our Mission," Project on Government Oversight, https://www.pogo.org/about/.

46. "About Democracy Web: What Is Democracy Web?," Democracy Web, http://democracyweb.org/about-democracy-web.

47. "Mission, Vision and Values," Transparency International, https://www.transparency.org/whoweare/organisation/mission_vision_and_values.

48. "Mission" and "Background," USAspending.gov, https://www.usaspending.gov/#/about.

49. Ella Nilsen, "Sen. Elizabeth Warren Just Unveiled a Dramatic Plan to Eradicate Washington Corruption," *Vox*, August 21, 2018, https://www.vox.com/2018/8/21/17760916/elizabeth-warren-anti-corruption-act-bill-lobbying-ban-president-trump.

50. Bastian Obermayer et al., "The Panama Papers: Giant Leak of Offshore Financial Records Exposes Global Array of Crime and Corruption," International Consortium of Investigative Journalists, April 3, 2016, https://www.icij.org/investigations/panama-papers/20160403-panama-papers-global-overview/.

51. Ronald Kessler, *The Trump White House: Changing the Rules of the Game* (New York: Crown, 2018).

CHAPTER 7

1. Jeremy Diamond, "Trump Slams Globalization, Promises to Upend Economic Status Quo," CNN, June 28, 2016, https://www.cnn.com/2016/06/28/politics/donald-trump-speech-pennsylvania-economy/index.html.

2. Matt Novak, "That Time Republicans Smashed a Boombox with Sledgehammers on Capitol Hill," Paleofuture, May 9, 2016, https://paleofuture.gizmodo.com/that-time-republicans-smashed-a-boombox-with-sledgehamm-1775418875.

3. "U.S. Trade Policy: Free Trade and Globalization," Selous Foundation for Public Policy Research, http://sfppr.org/free-trade-and-globalization/.

4. Charles Hankla, "Economic History Shows Why Trump's 'America First' Tariff Policy Is So Dangerous," The Conversation, April 4, 2018, http://theconversation.com/economic-history-shows-why-trumps-america-first-tariff-policy-is-so-dangerous-92715.

5. Eric Levitz, "Trump Ends NATO Summit by Announcing a Diplomatic Breakthrough that Did Not Happen," *Intelligencer* (blog), *New York Magazine*, July 12, 2018, http://nymag.com/intelligencer/2018/07/nato-summit-trump-fabricates-agreement-on-defense-spending.html?gtm=bottom&gtm=top.

6. Ashish Kumar Sen, "The United States Stands Isolated at a Meeting of Its Friends," *New Atlanticist* (blog), Atlantic Council, June 9, 2018, https://www.atlanticcouncil.org/blogs/new-atlanticist/the-united-states-stands-isolated-at-a-meeting-of-its-friends.

7. Dilip Hiro, "America First Actually Means China First: 'Rivals' Are Stepping into the Vacuum Created by Trump's Isolationism," *Nation*, February 6, 2018, https://www.the nation.com/article/america-first-actually-means-china-first/.

8. Walter Williams, "Benefits of Tariffs May Outweigh Costs for Trump," *Daily Reflector*, March 14, 2018, http://www.reflector.com/Op-Ed/2018/03/14/Trump-s-Steel-and-Aluminum-Tariffs.html.

9. Shrutee Sarkar, "Economists United: Trump Tariffs Won't Help the Economy," Reuters, March 13, 2018, https://www.reuters.com/article/us-usa-economy-poll/economists-united-trump-tariffs-wont-help-the-economy-idUSKCN1GQ02G.

10. Josh Wingrove, "Economists Invoke Great Depression in Warning to Trump on Trade," *Bloomberg*, May 2, 2018, https://www.bloomberg.com/news/articles/2018-05-02/economists-invoke-great-depression-in-warning-to-trump-on-trade.

11. Michael Cannivet, "Trump's Tariffs Will Harm U.S. Steel Companies, Not Help Them," Real Clear Markets, March 19, 2018, https://www.realclearmarkets.com/articles/2018/03/19/trumps_tariffs_will_harm_us_steel_companies_not_help_them_103197.html.

12. "American Corporations Come Out against Donald Trump's Proposed Tariffs," *Economist*, March 21, 2018, https://www.economist.com/graphic-detail/2018/03/21/american-corporations-come-out-against-donald-trumps-proposed-tariffs.

13. Nick Carey, "The Financial Impact of Trump's Tariffs on Steel and Aluminum," Reuters, March 2, 2018, https://www.reuters.com/article/us-usa-trade-explainer/the-financial-impact-of-trumps-tariffs-on-steel-and-aluminum-idUSKCN1GE2WK.

14. Natasha Bach, "How Many American Jobs Could Be Lost Thanks to Trump's Steel and Aluminum Tariffs," *Fortune*, March 6, 2018, http://fortune.com/2018/03/06/trump-steel-aluminum-tariffs-cost-jobs/.

15. Bob Bryan, "Trump's Massive New Tariffs Could End Up Costing America 146,000 Jobs," *Business Insider*, March 6, 2018, https://www.businessinsider.my/trump-tariffs-on-aluminum-steel-could-cost-jobs-study-2018-3/.

16. Anviksha Patel, "Trump's Tariff Proposal Provokes Global Retaliation," *World Finance*, March 7, 2018, https://www.worldfinance.com/strategy/government-policy/trumps-tariff-proposal-provokes-global-retaliation.

17. Kate Gibson, "Trump Tariffs: Europe Releases List of Retaliation Targets," CBS News, March 16, 2018, https://www.cbsnews.com/news/eus-list-of-potential-targets-to-retaliate-for-trump-tariffs/.

18. Edward Helmore, "China Threatens 'Trump Country' with Retaliatory Tariffs Ahead of Midterms," *Guardian*, April 6, 2018, https://www.theguardian.com/business/2018/apr/06/china-us-tariffs-trump-country-midterms.

19. Alanna Petroff and Steven Jiang, "China Plans Tariffs on $60 Billion of US Products," *CNN Money*, August 3, 2018, https://money.cnn.com/2018/08/03/news/economy/china-us-tariffs-retaliation/index.html.

20. Emily Stewart, "Trump Says Tariffs Are Working 'Big Time.' Here Are 5 Pieces of Evidence That's Not the Case," *Vox*, August 5, 2018, https://www.vox.com/policy-and-politics/2018/8/5/17653632/trump-tariffs-trade-war-steel.

21. Andrew Tangel and Mike Colias, "Optimism for Manufacturers Upended with Trump's Tariff Pledge," *Wall Street Journal*, March 4, 2018, https://www.wsj.com/articles/tariffs-throw-wrench-into-manufacturers-plans-1520164800.

22. Lauren Thomas, "Trump Tariffs on Appliances, Electronics Will Hit American Consumers, Retailers Warn," CNBC, April 4, 2018, https://www.cnbc.com/2018/04/04/tariffs-on-appliances-electronics-would-hit-consumers-in-the-wallet-us-retailers.html.

23. Paul Wiseman, "Trump Tariffs May Imperil a Delicate Global Economic Rebound," AP News, March 11, 2018, https://www.apnews.com/5a104f3bec8e468ca17dcc6c9c2dbf67.

24. Tracey Samuelson, "Trump Grants Tariff Exemptions for Mexico and Canada," Marketplace, March 8, 2018, https://www.marketplace.org/2018/03/08/economy/trump-grants-tariff-exemptions-mexico-and-canada.

25. Michael Birnbaum, "EU, Brazil, South Korea and Others Get Temporary Exemptions from Trump's Steel Tariffs," *Washington Post*, March 22, 2018, https://www.washingtonpost.com/world/europe/eu-brazil-south-korea-and-others-get-temporary-exemptions-from-trumps-steel-tariffs/2018/03/22/9d0fac5a-2de4-11e8-8dc9-3b51e028b845_story.html?utm_term=.15cad4c8c84f.

26. Greg Ip, "The Flaw in Trump's National Security Tariffs Logic," *Wall Street Journal*, March 9, 2018, https://www.wsj.com/articles/the-flaw-in-trumps-national-security-tariffs-logic-1520612895.

27. John Brinkley, "Trump's National Security Tariffs Have Nothing to Do with National Security," *Forbes*, March 12, 2018, https://www.forbes.com/sites/johnbrinkley/2018/03/12/trumps-national-security-tariffs-have-nothing-to-do-with-national-security/#7972948c706c.

28. Bob Fredericks, "Trump Rips Fed Again for Hiking Interest Rates," *New York Post*, July 20, 2018, https://nypost.com/2018/07/20/trump-rips-fed-again-for-hiking-interest-rates/.

29. Paul Mozur and Raymond Zhong, "In About-Face on Trade, Trump Vows to Protect ZTE Jobs in China," *New York Times*, May 13, 2018, https://www.nytimes.com/2018/05/13/business/trump-vows-to-save-jobs-at-chinas-zte-lost-after-us-sanctions.html.

30. Jack Crowe, "China Contributing $500 Million to Trump-Linked Project in Indonesia," *National Review*, May 14, 2018, https://www.nationalreview.com/news/china-contributing-500-million-trump-linked-project-indonesia/.

31. Brent Griffiths and Annie Karni, "Trump Says He'll Help Chinese Company That Violated U.S. Sanctions," *Politico*, May 13, 2018, https://www.politico.com/story/2018/05/13/trump-zte-china-sanctions-korea-iran-584244.

CHAPTER 8

1. Robert Longley, "What Is Federalism? Definition and How It Works in the US: A Government System of Shared Powers," ThoughtCo., August 3, 2018, https://www.thoughtco.com/federalism-powers-national-and-state-governments-3321841.

2. "The Ratification Debate," Judicial Learning Center, http://judiciallearningcenter.org/the-ratification-debate/.

3. John Judis, "Federal Government Is More Powerful Than State Government," *New York Times*, July 16, 2013, https://www.nytimes.com/roomfordebate/2013/07/16/state-politics-vs-the-federal-government/federal-government-is-more-powerful-than-state-government.

4. Linda Monk, "The Commerce Power," *Constitution USA with Peter Sagal*, PBS LearningMedia, http://www.pbs.org/tpt/constitution-usa-peter-sagal/federalism/commerce-power/.

5. "Ratification Debate."

6. Ugonna Eze, "The Anti-Federalists and Their Important Role during the Ratification Fight," *Constitution Daily* (blog), National Constitution Center, September 27, 2017, https://constitutioncenter.org/blog/the-anti-federalists-and-their-important-role-during-the-ratification-fight.

7. For a discussion on the Tenth Amendment, see Gary Lawson and Robert Schapiro, "Common Interpretation: The Tenth Amendment," National Constitution Center, https://constitutioncenter.org/interactive-constitution/amendments/amendment-x.

8. Judis, "Federal Government Is More Powerful."

9. "Nullification Proclamation," Web Guides: Primary Documents in American History, Library of Congress, https://www.loc.gov/rr/program/bib/ourdocs/nullification.html.

10. Rebecca Onion, "A WWI-Era Memo Asking French Officers to Practice Jim Crow with Black American Troops," *Slate*, April 27, 2016, https://slate.com/human-interest/2016/04/secret-information-concerning-black-troops-a-warning-memo-sent-to-the-french-military-during-world-war-i.html.

11. Randy St. Laurent, "History of the Anti-Lynching Law," *County Press* (MI), February 8, 2012, https://thecountypress.mihomepaper.com/articles/history-of-the-anti-lynching-law/.

12. Office of the Historian, "Anti-Lynching Legislation Renewed," *Black Americans in Congress*, History, Art, and Archives, US House of Representatives, https://history.house.gov/Exhibitions-and-Publications/BAIC/Historical-Essays/Temporary-Farewell/Anti-Lynching-Legislation/.

13. Sheryl Gay Stolberg, "Senate Issues Apology over Failure on Lynching Law," *New York Times*, June 14, 2005, https://www.nytimes.com/2005/06/14/politics/senate-issues-apology-over-failure-on-lynching-law.html?mtrref=www.google.com&gwh=50742255DA64262649E5477AF06091B9&gwt=pay.

14. Eli Watkins and Ted Barrett, "Senate Passes Anti-Lynching Bill in Renewed Effort to Make It a Federal Hate Crime," CNN, February 14, 2019, https://www.cnn.com/2019/02/14/politics/senate-anti-lynching-harris-booker/index.html.

15. Josh Sager, "Why Conservatives Love 'States' Rights,'" Progressive Cynic, October 29, 2012, https://theprogressivecynic.com/2012/10/29/why-conservatives-love-states-rights/.

16. Daniel Medwed, "The Evolution of 'States' Rights' in the Age of Donald Trump," WGBH News, July 26, 2017, https://www.wgbh.org/news/2017/07/26/news/evolution-states-rights-age-donald-trump.

17. Philip Rucker, Robert Costa, "Bannon Vows a Daily Fight for 'Deconstruction of the Administrative State,'" *Washington Post*, February 23, 2017, https://www.washingtonpost.com/politics/top-wh-strategist-vows-a-daily-fight-for-deconstruction-of-the-administrative-state/2017/02/23/03f6b8da-f9ea-11e6-bf01-d47f8cf9b643_story.html?utm_term=.ec9fb3d57c9f.

18. Evan Isaacson, "Environmental Federalism and Scott Pruitt: We've Been Here Before," *CPR Blog*, Center for Progressive Reform, February 27, 2017, http://www.progressivereform.org/CPRBlog.cfm?idBlog=0216CC4F-DF1C-585A-30A67316557ED2F4.

19. Nadja Popovich, Livia Albeck-Ripka, and Kendra Pierre-Louis, "78 Environmental Rules on the Way Out Under Trump," *New York Times*, December 28, 2018, https://www.nytimes.com/interactive/2017/10/05/climate/trump-environment-rules-reversed.html.

20. Darryl Fears, "Trump Administration Halted a Study of Mountaintop Coal Mining's Health Effects." *Washington Post*, August 21, 2017, https://www.washingtonpost.com/news/energy-environment/wp/2017/08/21/trump-administration-halted-a-study-of-mountaintop-coal-minings-health-effects/?utm_term=.5dd7c97345ea.

21. George Ochenski, "States' Rights—The Other Side of the Coin." *Missoulian* (MT), February 12, 2018, https://missoulian.com/opinion/columnists/states-rights-the-other-side-of-the-coin/article_81ed5833-9706-5893-8271-3def0537469f.html.

22. Michael Greshko et al., "A Running List of How Trump Is Changing Environmental Policy," *National Geographic*, November 9, 2018, https://news.nationalgeographic.com/2017/03/how-trump-is-changing-science-environment/.

23. Mary Fan, "How Sanctuary Cities Can Protect Dreamers," *Fortune*, September 7, 2017, http://fortune.com/2017/09/07/daca-program-sanctuary-cities-donald-trump-dreamers/.

24. Stephen Dinan, "Sessions Likens California Sanctuary Laws to Slave-State Nullification," *Washington Times*, March 7, 2018, https://www.washingtontimes.com/news/2018/mar/7/sessions-calif-sanctuary-slave-state-nullification/.

25. David Caplan, "Justice Dept. Suing California over Sanctuary Laws, Gov. Brown Calls It a 'Political Stunt,'" ABC News, March 6, 2018, https://abcnews.go.com/Politics/justice-dept-suing-california-sanctuary-laws-gov-brown/story?id=53570616.

26. William Watkins Jr., "Sanctuary Cities Are Not the New Nullification Crisis," Independent Institute, May 23, 2017, http://www.independent.org/news/article.asp?id=9081.

27. Melina Delkic, "Do Republicans Still Believe in States' Rights? Sessions's Marijuana Policy Is Ultimate Test," *Newsweek*, January 6, 2018, https://www.newsweek.com/republicans-still-believe-states-rights-marijuana-policy-772611.

28. Chad Terhune, "Leading Republicans See a Costly Malpractice Crisis—Experts Don't," *Kaiser Health News*, January 4, 2017, https://khn.org/news/leading-republicans-see-a-costly-malpractice-crisis-experts-dont/.

29. Will Costello and Sumner Park, "Most States Refusing to Provide Voter Data to Trump Election Panel," *The Hill*, June 30, 2017, https://thehill.com/homenews/state-watch/340289-19-states-refusing-to-provide-voter-data-to-trump-panel.

30. Peter Montgomery, "Trump's Election Integrity Commission: The Lies and the Cold, Hard Facts," People for the American Way, July 2017, http://www.pfaw.org/report/trumps-election-integrity-commission-the-lies-and-the-cold-hard-facts/.

31. Scott Simon, "Goodbye to a Commission Established to Solve a Nonexistent Problem," NPR, January 6, 2018, https://www.npr.org/2018/01/06/576190657/goodbye-to-a-commission-established-to-solve-a-nonexistent-problem.

32. Michael Stratford, "Trump Endorses States' Rights—But Only When He Agrees with the State," *Politico*, April 2, 2018, https://www.politico.com/story/2018/04/02/trump-states-rights-education-sanctuary-drilling-492784.

33. Kurtis Lee, "Meet the 6 Governors Leading the Charge against the Senate Health Plan," *Los Angeles Times*, July 2, 2017, https://www.latimes.com/politics/la-na-governors-healthcare-20170702-htmlstory.html.

34. Joe Perticone, "Top Senate Republican Threatens Jeff Sessions over Marijuana Policy Change," *Business Insider*, January 4, 2018, https://www.businessinsider.com/jeff -sessions-marijuana-policy-cory-gardner-2018-1.

35. Thomas Mitchell, "Trump, Gardner Strike Marijuana Deal after Sessions Memo Fallout," *Westword*, April 13, 2018, https://www.westword.com/marijuana/colorado -cannabis-and-fashion-industries-explore-sustainability-together-11322095.

36. Jen Mishory and Yan Cao, "Four Things DeVos Gets Wrong about State Laws Protecting Borrowers," Century Foundation, March 12, 2018, https://tcf.org/content/com mentary/four-things-devos-gets-wrong-about-state-laws-protecting-borrowers/?session=1.

37. Monique El-Faizy, "US Cities, States Vow to Honour Paris Climate Accord despite Trump's Withdrawal," France24, June 2, 2017, https://www.france24.com/en/20170601 -cities-states-companies-climate-paris-agreement-trump.

38. Angela Hart, "California's War against Trump Is Costing Taxpayers Millions," MSN News, October 3, 2018, https://www.msn.com/en-us/news/us/californias-war -against-trump-is-costing-taxpayers-millions/ar-BBNSwJF.

39. Alan Gomez, "California Sues Trump Administration over Census Citizenship Question," *USA Today*, March 27, 2018, https://www.usatoday.com/story/news/nation/ 2018/03/27/california-sues-trump-administration-over-census-citizenship-question/ 462241002/.

40. Hansi Lo Wang, "More Than 2 Dozen States, Cities Sue to Block Census Citizenship Question," NPR, April 3, 2018, https://www.npr.org/2018/04/03/ 599159295/17-states-7-cities-sue-to-remove-2020-census-citizenship-question.

41. Lydia Wheeler, "Supreme Court to Hear Census Citizenship Case This Term," *The Hill*, February 15, 2019, https://thehill.com/regulation/court-battles/430239-supreme -court-agrees-to-hear-controversial-census-case-this-term.

42. Dan Levine, "In Trump Era, Democrats and Republicans Switch Sides on States' Rights," Reuters, January 26, 2017, https://www.reuters.com/article/us-usa-trump -legal-analysis/in-trump-era-democrats-and-republicans-switch-sides-on-states-rights -idUSKBN15A1H1.

43. Dominic Fracassa, "California Files First 'Sanctuary Cities' Lawsuit from a State," Governing, August 15, 2017, https://www.governing.com/topics/public-justice-safety/tns -california-sanctuary-cities-lawsuit.html.

44. Josh Gerstein, "California Files Suit over Trump Sanctuary City Policy," *Politico*, August 14, 2017, https://www.politico.com/story/2017/08/14/california-trump-sanctuary -city-grant-lawsuit-241623.

45. Xavier Becerra, "California AG Becerra discusses Trump, DeVos, and Gun Safety," *Andrea Mitchell Reports*, MSNBC, March 12, 2018, http://www.msnbc.com/andrea-mitchell -reports/watch/california-ag-becerra-discusses-trump-devos-and-gun-safety-1183797315813 [transcription by the author].

46. Lorraine Chow, "Trump Administration Sued for Suspension of Clean Water Rule," EcoWatch, February 7, 2018, https://www.ecowatch.com/clean-water-rule-lawsuit -2532176300.html.

47. John Stoehr, "The GOP Only Selectively Cares about States' Rights," *Washington Monthly*, January 10, 2018, https://washingtonmonthly.com/2018/01/10/the-gop-only -selectively-cares-about-states-rights/.

48. "Democrats Adopt States' Rights Platforms," *Gazette* (Colorado Springs), December 7, 2016, https://gazette.com/opinion/editorial-democrats-adopt-states-rights-platforms/article_b8780d54-381d-52cf-b98e-d82e9eda7b1a.html.

49. Garrett Epps, "When Republicans Attack States' Rights," *Atlantic*, March 13, 2018, https://www.theatlantic.com/politics/archive/2018/03/when-republicans-become-anti-states-rights/555362/.

50. *Bush v. Gore*, 531 U.S. 98 (2000).

51. *District of Columbia v. Heller*, 554 U.S. 570 (2008).

CHAPTER 9

1. Julia Zorthian, "The Future of Bipartisanship in Congress Might Be Road Trips," *Time*, March 16, 2017, http://time.com/4703631/beto-o-rourke-will-hurd-road-trip-congress/?xid=homepage.

2. Sonia Sotomayor, "Supreme Court Justice Sonia Sotomayor at Stanford Law School," interview by Mary Elizabeth Magill, C-SPAN video, 1:13:39, recorded March 10, 2017, originally aired April 14, 2017, https://www.c-span.org/video/?424802-1/stanford-university-hosts-discussion-supreme-court-justice-sonia-sotomayor, at 17:17–25:22.

3. Mara Liasson, "Measuring McCain and Obama's Bipartisan Efforts," NPR, July 2, 2008, https://www.npr.org/templates/story/story.php?storyId=92111942.

4. Jeff Zeleny, "Initial Steps by Obama Suggest a Bipartisan Flair," *New York Times*, November 23, 2008, https://www.nytimes.com/2008/11/24/us/politics/24bipartisan.html?mtrref=www.google.com&gwh=4490F5A1AD37034197ABB43CC8F144B1&gwt=pay.

5. Cyrus Tashakkori, "Obama's Attempts at Bipartisanship: A Chronological Review," Modest Proposal, October 12, 2012, http://www.themodestproposal.com/?p=151.

6. Bill Scher, "Obama's Unsung Bipartisan Legacy," *Real Clear Politics*, January 16, 2017, https://www.realclearpolitics.com/articles/2017/01/16/obamas_unsung_bipartisan_legacy_132798.html.

7. "Obama Reaches Out to Republicans on Health Care, but Bipartisan Bill Looking Unlikely," Fox News, July 18, 2009, https://www.foxnews.com/politics/obama-reaches-out-to-republicans-on-health-care-but-bipartisan-bill-looking-unlikely.

8. "Individual Health Care Insurance Mandate Has Roots Two Decades Long," Fox News, June 28, 2012, updated December 23, 2015, https://www.foxnews.com/politics/individual-health-care-insurance-mandate-has-roots-two-decades-long.

9. John Farrell, "Conservatives Run from the Individual Mandate They Once Embraced," *U.S. News & World Report*, April 19, 2010, https://www.usnews.com/opinion/blogs/john-farrell/2010/04/19/conservatives-run-from-the-individual-mandate-they-once-embraced.

10. Ross Baker, "Set the Health Care Record Straight: Republicans Helped Craft Obamacare," *USA Today*, August 1, 2017, https://www.usatoday.com/story/opinion/2017/08/01/set-health-record-straight-republicans-helped-craft-obamacare-ross-baker-column/523952001/.

11. Meghan Foley, "The Irony of Obamacare: Republicans Thought of It First," Cheat Sheet, October 4, 2013, https://www.cheatsheet.com/money-career/the-irony-of-obamacare-republicans-thought-of-it-first.html/.

12. Baker, "Set the Health Care Record Straight."

13. Sam Stein, "Robert Draper Book: GOP's Anti-Obama Campaign Started Night of Inauguration," *Huffington Post*, April 25, 2012, https://www.huffpost.com/entry/robert-dra per-anti-obama-campaign_n_1452899.

14. Ewen MacAskill, "Democrats Condemn GOP's Plot to Obstruct Obama as 'Appalling and Sad,'" *Guardian*, April 26, 2012, https://www.theguardian.com/world/2012/apr/26/democrats-gop-plot-obstruct-obama.

15. Paul Waldman, "The Projection Party: The Republican Fantasy of Barack Obama's 'Divisiveness,'" *American Prospect*, August 27, 2012, https://prospect.org/article/projection-party.

16. Chad Livengood and Jonathan Oosting, "Trump to Black Voters: 'What Do You Have to Lose?'" *Detroit News*, August 19, 2016, https://www.detroitnews.com/story/news/politics/2016/08/19/trump-chairman-resigns-ahead-mid-michigan-rally/88996014/.

17. Jonathan Chait, "How Republicans Gamed Budget Rules to Pass Their Tax Cut," *Intelligencer* (blog), *New York Magazine*, November 15, 2017, http://nymag.com/intelligencer/2017/11/how-republicans-gamed-budget-rules-to-pass-their-tax-cut.html.

18. Sarah Binder, "Three Reasons Republican Senators Will End Up without Real Tax Reform," *Washington Post*, November 30, 2017 https://www.washingtonpost.com/news/monkey-cage/wp/2017/11/30/three-reasons-republican-senators-will-end-up-without-real-tax-reform/?utm_term=.609b74b4279e.

19. Jim Newell, "The Dreamer Deal That Wasn't," *Slate*, January 11, 2018, https://slate.com/news-and-politics/2018/01/a-bipartisan-group-of-senators-struck-a-daca-deal-but-can-it-go-anywhere.html.

20. Gabrielle Levy, "Trump Trashes Gang of Six Immigration Deal, Lawmaker Confirms 'Shithole' Remarks," *U.S. News & World Report*, January 12, 2018, https://www.usnews.com/news/national-news/articles/2018-01-12/trump-trashes-gang-of-six-immigration-deal-lawmaker-confirms-shithole-remarks.

21. Pope Francis, "Full Speech of Pope Francis' Address to the Joint Meeting of the U.S. Congress," National Federation of Priests' Councils, September 24, 2015, http://nfpc.org/uncategorized/full-text-of-pope-francis-speech-to-congress/.

22. Cristina Marcos, "Lawmakers Set Up Bipartisan Problem Solvers Caucus for New Congress," *The Hill*, February 3, 2017, https://thehill.com/blogs/floor-action/house/317764-bipartisan-lawmakers-set-up-problem-solvers-caucus-for-new-congress.

23. Aneesh Chopra, "Government to Entrepreneur Mindset: Aneesh Chopra & Farzad Mostashari, MD: NOW #179," interview by Steven Krein, StartUp Health Festival 2018, San Francisco, CA, January 9, 2018, YouTube video, 42:07, posted by StartUp Health, March 1, 2018, https://www.youtube.com/watch?v=FGtu7EQG_-g&list=PLkzfu6hnQEQF LIhIuvu_58MX2VB_Hx7y5&index=48, at 6:04–7:12 [transcription by the author].

CHAPTER 10

1. Paul Abrams, "What Karl Rove *Really* Had in Mind for a 'Permanent Republican Majority,'" *Huffington Post*, August 17, 2007, updated May 25, 2011, https://www.huffpost.com/entry/what-karl-rove-really-had_b_60947.

2. Steve Denning, "Understanding the Trump-Putin Bromance," *Forbes*, July 29, 2018, https://www.forbes.com/sites/stevedenning/2018/07/29/understanding-the-trump-putin -bromance/#4bbd22a675b1.

3. Richard Cohen, "Trump Is a Modern-Day McCarthy," *Washington Post*, February 5, 2018, https://www.washingtonpost.com/opinions/trump-is-a-modern-day-mccarthy/2018/ 02/05/7805dfac-0aa2-11e8-8b0d-891602206fb7_story.html?utm_term=.452253e28c58.

4. Lisa de Moraes, "Carl Bernstein Blasts Media Falling for Donald Trump's Joe McCarthy-esque Dueling-Memos Side Show," *Deadline Hollywood*, February 7, 2018, https:// deadline.com/2018/02/carl-bernstein-donald-trump-is-joe-mccarthy-demagogue-authori tarian-treason-mccarthyism-video-1202280285/.

5. Elaine Kamarck, "Will the Trump Presidency Turn Out to Be Watergate, McCarthyism or Something Else Entirely?" *FixGov* (blog), Brookings, February 16, 2018, https://www.brookings.edu/blog/fixgov/2018/02/16/watergate-mccarthyism-or-some thing-else-entirely/.

6. Ruairi Arrieta-Kenna et al., "The 155 Craziest Things Trump Said This Election," *Politico Magazine*, November 5, 2016, https://www.politico.com/magazine/story/2016/11/ the-155-craziest-things-trump-said-this-cycle-214420.

7. Michael Steel, interview by Andrea Mitchell, *Andrea Mitchell Reports*, MSNBC, January 9, 2018 [transcription by the author].

8. Alec MacDonald, "The 13 Best Reactions to Trump Saying He Loves 'The Poorly Educated,'" Elite Daily, February 24, 2016, https://www.elitedaily.com/humor/donald -trump-loves-poorly-educated/1396865.

9. "Read a Full Transcript of the Joint Trump-Putin News Conference," CBC/Radio Canada, July 16, 2018, https://www.cbc.ca/news/world/trump-putin-summit-full-tran script-1.4749475.

10. Zeke Miller and Lisa Mascaro, "Trump Backs Down, Says He Misspoke on Russia Meddling," AP News, July 17, 2018, https://www.apnews.com/bf62711854b6482c88a 611391db05a7d.

11. Colby Hall, "CNN's Abby Phillip: Trump Hired Matt Whitaker as Acting AG because of His Anti-Mueller Rants on TV," *Mediaite*, November 9, 2018, https://www. mediaite.com/tv/cnns-abby-phillip-trump-hired-matt-whitaker-as-acting-ag-because-of -his-anti-mueller-rants-on-tv/.

12. Eileen Sullivan and Katie Benner, "Trump on Friday: 'I don't know Matt Whitaker.' Trump Last Month: 'I know Matt Whitaker,'" *New York Times*, November 9, 2018, https:// www.nytimes.com/2018/11/09/us/politics/matthew-whitaker-donald-trump.html.

13. Bob Woodward, *Fear: Trump in the White House* (New York: Simon & Schuster, 2018), pp. 225, 308, 286.

14. Jill Colvin, "Trump Says He's 'Like, Really Smart,' 'A Very Stable Genius,'" *U.S. News & World Report*, January 6, 2018.

15. Ken Meyer, "Trump Reads Statement Admitting Russia Meddled, Then Ad-Libs: 'Could Be Other People Also,'" *Mediaite*, July 17, 2018, https://www.mediaite.com/tv/ trump-reads-statement-admitting-russia-meddled-then-ad-libs-could-be-other-people-also/.

16. Robert S. Mueller III, *Report on the Investigation into Russian Interference in the 2016 Presidential Election* (U.S. Department of Justice, March 2019), https://www.justice.gov/ storage/report.pdf.

17. Dylan Scott, "Former CIA Director: Trump-Putin Press Conference 'Nothing Short of Treasonous,'" *Vox*, July 16, 2018, https://www.vox.com/world/2018/7/16/17576804/trump-putin-meeting-john-brennan-tweet-treasonous.

18. Donald Trump (@realDonaldTrump), "The Mueller probe should never have been started in that there was no collusion and there was no crime," Twitter, March 17, 2018, 5:12 p.m., https://twitter.com/realdonaldtrump/status/975163071361683456?lang=en.

19. Robert S. Mueller III, "Russian Government Outreach and Contacts," *Report on the Investigation into Russian Interference in the 2016 Presidential Election*, vol. I, sec. V.C. (U.S. Department of Justice, March 2019), pp. 180–88, https://www.justice.gov/storage/report.pdf.

20. Kenneth Walsh, "The Decline of Character: Americans Used to Look at Their President as a Role Model; Not Anymore," *U.S. News & World Report*, February 2, 2018, https://www.usnews.com/news/the-report/articles/2018-02-02/with-trump-character-doesnt-matter.

21. Katherine A. S. Sibley, "Does Character Matter in a President?" *Asbury Park (NJ) Press*, July 28, 2017, https://www.app.com/story/opinion/columnists/2017/07/27/presidential-character-important-trump/104039296/.

22. Robert Weissman, "Character Is Destiny, and Donald Trump's Character Is Ours," *Dallas Morning News*, April 15, 2018, https://www.dallasnews.com/opinion/commentary/2018/04/15/character-destiny-donald-trumps-character.

23. "'I Love the Poorly Educated'—Read Donald Trump's Full Nevada Victory Speech," Quartz, February 24, 2016, https://qz.com/623640/i-love-the-poorly-educated-read-donald-trumps-full-nevada-victory-speech/.

24. Ian Schwartz, "David Brooks: Trump Supporters Are 'Tuned Out'; His 'Chaos' 'Doesn't Rise to the Level of Consciousness," *Real Clear Politics*, March 17, 2018, https://www.realclearpolitics.com/video/2018/03/17/david_brooks_trump_supporters_are_tuned_out_of_his_chaos_doesnt_rise_to_the_level_of_consciousness.html.

25. Max Boot, "Trump Is a Character Test for the GOP," *USA Today*, February 29, 2016, https://www.usatoday.com/story/opinion/2016/02/29/trump-tests-republicans-max-boot/81123934/.

26. Edward Alden, "The Roots of Trump's Trade Rage," *Politico Magazine*, January 16, 2017, https://www.politico.com/magazine/story/2017/01/the-roots-of-trumps-trade-rage-214639.

27. Ta-Nehisi Coates, "The First White President: The Foundation of Donald Trump's Presidency Is the Negation of Barack Obama's Legacy," *Atlantic*, October 2017, https://www.theatlantic.com/magazine/archive/2017/10/the-first-white-president-ta-nehisi-coates/537909/.

28. Gabriella Baczynska and Steve Holland, "Trump Shoves Fellow NATO Leader Aside on His First Summit," Reuters, May 25, 2017, https://www.reuters.com/article/us-usa-trump-europe-montenegro/trump-shoves-fellow-nato-leader-aside-on-his-first-summit-idUSKBN18L2FK.

29. Donald Trump (@realDonaldTrump), "Why does @BarackObama always have to rely on teleprompters?" Twitter, March 19, 2012, 11:39 a.m., https://twitter.com/realdonaldtrump/status/181812278780379137?lang=en.

30. Jonathan Lemire, "Trump Turns to Object of His Ridicule: A Teleprompter," AP News, June 7, 2016, https://www.apnews.com/a3cc4937aa4043b4809974d4c6409be3.

31. Nana Ariel, "What the Teleprompter Tells Us about Truth, Trump, and Speech," *Aeon*, February 2, 2017, https://aeon.co/ideas/what-the-teleprompter-tells-us-about-truth -trump-and-speech.

32. Andrew Buncombe, "Trump Has Proved He Can Read off a Teleprompter but That Doesn't Make Him Presidential: The Bar Has Been Lowered So Much, People Get Overly Excited When He Keeps to the Script," *Independent*, January 31, 2018, https:// www.independent.co.uk/voices/donald-trump-state-of-the-union-address-melania -teleprompter-a8186496.html.

33. Francine Prose, "The Sad Truth about Teleprompter Trump," *Guardian*, August 25, 2017, https://www.theguardian.com/commentisfree/2017/aug/25/donald-trump -teleprompter-speech.

34. Emma Dibdin, "Donald Trump Is Pretty Sure That Barack Obama Likes Him," *Marie Claire*, February 7, 2017, https://www.marieclaire.com/politics/news/a25268/donald -trump-barack-obama-relationship/.

35. Alex Thompson, "Trump Gets a Folder Full of Positive News about Himself Twice a Day: It's Known as the 'Propaganda Document,'" *Vice News*, August 9, 2017, https://news .vice.com/en_ca/article/zmygpe/trump-folder-positive-news-white-house.

36. Amber Phillips, "Want to Change Trump's Mind On Policy? Be the Last One Who Talks to Him," *Washington Post*, April 28, 2017, https://www.washingtonpost.com/news/the -fix/wp/2017/04/14/want-to-change-trumps-mind-on-policy-be-the-last-one-who-talks-to -him/?utm_term=.378e569be385.

37. Aaron Blake, "Obama and Trump: The Ticktock of a Truly Bizarre Relationship," *Washington Post*, March 6, 2017, https://www.washingtonpost.com/news/the-fix/wp/ 2017/03/06/obama-and-trump-the-history-of-a-truly-strange-relationship/?utm_ term=.33786a2305e9.

38. Kevin Liptak, "Read the Inauguration Day Letter Obama Left for Trump," CNN, September 5, 2017, https://www.cnn.com/2017/09/03/politics/obama-trump-letter -inauguration-day/index.html.

39. Dan McAdams, "The Mind of Donald Trump: Narcissism, Disagreeableness, Grandiosity," *Atlantic*, June, 2016, https://www.theatlantic.com/magazine/archive/2016/ 06/the-mind-of-donald-trump/480771/.

40. Jamelle Bouie, "The Republican Base Might Not Be as Scary as It Looks," *Slate*, July 22, 2018, https://slate.com/news-and-politics/2018/07/the-pro-trump-republican -base-that-many-politicians-fear-may-be-shrinking.html.

41. Carroll Doherty et al., "Trends in Party Affiliation among Demographic Groups," US Politics and Policy, Pew Research Center, Washington, DC, March 20, 2018, http:// www.people-press.org/2018/03/20/1-trends-in-party-affiliation-among-demographic -groups/.

42. Elaine Kamarck, Alexander Podkul, and Nicholas Zeppos, "Trump Owns a Shrinking Republican Party," *FixGov* (blog), Brookings, June 14, 2018, https://www .brookings.edu/blog/fixgov/2018/06/14/trump-owns-a-shrinking-republican-party/.

43. Amanda Taub, "The Rise of American Authoritarianism," *Vox*, March 1, 2016, https://www.vox.com/2016/3/1/11127424/trump-authoritarianism.

44. Clare Malone, "'Reluctant' Trump Voters Swung the Election. Here's How They Think He's Doing," FiveThirtyEight, April 18, 2017, https://fivethirtyeight.com/features/ reluctant-trump-voters-swung-the-election-heres-how-they-think-hes-doing/.

45. Nate Silver, "Donald Trump's Base Is Shrinking," FiveThirtyEight, May 24, 2017, https://fivethirtyeight.com/features/donald-trumps-base-is-shrinking/. Silver used data from over a dozen polling firms.

46. Steven Shepard, "Trump Hits New Polling Low as Base Shrinks," *Politico*, August 9, 2017, https://www.politico.com/story/2017/08/09/trump-polls-base-polling-241425. In addition to Trump's declining overall approval, Shepard notes "the percentage who approve strongly—one way to measure the size of Trump's most fervent supporters—is also at a new low: just 18 percent."

47. Kristen Soltis Anderson, "Data Show That Trump's Real Base Is 24 Percent of the Electorate," *Washington Examiner*, August 15, 2017, https://www.washingtonexaminer.com/data-show-that-trumps-real-base-is-24-percent-of-the-electorate.

48. Howard Dean, interview by Andrea Mitchell, *Andrea Mitchell Reports*, MSNBC, August 15, 2017 [transcription by the author]. Dean's "10 or 15%" was reached by subtracting the 21–24% base from Trump's 34–36% overall job approval numbers that polls showed at that time.

49. John Dean, "Trump's Base: Broadly Speaking, Who Are They?" Verdict/Justia, February 16, 2018, https://verdict.justia.com/2018/02/16/trumps-base-broadly-speaking.

50. Robert Schlesinger, "The Incredible Shrinking President," *U.S. News & World Report*, August 18, 2017, https://www.usnews.com/opinion/articles/2017-08-18/bad-news-for-trump-keeps-coming-as-his-standing-with-his-base-erodes.

51. Carl Cannon, "Five Tribes of American Voters," *Real Clear Politics*, October 18, 2018, https://www.realclearpolitics.com/articles/2018/10/18/five_tribes_of_american_voters_138390.html. The Real Clear Opinion Research study was led by John Della Volpe, CEO of SocialSphere and Director of Polling at the Harvard Kennedy School's Institute of Politics.

52. Washington Post-ABC News Poll, "Frustrations with Economic and Political System, and How Americans Weigh Trump's Agenda Ahead of 2020 Election," *Washington Post*, April 30, 2019, https://www.washingtonpost.com/page/2010-2019/WashingtonPost/2019/04/29/National-Politics/Polling/release_549.xml?tid=a_inl_manual&tidloc=6.

53. Washington Post-ABC News Poll, "Q: Assuming Trump Is the Republican Candidate for President in 2020, Would You Definitely Vote for Him, Would You Consider Voting for Him, or Would You Definitely Not Vote for Him?," *Washington Post*, April 30, 2019, https://www.washingtonpost.com/page/2010-2019/WashingtonPost/2019/04/29/National-Politics/Polling/question_21381.xml?uuid=Ba03pmplEem75xx5j7gFNg.

54. Harry Enten, "Trump's Popularity Has Dipped Most in Red States," FiveThirtyEight, September 18, 2017, https://fivethirtyeight.com/features/trumps-popularity-has-dipped-most-in-red-states/.

55. Charlie May, "New Poll Reveals Donald Trump Is Losing Support from a Key Part of His Base," *Salon*, August 2, 2017, https://www.salon.com/2017/08/02/new-poll-reveals-donald-trump-is-losing-support-from-a-key-part-of-his-base/.

56. Chris Kahn and Tim Reid, "Trump's Popularity Is Slipping in Rural America: Poll," Reuters, October 9, 2017, https://www.reuters.com/article/us-usa-ruralamerica-poll/trumps-popularity-is-slipping-in-rural-america-poll-idUSKBN1CE162.

57. Gregory Krieg and Ryan Struyk, "Is Trump's Base Fraying?" CNN, December 8, 2017, https://www.cnn.com/2017/12/08/politics/donald-trump-base-pew-poll/index.html.

58. Sharon Bernstein and Chris Kahn, "As Elections Near, Many Older, Educated, White Voters Shift Away from Trump's Party," *Reuters*, April 9, 2018, https://www.reuters.com/article/us-usa-election-healthcare-poll/exclusive-as-elections-near-many-older-educated-white-voters-shift-away-from-trumps-party-idUSKBN1HG1I6.

59. Emily Elkins, "The Five Types of Trump Voters: Who They Are and What They Believe," Democracy Fund Voter Study Group, June 2017, https://www.voterstudygroup.org/publications/2016-elections/the-five-types-trump-voters.

60. James Hohmann, "Trump Voters Have Buyer's Remorse in North Carolina Focus Group," *Washington Post*, November 16, 2017, https://www.washingtonpost.com/news/powerpost/paloma/daily-202/2017/11/16/daily-202-trump-voters-have-buyer-s-remorse-in-north-carolina-focus-group/5a0d0c8a30fb045a2e003078/?utm_term=.e7165dd63d04.

61. Kyle Kondik, "Center for Politics Poll Takes Temperature of Trump Voters at 100-Day Mark," *UVA Today*, April 26, 2017, https://news.virginia.edu/content/center-politics-poll-takes-temperature-trump-voters-100-day-mark.

62. Edward-Isaac Dovere, "Pittsburgh Focus Group Tanks Trump," *Politico*, August 29, 2017, https://www.politico.com/story/2017/08/29/trump-pittsburgh-focus-group-242158.

63. John Bowden, "Focus Group: Trump Risking Supporters by Picking Twitter Fights," *The Hill*, November 18, 2017, https://thehill.com/homenews/administration/361020-focus-group-trump-losing-supporters-by-picking-twitter-fights.

64. Michael Ritchie, dir., *The Candidate*, written by Jeremy Larner (Burbank, CA: Warner Bros. Pictures, 1972).

65. John Sides, "Did Enough Bernie Sanders Supporters Vote for Trump to Cost Clinton the Election?" *Washington Post*, August 24, 2017, https://www.washingtonpost.com/news/monkey-cage/wp/2017/08/24/did-enough-bernie-sanders-supporters-vote-for-trump-to-cost-clinton-the-election/?utm_term=.a1ef32b86e1a.

66. Omri Ben-Shahar, "The Non-Voters Who Decided the Election: Trump Won because of Lower Democratic Turnout," *Forbes*, November 17, 2016, https://www.forbes.com/sites/omribenshahar/2016/11/17/the-non-voters-who-decided-the-election-trump-won-because-of-lower-democratic-turnout/#3a4ad51f53ab.

67. Sarah Zheng, "How China Hit Donald Trump's Supporters Where It Hurts as Tariffs Target Republican Party's Heartlands," *South China Morning Post*, April 5, 2018, https://www.scmp.com/news/china/diplomacy-defence/article/2140464/how-china-hit-donald-trumps-supporters-where-it-hurts.

68. Jen Hayden, "Red-State Voters Are Starting to Panic over Trump's New Tariffs," *AlterNet*, April 4, 2018, https://www.alternet.org/2018/04/red-state-voters-are-starting-panic-over-trumps-new-tariffs/.

69. Dan Balz, "Trump Does More Damage to Himself Than His Opponents Ever Manage to Do," *Washington Post*, January 13, 2018, https://www.washingtonpost.com/politics/trump-does-more-damage-to-himself-than-his-opponents-ever-manage-to-do/2018/01/13/067ce484-f878-11e7-a9e3-ab18ce41436a_story.html?utm_term=.61978c2ac707.

70. Rick Wilson, "When Will Republicans Learn That Donald Trump Hates Them?" *Daily Beast*, July 21, 2017, https://www.thedailybeast.com/when-will-republicans-learn-that-donald-trump-hates-them.

71. Robert S. Mueller III, "Executive Summary to Volume II," *Report on the Investigation into Russian Interference in the 2016 Presidential Election*, vol. II (U.S. Department of Justice, March 2019), pp. 3–6, https://www.justice.gov/storage/report.pdf.

72. James Warren, "Trump, the Third-Party Candidate? How 2020 Could Shake Out to Be a Bizarre, Three-Way Race," *U.S. News & World Report*, February 14, 2018, https://www.usnews.com/opinion/op-ed/articles/2018-02-14/how-trump-could-be-a-third-party-candidate-in-2020.

73. Doug Sosnik, "Trump Is on Track to Win Reelection," *Washington Post*, October 6, 2017, https://www.washingtonpost.com/opinions/trump-is-on-track-to-win-reelection/2017/10/06/91cd2af0-aa15-11e7-850e-2bdd1236be5d_story.html?utm_term=.85cd05d19649.

74. Graham Vyse, "How Trump Wins Reelection," *New Republic*, February 26, 2018, https://newrepublic.com/article/147119/trump-wins-reelection.

75. J. D. Vance, *Hillbilly Elegy: A Memoir of a Family and Culture in Crisis* (New York: HarperCollins, 2016).

76. David Smith, "President Mike Pence? Dems Should Be 'Careful What They Wish For,' Experts Say," *Guardian*, May 21, 2017, https://www.theguardian.com/us-news/2017/may/21/mike-pence-president-democrats-conservatives.

77. Will Drabold, "Here's What Mike Pence Said on LGBT Issues over the Years," *Time*, July 15, 2016, http://time.com/4406337/mike-pence-gay-rights-lgbt-religious-freedom/.

78. Jane Mayer, "The Danger of President Pence," *New Yorker*, October 16, 2017, https://www.newyorker.com/magazine/2017/10/23/the-danger-of-president-pence.

AFTERWORD

1. Adam Gopnik, "Being Honest about Trump," *New Yorker*, July 14, 2016, https://www.newyorker.com/news/daily-comment/being-honest-about-trump.

2. Mickey Edwards, "Burning the Constitution," *Aspen Institute Journal of Ideas*, December 1, 2017, https://www.aspeninstitute.org/longform/aspen-ideas-winter-2017/burning-the-constitution/.

3. Robert S. Mueller III, "Russian Government Outreach and Contacts," *Report on the Investigation into Russian Interference in the 2016 Presidential Election*, vol. I, sec. V.C. (U.S. Department of Justice, March 2019), pp. 180–88, https://www.justice.gov/storage/report.pdf.
Mueller's report did not recommend criminal conspiracy charges against Americans for actions undertaken with Russians. Mueller based that decision on (a) the absence of "scienter," i.e., that the person under scrutiny entered into a criminal conspiracy knowingly and willfully, and (b) the inability to establish the value of campaign assistance in the forms of information and material damaging to one's opponent. Yet scienter could have been interpreted as a matter of whether the person knowingly and willfully engaged in the actions that they undertook; this interpretation would have set a standard that is less favorable to a person who was a target of the investigation. The higher standard for scienter also derogates from the maxim that "ignorance of the law is no excuse." The inability to establish a precise monetary value on campaign assistance in the forms at issue disregards the substantial benefit, or value, that information and damaging material confer upon a campaign, and unduly emphasizes the valuation calculation for such assistance. Since Mueller's decision (that criminal conspiracy charges were not provable beyond a reasonable doubt) was based

on technical distinctions, the facts surrounding collaboration or collusion with Russians remain condemnable and appropriate for congressional action.

4. Robert S. Mueller III, "Executive Summary to Volume II," *Report on the Investigation into Russian Interference in the 2016 Presidential Election,* vol. II (U.S. Department of Justice, March 2019), pp. 3–6, https://www.justice.gov/storage/report.pdf.

Mueller's report cited Department of Justice policy that prevents a sitting president from being indicted. Mueller indicated that his adherence to this policy forestalled him from considering obstruction of justice charges. However, he provided evidence of Trump's actions that gave rise to obstruction of justice concerns that would warrant charges if the party engaged in such actions were not a sitting president. Mueller asserted that he was also impeded by his inability to receive Trump's oral testimony in response to questioning, as that would provide direct evidence of Trump's state of mind when taking the actions that gave rise to obstruction of justice concerns. Mueller indicated that he did not insist on Trump testifying because, if Trump refused to comply, the normal enforcement procedure via a subpoena was not available due to the policy that prevents a sitting president from being indicted. Thus, Mueller needed Trump's oral testimony to substantiate an obstruction of justice charge but was unwilling to require it. Because Mueller's decision was based on these technicalities, the relevant facts remain condemnable and appropriate for congressional action.

5. Lawrence Tribe, interview by Fareed Zakaria, *Fareed Zakaria GPS,* CNN, April 14, 2019 [transcription by the author].

6. "Trump to Senators: 'You're Afraid of the NRA,'" *VOA News,* February 28, 2018, https://www.voanews.com/a/trump-tells-senators-youre-afraid-of-national-rifle-association/4274949.html.

7. David Roads, "If You're Not Part of the Solution, You're Part of the Problem," *Philosiblog,* December 11, 2013, https://philosiblog.com/2013/12/11/if-youre-not-part-of-the-solution-youre-part-of-the-problem/.

LIST OF TERMS AND ENTITIES

Graham, Senator Lindsey
Grant, President Ulysses S.
Grassley, Senator Chuck
Great Society initiative
Green Seal
Group of Seven (a.k.a., G7) largest advanced
    economies
Guantanamo Bay
Gurfein, Judge Murray

Haberman, Maggie
Haiti
Haley, Nikki, former Ambassador to the
    United Nations
Hamilton, Secretary Alexander
Hannover, Germany
Harding, President Warren G.
Harley Davidson
Harris, Senator Kamala
Harrison, President Benjamin
Hart, Gary, former Senator
Harvey Weinstein
Hastert Rule
Hastert, Denny, former Congressman and
    Speaker
Hays, Wayne, former Congressman
Head Start Program
Health and Human Services, US
    Department of
Heller, Senator Dean
Helsinki, Finland (site of Putin-Trump 2018
    Summit meeting)
Henry, Patrick
Henry, Patrick
Heritage Foundation
Hickenlooper, John, former Governor
Hicks, Hope
Hispanic/Latino Americans
Historically Black Colleges and Universities
Holder, Eric, former Attorney General
Holt, Lester
Homeland Security, US Department of
Hoover, J. Edgar
Hoover, President Herbert
Housing and Urban Development, US
    Department of

Huawei
humility
Humphrey, Hubert, former Vice President
Hunter, Congressman Duncan, Jr.
Hurd, Congressman Will
Hurricane Katrina
Husted v. A. Philip Randolph Institute
hypocritical

Idaho
identity politics
Idlib Province, Syria
immigration
Immigration Act of 1924
Immigration and Customs Enforcement
    (ICE)
impeachment
Implicit Association Test, Harvard
    University's Project Implicit
Inaugural Address, President Lincoln's
    Second
incivility
India
Indiana
individualism
Indonesia
industrial revolution
inept
Instagram
insult
intellectual property
Intelligence Community
interdependence
interest rate
Interior, US Department of
International Monetary Fund
international order, the
Interstate Commerce Clause
Investor's Business Daily
Iran
Iran Nuclear Deal (a.k.a., Joint
    Comprehensive Plan of Action,
    JCPOA)
Iraq
Iraq War
Ireland